CAREER DEVELOPMENT AND AND JOB TRAINING

CAREER DEVELOPMENT AND JOB TRAINING

A Manager's Handbook

James G. Stockard

amacom

A Division of American Management Associations

Library of Congress Cataloging in Publication Data

Stockard, James G
  Career development and job training.

  Includes index.
  1. Employees, Training of--Handbooks, manuals, etc.
2. Personnel management--Handbooks, manuals, etc.
I. Title.
HF5549.5.T7S698   658.31'243   77-12978
ISBN 0-8144-5449-6

© 1977 AMACOM
A division of American Management Associations,
New York.
All rights reserved. Printed in the United States of
America.

Second Printing

To THE MEMORY OF MY FATHER

James Carl Stockard
1886–1971

WHOSE STERLING CHARACTER AND EXCELLENCE IN MANY
PURSUITS INSPIRED MY CONTINUING GROWTH
AND DEVELOPMENT

PREFACE

WHEN the natural gas supply dwindles and is turned off in a plant or school system during a frightfully cold winter, it is a stark reminder of our national energy problem. When a member of one's immediate family or a neighbor's suddenly must go on the welfare rolls (or is taken away to prison or a mental institution or the morgue) for lack of a marketable skill and a self-fulfilling job, we are acutely aware that something is amiss in our systems for human resources development. On both fronts, many of us are not attacking the root causes but the symptoms—the environmental abuses and consumer ripoffs, growing welfarism, unemployment levels, and crime everywhere.

This book deals with what I consider to be the root causes of inadequate human resources development in the United States. It calls for a national commitment, industry by industry and employer by employer, to adopt systems that will more nearly ensure the maximum development and utilization of every individual in our society in relation to his or her potential for growth and development. This means development and utilization to the point where the personal dignity, the innate talents, and the acquired knowledge, skills, and abilities of the individual will have been properly recognized, rewarded, and recorded.

This is a practical handbook, in four parts, for accomplishing this objective. The parts equate to the four basic steps in a sound approach to employee education, training, and career development: sorting out the needs (Part I), planning and developing solutions (Part II), delivering new knowledge and skill (Part III), and examining results and determining the future course of action (Part IV). Broad policy issues, management objectives and options, and operational strategies and techniques are detailed candidly.

A central thesis is that the best results are obtained when continued training and career development is undertaken as a joint-venture relationship between employer and employee, with each making a continuing series of logically sequenced and timed inputs to form durable building blocks. Within every organization, one can find people at all levels of responsibility and in every occupational category who are skilled in the art of discovering people of promise and in guiding them informally to greater heights. Such people, herein titled "people developers," make a significant contribution to our social, political, and economic life. They should be identified and encouraged. They may or may not be supported by institutionalized groups of training and development specialists who understand the state of the art, and who can marshal the necessary resources and use the tools of the trade intelligently.

It is time for our thinking about training and development to move beyond the parameters of a single classroom to the concept of modern "delivery systems" for the efficient transfer of knowledges, skills, and abilities to our decentralized forms of trade, commerce, and public service. The costs of constantly moving people to central training locations for updating their knowledge of science, technology, and management are economically prohibitive. Similarly, it is time for less lockstep training for groups of people, and more training and development oriented to individual needs on a learner-paced scale.

There is no shortage of training methods, materials, and devices. The secret is to orchestrate the best of these at the right places, in suitable learning environments, at the best time, and with the full support and active participation of top management. And above all, we need more thorough follow-through and evaluation of results from a cost-effective standpoint as a basis for adjusting the future course of action where necessary.

Since supervisors and executives are sometimes a part of the problem of human resources development, Chapters 7, 14, and 15 are included as a contribution to the long-range task of building new leadership for organizations and new support for the development of human potential. Obviously, and notwithstanding the claims of a carnival of faddists to the contrary, supervisor training is more than an 80-hour course, and executive development is more than a few weeks or months of training at an in-service or outside facility.

I am firmly convinced that a cornerstone of human resources development is an integrated personnel system in which better selection, placement, performance appraisal, and career counseling are essential and are desperately needed in today's systems. Although some personnel specialists might pursue a different sequence of presentation to accomplish such an objective, I have arranged the contents of this book in what I consider is a logical and most effective procedure for effecting an integrated system. As an aid to the administrator or executive who is ready and willing to reconstruct the human resources of his or her organization, each of the four basic steps, or parts, contains overviews of the central themes addressed in the individual chapters therein.

Finishing touches were put on the manuscript shortly before the Carter administration took office. It therefore seemed appropriate to include some thoughts on how the federal establishment can better come to grips with its people problems. Appendix I is essentially an open letter to all members of that and all future administrations who may have some responsibility for dealing decisively with the people-power factor in the federal establishment. Appendix II is a set of guideposts for individuals who may from time to time consider casting their lot with the public sector at the national level.

I would be remiss if I failed to mention my debt to, and great respect for, the countless training and development practitioners and their "people developer" colleagues with whom I have been associated throughout the world for some 40 years, in both the private and public sectors. I would simply say to them: Work on, even harder, for your reward will doubtless come after reincarnation in another world where things will be different and your masters will perhaps be more appreciative of your unique talents and untiring efforts.

James G. Stockard

CONTENTS

PART ONE

Sorting Out the Needs

I T is the purpose of this part to examine (1) the overall national problems in people development and the facts as they presently exist; (2) how these findings relate to organizations; and (3) to what extent people development can be applied in individual companies. Overviews of these subjects are presented and recommendations specific to them are given at the end of each chapter.

Chapter 1. People Development—An Acute National Problem

The United States has a finite supply of certain natural resources and is beginning to turn its attention to the discovery and development of alternatives. At least there is public recognition of the problem in this area.

With respect to its *human* resources, there are many symptoms to suggest that the nation has a false sense of security. The original level of American craftsmanship and the attitude of individuals providing services to the consuming public have eroded conspicuously. Counseling and education systems are channeling many individuals into the labor force who are not properly motivated or qualified in the basics. Therefore, the infrastructure on which our industry, business, and public service sectors have traditionally depended may be weakening. Many graduates of educational institutions in specialized fields are having to take sustenance-type jobs and are therefore underemployed, at least in their own eyes. Consumerism and environmentalist movements have cropped up extensively to combat these mismanagement symptoms of our people development responsibilities. Politicians are exploiting public concern over another of the symptoms, welfarism, which is the status to which many workers have retreated after fruitless searches in the "school of experience and hard knocks" for identity and a meaningful occupational role.

Poorly managed organizations in all sectors of the economy have aggravated the problem. The clues to this mismanagement include absentee management, top-heavy and bureaucratic organizations, and abuse of equal opportunity through the practice of seniority, nepotism, and discrimination based on sex or racial and ethnic origin.

Chapter 2. Assessing Organization Development Needs

It is not unusual for organizations to overlook training and development needs created by management decisions. To assume that only new employees need training and that an hour or so of orientation will suffice is an indicator of shortsighted planning. People development needs stem from origin, internal dynamics, and external influences that vitally affect an organization's future. Some leaders fail to grasp the true meaning of their organization's charter, franchise, license, or enabling legislation. Others fail to see training and development implications in their product and service line as it changes to conform to customer or client demands.

The health of the economy, the political climate, and technological advances have direct impact on the people development function. Automation, centralization, decentralization, organization and management system changes, rapid expansion, reduction in force, leadership style changes, work simplification, budget formulation, labor/management contracts and agreements, performance appraisals, and community pressures are among the many factors that can trigger the need for people development.

Chapter 3. Identifying Target Audiences and Individual Training Needs

It is a given in this book that the *organization's* need for enlargement of its reservoir of knowledge, skill, and abilities takes precedence over the training and development of the individual employee as such. The leaders of many organizations sense that the members of their staffs need additional training, but apparently they do not know how to identify their specific needs. This makes such managers susceptible to canned, faddish, alleged cure-all courses that are introduced with great fanfare. These courses may be adopted and mandated for vast numbers of employees without regard for their individual requirements at particular stages in their growth and career development.

It is feasible to identify certain target audiences for which a specific training experience is a logical need at a particular stage of their development. For example, shortly before or after an individual begins to supervise other employees for the first time, it is well to provide a course in the basics of supervision. To the extent that an organization has a number of such employees reaching this stage simultaneously, they can be assembled in a homogeneous group and encouraged to interact on common problems.

There is a wide variety of approaches to finding individual training and development needs. A representative assortment of 26 such methods is discussed in Chapter 10. Heading the list are job analysis and day-to-day supervision, which, when used together, are most effective.

1

People Development— An Acute National Problem

O UR natural resources are dwindling. Environmentalists are speaking, but our action and lack of action suggest that we are not hearing them.

We appear to be very rich in human resources, especially when one considers the great mix of people in the United States from so many ethnic, religious, and national origins. However, we may have a false sense of security in availability of the *useful* human resource, and that is the subject of this book.

The Problems and the Facts

In examining this question, one might start with the unwritten national policy of achieving and maintaining a goal of zero population growth. Long strides are being made toward that goal—some by deliberate family planning methods and basic change in lifestyle; some by use of the pill, vasectomy, and other birth control procedures; and still more in the highly controversial abortion clinics. From a practical viewpoint, a declining population means fewer

5

workers, all of whom must be proficient in their chosen occupations.

The burden of this book, then, is to try to point the way to a national commitment for the creation of systems, both private and public, that will more nearly ensure the maximum development and utilization of every individual in our society, in relation to his potential growth and development. This means development and utilization to the point where human dignity, innate abilities, and acquired skills of the individual will be properly recognized, rewarded, and recorded. It also means that the individual will be able, at each milestone in his life, to look back with the same sense of satisfaction and self-fulfillment that an engineer feels when he looks at an edifice he has built and knows he must surrender it to the owners and walk away.

It appears at times that—as parents, educators, social scientists, economists, labor leaders, employers, personnel managers, and others—we are almost bankrupt in terms of our ability to provide the necessary environment, policies, funds, and guidance for the maximum development and utilization of human resources. Consider a few examples with which we are all familiar.

The vast majority of sales clerks in department stores apparently know little or nothing about the merchandise they preside over. National and local advertising brings customers to the store. The clerk, often a "moonlighter," barely knows how to ring up the sale. A question from the prospective customer often meets with passiveness or even hostility. How refreshing it is to find a specialty shop where the clerks genuinely know the merchandise they sell and can intelligently help you make a decision on whether or not to buy, and—should you decide to buy—what size, model, or color, and how best to use the item to enjoy and profit from it fully.

You buy a new automobile for several thousand dollars. You actually may have to take it back to the dealer as many as ten times to get all the bugs out of its performance. Reportedly, cars assembled on Mondays are the worst of the lot, because temporaries are used on Mondays to take the place of the many regulars who fail to make it to the plant after the weekend. Research studies have some interesting things to say about the low morale and productivity of people who work on routine, monotonous jobs, and this may well account for some Monday absences at automobile plants.

You search the "yellow pages" in hopes of finding a knowledgeable, responsive, and reasonable firm to fix some household appliance. You know what your batting average in this search has been.

You have had your encounters with computerized systems of billing and with computers in general. The computer itself is a marvelous invention, remarkably accurate, and we are using it constructively in countless ways, but it is poorly trained, careless people who usually cause the computer to err and frustrate you.

A jet airplane crashes, resulting in a tremendous loss of life and the influence those lives might have had on others had they continued. Months later, the cause is all too often attributed to "human error."

A high-rise housing complex in the central city of some metropolitan area is suddenly deserted by tenants only a few years after construction and occupancy. The building deteriorates rapidly, and is soon dynamited and reduced to rubble. The root cause of such failures has typically been poor management, which is overcome by insolvable problems of security, finance, community relations, and normal maintenance. Pathetically, there was no facility for training housing managers in the United States until the National Center for Housing Management was established in Washington, D.C., in 1972 by Executive Order 11668.

It is generally agreed among consumers that the United States is losing its expert craftsmanship—a quality in which it originally prided itself. Quality controls, to the extent that they exist, are not yielding quality products—a degradation that Ralph Nader exploited successfully. Equally bad is the picture in many government agencies at federal, state, and local levels. Here, the so-called merit system has not always run on merit tracks. Public servants are frozen out of equal opportunities for employment, career development, promotion, upward mobility, and a self-fulfilling career. Only token efforts have been made to comply with fair employment and affirmative action regulations in many organizations.

For example, in the police department of one of the nation's ten largest cities, a minority group applicant who was otherwise well qualified in the eyes of the decision maker was passed over because investigation revealed that he had "tied another person to a tree and assaulted him"—an act later discovered by an investigator to have been committed by the applicant at age 6 against a six-year-old buddy!

By no means can the examples of malpractice be limited to such occupations. The crisis in malpractice suits suggests that something is wrong in the medical profession. Law firms, realtors, insurance companies, oil companies, pharmaceutical manufacturers, food processors, and countless others are constantly being charged with "rip-off" practices. Sometimes it is a defect in knowledge or skill that is disclosed by research. Sometimes it is a dreadful neglect of ethical standards.

The Underlying Problem

If all or any part of these indictments is true in your experience, why do you think it is? The thesis of this book is that all too frequently the individual worker is left to shift for himself in the "school of experience"—a school more or less synonymous with learning by trial and error. That well-known school was once described by industrialist Henry Ford, who said: "The School of Experience may be all right but the trouble is the graduates are too old to go to work."

It may also be true that the school of experience encompasses (for many) the schools they attend, the particular employers they connect with, and the employment world generally. They get no counseling or they get inadequate counseling in junior high school, where the need begins. They land in an educational institution of higher learning and there they get even less attention. Perhaps they go directly from a weak secondary school system to the labor market where, they soon discover, they failed to learn how to think, reason, solve problems, communicate, and use the tools that enable them to continue the development of their minds and bodies.

Disadvantaged individuals are doubly handicapped when they find themselves with an employer who cares too little or not in the least about the idea of systematic training and career development programs, true merit principles, and the other aspects of sound personnel management. Furthermore, this may happen not once but many times during a whole series of employment experiences. Eventually, the individual reaches the age (say, 40) that is categorical disqualification—in the eyes of many employers—for promotion to positions holding much promise. This moment of reality leaves an individual with a feeling of utter futility, about the same feeling the occupants of a busy household have when the electricity suddenly goes off on a hot night during a rainstorm. Everything shuts down in the home and the electricity may not be restored for hours. In the life of the individual whose career opportunities are blocked by lack of training and development opportunities, nothing much may happen for *years*—if ever.

Waste Products of Our People Development Systems

We hear a great deal about high school dropouts. In a county in northern Virginia, which prides itself on having one of the nation's foremost public school systems, the dropout rate runs 5 percent per year from the time children reach about the seventh grade.

The dropout is a sad case, mostly because parents and child both know how empty-handed the child will be when he ventures into the world to try to make it on his own. Perhaps a much sadder situation is the case of the child who "finishes" high school and gets a diploma without having acquired the fundamental abilities for reasoning and communicating. Without these capabilities or any vocational skills—such as industrial arts, home economics, and clerical practices—with which to get and hold the first job and establish a home, what then? This is probably true of the lower quartile if not the lower half of the scale among most high school classes.

Another group the business world has to contend with is the overeducated—people who have kept on the education treadmill until they have not one degree but two, three, or four, without a single substantive work experience unless it is that of teaching others who were jogging the education track. People can lose their verve, their perspective, and their usefulness in the practical world of work by lingering too long in a catacombed academic world, by not interfacing job application with theory, or by accepting as gospel the doctrine of professors who have been stationary at a podium through the years.

Another class of unfortunates who are a drag on the efficiency of the labor force comprises the misguided people who were pushed at an early age by their parents into a father/son or mother/daughter mold that was not a good fit. Father is a lawyer, doctor, or candlemaker, so son must be one. Mother is a musician, so daughter must be one. Parents can attach strings to the higher education purse in subtle ways, and the child may end up in a field for which he or she has little or no aptitude or interest. Guidance systems in schools, nonexistent or weak, fail to retrieve the misguided in time to save them.

Still another category is plainly that of the migrant. These people, for one reason or another, are constantly shifting about from place to place and from employer to employer until their employment history becomes checkered and suspect. Some mobility, both geographical and occupational, can be an accelerating growth experience, but too much is a liability. At some point, the individual has to submit to a series of real training and development experiences, and must give sustained performance of fully acceptable quantity and quality.

All these waste products of our people development systems add complication upon complication to the problems of people development, even in organizations that have the best of intent, policies, and practices.

Effects of Poor Management

Let no reader conclude that the *senders* of people to the marketplace and to the government offices—homes, high schools, colleges and universities, employment agencies, and others—or that the *members* of the potential labor force themselves are the sole trouble spots in the equation of people development. The *receivers* must share the guilt, for the ineffective management of many enterprises and government installations contributes much to the problem. Add to this the human resource exploitation factor.

For example, some organizations are not managed at all. Supposedly, they have a form of absentee management, one that is monitoring from afar the work of individuals who serve the organization's public. Take the situation in a housing development that has only a dimly lit lobby with some unsightly mail boxes. The "management" is a telephone number!

Next we find organizations that are so layered with unnecessary levels of supervision and management that upward and downward communications never penetrate the barriers. The chain of command on an organization chart resembles a tall totem pole. Preoccupation with formalities and details, procrastination, indifference, and lack of simple awareness of the problems at the operating level lead many organizations to minimal concern with developing people for maximum productivity and service. Only when a consumerism leader or a disgruntled client takes the initiative and complains to top management is there serious effort to reexamine the system for delivering goods and services to the customer's or client's satisfaction.

Then there is the industry or business or public service group that suffers from the disease of seniority. There is no deadlier killer of incentive and dedication. Promotions in such organizations are handed out routinely on a seniority basis. Labor/management contracts are ratified by management without an argument when seniority is inserted by unions as the overriding factor that decides job assignments, transfers, layoffs, fringe benefits such as parking privileges, room assignments, and the like. Such organizations follow the course of least resistance when they follow seniority guidelines. When they do not institute intensive training and accelerated promotion agreements, do not promote the best qualified individual regardless of seniority, do not fire the least competent regardless of seniority, these organizations lose money and the price they pay is obviously passed on to the consumer in the form of higher costs, lower quality, delays, mistakes, and bad public relations.

Another charge we might as well lay at the doorstep of some managements is that of nepotism. This practice appears to be declining, but wherever it exists it creates an unhealthy atmosphere, suspicion, recrimination, resentment, and friction. Favoritism instead of equity is the rule in such organizations, and communications are impaired because people are afraid of having their views passed along by a relative at one level to higher levels where next of kin or even a distant relation may be perched in a decision-making position.

We also have organizations whose leaders have had an unfortunate experience or lack of experience on their way to the top, and therefore they are hard-nosed about proposals to provide growth opportunities to their juniors on the way up. They say, "I learned my work the hard way. Let the newcomers do the same!" For example, when presented with a significant training proposal that might have improved service and productivity (not only in his bureau of a major federal staff agency created to serve all other civilian agencies), an executive pounded the desk and proclaimed that his job was to run the program, not to "hold school." He had worked his way up to a senior executive position through seniority, a little politics on the side, and a commanding tone of voice. He was a graduate of the school of experience, and he commended it to others, sneering at other schools.

Finally, we find both private and public organizations that have seemingly prospered because they have had through the years a unique product or service to offer, somewhat like a police department, a utility, city hall, a local newspaper, a tax collector, or a court system. Many of these organizations are disinclined to have strong programs for the training and development of people because they are certain that nothing short of an earthquake will shake up their constituencies enough to make them demand better management.

Supply and demand is the economic principle at work here. People
will pay more and overlook inefficiency if it is a product or service
they *must* have. (Have driving habits changed noticeably since the
sharp rise in the price of gasoline?)

Shifting Social Stresses on People Performance

The twentieth century has been momentous, to say the least. Automobiles, airplanes, radio, television, radar, computers, atomic energy, and space vehicles are only the most conspicuous of the great
scientific and industrial discoveries. Social revolutions, wars, political
upheavals, and economic disasters have added another dimension to
change. During the past two decades alone, the individual employee
in the United States has been steadily confronted with new and more
complex phenomena in his work, demanding new levels of knowledge, skill, and understanding. For example, he must (1) install,
operate, maintain, or manage far more sophisticated systems and
capital equipment; (2) work within a vastly more decentralized organization; (3) interact as a member of constantly changing racial and
ethnic mixes of people; (4) face physical hazards constantly growing
out of the environment, new technology, and unprecedented crime
in urban areas; (5) perform within very sensitive and elaborate la-
bor/management contracts and agreements; and (6) observe new
laws and court rulings that have narrowed the discretion of supervisors and managers in making decisions where the civil rights and
individual liberties of employees are involved.

All these shifting stresses require adjustment on the part of people who create the gross national product (GNP). Training and development can do three things to facilitate smooth adjustments to
social, economic, and political change: increase knowledge, develop
new skill, and improve attitudes.

Vital Policy Considerations

Once an organization makes the commitment to develop its
human resources, a whole array of vital policy considerations
present themselves. Evaluating and choosing from among these will
determine the course of action to be taken, which may very well perpetuate itself throughout the life of the organization. For example,
an official of the U.S. Forest Service was asked to explain how his

agency has managed to maintain its continuity of sound career development through the years. He thought for a moment and said, "It has always been that way. We have always had a professional forester as administrator, and all our administrators have supported career development as a philosophy. In fact, every supervisor knows that career development is a vital part of his job." One of these administrators, Richard E. McArdle, during a luncheon talk on executive development, said, "When the trees start to die back at the top we know something is wrong in the forest."

In other words, the climate of an organization has to be right from the top down, and that climate must permeate all levels of supervision. Further, some provision must be made in shaping the organizational structure to provide a central point of coordination, encouragement, and technical direction. Without an organizational element with full accountability for results, the people development function is distributed thinly on the heads and shoulders of everyone in the chain of command, and consequently may fall through the cracks. Full accountability for favorable results is needed.

The short-term and long-range organization development needs of an organization must be assessed from time to time. Findings create new agendas for the training and development activity.

Target audiences of whole categories of employees, such as new hires and new supervisors, must be identified. Even more critical is the determination of individual training and development needs, and these needs are constantly changing as employees mature and reach new levels of responsibility.

Organizations need to decide how they will meet organization and individual development needs. Will they use in-service training programs or depend largely on outside educational and training facilities? Can the training and development effort be left largely to operating officials and their on-the-job training (OJT) facilities or must the central training unit have the initiative for planning, organizing, and directing training programs to ensure quality control?

How can sufficient resources be marshaled to meet continuing education and training needs? It takes money, space, staff, materials, and equipment.

Where can the people developers be found? By what selection standards should they be identified? Does one look for subject-matter experts and count on them to be able to teach successfully? Or does one find expert teachers, give them a cram course in the subject, and supply them with some good materials?

What about the learning environment? Space is usually so precious that training lacks priority in the allocation of prime space. The state of the art in teaching is now such that any old space will not do. Individual study carrels, language labs, computer-assisted instruction, videotape systems, simulators, and other paraphernalia of modern instructional technology are examples of things that are demanding special attention in the design of the learning environment.

As organizations decentralize, and many do as they grow, they encounter the problem of how to move technical know-how from point of origin to point of use. The U.S. Postal Service, for example, has over 30,000 post offices (over 40,000 separate structures) where postal employees need continuing training in order to do their work intelligently. In 1971 it came to grips with the problem of developing a delivery system that would incorporate the best-known ways of moving the mail throughout its far-flung domain. The first step was to establish the Craft Training Center under the leadership of this author. The next step was to design the training strategy and direct production of curriculum materials and special equipment, and to train instructors. From this initial training center, a national network of 200 centers for training postal employees was developed. A similar system was organized for the Bureau of the Census by preparing a standardized, pretested program for training 134,000 enumerators located at 5,000 stations throughout the United States for a periodic census.

The preparation of curriculum materials is a policy issue that needs attention. Capital cost, production time, quality control, and relative effectiveness are major curriculum materials considerations.

The training effort for each project requires organization and management, once the materials have been produced, assembled, and placed under a distribution control system. The selection of participants in itself can be a major undertaking.

Provision has to be made at the inception of each training and development program for evaluation and for measuring the results in terms of impact on productivity and service.

Provision must be made for follow-through to ensure the fullest results from the investment on both management's part and the individual's. This means counseling, inquiries of the trainee's supervisor, and feedback to the program planners for modifying future programs and to line-management officials for modifying operational procedures and policies.

A continuing program of developing and redeveloping the training and development staff and persons who augment that staff on an ad hoc basis must be maintained. People developers, like the cobbler's children, cannot be neglected.

Every organization is learning things as it goes about its task of developing people for greater output and richer self-fulfillment. It is obliged to record this experience in appropriate journals, to run demonstration projects, and to accept its fair share of fellows, interns, and graduate students.

This book addresses these and other vital policy issues.

How People Learn

Educators, training specialists, and other people developers have discovered that the best and quickest learning is not by rote, lockstep memory, and recitation. Instead, it is now generally agreed that people learn

At different rates.
Through different media.
Under different physical conditions.
Under different degrees of guidance.
From each other.

Traditional instruction features lectures and lecture-discussions. Modern instruction is highly interactive, participative, and experiential. It is a learning-by-doing-under-trained-guidance system. Learning at different rates suggests multiphased teaching. Learning through different media points to multimedia teaching. Learning under different physical conditions can be translated into a plan for staging part of the teaching as OJT, some in the classroom, some in a laboratory or workshop, and even a part of it as live-in experiences in the living quarters and at the dining-room table. Learning under different degrees of guidance means providing the setting for learning in large groups, in small groups, tutorially, and from the supervisor during the OJT phase. Learning from each other dictates the use of such modern experiential methods as role playing, videotaping, analysis of critical incidents, and the like.

Technology for Transfer of Knowledge, Skill, and Understanding

From the time the Link trainer was introduced as a method of training airplane pilots by simulating the conditions of flight, things have been happening increasingly in educational and training technology.

By the late 1940s the U.S. Navy maintained the Special Devices Center on Long Island, N.Y., with a diverse collection of systems and devices to facilitate teaching and learning. Among these was a model classroom, which was studied by line officers and duplicated on naval vessels. The Center also experimented with closed-circuit television.

Today, the state of the art is far beyond that point. Videotape systems are used extensively in training, the instant playback feature being especially useful for third-person training such as sales procedure, interviewing, investigative work, public relations, and the like. Computer-assisted instruction is also gaining momentum. For example, decentralized organizations can train sales and maintenance representatives without having them travel off premises as long, as they have input and output devices connected by leased telephone lines. And career management systems can be monitored by computers and coordinated with personnel actions and new training requirements.

The whole new concept of teaching is individualized, learner paced, and often assisted by teaching machines. Much of it is an outgrowth of the research and writings of psychologist B. F. Skinner of Harvard, whose work laid the basis of programmed instruction. Now you can find professionals, paraprofessionals, blue-collar workers, elementary school students, housewives, and countless others working away on their own initiative—interacting with preprogrammed material, either on the printed page (unconventionally printed) or in a small machine that looks more like a child's toy than something related to one's bread-and-butter line.

In fact, individualized learning systems have reached the stage where one can find whole elementary schools with teachers functioning inconspicuously in the background, in classrooms without walls, as children individually or in small clusters delve into subjects. Learners no longer interact and compete primarily with each other, and they are no longer being "talked at" by the teacher standing in the front of the classroom, with desks regimented in straight rows and screwed to the floor. It is a whole new world for both the teacher and the learner.

Campuses without Walls

"Classrooms without walls" were followed into the twentieth century by college and university campuses without walls. For example, the Graduate School, U.S. Department of Agriculture, Washington, D.C., has an annual enrollment of more than 30,000 individuals from the community at large. It has no campus in the traditional sense. Instead, its administrative staff is located in a government building near the Mall that runs between the Lincoln Memorial and the Capitol.

The Graduate School does its teaching after normal business hours in some 50 borrowed and rented facilities in metropolitan Washington; for special seminars and institutes, it conducts retreats within a half-day's drive from Washington. It has an extensive correspondence-course program that is administered nationally, and conducts programs on educational television facilities.

This school is just one campus without walls in the Washington area. Many of the city's 35 or more institutions of higher learning are competing for the same student body; moreover, there is a growing list of universities from all over the United States hanging out their shingles in Washington for off-campus business. Among these are Central Michigan University, University of Chicago, University of Oklahoma, and University of Southern California. Some of the Washington-based institutions have begun to reciprocate by finding markets for their curricula elsewhere in the world. The University of Maryland is a good example; it has followed United States military agencies around the world, providing off-campus courses that can lead to a degree.

Many of these campus-without-walls institutions almost let the student write his own ticket with respect to the mix of courses, sequencing, and pacing. CMU permits a student to complete a three-semester-hour course in two weeks of intensive effort, in contrast to the traditional semester of 15 or 16 weeks. The key point is flexibility—catering to the needs of organizations and people instead of letting curriculum, faculty, and methods of instruction become hardened.

Recognition of the Training and Development Function

It took the Congress of the United States 182 years to bring itself to the point of willingness to recognize the training and development function in the federal civil service, and it did so by enacting the Government Employees Training Act (see Appendix I). Even then, it stopped short in its public policy declaration of recognizing that training and development is intrinsically valuable to people so that they have greater opportunity for merit appointments, protection from arbitrary removal, leave, retirement, and health and insurance benefits. The policy is explicitly a public policy that aims to promote efficiency and economy in government.

While the Pendleton Act of 1883 established a merit system, and a dozen or more amendments have reinforced the benefits to the civil servant, nothing in that Act demonstrates the will of the Congress to develop human resources for the sake of people development. It is a one-way street.

Contrast our agricultural research centers devoted to the serious study of methods designed to accelerate the growth of chickens, beef cattle, swine, and other forms of livestock that serve people. Why not some proportionate concern for the maximum development of the nation's *people,* who serve in other ways?

One may reason that education is a matter properly left to states and local communities, that in a democracy the people should determine their own destiny and the national government should take the initiative only when a significant group of people fail to find other means of furthering their training and development. This argument fails because the states and communities on the whole are farther behind than the federal government in meeting the needs of their employees for new knowledge and skill commensurate with their changing requirements. Some assistance is provided, however, by the Intergovernmental Personnel Act, PL 91-684, Jan. 5, 1971. This Act enables the states to have many of their state and local employees trained in U.S. government facilities.

Defining the Training and Development Function

The work of a training and development unit is diverse and complex. In 1971 the Craft Training Center of the U.S. Postal Service, Maryland, after its first year of operation was engaged in the following activities:

    I. *Administration*
        a. Day-to-day communication
        b. Administrative correspondence
        c. Representation at conferences and meetings
        d. Delegation of authority and responsibility for action
        e. Organizational planning
        f. Staff appraisal/counseling and development
        g. Progress reporting in administrative channels

II. *Supervision and Management*
    a. Day-to-day supervision of people
    b. Project management, overall
III. *Program Planning*
    a. Resource planning
    b. Facility planning
    c. Personnel planning
    d. Administrative systems planning
    e. Procurement and distribution planning
    f. Equipment planning
    g. Liaison with academic community
    h. Timetable planning
IV. *Systems Engineering*
    a. Studying postal technology, present and projected
    b. Applying the state of the art in educational technology
    c. Demographic studies of target populations
    d. Analysis of man/machine interaction factors
    e. Task analyses
    f. Developing basic conceptual designs
V. *Program Development*
    a. Exploration of training needs
    b. General program planning
    c. Coordination with client representatives
    d. Coordination with in-house specialist groups
    e. Setting behavioral objectives
    f. Developing control system for project management purposes (lattice)
    g. Developing evaluation design
    h. Developing contract conditions
    i. Overseeing work of staff members who write instructional materials
    j. Overseeing work of freelance instructional material writers
    k. Monitoring contractors (includes orientation of contractors)
    l. Organizing and administering field tests
    m. Modification of instructional systems, programs, materials, devices
VI. *Installation Services*
    a. Interpreting models (space, curriculum, hardware, staffing, funding, etc.)
    b. On-site technical assistance during local installation

       c. Providing ad hoc teaching and counseling services

       d. Reviewing preliminary sketches and final working drawings and technical specifications for space layouts

VII. *Teaching*

       a. Briefing others preliminary to new system or program start-ups

       b. Instructor or trainer training

       c. Guest lectures

       d. Counseling and guiding persons in learning situations; for example, interns, understudies, summer students, research fellows

VIII. *Consultative Services (quality assurance)*

       a. Briefings; for example, PEDC delivery system, software line, prototype experience

       b. Preparing and presenting formal proposals

       c. Technical assistance to ongoing systems and programs

IX. *Informational Activities*

       a. Supplying informational media (in house) with background material

       b. Ditto for outside groups

X. *Support Services*

       a. Providing support services to professional staff of CTFC

       b. Providing support services to the field

XI. *Evaluation*

       a. Before and after cost studies

       b. Cost/benefit studies

       c. Scientific sampling of the job performance of trainees

       d. Upward mobility studies

       e. Retraining studies

XII. *Self-Development Activities*

XIII. *Leave and Excused Absences*

       a. Annual leave

       b. Sick leave

       c. Holidays

Building Blocks

In concluding this first chapter it needs to be said that people development is fundamentally like the building process of the construction industry. A bricklayer soon learns that he cannot just throw the bricks indiscriminately at a structure and have them fit automatically into place properly. He must lay each brick precisely in accordance with the overall design and the principles of brick construction. Likewise, the supervisor, the manager, the training and career development specialist, and the individual himself are all "bricklayers" in the sense that they contribute to the individual's growth and development. Each training experience needs to be put in place as if it were a building block because each training experience must relate to, and form an interlocking support for, other training experiences.

Conclusion

The leadership of every organization should honestly and objectively reexamine its policies and practices with respect to people development, taking into account such factors as the hierarchy of human needs, how people learn, the exciting new teaching technologies, the concept of continuing education and training, and the phenomenon of campuses without walls.

On the basis of such findings, leadership should act affirmatively to develop the commitment, the conscience, and the capability for dealing effectively with its people development problem, keeping in mind the following quotes:

> *The School of Experience may be all right but the trouble is the graduates are too old to go to work.* Henry Ford

> *He is idle who might be better employed.* Socrates

2

Assessing Organization Development Needs

Before in-depth examination of an organization to learn what needs to be done to ensure its continuity and the sound, efficient control of its operations, one needs to look at the circumstances of its origin.

Reviewing the Needs

The enabling document of our own nation is the Constitution of the United States, a copy of which appears in any good encyclopedia. The famous preamble to the Constitution sets the tone for the Articles that follow it:

> We, the People of the United States, in order to form a more perfect Union, establish justice, insure domestic tranquility, provide for the common defence, promote the general welfare, and secure the blessings of liberty to ourselves and our posterity, do ordain and establish this Constitution for the United States of America.

The operations of at least three major federal departments of government—Defense, Justice, and Health, Education and Welfare—are grounded in those few words.

In Article I, Section 2, the Constitution stipulates a large undertaking on a continuing basis for the U.S. Bureau of the Census, Department of Commerce:

> Representatives and direct taxes shall be apportioned among the several states which may be included within this Union, according to their respective numbers. . . . The actual enumeration shall be made within three years after the first meeting of the Congress of the United States, and within every subsequent term of ten years, in such manner as they shall by law direct. . . .

Census experts have faithfully complied with this constitutional requirement since 1790, when the first census was taken. However, from the Watergate scandals (1972–1974) came evidence that several federal investigative agencies (CIA, FBI, and IRS) had overstepped their legal authority by encroaching upon individual liberties without due process of law.

In the case of a small business, the application for license probably expresses the intent and purpose of the business adequately. Corporate entities have by-laws and articles of incorporation that articulate the mission and other particulars in elaborate detail. Community groups—such as local parent-teacher associations, churches, and service clubs—have enabling documents to regulate their activities. For example, the first object of the National Congress of Parents and Teachers, to which all local units subscribe, states: "To promote the welfare of children and youth in home, school, church, and community." We pride ourselves in being a nation of laws and we carefully codify our federal, state, and local laws to guide citizens.

Any training and development specialist is well advised to square his program planning with the fundamental precepts expressed in the enabling document of his employer. Moreover, he needs to reflect on these precepts and ask a few hard questions until he is certain he grasps the full meaning of the rhetoric. If his company exists to produce goods and services, he may well ask, "Production for what?" If he concludes that the founders were solely in search of materialism, and this goal is repulsive to his own outlook on life, it may be time to begin casting about for other employment. On the other hand, his scrutiny of the origins may be a source of inner renewal and inspire the creation of an exemplary people development program.

Analyzing Product and Service Lines

What makes a product or service line "good"? Let us look at a few well-known models for clues that explain their success and continuity.

Henry Ford made his reputation by producing a single product well—the model T Ford. When pressured to offer the product in assorted colors, he reportedly agreed to make it in any color the public wanted, "as long as it is black."

The National Geographic Society, a quasi-public entity, was organized in 1888 "for the increase and diffusion of geographic knowledge." Eighty-nine years after its origination, the Society proudly credits itself with a wide array of products and services. These include extensive research and explorations, reported in the *National Geographic;* distribution of educational materials; releases to the news media; exhibitions; and a special publication for children in the eight-to-twelve age group.

Another example of public service is the Smithsonian Institution, also headquartered in Washington, D.C. Started from an idea and generous grant from the Englishman James Smithson "for the increase and diffusion of knowledge," and founded by an Act of Congress in 1846, it is the United States national museum and a repository rich in holdings that trace our social and economic development. It is a consortium of structures in Washington ranging from a vast zoo to a contemporary art collection and housing many originals used in our search for new frontiers ranging from space vehicles and agricultural technologies to home improvement artifacts.

One other public agency is the U.S. Patent Office, which has quietly continued its tedious task of researching patent and trademark applications and regulating this aspect of our economic life since 1790.

In the private sector, we find a "fast food" chain that exists on its hamburger reputation, claiming sales of billions of hamburgers. It has a whole "university" setup in the South for training new managers. Managers pause 5 minutes daily, at 11:00 A.M., according to a former personnel supervisor, to administer a small capsule of training to employees on the best-known way to do some task in the business.

From these examples, it is obvious that the training specialist must focus on the *nature* of products and services, and their claim to quality (for example, "99.44% pure soap"). Pending changes in the line may suggest the direction and priorities for training and development programs. Analysis should include the history, manufacture, uses, limitations, and advantages of each item. Orientation materials, clerical training, supervisor training, manager training, and many other aspects of training and development are hinged to the basic products and services. Introduction of new methods and technology may require expansive training direction. For example, when the U.S. Bureau of the Census introduced the first computer into its statistical processing operations in connection with the 1950 Census of the United States, training programs for unprecedented types of work had to be devised and administered.

Economic and Political Fluctuations

Barometers of the economy have to be read constantly. These include such phenomena as recessions, inflation, technological innovations, crises in the continuing supply of such basic commodities as petroleum, excessive unemployment, crime levels, labor-management strife, crop failures, production surpluses, money-market conditions, stock-market fluctuations, and new government initiatives.

The proceedings of legislative bodies are a good barometer of the political climate. For example, the *Congressional Record* is a faithful playback of the proceedings of the Congress of the United States; it is on the desk of each Congressman on the morning of the first workday following the day of Congressional business reported, and any citizen can subscribe to the issuance. The concerns of the people are presumably reflected in the words and actions of their political leaders.

Other public arenas for influencing social, economic, and political progress, since the 1970s began, have existed in the form of certain nonpartisan, nonprofit, grass-roots ventures. One is a lay-group movement known as "consumerism," which was launched dramatically as a critique of automobiles by Ralph Nader's *Unsafe at Any Speed.* Another is Common Cause, which was started by John Gardner, a former secretary of the Department of Health, Education and Welfare. Within five years it became a 300,000-member self-styled citizens' lobby united in its concern about government. Other citizen movements with more or less common constituencies include those in support of public television, the ecology campaign, and the promotion of facilities to house the performing arts. The newsletters

and special reports of such groups record the reforms won through
their efforts and may indicate the need for training and development in organizations affected by them.

Impact of Automation

Increasingly, capital investment in fully or semi-automated equipment has displaced people in the production of goods and services.
The old-fashioned telephone switchboard and its operators with
headsets have long ago been replaced by automated equipment.
Hotel and plane reservations are made instantly by automated
means.

One of the last frontiers of the labor-intensive world in the
United States is the U.S. Postal Service. It, too, is busy converting to
semi-automated methods of mail processing. Another familiar area in
which people were needed in relatively large numbers is the automobile service station, but even here the work force is diminishing
as faster pumps and self-service policies of the stations become common.

Computers have probably made the largest single impact on
manual operations, but there are countless others—hydraulic lifts,
mechanical ditch diggers, giant earth-moving equipment, conveyor
belts, automatic elevators, 360-degree revolving cranes on construction projects, farming equipment, automated factory operations,
communications systems, and closed-circuit television.

Automation can dramatically change training requirements. An
intelligent training specialist keeps his eyes and ears open for signs
of imminent impacts on the work of his employer.

Organization and Management Questions

The people developer needs to know the organization of his employer intimately, and also the management style by which it gets
things done. Does it have a "tall" chain of command with many levels
of supervision, or does it have a "flat" organization with a liberal
delegation of authority commensurate with responsibility?

Does it practice the traditional "line and staff" format in its division of labor—the doers and the thinkers—or does it keep a pragmatic organization by building action into functional teams and

around individuals whose "time has come" to provide leadership?

Does it rely essentially on participative management rely on a hierarchy of benevolent autocrats? For example, when faced with drastic changes resulting from new legislation, technology, labor contracts, or product and service changes, does it use two-way communication and training to make the conversion, or does it decree changes by sharp commands?

Are its supervisors concerned very much with people or only with production? Are its executives generalists or subject matter specialists? Are jobs ever engineered to fit people or do they remain rigidly fixed?

Does the organization have a "delivery system" for getting a multiplier effect and for moving technical and management know-how from a central point to the many points of use? Does it practice a program of quality control and assurance? Does it pretest its policies, procedures, and training methods? Does it have a career system and a history of career development programs?

Does the organization use systems and methods analysts to accomplish management improvements, or does it try to speed up inefficient old systems and methods to get out more production? Does it use internal audit concepts effectively to check on accountability and compliance with laws, policies, and procedures, or does it wait for external audits to smoke out its shortcomings?

Production-Oriented Teams

Training specialists are accustomed to concluding a training program only to have the participants praise the content and the methods used but to comment in unison, "You should have given it to our bosses." Give it to their bosses and you are likely to get the identical response. This willingness to finger higher echelons suggests that upward and downward communication is imperfect, that there is too little team effort in solving production problems.

One way to combat this tendency is to periodically assemble vertically structured teams and have a series of working sessions. The teams should include representatives from three or four levels in the chain of command. At least one senior executive should be present. Such sessions, if well run by a seasoned training specialist, can accomplish much. They reestablish communication among the people

who should be communicating with each other. They afford the
training specialist an opportunity to review the fundamental principles of sound organization and management.

Sessions of this kind get the team started on solving specific production problems that need attention. When a participant says, "We
could cut delivery time if the people upstairs would . . . ," the participant from "upstairs" becomes personally involved, and the two of
them may spin off from the main group and work out a solution.
Out of such incidents, the trainer finds opportunities to clinch a
principle in the minds of all participants. This is better training than
straight lectures on principles.

Work Simplification

Traditionally, most organizations seek management improvement in one of two ways. One way is to have a centrally based team
of organization and methods (O&M) experts descend on a worri-
some area of operations and sweat out a new way. The other conventional approach is to contract with an outside group to do the
job. Each method has its advantages and disadvantages. Too
frequently, nothing much happens in the end except a hassle, and
there are no lessons learned of enduring consequence by the people
who have to get out the work. No people development occurs.

A far more constructive approach is a process known as "work
simplification." It can be a yardstick for measuring organization development needs. It can stimulate growth and development on the
part of first-line supervisors and all higher levels of management.

In 1945, the U.S. Bureau of the Budget, under the directorship
of Harold D. Smith, introduced a version of work simplification and
some noteable results were obtained for a few years until it died out.
Selected private firms have made use of it and some claim excellent
results. For example, one electronics products company claims that
10 percent of its net profit annually is attributable to beneficial
suggestions for work simplification contributed by its employees.
One consultant (Alan Moganson) has made a lifetime career of
teaching work simplification and consulting with over 500 firms that
were interested in its use.

Work simplification, in essence, is a scheme for attacking the procedural problems of large organizations by teaching line supervisors
and their subordinates how to analyze and improve methods. Every
supervisor needs certain basic skills, such as the skill of instruction,

the skill of improving methods, and the skill of working with people. Part of this management job is to simplify operations, eliminate red tape, get out more work with less manpower, materials, and equipment. If the supervisor practices participative management methods, his subordinates will become interested and involved in finding and perfecting better ways.

Management experts have long agreed that at least 80 percent of the ideas for improving a job originate with the people who do the job. Why not enlist them in the work simplification effort? Why pay outsiders to come in, pick their brains, and sell the results back to senior executives? This use of external consultants diminishes the respect management has for its labor force because it is left to wonder why someone inside the place did not think of the improvements. Work simplification consists of a series of basic tools, including work distribution chart, process chart, and work count. The data collected by these devices, when analyzed, can point the way to elimination, combination, rearrangement, or simplification of tasks and steps.

Work simplification results are not automatic. Active support of top leaders is critical. A mechanism for generating quick, official response to beneficial suggestions is needed. The employer must fairly and generously reward (financial and recognition) those who contribute ideas worthy of adoption. The program must have continuity and there should be special occasions for recognizing the harvest of useful work simplification ideas. Annual stockholder meetings, incentive award presentations, house organs, retirement parties, recruitment literature, and special reports are but a few of the ways to give recognition. The work simplification program needs an effective coordinator, and the training specialist is a logical candidate for this post.

The Budget—Key to Organization Development Needs

The budget of any organization can be the best instrument for sound planning. The real planning is not done by a professionally trained planner, though such individuals can be extremely useful as a catalyst of ideas and for coordinating the consideration of issues affecting the budget. The only planning with any meaning and ultimate payback is that done by the concerted efforts of supervisors, managers, and senior-level officials with the help of their respective staffs.

In the give and take of budget formulation, and in the prose and money figures that flow forth as the basis for future operations, one can see long-range, intermediate, and short-term goals and objectives. The need may be clearly indicated for such things as organizational adjustments, new technology, training and retraining, communications, problem solving, new decisions, stricter accountability, and increased attention to public relations.

In brief, the training and development specialist is well advised to become an integral part of the budget planning process. Through a network of people developer counterparts, the specialist can perhaps influence the inclusion of items in the budget that will advance the objectives of organization development through people development.

Budget execution is the other side of the coin. Operating officials have considerable discretion in the allocation of authorized funds as long as projects are compatible with the basic mission. The training specialist is adept at writing, illustrating, and packaging proposals; this skill is not universal, and some busy operating officials are therefore pleased when the training specialist lends a hand in making a program ready for operational stages. In short, the specialist may be glad to obtain an allowance in the budget for some needed training in return for some good staff work in putting the plans together.

Labor/Management Contracts and Agreements

A signed and sealed contract or agreement symbolizes the long struggle between labor leaders and the management of a company or government agency. The language of such documents usually represents a delicate compromise between the extremes of two pre-bargaining positions. Nevertheless, it lays out the terms and conditions that management has agreed to live by during the contract period; that is, the specified improvements in pay, fringe benefits, and working conditions.

As management makes the reforms it has pledged in writing to make, some training and development will be needed. Executives will need briefing. Managers and supervisors will need training in specific new procedures. Perhaps some organization refinements and systems changes will be needed. Additional planning is required. Policy and procedure issuances may be needed. More significantly, *attitudes* of the decision makers may have to be adjusted. For example, officials who may have been giving lip service and a wink to affirmative action policies may be faced with a choice between reform and litigation.

It is pure folly for management people to ignore or to underestimate the voice of labor spokesmen. Experience has shown that they are seldom in the position of not having done their "home work." They have a direct channel of communication to employees; management tends to hear nothing from employees, or get its information late, indirectly, and filtered.

Performance Appraisals

While most appraisal systems result in a net loss in cost/benefit terms, the end products of such systems may give a few clues to organization development needs. If an experienced training and development specialist were to sample a stratified sample of such ratings for the entire organization, he or she might well glean some trends, or an underlying tone or theme. By then having a dialogue with management officials, the specialist could dwell on specifics. For example: Customers are complaining about lack of courtesy; new clerical employees are marginally skilled and are making excessive errors; first-line supervisors are generating many grievances; the position classification system is slow and allegedly inequitable; there is an imbalance in work load; the merit promotion system is not working; some people have gone far beyond the call of duty without proper recognition; the published organization chart is obsolete and a source of embarrassment.

Performance appraisals may be the best mirror of emerging leaders. They may also be signaling for selected individuals to get mid-career training or executive development. The work of some appraisers may identify them as having true perspective on sound organization and management. Supervisors and managers who do an honest, thorough, constructive job of performance appraisal are actually a part of the people development crew of an organization. They carry, with or without commensurate pay and recognition, the greatest responsibility for the continuity of ongoing operations. Unfortunately, many of them may be underrewarded for their gallant efforts for years, if not forever.

Other Ways and Means

There is no magic set of ways to get at organization development needs. The task is somewhat like that of a diagnostician or a pathologist. Given a symptom or series of known conditions, such specialists usually show great brilliance in diagnosing and prescribing a course of action. Intensive research may be needed just before they announce their conclusion, and the principal in the case may want to consult with peers or even remote sources of expertise.

The training and development specialist may be influential enough to get senior executives long enough away from their usual place of business to a retreat where they can engage in some soul searching on those occasions when they are faced with hard decisions. During the retreat, the people developer may find it appropriate to introduce some resource people who can point up options that are beyond the parameters of the decision makers' experience.

It is not unusual for senior executives to buy time for their major decisions by appointing task groups or committees to gather more data and to present them graphically. A field inspection trip may be suggested. A conference with delegates from consumer groups or employee organizations may be in order. The use of experts such as mathematical statisticians, actuaries, certified public accountants, and attorneys can be productive.

Organization development, like the development of individuals, should be undertaken in the spirit of universal craftsmanship with which all true craftsmen are imbued. The dynamism and pragmatism permeating the processes of organization development are best met by individuals with a high order of intelligence, ingenuity, and a thorough understanding of how organizations and individuals do their best work.

Conclusion

People development is a function that must primarily serve the productivity goals of the organization itself. Since the needs of individual employees for further training and development must therefore be related to organization needs, systematic inventories should be taken, at the direction of top management, using the check list suggested in the overview to this Part I. In other words, every barometer of productivity affected directly or indirectly by people performance should be checked periodically both before and after the input of more training.

3

Identifying Target Audiences and Individual Training Needs

The timely and precise identification of training needs starts with the determination of knowledges, abilities, and skills essential for maximum effectiveness in an organization's positions at all levels of responsibility. With the possible exception of institutions whose mission is the education or training of people, an *organization's* requirements with respect to training take precedence over those of individuals.

Getting the Best Results

The systematic approach called "job analysis" is probably the best known way to assemble valid information about the necessity for training in an organization. Job analysis is also helpful in determining the training needs of the typical employee for any given position; however, one cannot safely generalize that all employees should have identical training for a particular job. This chapter provides a rationale for the use of job analysis and a brief description of the method.

There are numerous other ways to isolate the training needs of individuals at specific stages of their growth and development. This chapter also lists some alternative methods and annotates each one briefly.

In its advice to federal departments and agencies on the determination of training needs, the U.S. Civil Service Commission offers some useful criteria:

Agencies will get best results when reviews of training needs:
—Are conducted in a planned and systematic manner.
—Are conducted both at local levels to identify specific, local needs and at agency levels to identify general, overall needs.
—Are based on realistic assessment of organizational conditions and operating problems as well as on an overall assessment of the performance of the agency's work force.
—Take into consideration future program and staffing needs, and potential for meeting those needs, including the potential of employees for advancement within their present occupations or for assignment and advancement within other occupations in the agency.
—Provide reasonable opportunity for employees and employee organizations to express their views on training, especially any which management determines that employees shall take.
—Identify all significant needs, regardless of whether they can be met with available resources.
—Represent the conclusions of line management as well as the views of personnel and training staffs.
—Cover training requirements imposed by authority outside the agency (for example, the supervisory training requirement imposed by the Commission).[1]

Logical Target Audiences

The Hoover Commission reported to the Congress of the United States, in 1955, that the federal employee most needs training at three major points in his career, as follows:

First, on his entrance to public service his agency should make certain that he has a basic understanding of the needs of the American public service. . . .

[1] *Federal Personnel Manual,* Subchapter 2, "Determining Training Needs," Sept. 1974, pp. 410–412.

> Second, as the employee advances in his field, there comes a time when he needs either advanced knowledge of his occupation, skill in supervision of others, or both. . . .
>
> Third, as the employee enters executive ranks he needs to gain a working knowledge of Government programs outside of his own, a more thorough insight into public attitudes and legislative issues and a more comprehensive view of the techniques of management.[2]

The training specialist has discovered these target audiences and he is accustomed, in cooperation with operating officials, to planning and managing training programs for these and various other *basic categories of employees,* or "target audiences." Twelve target audiences are described below, but the list will not necessarily be comprehensive for any particular organization.

ORIENTATION FOR NEW EMPLOYEES. A form of introduction to the mission, structure, leadership, programs, policies, and practices of the organization. It also covers the rights and privileges and responsibilities of the employee, and routine services available to him. It normally occurs on or about the day of entrance upon duty, though more enlightened employers are able to start the orientation before the new employee reports for duty, and they have ways of updating it after initial entry.

VESTIBULE TRAINING. It is the exception, not rule, when an employer uses the valuable form of vestibule training. For example, if a skilled clerk-stenographer is lost, the replacement should not necessarily be recruited and sent directly to the vacant desk. The replacement may be a person who was last employed years ago in a different industry or occupational field, and whose clerical skills are therefore rusty. Under the circumstances, it is better practice to assign the replacement to a central unit for indoctrination and temporary duty on work using the tools, systems, procedures, and terminology peculiar to his or her new employer. The supervisor will presumably be a master craftsperson who conducts the vestibule training unit in a manner empathetic to newcomers, and is skilled in coaching such people so that they quickly regain an acceptable proficiency level. In the interim, all operating groups awaiting the arrival of replacements can have work consigned to the vestibule unit so that the work force there is engaged in real production instead of training exercises. Persons are released from vestibule units individually as they reach proper performance standards.

[2] *Personnel and Civil Service,* a report to the Congress by the Commission on Organization of the Executive Branch of the Government, Feb. 1955, pp. 48–49.

For example, the Federal Highway Administration uses vestibule training for typists and stenographers. The Bureau of the Census made extensive use of the technique in training several thousand coders and editors for the 1950 Census in Suitland, Maryland. An air-conditioning equipment manufacturer places all incoming secretaries in a vestibule unit for approximately three weeks.

APPRENTICESHIP AND CRAFT SKILLS TRAINING. Both private and public sectors have occupations that lend themselves to apprenticeship training under standards regulated by the Bureau of Apprenticeship, U.S. Department of Labor. One person learns from another in such trades as carpentry, plumbing, electrical work, and bricklaying. Specific time requirements must be met for each content element, and certain performance tests and self-study courses are stipulated. When all requirements are met, the apprentice is eligible for advancement to the journeyman level.

Organizations that do not participate in formally affiliated apprenticeship programs may have their own programs of craft skills training. A typical case of in-service training is the U.S. Postal Service, which has seven recognized "crafts," including postal clerk and postal carrier.

SUPERVISORY TRAINING. Employees who are designated to supervise other employees, but who do so for the first time, receive special courses of instruction. These courses average about 80 classroom hours in length, and include instructional techniques, methods improvement, employee relations, and administrative management procedures.

OFFICE SKILLS TRAINING. Refresher training in mechanical skills and basic education skills (reading, mathematics, language arts, and general science), new systems, methods, and equipment is given to clerical employees and secretaries. For example, secretaries may receive special training in handling communications systems, correspondence, records management procedures, and security classification.

TRAINING OF TECHNICAL, PROFESSIONAL, AND SCIENTIFIC PERSONNEL. The specialized personnel classification includes a wide variety of personnel whose work is above the craft and office skills level of responsibility and is not primarily administrative or managerial in nature. For example, an electronics repair person for sophisticated equipment is considered a "technician." The engineers who design such equipment are "professionals." Research people who discover new knowledge with which new equipment can be designed are the "scientists." These classes of personnel have to be kept updated at such places as universities and manufacturers' schools and at on-site applications of prototype equipment.

SPECIAL TRAINING. Every organization is subject to serious and sometimes abrupt change—changes in headquarters, systems, methods, equipment, organization, working languages, policies, and other factors. Emergencies may occur. Seasonal and cyclical events demand special training. Such training may be beamed broadside at all operational personnel or at an isolated group of employees in a limited occupational class. It may be conducted in a formal manner, with proper advance planning, or it may be done quickly and informally on a word-to-mouth (briefing) basis or through cadres.

MIDDLE-MANAGEMENT TRAINING. When a supervisor begins to supervise other supervisors or supervisors of supervisors—when he begins to manage—he needs additional training, and most employers recognize this need. An example is the administrative officer who has primary responsibility for the personnel management, budget, and administrative service functions of a division of, say, 100 or more employees. This officer will normally have three to five supervisors in the group, and the supervisory problems will be different from those of a first-line supervisor.

EXECUTIVE DEVELOPMENT. Persons who manage the managers are "executives." The principles of supervision and management are about the same at first-line supervisor and executive levels, but the manner of applying them and evaluating the results are entirely different. Subtleties can be learned in experiential methods of training such as role playing, videotaping, and simulated situations involving critical incidents. Additionally, the executive should seek interpretation of the new initiatives of the organization and industry, the political climate, legislative issues, community pressures, and the like. Persons who are compelled to stay at their desks the year round soon become bureaucrats and lose their perspective.

PRERETIREMENT TRAINING. Progressive organizations conduct preretirement sessions for employees whose age category suggests the need for expert advice on such matters as investments, insurance, estate planning, health maintenance, leisure-time activities, retirement-home considerations, postretirement income possibilities, and related information. Outside resource people are usually brought in to conduct such sessions.

TRAINING OF INCOMING GROUPS FOR CAREER DEVELOPMENT PROGRAMS. The more progressive organizations have established policies of making an input into their career development channels periodically. Inputs from external sources may be young professionals, such as engineers or social scientists, management trainees, or work/study students engaged under "co-op" plans with educational institutions. Inputs from internal sources may be individuals who have been competitively selected from the ranks for presupervisory training, management training, upward mobility, and the like.

Inputs may also be lateral entries, at any level, as advocated for the federal career system by The American Assembly of Columbia University in 1954. The Assembly offered this advice:

> The Federal career system should be cut to the pattern of American customs and institutions. A closed, self-contained system is not in the American tradition. The Federal Service should provide both for promotion from within and for the lateral entry of personnel, particularly in the middle and higher grades. It should be open to interchange with the other fields of American life—business, trade unions, universities, the professions, state and local governments. Such exchanges benefit both the Federal Service and these groups, and our society is the richer. Efforts to close the door on such interchange should be vigorously resisted. (*The Federal Government Service: Its Character, Prestige, and Problems,* Final Edition, 1954, page 184).

COMPLIMENTARY AND FEE-FOR-SERVICE TRAINING. The Government Employees Training Act (1958) requires all federal departments and agencies to share their training facilities with each other on a space-available basis, and they may charge a reasonable fee for the service. The Intergovernmental Personnel Act requires the federal government to share its training facilities with state and local governments. The Mutual Security Assistance Act, under which the United States foreign-aid program operates, requires all federal agencies to assist less developed countries with which the United States has an agreement to provide economic and technical assistance. Industrial organizations frequently share their training facilities. Therefore, it is common to have a number of foreign nationals observing or participating in formal training courses conducted by both public and private organizations.

Adding a Training Entitlement Factor to the Merit System

Merit systems, to which most governmental units in the United States are committed by law in their personnel management actions, promise a multitude of benefits to the employee, but they stop short of promising any training. Instead, they prod employees to continue their efforts after hours in order to realize more "self-education, self-training, and self-improvement." In the meantime, the employer is probably making profound and sometimes abrupt changes in the employee's working conditions, systems, methods, equipment, tools, and the like.

More specifically, merit systems *guarantee* certain fundamental rights and fringe benefits to individuals—merit appointment, protection against arbitrary removal, uniform pay, leave, retirement plan, health and insurance program subsidies, right to join or refrain from joining a union, affirmative action programs (for minority group employees and women), veterans benefits, out-placement service, and others. Unfortunately, training and career development are not included by law, ordinance, or policy in this list of guarantees. Training for the merit system employee, whether in public or private employment—starts and stops at the discretion and sole initiative of the employer, who is *usually an immediate supervisor*. Such a system, which essentially is the nomination system, can prove the saying about "Making the rich richer and the poor poorer"—and often does.

There are at least four good reasons for adding a training entitlement factor to the merit system of employment. First, during the past two or three decades the typical employee in both government and industry has been confronted with new and more complex phenomena in his work, demanding a new level of knowledge, skill, and understanding. For example, he must (1) operate or manage far more and increasingly complex capital equipment; (2) install, operate, maintain, or manage more sophisticated systems; (3) work within a vastly more decentralized organization; (4) interact as a member of new racial and ethnic mixes of people; (5) face physical hazards constantly growing out of the environment, new technology, unprecedented crime levels, and disturbed urban conditions; (6) function within the context of very sensitive and elaborate labor-management contracts and agreements; and (7) observe new laws and court rulings that have narrowed the discretion of supervisors and managers in decision making where the civil rights and individual liberties of employees are involved.

Second, the aftermath of a manufacturing or human error can be exceedingly serious in our society. Because remotely produced and managed goods and services are being increasingly automated, it is costly and time consuming to recall thousands of defective automobiles or cans of soup that have already trickled through the distribution system. By the time the error is discovered and recall is announced, the product or service will have become hazardous to life and property, costly, and counterproductive in GNP terms. It is a gross underestimate of the citizens to assume that they cannot and do not associate marginal service, unconscionable delays, and bad decisions with inadequate training of the worker or ineffective supervision and management, or both. Training is the best known insurance against the occurrence and recurrence of human errors.

Third, when marginal employees without the necessary training to perform increased duties and responsibilities clog up career channels, numerous "brakes" automatically engage in an organizational element—morale, productivity and service, efficiency, upward mobility, organization development, and human growth. When the decision is left to the discretion of a supervisor as to whether or not an individual receives additional training and development, the operating unit may be destined to stagnate and continue for years without the spark of innovation and creativity that can come from training experiences. Many supervisors are known to be guilty of discarding training announcements rather than post or circulate them among their subordinates and run the risk of losing production time. Such conditions often lead to another form of organizational disease—reorganization. The insecurities and other ramifications that flow from reorganization could fill a whole chapter in this book.

Fourth, the law and policymakers are trailing, not leading, the people because it is apparent that public acceptance of employee training is already a reality. Complaint after complaint indicates that the taxpayers and consumers feel that they are paying more and getting less than ever before for their dollars.

It is not hard to imagine what the public reaction would be if (1) a military service recruit were sent into battle without training in modern weaponry; (2) a commercial pilot were sent into the air without special training in the equipment he is assigned to fly; (3) a new subway system should be inaugurated with bus drivers who lack special training in driving subway trains; (4) the superintendent and staff of a new nuclear power plant were reassigned from a coal-fueled power plant without special training; (5) NASA, in the interest of keeping costs down and winning the race to the moon, had shot test pilots into orbit without special training. Obviously, in these cases, the public would be "up in arms" and would demand immediate inquiry and reforms in legislation and regulations. Equally clear is what the impact on public reaction would have been had the Congress not seen fit to enact after World War II the GI Education

Benefit Act, which afforded *certain rights to the individual* by enabling the returning veteran, at public expense, to continue his disrupted education and make a smoother transition to civilian life.

For these and other reasons, the case is compelling for making training an entitlement at specified, predetermined junctures in one's career. It is, and should continue to be, management's prerogative to hire, reassign, promote, and separate individuals for justifiable cause. Once new work assignment initiatives are taken by the employer, for which additional training is a reasonable necessity, the individuals should have a right to receive timely training of an amount and type appropriate to their needs, and the training should be administered in an environment fully conducive to effective learning.

Some Specific Methods for Identifying Individual Training Needs

No inventory of means for finding individual training needs can ever be exhaustive. A need can be discovered through formal counseling or quite accidentally during person-to-person conversation in such places as the golf course, the lunch room, or the car pool. The means are limited only by the imagination, finesse, keen oversight, and practical judgment of the supervisor, manager, executive, administrator, training specialist, and the individual. A number of procedures are suggested below for identifying training needs of the individual.

JOB ANALYSIS. Job analysis is a generic term covering diverse techniques and end products. The fundamental idea is to find out as much as possible about a particular *job,* as distinguished from an individual person who may temporarily be the incumbent. The U.S. Department of Labor is credited with a benchmark piece of work in its original development of the dictionary of occupations in the United States. In order to produce the original edition of the dictionary, the Department's technicians developed a classical approach to job analysis, which may be defined as follows:

> Job analysis is the systematic review of a job (group of similar positions) to ascertain objectively the: duties, educational requirements, specific knowledges required, experience required, knowledges acquired on the job, physical effort, responsibilities, and working conditions.

Job-analysis results can be critical in grading and setting pay for jobs; in recruitment, selection, and placement; in training and development; in performance appraisal and counseling; and for selection-out purposes.

The analysis is best obtained by using a pretested, standardized form completed by an experienced analyst who knows how to probe objectively and ask quality questions of respondents. Job-analysis conclusions can be deceiving, since there is always the rare individual who can or cannot perform at his best despite the available methods and tools, and prevalent working conditions. For example, the deaf typist is usually a whiz in noisy work situations in comparison to the typist with normal hearing.

When it is not feasible, within the available resources of an organization, to make a thorough job analysis of its jobs using the Department of Labor methods, an acceptable substitute for many jobs is one that can be done by the supervisor after a few hours of special training, and which is less time consuming. The supervisor divides the work of his unit into "jobs," each of which has five or six steps and a definite beginning and end. He then makes a "job breakdown" for each job on a separate sheet of paper with a line drawn down the middle. He carefully lists the principal steps in proper sequence on the left side of the sheet; opposite each step he lists the key points that (1) make it easier to do, (2) will make or break the job, and (3) may injure the worker if not observed.

As each new employee enters the unit, the supervisor can draw from a file of job breakdowns those that are appropriate to the individual training of the employee. The supervisor should know from experience which steps and key points require special attention in training. Job breakdowns, like job analyses, have various other uses in good supervision and management.

DAY-TO-DAY SUPERVISION. There is no substitute for the day-to-day supervisor/employee relationship in determing the real training needs of an individual, provided the relationship is a healthy one based on frequent communication. Both the supervisor and the employee know when there is a shortfall of production, quality, and manner of doing the job in accordance with reasonable job-performance standards. Both know when job requirements change. Both know when those served are reacting adversely to the service or lack of service. The fact is that training needs are common knowledge in the local work situation. Even an individual's poor performance is known by co-workers, for they are a part of the work group and unsatisfactory work may be reflecting indirectly against them too.

Unfortunately, some training specialists have failed to recognize that the way to find out what is common knowledge on the work scene is to associate with operating people—not to sit in the personnel office and wait for the answer to walk in. This failure has been compounded by their tendency to import canned courses to meet *assumed* needs, depending on the endorsement of outside facilities that offer no job-related training, or by using "vacuum packed" courses made in the training office and imposed by administrators.

TRAINING INVENTORIES. Some organizations have a practice of taking periodic inventories of training needs, usually at annual intervals. Such inventories may be all right if enough planning goes into them. However, they tend to gather information on general training needs rather than specific training needs. For example, these inventories frequently report that training is needed in such subjects as human relations, effective writing, rapid reading, better listening, conference leadership, and telephone techniques. In other words, the demand is for superficial cures for symptoms instead of root causes. Poor writing can often be traced to a shallow or obsolete knowledge of one's specialized field. The inventory method can produce valid results when it is a genuine and diligent effort to get the facts, and not merely an armchair exercise. It should be pretested and key persons in supervisory and managerial positions should be briefed well in advance.

SELF-ANALYSIS. Self-analysis can help to identify valid individual training needs even at the executive level when it takes place in an atmosphere of mutual confidence. It is best used within the context of a career system, where all parties have commitments to fulfill, and where auxiliary systems are used on a continuing basis. A sound, honest approach to appraisal/counseling processes can set the stage for an individual to seriously and deeply reflect about his or her immediate and long-range training needs. An employee who knows the qualification requirements for gaining entry into a training program with accelerated promotion provisions has no difficulty in spotting his or her deficiencies.

MANAGEMENT IMPROVEMENT STUDIES. In-house management analysts are in a good position to identify individual training needs. They participate in organizational realignments, work simplification, work measurement studies, and systems changes. The success or failure of their efforts so often depends on whether or not employees accept and receive sufficient training in the new methods. For example, if an operation is being computerized, management has a vested interest in having associated personnel receive special training.

CONSULTANTS. Outside consultants and experts are often good

catalysts in the formulation of training programs because they work in numerous places and have contact with various problems. They, like the in-house analyst, are change agents and, in order to effect lasting change efficiently, they concentrate on who needs training in what, where, and when.

AUDITORS. Internal and external auditors who inspect for compliance with laws and regulations are still another source of insights into individual training needs. When they trace mistakes to the source, they generally discover that they were not caused by willful misuse of funds or authority but by ignorance and lack of training. Fortunately, auditors are beginning to broaden the scope of their concerns from fiscal matters to include program planning and performance in relation to organization goals and objectives.

TECHNOLOGICAL CHANGE. Ironically, buildings and capital equipment seem to get more attention than people in the business world. But investors are bent on making their capital asset investments live up to their expectations and therefore they readily see the need for service contracts, preventive maintenance, and even the training of operators and mechanics. The professional who programs the use of the equipment may not be so fortunate in getting initial training before the equipment arrives and on occasions when it is upgraded.

ACCIDENT REPORTS. The safety engineer and the safety training officer usually have well-established reporting systems for monitoring the incidence of accidents. An organization can panic over a sudden spurt in its accident rate and throw a disporportionate amount of its training resources into safety training. The accident rate may be erratic, depending on definitions, compliance with reporting requirements, and the whoopings of safety-campaign managers. Out of it all can be winnowed a few individual training needs, for a good accident report can establish the place, time, basic cause, and special circumstances surrounding the accident.

PRODUCTION RECORDS. Educational psychologists long ago discovered the value of a "learning curve." This tells that a learner experiences one or more plateaus in his or her progress to reach a satisfactory proficiency level of task performance. If a supervisor has time to plot learning curves for a statistically significant number of individuals (a hundred or more) in a given type of work, he will generally know when to apply special training that will speed up learning and production. This would be a good assignment for industrial engineers and management analysts. The cause of poor output is there in the basic production records, if only someone could, and would, spot it and act accordingly.

TRAINING COMMITTEES AND TASK GROUPS. Comments have already been made about the comparative value of training committees and training task groups (Chapter 2). The task group is especially recommended as a means of smoking out individual training needs. It can easily be combined with many of the other methods suggested above, such as job analysis, inventories, analysis of production records, and use of technological changes.

ADMINISTRATOR'S OBSERVATIONS. The administrator or manager in charge of an establishment is in an advantageous position to sense the need for individual training. This exectuve travels, confers, defends budgets, apologizes for goofs and excessive delays, reviews appeals and court actions, monitors production in relation to goals, signs mail, and issues reports. While the staff span of control may be only a private secretary and five or six executives, the manager's eye is roving over the entire spectrum of operations through multimedia monitoring systems.

CONFERENCES AND MEETINGS. Modern participative management induces a lot of decisions through advice-and-consent strategies. Out of such dialogue comes the realization that Tom, Dick, or Harriet, or all three will need special training before they can do what is needed.

QUALITY CONTROL SYSTEMS. The application of scientific sampling methods enables an organization to set tolerable error limits and regulate the amount of sampling to produce within such tolerances. For example, in statistical processing work the publisher may be satisfied with 98 percent accuracy in coding and editing steps. Adjustments are made in the level of sampling for employees who are still learning the work. An employee making 4 percent error would presumably have 50 percent of his work reviewed in order to reduce the error to 2 percent. Consistent deviation from acceptable norms points up individual training needs, including perhaps the supervisor's need for refresher training in how to instruct.

PERFORMANCE APPRAISAL. While most performance appraisal systems have many imperfections and are frequently worthless, they can be a valid source of individual training needs. This is particularly true when multiple judgments enter the appraisal process; that is, when an appraisal panel instead of the supervisor alone is used and the panel reports out only matters on which it is unanimous.

COUNSELING. Nearly every organization has people whose function it is to listen to the complaints of others. Most personnel offices have such people, called counselors. An alert counselor can often detect the need for specific kinds of training. Supervisors also have to do a lot of listening and counseling. A good training specialist will systematically debrief counselors and supervisors of information, and translate the findings into training needs of individuals.

BRAINSTORMING. It has been conclusively demonstrated that a group of people (any group) of average intelligence can "think wild" on a problem and produce some useful solutions. They need not be experts in the substantive area of the problem. Statistically, five of a hundred brainstormed ideas are likely to be worthy of implementation, at least in modified form. Many officials and supervisors tend to generalize that their units need training, but they cannot name the specific kinds of training needs. One way to resolve this question would be for the training specialist to meet with a group of such people and moderate a brainstorming session. It is considered improper and cause for dismissal from such sessions to "throw cold water" on suggestions of other participants. One person serves as recorder. A second group—knowledgeable management officials—evaluates all brainstormed suggestions.

IN-BASKET PROBLEMS. A reliable method for developing young executives is called the "in-basket" technique. The trainee is permitted to examine the contents of the in-basket on the desk of the senior executive daily, before the day's work begins. He or she analyzes each problem, tries to decide what action to take, and then waits for the senior executive to act. When the day ends, the senior executive counsels the trainee on the action actually taken, if any, and why or why not. With a slight variation of this strategy, the in-basket could be used as a barometer of training needs. The training specialist would, of course, be the one having a direct relationship with the senior executive for a period of time.

INCIDENTS. From every crisis in the management of organizations is likely to come the recognition of some training needs. The alert training specialist will be one of the first to arrive on the scene after a crisis has passed, and will collaborate with management officials in trying to discover how the crisis could have been avoided by the use of training as a management tool.

RESEARCH. The organized research and development technique is one of the surest ways to discover specific training needs. Suppose, for example, that an organization is considering a refresher course for its typists in order to improve their speed and accuracy. A controlled experiment can discover what the training input needs to be and at what rate in order to raise the proficiency of typists to the desired level.

TESTS. Paper-and-pencil tests, performance tests, oral examinations, and other forms of tests can isolate training needs. Many employers do not make enough use of this measuring device.

QUESTIONNAIRES. While questionnaires are closely related to other methods discussed above, and may be even an integral part of some, they deserve separate mention. They must be carefully designed by experts so that the bias of the respondent is minimized by the design of the questions. Every word has to be measured for readability, cultural bias, and other factors.

WORKSHOPS. Training begets training. When the workshop form of training is used, it is often discovered that participants lack understanding in some of the fundamentals that were taken for granted during the workshop design stage. In other instances, the demand for advanced training may grow out of workshops, which are, of course, never intended to do the entire job of training.

ANNUAL REPORTS. A serious and reflective job of preparing and analyzing an annual report can pinpoint individual training needs. They involve not only a technical editor in the reports office but also others from numerous organizational departments. Annual reports can illuminate units where training has been used to resolve operating difficulties, and prologize action in the ensuing year for units that have neglected to use training as a management tool.

RECORDS MANAGERS AND ARCHIVISTS. In exceptional cases one will find an organization that is enlightened enough to appoint an archivist, historian, or records management specialist to oversee the assembly, culling, preservation, and arrangements for future servicing of important records generated by program areas. Such organizations have foresight in planning future training needs, particularly for recurring seasonal or cyclical operations.

LABOR DEMANDS. Labor unions, less formal employee organizations, and professional societies are interested in seeing training used to bridge the gaps in the backgrounds of their members. An individual member may seek labor-group support when he or she sees training being used inequitably by management to place a peer in line for promotion. Labor groups demand training programs, such as apprenticeship training, so that their members will not have to serve a lifetime as "helpers." They demand pre-supervisor training so that their members will be more likely to succeed when they are elevated to supervisor or foreman.

PUBLIC DEMANDS. It is not likely that the consumerism movement can be wished away by suppliers. In fact, it can be expected to grow stronger unless the declining level of craftsmanship in our economy is reversed. As public and private producers become more responsive to consumers' demands for higher-quality products and services, they will begin to scrutinize their operations, in order to identify the cause and correct mistakes rather than fix the blame—and this can help detect individual training needs.

Conclusion

Organization hierarchies should stop pumping into their associate employees the "patent medicine" type of course and berating them for not responding to the treatment by delivering outstanding performance. Further, they should correct their fuzzy vision by focusing on certain target audiences of particular employees who have common inadequacies and can be intelligently grouped for training and development purposes. Finally, managements should use the wide assortment of tools available to them through existing in-house systems so that they can identify the specific training and development requirements of individuals from the time of employment to the time of separation. The key point is that employees must be treated as individuals—not as a faceless, nameless group about which the organization knows literally nothing.

PART TWO

Planning and Developing Solutions

Given that a people development problem exists, an alert management of an organization will be impelled to correct it. Perhaps the most crucial elements of a development program are those described in this Part II. Whether training and retraining programs will succeed depends on the care with which each part of the structure is formulated. Chapters 4 through 12 describe explicitly the elements of these parts. The following overviews emphasize the highlights of each chapter.

Chapter 4. Structuring the Development Program

Many organizations do not seem to have any management philosophy. Instead, they are run by persons who react to day-to-day crises. Their leaders do not act positively within the parameters of a well-conceived set of guiding management principles and processes.

Other organizations know where they want to go from a management standpoint, but they are never quite able to convert their philosophy into practical policies and practices. They are not skilled in the use of such tools as policy and procedure manuals, handbooks, orientation programs, audiovisual aids, slogans, posters, and other means of communication.

With respect to the people development function, inept organizations are unsure about its placement in relation to functions affecting the acquisition, development, utilization, and loss of human resources. They generally associate it with the routine paperwork and the regulatory-type function in the typical personnel office. Such organizations stifle the initiative and creativity that many training and career development specialists bring to their work.

Organizations that do not prepare to develop career systems and career development programs for continuing use are making a tragic mistake. It may be that they lack interaction with educational institutions of the community in which they operate. This means that they are without manpower supply lines and must rely on such sources as walk-ins, classified ads, personal and political patronage, employment agencies, and the like. The uncertainties of such labor markets compound both management and operations for an employer.

Chapter 5. Evaluating Sources of Help

The individual charged with coordinating people development activities of a sizable organization is the orchestrator of events. He or she must therefore be adroit in the identification and assessment of the various sources of technical assistance. Both internal and external sources of help are available, but no organization can rely exclusively on either of these main sources. Balance and flexibility are essential in marshaling effective people development capability at appropriate places when needed. There is a surprising amount of people development talent within most organizations. One of the central theses of this book is that people developers stud every level of responsibility and every area of occupational endeavor, and are not peculiar to institutionalized units that claim expertise in the training and development of employees.

Some places are more logical than others in which to look for in-house talent for the people development movement. Subject-matter specialists, on whose brainpower and experience the organization runs, are probably the best source. Librarians, public information offices, labor leaders, executives, field offices, and audiovisual presentation groups are also good sources.

External sources offer both advantages and disadvantages, but an organization cannot expect quality results if responsibility is relinquished to a contractor. A carefully drafted contract is fundamental, but it must be controlled by good monitoring of contract performance. There is a wide field of choice externally—individuals, educational institutions, consulting firms, business and industrial firms offering training and education services as a secondary or incidental line, professional societies, governments, and organizations dealing primarily in education and training services.

Chapter 6. Marshaling Resources

It takes physical energy to produce the additional physical energy that runs various household appliances. Similarly, it takes a continuing input of combined human and organizational resources to develop productive human resources. These resources include space, time, equipment, authority, money, manpower, materials, and management—a combination conveniently labeled with the acronym "STEAMMMM."

An apt definition of management is "the process of guiding human and physical resources into dynamic organization units that attain their objectives to the satisfaction of those served and with a high degree of morale and sense of attainment on the part of those rendering the service." Therefore, besides the major categories of human resources, the two additional dimensions required by the resource development equation are the people to be developed and the clients ultimately to be served by those people. The former must feel self-fulfilled in the level of service they *give,* and the latter must be pleased with the level of service they *receive.*

The marshaling and application of each of the principal resources required in people development is in itself a painstaking project. For example, haphazardly arranged space used for the training and development of people can easily have a counterproductive effect. The resources needed should be as deliberately marshaled and well planned, and as well articulated and defended, as those for any other major program activity. To make people development an incidental, uncoordinated, poorly funded program is as ill advised as the practice of the American pioneers who ate their seed corn in winter and left none to plant in the spring.

Chapter 7. Finding People Developers

The discovery of people developers is not an easy task, and is complicated by the fact that they are usually already employed by other organizations. Obviously, not all are associated with institutionalized units that have this function as their regular activity.

There are two categories of people developers: those who work in training and development units, each unit normally being a part of a personnel office; those made up of people who perform the function without benefit of title. The first category has a number of titles that designate the level and specific kind of work done. For these people, guidelines or qualification standards are necessary as a basis for making an intelligent search. Guidelines can be divided into negative and positive criteria, or things to look for and not to look for. A conscious recruitment effort is made only for persons to staff institutionalized units. There is a great deal of experience on recruitment, selection, and placement, which should be taken into account in these searches. As a rule, the larger the field of candidates developed by recruitment, the better the ultimate selection, and multiple judgments surpass single judgments. People developers stud all parts of an organization. The challenge is therefore in discovering such persons, channeling their talents, and giving appropriate recognition and encouragement to facilitate their efforts.

Chapter 8. Designing the Learning Environment

Nothing inhibits training, for both the learner and the trainer, more quickly than improvised space with shabby furnishings. Yet, on the whole, the typical physical environment set aside by employers for teaching adults new knowledge and skills is deplorable. Frequently, the "training room" is a place not adaptable for most other purposes.

The space needs of the people development activity cannot be generalized. They vary widely among organizations and even within the same organization. For example, the fire department may need an area where it can create fires, explosions, and other hazardous conditions as a simulated firefighting situation for training purposes. A group of executives may require a retreat well removed from the city and the stresses of their offices.

Of the more formal types of training and development space requirements, three categories are identified: the single-purpose training room, the general-purpose employee training and development center, and the institute or staff college. Experience has shown that a number of physical and environmental features in each of these four types make them far more functionally effective than they would be without expert planning.

Chapter 9. Engineering Delivery Systems

The transfer of knowledge, skill, information, and understanding from appropriate sources to points of need has become an increasingly complex aspect of the people development process as decentralization and other organizational changes have occurred. Many organizations have only two choices: uprooting their employees and sending them hundreds or thousands of miles for training and development; or doing nothing because of the awesome costs. For example, the U.S. Postal Service, with nearly three-quarters of a million employees, could never afford to move all its employees even once for training.

This chapter uses five actual case histories of massive delivery systems, drawn from the author's experience, to demonstrate the economic feasibility and general viability of the delivery system concept. Delivery systems, once in place, can be continuing conveyors of training and development opportunities by offering new inputs of knowledge and skill-building instruction to employees who work a distance away from the source of the best-known job methods.

From the five case histories a list of guidelines is formulated as a pattern for any organization in the design and installation of its own delivery system, which obviously must be tailored to the special requirements of that organization.

Chapter 10. Selecting Training and Development Methods

People development is at best an art. There is little or no possibility that it can ever become a science. Since the needs of individuals and organizations differ so widely, the process of coordinating them requires much creativity and innovation.

Of course some basic guidelines are available to assist in meeting the specific requirements of organizations and individuals. For example, the methods used should encourage full response of the participants by stimulating them to interact with the instructor, the program content, and other participants. Also, certain cautions serve as guardrails against using nonproductive instructional approaches.

The growing assortment of training methods can be broadly categorized: (1) methods generally used on a one-to-one basis in day-to-day supervisory relationship (e.g., the outmoded apprenticeship method); (2) conventional methods that are best used in group training situations (e.g., the training conference); (3) methods having an experiential approach and best used away from the normal work situation (e.g., case study); and (4) some newer methods used away from the job and having an individualized, learner-paced feature (e.g., programmed instruction).

Chapter 11. Producing Curriculum Materials

Four perfectly acceptable strategies provide necessary curriculum materials for the training and development staff. These include beg or borrow, purchase of commercially available materials, production with in-house capability, and contracting for outside assistance. Circumstances such as time frame, budget, and nature of the training need will dictate the choice of strategy. The ability to move at all times with the best strategy is an enviable position.

The two essential kinds of curriculum materials are classified as written and audiovisual. Written materials include basic items such as trainers' guides, experiential exercise materials, reference manuals, and handouts. Audiovisual materials are motion pictures, sound filmstrips, slides, videotapes, photographs, overhead projector transparencies, exhibits, and models.

The choice of prepared materials and the production of original materials is dependent on high-level quality assurance and cost effectiveness. The trainer's guide is an indispensable means to this end because it states priorities, sequences, outlines, and times, and orchestrates the material to be covered, the audiovisual aids to be used, and the participant interaction. The scope-of-work element of the contract and monitoring of the outside contractor who produces the materials are also critical for quality results.

Chapter 12. Assembling and Controlling Training Aids

Training aids support people development programs in a growing number of ways, but their exclusive use is poor practice even for the simplest type of program. Knowledge of the market and the capability and limitations of each audiovisual (A/V) device is one of the many technical qualifications needed by the training and development specialist.

Just as a good craftsman has to choose tools for a specific job, the training and development specialist has to choose a basic set of A/V aids and an experience-tested strategy for meeting the A/V requirements for large-scale operations. Chapter 11 discussed the ways to meet these requirements—a four-option scheme comprising beg or borrow, purchase of commercially available units, production with in-house capability, and contracting for outside assistance in building units to one's specifications.

Large private enterprises, or public service organizations such as the federal government, strive constantly for a program of standardization and interchangeability in A/V aids. The procurement system seldom if ever *asks* the training and development specialist what he or she needs. It continues to grind out products of designs and unit costs gauged only by what the traffic will bear. This results in excessive and inequitable expenditure of vital resources, and deprives training programs of funding because the using organizations cannot afford the greater unit costs of large-scale operations.

4

Structuring
the Development Program

Under New Management is the language of a sign that often marks the spot where a small business has failed and new owners have taken over to try to make a go of it. The real message could be that the last management had no philosophy at all or had one that failed to recognize that the people it employed were its most precious asset.

The U.S. Department of Commerce has for many years offered technical assistance to small businesses in the form of a series of pamphlets, the hard core of which is modern management. Modern management is, of course, heavily weighted with people development.

Adopting a Management Philosophy

One of the leading spice manufacturers in the United States has consistently practiced a philosophy of "multiple management."[1] Es-

[1] McCormick & Co., Inc., Baltimore, Md. 21202.

sentially, this philosophy recognizes the intrinsic worth of people to the business by providing for such systems as "Junior Boards" to gain the full participation of rank-and-file employees in the formulation of company policy. Employees are so thoroughly oriented to the company's objectives and internal operations that individuals least responsible for results, such as elevator operators, share in the public relations program by answering questions of visitors with factual, interesting data.

A classic example is one of the nation's leading department stores, which for decades has proclaimed this management philosophy: "The customer is always right."[2] A similar philosophy is reflected in the iron-clad guarantee of Sears, Roebuck and Company: "Satisfaction guaranteed or your money back."

One could stand at the door of the retail outlets of these firms and probably tally a significant number of people who kept returning to the stores because of their management philosophy.

Detailed reviews of the mission, organization, and effectiveness of federal departments and agencies by citizen review commissions and leading consulting firms have, on several occasions, singled out the personnel management philosophy of the Tennessee Valley Authority as an outstanding example of public personnel management in action. Countless other agencies of the federal government have been absorbed by superagencies, have had their names changed, and have virtually lost their identity. TVA, with a sound people development philosophy, continued for 40 years after the Great Depression to build people participation as carefully as it built dams, hydroelectric plants, recreation facilities, and other advantages for its customers.

A retiring industrial relations executive of the Standard Oil Company of New Jersey, when asked "How do you develop executives at your company?" answered: "We hire field hands!" His response reflected confidence in the development potential of individuals, and an awareness of the company's responsibility for helping to develop the potential of field hands for positions of greater responsibility.

Since 1944 the U.S. Civil Service Commission has offered federal departments and agencies the opportunity to select from its Management Intern Register those individuals eligible for high risk/high reward training and promotion programs. The use of the plan is optional, not mandatory, for agencies. Some were quick to see the value of such a plan for developing new leadership at managerial

---

[2] John Wanamaker, Inc., 13th & Market Sts., Philadelphia, Pa. 19101.

levels; other agencies made little or no use of the Register. It would be an interesting piece of research to trace the upward mobility of interns and to analyze the evolution of organizations using interns and compare the results to those that have not practiced the infusion of new blood. In all the successful cases it would be apparent that the leadership of certain organizations had adopted a management philosophy, that the philosophy related to the human element, and that a commitment had been made to people development. Commitments to people, like commitments to build, imply an agenda for action in decades ahead. With each generation a new corps of people developers has to be identified, educated, oriented, and equipped for leadership. Once the chain of continuity is broken, the organization soon deteriorates, and the same old announcement, "Under New Management," goes back on the storefront or government office door.

Converting Philosophy into Policies and Practices

A wise old bureaucrat once said, "Any policy worth being a policy needs to be written down." As organizations grow, their need for a policy manual becomes more important. Perhaps a one-person business may operate efficiently when its philosophy, policies, and procedures are centered in the proprietor who practices them as an unconscious part of daily dealings with customers. However, if a partnership is formed or the business begins to expand and to hire subordinates, the beginnings of a policy manual begin to crop up as little "Notices" are posted near the entrance, at the cash register, and elsewhere. This also happens in government offices.

An organization needs a great deal of help when it becomes so sophisticated in its operations that it needs to institutionalize its people development policies in a policy and procedures manual. Then it is time for employees at all levels of responsibility to participate. An experienced management analyst can do the writing, but the input of the individuals affected in doing the work of the business or government office is far more important.

The analyst should interview a carefully selected sample of key people—managers, supervisors, secretaries, line executives, field officials, people in the mail room and public information office, and others. It is a good idea, also, to talk with a sample of customers or recipients of service to find out what concerns them about the organization's performance and what ideas they have for reform. The analyst can, on the basis of such findings, produce a first draft of realistic policies and procedures pertaining to the training and development of people in the organization.

Full participation of employees is needed in the final review and revision of a policy manual. For example, at what stages in an individual's career should new training experiences be assured? How much responsibility does the employee have for self-training and self-development? Under what circumstances can the individual become a self-nominee for a training program?

There are numerous ways, besides a formal policy and procedures manual, in which an organization can promulgate its basic policies that stem from its philosophy, but the manual is administrative law, a point of reference in handling questions that require interpretation and in settling disputes that may go as far as the courts. Although a policy manual may at times gather dust, it can be a dynamic referee in problem situations.

Many organizations issue employee handbooks and orientation kits to new employees. Emphasis should be made in such materials on people development. The next exposure of new employees to this philosophy may be in orientation sessions, which are generally scheduled on, and unfortunately limited to, the day when the new employee enters upon duty.

Motion pictures and other audiovisual aids are produced in some agencies as a means of orientation and for public relations purposes. The management philosophy and policies with respect to people development can be a theme or subtheme of these productions.

Another excellent means of setting the tone for people development in an organization is the slogan. Important political campaigns have been won with slogans, and it should be feasible to win the goodwill of employees and an organization's public by repeated use of slogans with a message. Practically everyone is familiar with these messages: "All the News That's Fit to Print," "When Better Cars are Built Buick Will Build Them," and "We Try Harder." The writers of these slogans may well have been aiming them at two audiences: their employees and their customers and potential customers. A management improvement strategy known as "Zero Errors," which some organizations practice, should have a double-edge effect on employee and customer alike.

Other organizations have cultivated their climate by advancing their policies through poster programs. Still others have done it through house organs, newspapers, and magazines. Pay envelope enclosures, lunchroom literature, annual campaigns, reports to stockholders, incentive award programs, letters of commendation, and luncheons are among the many other measures that can be used effectively to advance people development policies.

Essentially, the campaign of the leaders of any organization to set the tone and secure the cooperation of its chain of command in the processes of people development is not unlike the strategy of any other successful campaign; for example, political campaigns, fund raising campaigns, sales campaigns, and recruitment campaigns.

Anchoring the People Development Function Organizationally

Traditionalists in personnel management are unalterably opposed to making the training and development (people development) function a separate and independent entity. Personnel functions include wage and salary administration, employment (recruitment, selection, and placement), labor/management relations, and personnel transactions and records. There are pro and con arguments for associating training and development with other people management functions. One federal director of personnel once described personnel management as the art of "getting, using, and losing" people. Interestingly, while he always wanted training as a personnel function in his department, he failed to recognize it in his simplisitc definition. He had come from a state that is far from the top rank of merit system states, and he understood patronage better than he did merit systems. He found little time for the thoughtful planning and direction of training and development programs.

The day-in and day-out business of recruitment, selection, placement, promotions, position classification, grievances, meetings, reports, correspondence, telephoning, and union demands is more than enough to fully occupy a personnel director. Such people soon become *case oriented* and must work hard to move the contents of their "in" box to their "out" box. They seldom find time in their schedule to contribute to and support constructive *programs* that upgrade the skills, knowledge, attitudes, and future potential of employees. However, training and development is not unrelated to the basic personnel management functions; in fact, a fully integrated personnel management system does include training and development. For example, a position classification survey may uncover legitimate grievances, placement problems, and the need to strengthen supervision, recruitment, selection, and promotion processes in an organizational element. Training and development can contribute to the solution of all these problems.

This is definitely not to say, however, that the people development function should be centered organizationally in the central personnel or industrial relations office. Government departments and agencies are each required to have a director of personnel at the headquarters level. Large business and industrial firms usually have a vice-president for industrial relations. In government, the director of personnel typically reports administratively to the Assistant Secretary for Administration, and the latter typically reports to the second-ranking political administrator, called "under secretary." A good place to assign the training and development function is to the assistant secretary for administration, usually on the same level as the director of personnel. The training and development staff at this highest level should be quite modest in size, perhaps only a senior specialist, a research assistant, and a secretary.

Individual personnel actions (paper transactions) and the substantive program activities to develop the knowledge, skills, and abilities of the employee are more effective when separated. The two basic functions can coexist and be supportive of each other without being centralized.

Those who do not approve of centralization present persuasive arguments. They contend that the director of personnel is "consumed" by the pressure of labor/management relations matters and individual transactions. This leaves little or no time to weigh and decide training and development program issues. Therefore, the function that may well offer the greatest promise for solving an organization's problems of production and service may suffer a slow death from benign neglect.

The training and development specialist can be a positive, constructive force in providing counsel directly to a high-level administrator. The specialist is experienced in identifying leadership potential and developing leaders at all levels, and this is precisely what top management wants. Top management can also use a specialist in spotting production bottlenecks. The specialist can be a roving troubleshooter and can therefore offer solutions to specific problems faster than a bureaucratic chain of command. He or she can use the tools of job analysis and work simplification to assemble factual data and develop behavioral objectives.

At the first subdivision (bureau, in the federal government; or department, in the private sector), there should be a staff of training specialists and support personnel commensurate with the size of the organization to be served. Here is where training and development programs to meet practical problems of production get organized, the curriculum materials get produced, participants selected, and the actual training done. This staff needs to have some elasticity to absorb the work load resulting from swift organizational adjustments, programmatic changes, cyclical events, and the like. It may be a staff of 6 on the average, but at times it may expand temporarily to 20 or 30. Or, if expansion is undesirable, it may hire outside resources for training purposes.

Finally, at the second subdivision (division, in the federal government, and division or branch in the private sector) there should be a training representative who can relate to the two higher levels of training and development. This person is in a liaison relationship. Periodically, the training representative serves on ad hoc task groups and committees to identify training needs, distributes and interprets communications about training, works on selection and evaluation panels, instructs, compiles data for training reports, and does other related things.

Stimulating Support Through Task Groups

Many training specialists have promoted the establishment of training committees and have later regretted the move. Their good intentions are always to manage the involvement of key people in the training and development activities. The membership of such committees is likely to include senior staff and operating officials—individuals who are straining to do the "must" things imposed by the 40-hour week.

Training committee meetings, as do other types of committees, usually take the greater part of a morning or afternoon and put the executive farther behind in routine official duties. The committee member has the choice of attending, sending an alternate, or cutting the meeting. If the executive attends, he or she may be there in body only, so the chances are about one in four that the training chief will have the kind of attendance and participation wanted. Meeting after meeting may then be canceled, until the projects the specialist wants are blocked by inaction. No progress is made in obtaining the desired endorsement of the training committee, which, under the circumstances described, is neither informed nor actively supporting the training project. Thus, the specialist is hobbled, even though a sympathetic committee of high-priced, standby talent is ostensibly ready to offer support.

The task group conference is a superior approach for a variety of reasons. The training specialist needs an ever-expanding base of support for people development programs. A task group is a problem-solving group. The problem may be to do some fact finding such as making a job analysis of a key position in the scheme of operations to determine the what, why, when, where, and how of a job for effective performance. The task group members may be subject-matter experts whose problem is to develop a working outline for an A/V production or a trainer's guide. Regardless of what the problem may be, the task group is disbanded when its work is complete. However, it is not forgotten by the training specialist and the task group does not forget the training specialist. Mutual respect has been established. Further, the fact that the members were consulted for their expertise tends to enlist them as supporters of the people development movement. Because they do not necessarily have chain-of-command responsibilities, and are not members of a standing training committee in which conclusions would be final, they are not so upset by delays or failures of the training specialist to act in strict accordance with their counsel. As each new problem is faced, a new task group can be formed for one-time service. Thus, the training specialist gets a multiplier effect as time passes.

The task group is an excellent vehicle for talent searches. The training specialist sees numerous people in action in the course of a year. Some will respond and stand out better than others. The training specialist is therefore in position to advise senior executives on moves that can further the group member's organizational development objectives.

Former task group members are in position to spread management philosophy on employee training and development throughout the organization. As new programs are announced, they are more inclined to nominate subordinates for participation. They are more receptive to persons on rotational work assignments. They are logical recipients for selected mail-outs of professional journal articles. They may be invited to serve as luncheon speakers, as members of boards of expert examiners in the selection of new trainees for special training programs, or as contributors of case histories and critical incidents to the reservoir of experiential curriculum materials. In short, task group constituencies are promising candidates for the people development network.

Building Career Systems and Career Development Programs

Psychological studies have shown that an alarmingly high percentage of working people (50 percent or more) are unhappy in their jobs. How people choose, or fail to choose, a line of work is complicated by a myriad of factors, including pure chance and luck. It will take concerted effort on the part of the community at large to fully correct the occupational maladjustment picture, and one place where the effort must begin is the employment world itself. This is logical because most people devote more time there than they do in any of the other developmental institutions of home, school, church, service clubs, labor union, and the like. The essential elements of such a program are discussed below primarily for the benefit of employers.

COMMITMENT. Nothing can, will, or should happen until responsible, accountable leadership of the employing organization fully commits itself to a positive, affirmative, self-disciplined, properly funded, institutionalized system of people development. The commitment must be documented, and it must be communicated from the highest to the lowest levels of the organization and to the community at large—not once but repeatedly through multimedia channels. It must be conceived out of a genuine desire to build strength and continuity into the organization in order to fulfill its broad objectives. In so doing, it must help its employees grow and achieve a generous measure of self-fulfillment. If the commitment is for image-building purposes only and lacks integrity, it is destined to be counterproductive and will ultimately fail dismally. A fallout of distrust and discredit of the organization and its clients will most likely occur.

COOPERATIVE APPROACH. Career systems and career development programs should be joint undertakings of line and staff people. The line officer has the inherent responsibility for getting a program of work accomplished. To meet goals, the officer must have the authority to use resources within the limits of the objective as long as these resources are applied within the framework of law and the employer's policies. With each such grant of authority goes the responsibility for assisting in the planning necessary to assure the availability of future resources, one of the most important of which is manpower. No line officer can relinquish this planning responsibility to a staff office such as personnel or finance. Neither can these offices substitute their judgment for that of the line operator and attempt to make accurate decisions as to the future manpower requirements of each operating unit, or the individual training needs of employees, or the best promotion and utilization moves.

TAILORING TO FIT. The business world, while in many ways more advanced than the federal government in the utilization of manpower resources, cannot manufacture manpower plans of universal interchangeability. Professional literature can offer only theory and guidance in terms of broad principles and some case histories. There are no quick, ready-made answers. Line and staff officials have to come to grips with the problem from a purely analytical standpoint and develop a strategy that considers the special needs and conditions with which their organizations are confronted. Developmental efforts should always be pretested on a small scale, time permitting.

There are several conventional ways in which to classify career systems. These are considered below.

Program versus Organization Careers. The "program" type of career builds on specialized knowledge and skill in some area such as finance, maintenance, construction, and customer relations. An "organization" career tends to follow the principle of planned mobility, cutting across program lines.

Closed versus Open Careers. "Closed" career systems bring people in at the junior levels only and promote from within (as in the military service). "Open" career systems permit entry at any level, subject to qualification standards.

Job-Oriented versus Rank-in-Corps Career Systems. Job orientation emphasizes the job to be performed and strives to grant equal pay for equal work. Rank-in-corps status focuses on the person, and is usually associated with careers of highly mobile people (as in the U.S. Foreign Service, or in the British Civil Service during the days of its far-flung colonial empire).

Career Cone—An Appraisal Device. This method of tailoring a career involves a technique in which the end products are called "career cones." A career cone is a useful device for analyzing the career development needs and upward mobility potential in any organization as a whole or for any element or specialized field therein. It is easily constructed on a piece of graph paper, using the data on the number of authorized positions in the area studied. A detailed explanation is given in Appendix II. Briefly stated, the first step is to draw a vertical line (the ordinate) down the middle of the sheet. Step 2 is to find the number of positions at the lowest grade level and divide this number by 2. Then, at the base of the sheet, plot points equidistant from the ordinate; the horizontal line on the graph paper connecting the two points is the abscissa. Proceed up the sheet, entering two points for each pay grade. Connect the points plotted with a curve to form a configuration symbolizing the parameters of existing career paths.

A diamond-shaped cone is believed by most personnel experts to be optimal. Hour-glass configurations and bulblike configurations with a tall stem are examples of situations where opportunity appears to be very limited. Stagnation, frustration, high turnover, lower productivity, and related problems presumably abound in such situations. However, there are usually some remedies for any bad career situations that are pointed up graphically by a career cone. For example, Frederic Herzberg's job-enrichment and job-enlargement theory may help. It may be possible to realign and consolidate some functions to provide lateral and then vertical movement. Individual training agreements and other techniques can be used to accelerate solving the problem of closing a gap in skill and knowledge.

PROPER TIMING. The General Services Administration (GSA) introduced a career management program at about the same time as it reappraised its organization and prepared for its second decade of service to customer agencies. During the first decade of its history, dating from 1949, GSA was steadily shrinking its personnel as technological improvements were found and as refinements in its organization were suggested by operating experience. The timing of its new program also considered an accelerated retirement rate resulting from a liberalized federal retirement plan. Flexibility is the key. One part of an organization may be ready for career planning and development while another may not be.

COMPREHENSIVENESS. The trend in merchandising in the United States for a long time has been the one-stop place. One finds it in large department stores, in food supermarkets, and in modern shopping centers. In England, the specialty shop still prevails. In career systems and career development planning, comprehensiveness is indicated. Some organizations seem to expend a vast amount of time, money, and energy in their annual recruitment campaigns, but their programs and plans for utilizing new talent do not have the same sparkle. Other organizations emphasize appraisal, training, records, utilization, counseling, or something else. It is next to impossible to find an organization that has an aggressive, positive plan for applying all these tools to the manpower problem in a cohesive, integrated, and comprehensive manner.

COORDINATION. Any program, regardless of how well conceived, will soon disintegrate unless it is actively coordinated at all levels. Coordination in the early stages is critical. This principle is clearly demonstrated in community development projects such as schools, libraries, parks, and recreational facilities. Citizen participation at all stages is essential to the success of the project. One sees the principle revalidated repeatedly on the political scene. There is no substitute for coordination.

BUILT-IN PROGRESSION. A good career system has some of the features of an escalator. People normally enter at one level and move to the next level where they wish to accomplish something. They may get on again later and go to a higher or lower level. The escalator and career systems are conveyors. Too many people can clog up either conveyor and cause injury to others. It is a low-risk/high-reward contrivance. Some career development programs, such as the management intern programs of the federal civil service, are designed as high-risk/high-reward systems.

A career system might be compared also with a large canal such as the Panama Canal, which has provisions for gates and locks to permit ships to negotiate the waterway at a controlled rate of speed. Obviously, the ship must meet certain basic requirements. It cannot be too wide. It must proceed at an assigned speed. The pilot and the gate-and-lock attendants have to be skilled. All systems have to be in a "go" position. The system can become clogged by a malfunctioning ship or by malfunctioning people.

Building Bridges to the Community

Before an organization with a strong commitment to do some people development work can get started, it needs to build some bridges to the community to ensure a steady flow of human resources with potential for training and development. Organizations that rely heavily on walk-in applicants and political or quasi-political referrals are in for many surprises—seldom pleasant ones. Walk-ins are about as reliable a source of manpower as street peddlers are a reliable source of merchandise for retail stores.

Private and public organizations need established bridges to high schools, trade schools, business colleges, community colleges, junior colleges, undergraduate colleges and universities, and graduate schools. Regular visits are needed once or twice a year to build rapport, communicate requirements, and interview promising candidates.

Some institutions have work/study arrangements that enable both employer and potential employee to pretest each other. Other institutions like to have graduate students, fellows, and their own professors negotiate research assignments with employers as a means of gaining realistic insights into the business world.

College students frequently seek summer employment in order to help defray their college expenses. Secondary schools, colleges, universities, and some employers practice a policy of granting sabbatical leave. Recipients of such fringe benefits are usually very serious in their research endeavors, their objective being to gain new knowledge and methods to take back and apply on their job. They also may be favorably impressed by the place where they do their sabbatical project, and therefore can be ambassadors of goodwill and possible recruiters who guide others to the employer for careers.

There is no substitute for an open door to welcome people who join an organization to work, contribute, and learn things. The conduits so established simulate a giant telephone trunk line containing numerous small wires. This trunk line is virtually free to the employer when measured in terms of cost-benefit returns.

Launching and Administering Career Development Programs

A good strategy for launching a career development program has at least seven basic processes, all of which should be accomplished within the context of the career system elements discussed above. The following brief description of these processes will be discussed at greater length elsewhere in this book.

ASSESSMENT OF FUTURE MANPOWER NEEDS. Fact-finding is the starting point. Creating a task group made up of both line and staff people is a good way to organize the effort. Many vital factors must be considered carefully. A substantial safety factor should be allowed when calculating the absolute minimum future manpower requirement. The career development program will normally provide for a systematic flow of high-potential talent at the entrance level. Ideally, there should be a reasonable balance between the number of new hires at the entrance level and the number at the journeyman or higher levels. The practice of hiring exclusively at the entrance level can soon lead to stagnation, just as consistent hiring at journeyman and higher levels aborts the career development concept. Honest, forthright attention must be given to affirmative action objectives so that reasonable proportions of minority ethnic groups and women in all occupational classes and pay levels will be maintained.

RECRUITMENT AS A FUTURE RESOURCE. The resourceful employer who has an eye on the future constantly reviews his available sources of labor supply so that he can eventually have a bank of more candidates than he has vacancies to fill. If he has built the bridges suggested above, his task will be much less burdensome when sudden vacancies must be filled.

The recruiter needs to know the answers to some questions in advance. For example, he thinks "qualified for what—today's job or tomorrow's?" as he considers each candidate. Choosing the best candidates is the next challenge. Personal interviews have been found to be hardly more reliable than the toss of a coin. A mix of methods is the best—a combination of such techniques as careful vouchering, group oral examinations, trial performances before career appointment through summer and work/study programs and internships, and selection panels instead of single interviews.

APPRAISAL. It is counterproductive for an enterprise or public service group to go to the extremes of protecting its investment in buildings and equipment—insurance, maintenance contract, modernizations, and safety measures—and do so little to ensure a fair return on its investment in human resources. Unfortunately, most attempts to devise objective appraisal systems have been utter failures. Practically everything is wrong with these systems. They are usually intended as all-purpose tools, which lump together appraisal techniques and historical records and serve as a basis for incentive awards, promotions, training, penalty actions, and diverse other actions. The employee's appraisal is usually done on his or her appointment anniversary, and is expressed in language not easy to interpret—pluses, minuses, check marks, percentages, adjectives, and phrases.

A plain sheet of paper and plain written English probably comprise the only universally intelligible system among English-speaking people. And instead of rating by the calendar, why not do it when something significant happens? For example, when the employee gets a change in duties, supervisors, systems, or duty station? Why not use separate guidelines when appraising for promotion, training, placement, special recognition, penalty action, and separation from the service? Appraisal is a vital step in career development. It is counterproductive if done carelessly, hurriedly, on an awkward form, or in a language to which the reader has no key.

COUNSELING. Good counseling should follow good appraisal. If the employer expects continuing self-improvement, as he should, the employee needs a qualified counselor as much as he needs a doctor when he is ill. And there are no all-purpose counselors. Some can counsel only on how the career system works; that is, what the requirements are for moving from one grade or pay level to another or from one field of work to another. Others, usually working as vocational counselors, are qualified to counsel on the advantages and limitations of careers in selected fields. Others can administer aptitude tests to measure an individual's special interests and potential for certain lines of work.

The best counseling for the typical employee is a responsibility shared by educational institutions and employers. Every organization has a few "people developers" who are wise, empathetic, and patient enough to take younger people under their wing and, as in the age-old apprentice systems, "help them learn their trade." In other words, psychologists and professional counselors have no monopoly on counseling.

TRAINING AND DEVELOPMENT. Some organizations follow fads in training and try whatever is popular. Some employees continue taking courses indefinitely, their patchwork academic record leading to no useful objective. On the other hand, a single training experience such as a 40-hour course in basic supervision should never terminate the training experience. Obviously, as the Hoover Commission studies of the federal civil service in the early 1950s recognized, the employee needs different training at different stages of his growth, a process that continues until he is ready for his preretirement counseling.

A joint venture or working partnership between the employer and the employee, aiming for reasonable and attainable milestones, is the best solution. The employee can show his good intentions by investing after-hours time. The employer can match the employee's contribution by investing dollars and, under special circumstances, excused time off from work. Some organizations have projected and documented long-range (5–10 years) career development commitments. Most commitments are never realized because there are too many variables in the equation. The foundations cited above should be in place, and teamwork on the part of the supervisors, managers, and executives should be used (not abused) to implement the career system as conceived.

If an organization is large enough to afford a training and development specialist, the system is likely to work more smoothly. However, such a specialist is not essential if management does its part. The responsibility for monitoring and reporting on the results of career development programs should be focused in one individual or, at least periodically, in a task group. Basically, career development is the day-to-day, ongoing responsibility of the first-line supervisor and all levels of management.

An excellent model for a total training and development program is symbolized by the cross section of a steel I-beam (see Chapter 15). The early stages or formative years are represented by the base of the symbol. Planned mobility, in the form of rotating work assignments, helps the individual visualize various career opportunities, gain wider perspective, and meet a number of different supervisors who can appraise his or her performance and potential. The next phase should be a period of specialization during which the individual gains confidence and discovers self-identity by becoming a recognized expert in that specialty. Finally, as times passes, the employee broadens this capability and may assume executive responsibility over several related specialties, at least one of which he or she has mastered. Both the employee and the employer contribute to the employee's growth in various ways at all stages of this career development.

UTILIZATION. Utilization is the payoff phase and is more or less the litmus test of preceding steps. The design of the career system directly affects utilization. Systems that build rank into the person instead of the job have more flexibility in moving people, but they have some disadvantages. Multiple-judgment placement decisions are far superior to the single "czar" system. Advertising all vacancies within the organization is better policy than are secretly operated systems. The "rule of three" in certifying eligible candidates is a great deal better than a single-name certification. Special registers with at least three categories (best qualified, adequately qualified, and poorly qualified) have some advantages over the rule of three.

The key to utilization is a soundly conceived, smoothly operating *system*. The *system* finds the best qualified people in an organization for any vacancy. The supervisor of the position to be filled is happily presented with a *choice,* which is desperately wanted at times when, for example, a person with seniority or influence is the only candidate in sight. A career development program, having done its work over the years within the context of a good career system, means that the walk-ins, personal patronage, political pressures, and the countless other drags on the merit system have less chance of depriving capable employees of new opportunity.

ORDERLY SELECTION OUT. What if your favorite department store were suddenly to invoke a policy of having an employee stand at the exit from the street-level escalator and give each passenger a hard shove and a few harsh words? Many companies do, in a sense, maul people as they leave the organization after a lifelong career. No better public relations could be earned or no better future recruitment foundation could be laid than an employment policy that ensures that employees leave with their self-respect, dignity, ego, and sense of self-fulfillment intact, and that they have been fairly and equitably treated. A graceful departure, invitations back on special occasions, farewell parties on company time, all these are better than any form of paid advertising for new employees. One of the mildest terms invented by personnel people is that of "selection out," a euphemism adopted by the foreign service of the State Department. The term, however, does not relate only to retiring employees. An individual can get selected out when departmental objectives change so drastically that the employee's qualifications are no longer adequate.

Conclusion

Organizations require continuous accountability for utilization and performance. They must give special attention to their communication systems for converting their best management philosophy into practical policies and practices in order to realize their goals and objectives.

The people development function should be removed from the traditional type of personnel office and anchored at a strategic place within the organizational structure where it can be a sensitive tool of top management to improve the quality, efficiency, economy, productivity, and general effectiveness of operations.

Career systems and career development programs should be designed and administered on such foundations as top management commitment, collaborative approaches, proper timing, comprehensiveness, and built-in progression. Input of trainees to such systems should be from labor markets that are known suppliers of persons of high potential. Such systems have to be capable of assessing future manpower needs, recruiting with an eye to the future, appraising and counseling people, making each training and development experience a purposeful building block, and contributing to the fullest utilization and occasional selection out of individuals.

5

Evaluating Sources
of Help

E ven in organizations large enough to afford an institutionalized training and development function, the unit is seldom adequate in size to plan, develop, and manage all people development activities it should. Curriculum development specialists, audiovisual technicians, classroom instructors, and others work under the supervision of the senior specialist or unit manager, whose major responsibility is to *manage* or *orchestrate* things. Therefore, the manager must be adroit in the identification and assessment of the various sources of assistance.

The internal and external sources of help discussed in this chapter have advantages and limitations. Deciding on the sequence in which to draw on various sources of help, choosing criteria for selecting a contractor, and managing the contractual relationship are procedures to be conducted carefully.

Internal Sources

It is folly to begin an outside search before internal resource possibilities have been exhausted. It is even worse to build too large a staff of regular full-time employees. Balance and flexibility are the keys.

It is generally true that outsiders have to be educated before they can help the training manager educate or train personnel in the organization. This process is time consuming and expensive. Moreover, outsiders generally cost more. Remember, too, that one of the finest developmental experiences one can have is the opportunity to teach. Therefore, the more a people developer can motivate teaching within his organization, the more the broader objectives of organization development and management are advanced and improved.

Readers will find the following inventory of in-house sources reasonably complete. The critique of each source and subsource is primarily the author's.

REGULAR TRAINING AND DEVELOPMENT UNIT STAFF. Depending upon its size and the integrity of the upper echelon chain of command, the regular training staff may be quite versatile and self-reliant. Some organizations are notorious for establishing a unit to carry on the training and development function and then prostituting its time by assigning it a scrubby set of irrelevant things to do—VIP photography, charity campaigns, socials, suggestion program management, dues collections, and assorted others. Under these circumstances, the regular staff has little time left for training work, and has even less credibility in the eyes of operating officials.

Another factor that may diminish staff stature in the hierarchy is that the regulars were not selected on a merit basis. For example, one may be assigned to training as a reward for long and faithful service to some cause—political or otherwise. Possibly the assignment was to get him off the "road," or "street," or "machines," or "his feet." Another member may have been "kicked upstairs" or eased aside because he was not doing very well where he was.

Credibility may also be affected if several regulars are highly competent but highly specialized and consistently overloaded. For example, one regular member of the staff may handle orientation and vestibule training for new personnel, but may be pressured because high turnover and business expansion make for many new hires. Another may be concentrating on safety training, including driver training, safety training for supervisors and managers, industrial safety for blue-collar workers, and the like. Another may handle training for clerical and secretarial personnel. Several members of the staff may be totally occupied in monitoring training contracts, maintaining liaison with operating officials, supervising field communications, and compiling administrative management details such as records and reports.

A shrewd training and development manager who can upgrade his regulars through the assignment of progressively more responsible projects can produce an amazing amount of creditable work in the course of a year. It is usually best to deploy them in various team configurations in order to cross train and build continuity into the staff.

SUBJECT-MATTER SPECIALISTS. A business or government unit without subject-matter expertise soon fails. Businesses without know-how close their doors or are bought out by a conglomerate. Government units get layered into a new superstructure, reorganized, or pushed aside so that they die a slow death from lack of resources. Healthy, productive organizations take pride in their staff of technicians, professionals, scientists, and managers. It is this staff that can be tapped by the training unit, and it can be done quite informally without paperwork and commotion.

For example, a large real estate firm may want to develop some audiovisual training aids for new salespersons. What better source of know-how than its sales force of 300 people? The training specialist can soon identify several of the more successful salespersons who will probably be pleased to have a role in the training project, provided it does not cut too deeply into their time for sales. The ways in which the specialist uses these sales talents are limited only by how they are channeled, the training budget, and their available time. The key to the use of subject-matter specialists in this case, and the principle is the same for other areas of expertise, is for the training specialist to have a good working relationship with the sales manager. Theoretically, the manager is the client, and therefore enters into joint venture with the training specialist, each contributing to the project. This is a sound approach, for it is safe to assume that one successful joint venture will beget more joint ventures. Eventually, the training specialist should find it feasible to use subject-matter specialists on task groups, and as advisers, resource people, conference leaders, trainers, role players, cadre leaders, and others who can contribute.

EXECUTIVES. Executives are the "softest touch" of all for the training manager. Practically without exception they dearly love to be asked to preside over the opening or closing of a training program or to make guest appearances for other purposes. Obviously, it is good office politics for them to get such visibility, and for the training manager it is supreme as a means of securing management's continuing support for training. Each executive so involved is more likely to become an advocate of the training and development program. It also offers the employee an unusual opportunity to have face-to-face meetings with executives. To the extent that the executive has to prepare for the part, it may serve as refresher training, and it may alert him or her to the possibility of personal development to cope with future executive demands.

From nearly every angle, the involvement of executives in the planning, development, and administration of training programs is useful and desirable. The participation of executives in exceptional cases can be a negative influence unless their objective is sharply defined in advance and the schedule is honored. The program is weakened for participants when the executive is allowed to abuse the schedule, tell offensive jokes, berate the participants, or stray into discussions of no value.

THE LIBRARY STAFF. The modern library is a far cry from the atmosphere and capabilities of old-fashioned libraries. Today, librarians are as qualified for, and as interested in, teaching as are educators and training specialists. Modern public school systems apply teacher standards as well as librarian standards to their school librarians and pay them on the teacher scale, which is usually higher than the public librarian scale. Today, school librarians are rich in technical knowledge on audiovisual equipment capabilities, mediated instruction methods, information retrieval systems, research methodology, curriculum planning, motivation, and related processes. They work in a dynamic setting, surrounded by books, periodicals, newspapers, research aids, and scholars who use their services.

Commercial or industrial libraries are not so generalized and are likely to concentrate on immediate interests, but their services include many of those offered in school libraries.

Librarians are categorically the most dedicated of people developers serving in any organization. The training staff is negligent if it overlooks this source of help, which is there every workday of the year, waiting to dispense information. The library staff can propose countless constructive ways to advance people development objectives and develop particular training programs, including but not limited to the following cooperative aids:

Develop bibliographies.
Assemble kits of relevant reading materials.

Conduct preliminary research and prepare briefs.

Collaborate with outside sources through its linkages with whole networks of other libraries.

Serve as advisers to curriculum development task groups.

Orient training group participants individually and during scheduled group visits.

Assist participants with home assignments.

Equip auxiliary classrooms where employees can pursue individualized study with mediated forms of self-instruction.

Maintain special shelf collections of materials of special relevance to ongoing training programs.

Develop mobile exhibits of library materials on topics of current interest.

Furnish quick-copy duplicates of articles and book excerpts to supply the training staff.

If the training officer has to try to work with an antiquated system in which the librarian insists on keeping all books on the library shelves at all times, except while in use at library tables by silent users, training specialists are advised to look elsewhere for assistance.

AUDIOVISUAL STAFF. Fundamentally, training specialists work with words and pictures. The Chinese were probably right when they equated one picture with 10,000 words. Ideally, the training and development unit should include a minimum of at least one illustrator, and when it can afford a larger audiovisual staff, it might add one or more visual presentation specialists.

A visual presentation specialist is a multimedia-minded individual with the capacity for visualizing, planning, and supervising the rendition of finished graphics work, such as diagrams, cartoons, photographic reproductions, flowsheets, charts, and similar illustrations. He or she also knows how to integrate and synchronize sound with visual media, choose locales, package the end product, prepare how-to-use booklets, and select appropriate equipment. One well-qualified visual presentation specialist can direct a crew of 15 to 20 A/V technicians of diverse skills and abilities, and also negotiate with and direct contractors when some of the work has to be farmed out. Additionally, the specialist may be a master craftsperson—a good artist, photographer, or writer.

The A/V staff may be organizationally separated from the training and development unit, depending upon such factors as the primary mission of the enterprise, its location, degree of centralization, peculiarities of organization, policy with respect to contracting work to outside groups, and supply and demand of A/V talent in the marketplace. For example, an advertising agency with a large commercial art staff probably would not have a separate A/V crew in its training unit.

PUBLIC INFORMATION STAFF. This unit is usually staffed by specialists whose primary skill is writing. However, it may include some visual presentation specialists, draftsmen, and illustrators. All talent and skill of the information staff are relevant to the training staff, but its target audience is different. The training staff presumably deals with topics in depth when it is teaching groups, whereas the information office prepares news releases and other items for an audience that is dispersed. But the public information staff can also assist the training staff by

Providing copious handout material to the training office.
Analyzing public complaints and suggesting areas in need of further training.
Assisting in the orientation of new employees, including new executives and administrators.
Writing scripts for A/V productions.
Preparing case histories and critical incidents for experiential training.
Assembling historical background of operational programs.
Furnishing statistical data for graphic materials and exhibits.
Arranging for publicity in news media about training programs.
Negotiating the use of local studios for shooting film and recording audio sequences.
Developing bidder lists for competitive bidding purposes.
Marshaling outside resource people who can dispense public information that might be unacceptable from the source (the familiar "plant").

In brief, the public information staff is another rich source of technical assistance to the training and development group.

FIELD PERSONNEL. Decentralized organizations may be large enough to have a training representative in each of its regions or large branch offices. Such personnel, used selectively on the basis of their known strengths and weaknesses, can be of tremendous value to the central training and development unit. Each field representative has a specialty and local resources from which to assemble practical material that will enlarge and enrich a centrally administered program. Logically, perhaps, these persons should be qualified trainers in order to get the multiplier effect among their target audiences. They are good spotters to help identify operating personnel and subject-matter experts to assist in program development and implementation. They can backstop the central unit by making advance arrangements for space, A/V equipment, housing, transportation, and other incidentals for making the program go smoothly when it moves to a particular field location.

Here is a note of caution. Field representatives often resent being cast as errand boys for headquarters teams. Therefore, it is desirable that they be given a balanced role, including a hand in all stages of the program from inception to follow-through and evaluation. Field representatives sometimes distinguish themselves to the point where they become logical choices for transfer and promotion to the central training and development staff.

LABOR LEADERS. Some managements ignore and even ostracize labor leaders to the point where nothing constructive ever comes from the relationship. This is unfortunate because task groups and training committees with labor representation can arrive at a reasonable meeting of the minds on how to get better paybacks from training. Perhaps even the big labor/management contract renegotiations would not so often reach an impasse if bits and pieces of negotiable matters were accomplished on a day-to-day basis in the normal course of business without a lot of fanfare. Labor's communication channels and powers of observation are just as good as management's—often better. Management has no monopoly on ideas for improving management and organization development. The input of labor in the identification of training needs, in program planning, and even in implementation could be a positive influence on people development.

TRAINING CENTERS. Large agencies of government and large commercial enterprises sometimes establish, in addition to their ordinary in-house training (such as off-job training and a small training unit in each major organizational segment), a vast training center to meet special needs. Several examples will illustrate this point. The Xerox Corporation has a magnificent and functionally designed training center at a site on the Potomac River near Leesburg, Virginia. It is a multimillion-dollar facility serving three principal target audiences—managers, salespeople, and maintenance technicians. The Foreign Service, U.S. Department of State, established the Foreign Service Institute several decades ago. Now, at Rosslyn, Virginia, it trains new Foreign Service officers, provides continuing training for all State Department professional personnel, and runs extensive foreign language training at satellite centers throughout the world. The Department of Defense operates the Industrial College of the Armed Forces at Ft. McNair in Washington, D.C., to keep its senior officers in the Army, Navy, and Air Force updated in the industrial and economic development capabilities of the United States. The Western Electric Division of American Telephone and Telegraph has a very modern executive development center in New Jersey for developing potential executives in the company.

Centers such as these can assist their parent agencies in special training programs in many ways. For example, the Army Management Engineering Training Agency (AMETA), at Rock Island, Illinois, teaches, performs research, and consults with its clients. Any army training specialist anywhere in the world should be able to draw on these capabilities, and probably does from time to time.

TEMPORARY PERSONNEL TRANSFERS. A training officer can go just so far in bargaining for the free and informal use of personnel assigned elsewhere in the organization. The requirement may last three to six months instead of a few hours or days. If more than incidental time is to be spent by a person from another department, the training officer should consult with that person's superior, explain the situation, and ask for approval. The executive may wish to request personnel action to arrange temporary transfer so that the departmental budget will not be affected and so that the assignment will be properly recorded in the transferee's personnel folder. The latter may be to the advantage of the person transferred when other positions are offered.

Repeated requests for temporaries from within the organization may become cause for concern among management, labor, and audit supervisors. If the training manager is pushed to this extreme because qualified assistance is lacking, he or she should make certain that the causes and conditions are duly recorded. Arbitrary raids on other departments for personnel may jeopardize not only the goodwill of operating people and senior executives, but may also reflect on the capability of the training manager or even on the value of the training program.

External Sources

One of the secrets of good management of training and development lies in knowing how to orchestrate internal resources with one hand, external resources with the other, and somehow to keep the two working efficiently and in harmony with each other and with the broad goals of the employer. There is a wide choice of external sources, some of which one can assume are pressing hard for one reason or another to gain a foothold inside the organization.

For example, the pressure may be a "loss leader" effort to gain some experience, or the endorsement of a company or public service group that will lend prestige and facilitate the negotiation of jobs with other employers. The training manager must know the resources of the local community and the contract training industry at large. Some of these sources may employ skilled sales representatives who know how to apply pressure on the training manager through executive and administrative channels. The representative may maintain a working relationship with political leaders and, when hungry for business or a choice contract, will persuade the politician or a member of the latter's staff to call or write the head of the training manager's organization. Contractors who rely on influence strategy instead of an earned reputation for quality work have at least one strike against them.

There are other things to watch for besides the approach of the sales representative. These will be mentioned as the several categories of external assistance are discussed below.

SHELF COURSES. People insist on rediscovering the wheel—repeatedly. The first place to look on the outside for help is the market for ready-made, self-instructional courses, provided the searcher has sufficient self-discipline and objectivity to resist the purchase of useless products and the ability to discriminate among applicable products.

For about $35 one can buy a book with a comprehensive listing of hundreds of such courses. One state university is now teaching statistics entirely by this method, and tests show that learning is as good or better than teaching by conventional methods. There is a particularly good collection of self-instructional courses in basic education skills and mechanical arts. Such courses are ingeniously designed to induce participation and get the participant interacting with the subject matter and usually with a simple teaching machine. The learner is not competing with other students—doubtless a factor that leads to high school dropouts—but is essentially competing with himself by pacing himself comfortably and recording his progress.

Many of these commercially available courses initially cost many thousands of dollars to develop and are available for a nominal fraction of that. There is an impressive and growing reservoir of self-instructional courses in the public domain. Taxpayers have made their investment once and should not have to make it repeatedly on subjects that change infrequently. Individualized, learner-paced courses have the advantage of being multipurpose. They can be used as a preliminary phase of training to orient, motivate, and suggest to the learner and trainer areas of strength and weakness. They can also be used as refresher training for follow-through purposes and for supplementary training.

It is dangerous to lean too heavily on self-instructional courses. They cannot do the job alone. People are better people developers than machines and cleverly constructed instructional materials. There comes a time in all learning when learners want to discuss their questions with other learners and with a teacher or someone else who knows more about the subject than they do.

TEMPORARY HIRES. If the need is urgent for training to get under way and the budget is limited, as it usually is, one is well advised to hire some short-term employees. Employment agencies can be helpful in identifying good prospects. Ads placed in appropriate media are often fruitful if the requirements are accurately and clearly written. Personal patronage (friend of a friend) is not so bad as merit system advocates would have you believe, as long as you are dealing in temporary hires instead of career service hires.

An individual hired one day may be able to begin work the next day, for he or she can bypass the preliminary procedures that an employer may organize and operate for permanent hires. The temporary hire may try harder if regular employment is an objective. Temporaries who have worked around for a number of different employers may bring to the job some unusually effective work techniques that are worthy of adoption. There are limitations to this source of help, too. If hires are not supplied by one of the many agencies registering temporaries, the first question to ask is why the person is unemployed.

INSTITUTIONAL SOURCES. Educational institutions, from secondary schools to graduate branches of universities, are a prime source of outside help. A discussion of these sources follows.

Colleges and Universities. These institutions have established pipelines to business, industry, and government through which they supply manpower at rates consistent with each interested employer's ability to absorb and the institution's ability to graduate qualified candidates. Institutions of higher learning are becoming increasingly flexible in their calendars and systems for class scheduling. In metropolitan areas, students can work during the daytime and attend classes at night; they can spread their courses over the whole semester or trimester, or in some institutions they can complete them without class attendance or by intensive attendance over a period of a few weeks. There are summers, holiday seasons, the privilege of taking a semester off for work, the formal work/study ("co-op") plan of some universities, sabbatical leaves for professors, and other possibilities.

Senior professors teach only a few hours a week and they expect to market a portion of their time to other employers for income supplement and research purposes. They are also interested in placing their graduate students and research grant fellows in situations where they can do some research on practical on-the-job work assignments. During a quinquennial United States Census of Agriculture, the Bureau of the Census employed scores of agricultural and trade college professors for several weeks, during Easter holidays, to serve as technical instructors of enumerators. Some institutions feature a service to public and private sectors, for a fee, which provides research, developmental, and operational expertise of the type required by training program managers. These groups travel far beyond their home bases; in fact, many are working around the world.

There are some cautions to heed. Institutions do not always practice a policy of deploying their first-rate talent on contract jobs. They hire directly from outside ranks on one day and the new hires may be on their way to domestic or overseas work sites on the next day. Marginal help is sometimes the result of recruitment practices that omit steps, such as a full field investigation. Moreover, all is not gold that glitters within the professorial ranks. The professor with the biggest name in town who hires himself out for fabulous rates may be half entertainer and half artist who can string a well-practiced set of clichés together and impress his audience, but who in fact has never applied or demonstrated the feasibility of his philosophy.

One more caution: Training managers looking directly to colleges and universities for contractual services are advised to watch the overhead factor. Overhead can run as high as 150 percent of direct costs because the university president's salary, the new football stadium, and other indirect cost items have to get a slice of the take from every contract job.

Junior Colleges and Community Colleges. These institutions provide a thirteenth and fourteenth year of schooling for young adults who are high school graduates. The junior college likes those who are definitely bound for four-year colleges. The community college is designed for those who have less commitment to a continuing academic education—students who are more concerned with the early acquisition of marketable skills in order to get on a payroll. Interestingly, however, 50 percent of the college and university new enrollments are now coming directly from community colleges.

Community colleges are working closely with local business and industry and gearing their curricula to known needs. They specialize in paraprofessional skill subjects such as drafting, electronics, bookkeeping, automobile mechanics, and clerical skills. Junior colleges and community colleges are local, practicable sources of assistance. In one instance they might be in position to pretest and validate a training program. In another, the faculty members may be able to provide valuable advice and assistance in curriculum design, or to teach a phase of the course in their facilities, or to detail some of their students to the employer to gain practical experience in working on some aspect of the training program.

High Schools. This level of our education system abounds in talent and is often overlooked. The talent is idled for several months yearly in most systems because the pattern established when we were an agrarian society required the children to help in the fields during the harvest of crops. Creative teachers can make real contributions to training programs, and lesson planning is their stock in trade. Moreover, they generally pay more attention to teaching methodology than college professors do, and they may be more currently knowledgeable than some college professors because they are in continuing education programs. Many communities now tie their higher salary scale to the teacher's commitment to continuing education programs.

In brief, high school teachers are an excellent source of talent, and their use by employers gives them the tremendous further advantage of being exposed to the realities of life in the real world of work for which they are preparing people. Much good counseling needs to be done at the high school level, and the teacher/student relationship is a good setting for the dissemination of advice and counsel on career opportunities in the business world.

PROFESSIONAL SOCIETIES. Every academic discipline and occupational specialty has some professional association for advancing and protecting its interests. For example, the American Society for Training and Development is the "union hall" for most training specialists. These societies and employee organizations have a keen sense of responsibility for the well-being of their members, and one of the services they offer is an employment clearinghouse. The larger ones have an office headquarters and employ a staff to coordinate its activities. The American Management Associations, with headquarters in New York City, has a long history of service to its worldwide membership through publications and training services. AMA courses are now dispensed by computer, like airplane and hotel reservations.

Professional societies are probably in as good a position as any source, if not better, for suggesting individuals who are between jobs or in the category of "old Turks" and semiretired. One can expect a society to hold itself reasonably accountable for its recommendations, since it will be around as long as the occupations it supports.

GOVERNMENTS. Reciprocity in the use of training facilities is common practice now. In fact, it is mandated by the Government Employees Training Act that various agencies share facilities on a space-available basis. State and local governments are using federal facilities, and underdeveloped countries are using federal, state, and local facilities authorized by foreign aid legislation.

The trend in the federal government is a proliferation of training centers within the larger agencies. The same is true of the larger companies in private industry, where the rationale is: "Anything a university can do for us we can do for ourselves better and cheaper." Administrators of an organization have more control over the doctrines taught if they own and operate their own training center. They have a staff of experts who can be given teaching tours. Much of the travel and per diem living expenses are saved. Scheduling is better controlled and coordinated with production. Administrators and senior executives are in a better position to make guest appearances if the training center is only a taxi ride away, or if the training center is in another city where the visit can be combined with other official business. The training is less likely to be degree-oriented in a center than in a university. These and other administrative considerations have influenced many organizations to establish their own training centers.

Among the federal agencies with whole *networks* of training centers are Army, Navy, and Air Force, Transportation, Postal Service, State Department, Internal Revenue Service, and the Civil Service Commission. The FBI has a large training facility at Quantico, Virginia. A consortium of law enforcement agencies has a large new center in Washington, D. C., known as the Consolidated Federal Law Enforcement Training Center. Many other agencies have centers at a single location. Others use stationary or mobile seminars, workshops, and institutes to meet agency training needs. Seldom do any of these training activities operate with 100 percent of their classroom seats reserved. Space can often be bought on a standby basis or on a percentage-of-space-available basis.

State and local governments all enjoy a reputation for excellence in certain areas of public service. Their training facilities should not be overlooked as good possibilities.

Finally, in the category of government sources, one should seriously consider the possibility of using the services of selected foreign governments for training purposes. We in the United States are still a "new kid on the block" in relation to European, Asian, and African cultures. For example, our tourist industry could probably learn a good many things from the tourist industry of Switzerland. Our railroad industry might well study railroading in nearly any country in Europe, in Japan, and in certain countries of Africa. The Paris subway is a model worth studying by United States cities with subways under their streets or on their drawing boards. Our urban park planners could learn some useful lessons in Asia; for instance, in Iran and Japan. Police administrations are apparently behind countless nations of the world in terms of maintaining security on the streets at night and in helping people feel more secure when using public transportation.

This is not to suggest that no public or private agency in the United States has ever used other governments as a source of new technical know-how. However, in those cases where it has been attempted, too frequently it was done on a "quickie" basis by sending one individual or a team abroad to confer and observe for a few days or weeks. This is not the way to gather new ideas. One must settle down and live there, and become a part of the system for a while. Most foreign governments in the more advanced nations also have training centers and staff colleges. For example, there are hundred-year-old staff colleges in Europe for preparing people for careers in postal, telephone, and telegraph operations, in contrast to our postal institute, which was opened in January 1968. We should cultivate more two-way streets to these overseas facilities, and adjust our laws and retirement plans if necessary to make such experience fully creditable.

Not only will the United States profit from the acquisition of new knowledge from other governments, but trainees also will benefit from the live-abroad experience. One gains better perspective on the United States as well as more accurate insights into the foreign culture where one is stationed. Preferably, the family of a participant should be encouraged to accompany the participant and their expenses should be subsidized. It will be a growth experience for the whole family, and they will return as broadened, more enlightened citizens.

CONTRACTORS. Training has become one of the largest industries in the United States. There is a wide range of capability among the enterprises engaged in the development and administration of training programs. This is related to the history of how some companies entered the market in the first place.

One company's entry may have emerged from an overseas marketing program that became overstaffed as sales diminished so that the staff had to be recalled and diverted to the domestic training market. Another may be the education and training division of a company that lost the bid for a major contract and was forced to find other work for the staff or let it go. It could be the engineering staff of such a company, which has not had a day's experience in training work. Another firm may be a consortium of professors who are marketing their available time. Still another may be second-career people. Consulting firms that do management improvement studies often include training recommendations and get an additional task order to follow through with the training program. Training "hardware" distributors sometimes get into the "software" business (preparation of curriculum materials) as a means of pushing more hardware sales.

The end product from a contractor is no better or worse than the *scope of work* against which the contract is bid in the first place. A fuzzy statement of the contract requirements is likely to produce a final report with fuzzy conclusions and recommendations. It will take more communication after the project is under way to compensate for a scope of work with gaps. Misunderstandings are generated by lack of specificity. For example, if the client is expecting the contractor to dry-run the program but fails to say so, then delay, cost adjustments, and misunderstandings are the inevitable result.

A clear understanding—preferably in writing in advance of the contract award—as to the caliber of persons who will perform the actual work is extremely important. To establish this, contractors may include with their proposals a portfolio of résumés of "associates" or staff available to the company. This can be very misleading, for the people who begin negotiations may be a different lot entirely from those who approve the contract, and may woefully lack the experience held by those whose résumés were included in the proposal package.

The market should be screened in advance of requests for proposals (RFP). Invitations should be sent to a minimum of three apparently qualified bidders. Seldom, if ever, should a sole source be unilaterally engaged. It is well, also, to conduct a prebid conference with interested bidders in the impartial offices of the contract officer or attorney. The RFP should include a penalty clause for noncompliance and specify the procedure for terminating the contractual relationship if the conditions are not met by either party.

It is well to remember that a low bid is not necessarily the best bid. Bids should arrive in the contract office, sealed, by the specified deadline. After a public opening in the presence of interested bidders, each one should be analyzed carefully against an experience-rated matrix of factors having particular concern for the organization buying the contract services. Another caution is to work closely with an experienced contracting officer and attorney before making any awards. This avoids the possibility of finding oneself paying not once for the development of curriculum materials, but over and over again. Developers also like to insert a clause giving themselves the copyright and sole rights to determine subsequent usage after one copy has been surrendered to the client. If the client wants more than one copy, which obviously is necessary, he may find himself being billed for $25 or some other figure for every kit ordered for every employee to be trained for as long as the course lasts.

Almost as essential as the scope of work is the requirement to monitor the contract at all stages as the work progresses. The contractor's priorities may suddenly change, employees may quit, or the project may start eating up its profits by taking longer than estimated. The monitor has to be eminently qualified for this assignment, and must be objective and above reproach in every respect. Upon these qualifications rests the success or failure of the project. If it should fail, there can be far-reaching implications.

Some Guidelines and Criteria

It is safe to say that there are no scientifically determined guidelines for deciding when to use internal sources of help on training projects and when to use outside sources or some combination of the two. It should be possible to make this decision easily, however, after some experience in contracting out and in using inside sources to develop a matrix to guide the training manager in making recommendations to superior officers. The stub of the matrix should include three possibilities: in-house, outside, and combination. The head of the matrix should include such experience-rated guidelines as these:

Number of participants to be trained?
Number of training locations?
Unit cost? (dollar bid divided by number of participants)
Timing? How soon must training begin?
Replication? Cycles? Finish date?
Quality control?
Should project be growth experience for agency staff?
Should project impact on agency's training and development consciousness?
Should project contribute to research on behavioral objectives, training needs, job analysis? If so, who can best do it?
How much flexibility will regular staff have with inside help? With outside help? With combination?
How will the project impact on continuing training programs and the regular staff's ability to manage them uninterruptedly?

It is equally difficult or harder to generalize about the order of preference among the categories of outside help. The chances of picking the best single contractor are comparable to those of picking the best apple in a large apple orchard. However, as an organization gains experience in contracting for training work, it becomes easier to judge the capability of bidders and the quality of their bid proposals. In the early stages of contractual relationships, a training manager may be well advised to engage a short-term consultant. With more experience, it should be possible to make a matrix, using a series of 10 to 12 factors, so that each bid can be rated on a three- to five-point scale. This matrix might include the following experience-rated criteria:

Experience of firm in education and training work?
Capability of staff resources to be committed to this project?
Local office or remote management?
Reference check findings?
Credit rating?
Feasibility of proposed steps to be used in producing end products?
Provision for supervision and quality control?
Support staff (adequacy, availability, qualifications, and so on)?

Reasonableness of bid in comparison with other bids? With project budget?

Impression made by bidder's representatives during prebid phase?

Past performance of bidder on projects, if any previously worked for this prospective client?

Recommended Procedure

The following guidelines should be used until the training manager develops a better set for himself out of practical experience in managing the training and development activities of the organization where he works.

1. Use inside help whenever possible.

2. If one needs to reach for outside assistance, draw on the several sources in the sequence in which they are listed above; that is, give first choice to shelf courses that are applicable and ready for use on a learner-paced, individualized basis, and give lowest priority to contractors.

3. When using contractors, proceed with deliberate speed in collaboration with a good contract officer and a good attorney. Prepare a detailed scope of work for the invitation to bid; weigh bids against experience-rated factors, and make an intelligent and defensible award; monitor faithfully; and record a fair appraisal (multiple judgment) of the contractor's work for future reference.

Conclusion

There is compelling evidence to dictate priorities when the limited capacity of the in-house unit requires an outside search for help in people development. If the thesis is that people developers are everywhere and the only problem is to identify them, it follows that an organization would be shortsighted to deprive itself of the finest people development experience of all by not affording its own staff the opportunity to assist in the development of their associates. Leaders should therefore commit themselves to this principle, allowing for exceptions when administrative considerations clearly indicate other courses of action.

If an organization must reach for external assistance, certain priorities should be observed. The following order of preference is recommended as a starting point, pending the evolutionary development of a matrix for scrutinizing the array of external source possibilities that one comes to rely on. Select in this order:

1. Shelf courses that specifically relate to the training needs of the target audience.
2. Temporary hires.
3. Educational institutions.
4. Professional societies that offer training and development services for a fee.
5. Government programs that sell space.
6. Private contractors.

When an organization elects to engage an external source of assistance other than direct hire, a set of precisely drawn requirements should be reduced to writing and a reasonable number of experienced sources should be invited to submit sealed bids by a deadline. The "scope of work" element of such documents is the critical element. Such arrangements should not be entered into without the advice and assistance of a good contract officer and a good attorney. Careful monitoring and a recorded critique of performance for future reference are essential.

6

Marshaling Resources

A THREE-DAY conference of executives from private industry once defined "management" essentially as the process of *guiding human and physical resources into dynamic organization units that attain their objectives to the satisfaction of those served and with a high degree of morale and sense of attainment on the part of those rendering the service.*

A shorter definition defines management as *the process of getting things done through others.* Some writers have coined a "3-M formula" as the best means of getting work done—money, manpower, and materials.

None of these concepts is fully satisfactory. The director of employee training and career development is basically a specialist/manager with a great volume of work constantly confronting him. What, if anything, does he need besides money, peoplepower, and materials? This chapter introduces an acronym for recalling the eight parts of a people developer's total requirement for getting work done in the most efficient and effective manner possible. These parts are *s*pace, *t*ime, *e*quipment, *a*uthority, *m*oney, *m*anpower, *m*aterials, and *m*anagement—the initial letters of which comprise the acronym STEAMMMM. It is easy to remember if one associates it with steam-power engines. Each component of the coined word is discussed below, with emphasis on the strategy most likely to

ensure that the particular resource is obtained in the quantity desired and at the right place at the right time.

Space (STEAMMMM)

Although space might appear to be the easiest of the resources to
marshal, it is nearly always the hardest to acquire. Even when it is finally made available after an incessant series of hassles with space
owners and managers and other space holders, one often winds up
with a submarginal location in poor condition. It may be in the basement, the attic, or an annex that is hardly fit for human habitation.
It may suffer from lack of cooling, heating, ventilation, noise
abatement, and insulation from distractions that impede learning. It
may be unsightly, drab, nonfunctional, poorly lighted, and marginally furnished. The chairs may be of ancient vintage and unsuitable
for arrangements that encourage participative and experiential
learning methods. The space may be located in a place hard to find,
inaccessible by public transportation, and without parking accommodations.

It is incomprehensible that some administrators permit the space
for the employee training and career development function to have
such low priority. Frequently, they are not surrounded by executives
who are training conscious and therefore mindful of including in
long-range space requirements and building plans the necessary
provision for suitable training space. A typical way to handle the
training space requirement is to authorize the training manager to
use a third-rate conference room, which is constantly being used as a
staging area for moves of various organization elements. In every
such move, the conference room must be relocated, and employees
sent to an all-purpose room for training often discover a sign,
"Moved to Room _____." They soon realize that training programs
are not considered very important by senior executives who allow
this to happen.

Even if the conference room reserved for the administrator's senior staff meetings were consistently available for training programs,
which it seldom if ever is, this is far from adequate. Conferences and
training sessions conducted in accordance with the current state of
the art are two distinctly different things. Training sessions require
more flexibility in the arrangement of the furniture than formal
conference rooms are prepared to accommodate. Training sessions
need a cluster of smaller breakout rooms for problem solving, role-

player preparation, buzz sessions, and related activity. Training sessions require rather elaborate provision for the use of multimedia equipment. Some training space requires stationary equipment of sizable proportions, such as simulators, prototypes, laboratory devices, input and output terminals for computer-assisted instruction, and safety gear. Elaborate wall space for exhibits, chalkboards, tack boards, magnetic boards, bulletins, and the taping of easel-pad pages is required in many types of training activities.

Training space must be space that can be converted into an accessible, functional, flexible, safe, comfortable, and inviting environment for learning. It should be regarded as one's office away from one's office, or one's home away from one's home. We add color, decor, acoustical materials, conveniences, "view," comfort, efficiency, multipurposefulness, and other advantages to our offices and to our homes. The same standards should guide us in designing and maintaining the space where people need to concentrate on learning new knowledges, skills, and perspectives.

What is the best road to take to realize one's objective? It is not easy, but here are some experience-tested strategies.

MASTER PROPOSAL OR PROSPECTUS. This should encompass all the known, continuing, and contingent requirements for training and career development space. All of the target audiences identified in Chapter 3 should be accommodated, together with some room for expansion and for facilities that have never been available to the organization in any form (such as an auditorium). Very little is ever accomplished by talk alone. A set of plans and specifications is an excellent basis for discussion at annual budget formulation time, or when the agency is contemplating the acquisition of new space, change of headquarters, or construction of a new, all-purpose building complex.

ANNEX BUILDING. The agency may already own or lease an annex building or other extra space that it is holding because of the land value or the possibility of future expansion. Take this space if it at least meets the test of accessibility, functional adaptability, basic comfortableness, and safety. It may not be so inviting as custom-designed space or your ultimate model, but it can compensate in other ways.

Otherwise unused space that is partially isolated from the main stream of agency operations has some distinct advantages, particularly if the employee training and career development activity is the sole tenant. The training manager can build an "extended family" environment in which all staff members will soon take pride in decorating to express their respective personalities. The staff develops a sense of self-sufficiency and control over its operations. Communication is improved internally because of the informality with which staff members can conduct their work and interpersonal relations. Morale and productivity may be stimulated by the team approach to problem solving.

SPACE RETRIEVAL AND REFURBISHMENT. It is well to conduct a search of all space in all buildings owned and occupied by the enterprise. Identify whatever space *appears* to be absolutely impossible, but which might be salvageable. Every organization has some of it or can readily make some by such methods as: clearing out dead storage of old equipment that can be surplused; culling inactive files and records, and either destroying them or dispatching them to a records management center where the cost of space per square foot is much less; or opening up space that has never been used for anything—attics, sub-basements, connecting tunnels, and the like. Chapter 8 deals specifically with how to convert existing space or design new space to serve the training function optimally. It is simply amazing what an enlightened architect or facilities planner who understands education and training requirements can do with space, light, color dynamics, wall and floor coverings, acoustical materials, glass, fabrics, and modern heating, cooling, and ventilation systems. The cost per cubic foot for converting existing space is a modest fraction of the cost of building new space. A comparative cost analysis may provide just the evidence needed to convince management of the desirability of going this route.

CO-OP ARRANGEMENTS. Another option is to canvass neighboring public and private agencies to analyze their situation. One may find that there is a state of general poverty among all agencies with respect to space that conforms to high standards, or one may find that one agency is relatively rich and is embarrassed by the plush space it has and the fact that it needs the space only about 30 percent of the time. It may be all too happy to negotiate a joint-use scheme, either without charge or on an out-of-pocket cost basis (utilities and custodial care).

MOTELS AND HOTELS. Many motels and hotels are allocating space during the design stage to training requirements of customers that need housing accommodations for participants. While such space is never suitable for all forms of training, it can serve reasonably well for supervisory, managerial, and executive development programs, and for seminars, workshops, and institutes for professionals and scientists. Specific agreements with respect to such facilities should be negotiated well in advance, and the division of labor should be clearly fixed in writing with respect to the backstopping of such space. Motels and hotels frequently offer such space without charge, provided they get to house and feed the participants for a minimum number of days. This solution should not be overlooked as a partial solution to the space requirements, but training managers are advised not to settle on this source as the permanent solution to required space problems. Many distractions in and around such places may detract from the learning environment and lessen the program effectiveness.

Time (sTeammmm)

Time is a finite resource within any given accounting period. What there is of it is as available as the oxygen we breathe. The challenge is in making the fullest possible use of the prime time available for employee training and career development programs, and to use some imagination and good planning in capturing peripheral time that can extend the total time span available to a program. Professional planners and systems analysts know how to exploit time to the fullest. Some proven methods for reducing the time to accomplish a work project, which may be useful to training specialists, are discussed below.

THE BUDGET. Perhaps the best-known and most commonly used method is the budget. Planning of the budget for any given fiscal year for federal agencies begins 18 months in advance. Planning in industrial and commercial organizations varies, from as little as 12 months to several or more years ahead. The budget year is divided into quarters, and expenditures are tracked and recapitulated quarter by quarter.

CHARTING AND ANALYSES. One of the most sophisticated techniques for time analysis was introduced in World War I by Henry Gantt (1861–1919), who developed the Gantt chart as an aid to orderly planning of work operations. This chart includes the steps necessary to obtain a final work result. The steps are worked out by projecting backward, step by step from end result to actions, their timing, and their sequence.

Program Evaluation Review Technique (PERT) charts were introduced by the U.S. Navy in connection with its Polaris Weapon Systems program in 1958. The DuPont Company introduced a similar technique about the same time, known as the Critical Path

Method (CPM). The critical path is the longest and most time-consuming method of obtaining the end result. In PERT and CPM, the tasks to complete a given project are meticulously charted to form a "network" that focuses on events and activities. Both PERT and CPM and network analyses are refinements and extensions of Gantt's significant work.

WORK SIMPLIFICATION. The method of work simplification is popular in some organizations. It uses work-distribution charts, process charts, and work counts to find better methods to do better work with less effort in less time without hurrying, and with greater safety and lower costs. It may result in doing the job better by eliminating unnecessary parts of the job, combining and rearranging the rest of the job, and simplifying the necessary parts of the job.

MANAGEMENT ANALYSTS AND INDUSTRIAL ENGINEERS. In-house specialists are engaged in studies of operational efficiency. These analysts and engineers are constantly searching for shortcuts to improve technology, quality controls, and other economy measures.

MANAGEMENT BY OBJECTIVES AND RESULTS. Another technique that has a sizable following among managers is called "Management by Objectives." Others call it Management by Objectives and Results (MOR). This process is a systematic approach to management which concentrates on the functions of planning and controlling. It encourages participative management in determining what must be done, how it must be done, when it must be done, how much it will cost, what constitutes satisfactory performance, how much progress is being achieved, and when and how to take corrective action.

TRAINING TIMETABLE. The training manager not only has to be concerned wtih careful husbandry of time allotted for meeting a specific training objective, but also has to use time advantageously in developing the training staff. Toward this end, a useful technique was introduced by the Training within Industry Service, War Manpower Commission, during World War II, through the "J" programs, which were used extensively in industry and government to train foremen and supervisors. Job Instruction Training (JIT), Job Methods Training (JMT), and Job Relations Training (JRT) were each a 10-hour, highly standardized training program for which trainers had to be certified by a special institute.

JIT included a device called a "training timetable." In the stub of the table the names of subordinates are listed by the supervisor. New names are added to the listing as new employees enter upon duty in the unit. In the heading of the table, the supervisor enters the jobs of work that have to be done by the several employees of the unit.

Using a code scheme, the supervisor may check a box to indicate that the employee has been trained to do a particular job; leaving the box blank may signify that the employee does not need to know how to do the job; and inserting a forward date represents a commitment to train the employee to do a job by the specific date for such reasons as to provide depth of coverage, to anticipate reassignments, or to provide a career development opportunity.

The composite picture resulting from this exercise, and from the continuous maintenance of the training timetable, has the same type of value that a TV monitor of pending plane arrivals and departures has to people in an airport.

PERIPHERAL TIME. Another consideration in the use of time as a resource pertains to peripheral time, that is, time that exists before and after the main event of a training and development program. There are times in the planning of a training program when it is just not possible to cover all content that needs to be covered. There are times when it is apparent that participants will begin the formal phase of a particular training program with a wide range of readiness for learning. On other occasions, participants will enter training with a vast unevenness in motivation. Some will have the will to learn and to apply the new knowledge and skill; others will approach the learning situation with indifference and passiveness.

In these and related circumstances, it is sometimes possible to make use of a pretraining phase. Mailouts, self-instructional materials, self-administering paper and pencil or performance tests, essays, home assignments such as professional papers, assigned reading, problem-solving exercises, and similar techniques can be used to good advantage by an imaginative program planner. It may also be possible to use individualized counseling and questionnaires to get a more precise fix on learning capability, readiness, and level of motivation. The point is that some of the pretraining time should be productive.

The same principle applies to the period just after the formal phase of a training program. Follow-through is an essential step in all good training, and should be an integral part of the planning. The post-training follow-through intervals should be predetermined. For example, the first action may occur within a few days, something else six months later, and again from one to two years after the end of the formal phase. These pretraining and post-training activities are not perceived by management to be a part of the training in terms of allocating time to a training project because the input of the employee usually occurs on the job or on his own time.

Desk and Wall Calendars. The training specialist's own calendar is always present, and the practice in some offices is to keep three wall calendars in full view—last month's, this month's, and next month's. Other training managers keep the whole year exposed on a large display board made of laminated materials and which will take grease pencil that can be easily erased. Production control boards, which are commercially available in the marketplace, are not so good. They require elaborate manipulation of pins, pegs, strings, and the like, and this clerical time is either not available or can be more profitably devoted to more productive activities. A faithful log of project developments in an ordinary manila folder is the minimum control needed on the history and status of a project.

Personal Diaries. Perhaps the simplest, and for many the best, time controller of all is the little daily diary for the calendar year. It is only about 2 inches wide, 4 inches long, and ½ inch thick, and fits neatly in a man's shirt pocket or lady's purse. It shows the week at a glance and allows 1 by 2 inches of space for noting each critical appointment, tasks to be done, and important happenings. Last year's calendar is pasted on the inside of the front cover, and next year's calendar is pasted on the inside of the back cover. This efficient planning tool, which can be purchased for a dollar or less, should not be out of reach from the time one rises until one retires. One can keep a few small sheets of note paper clipped to the current week's lead sheet for jotting down brainstorm ideas, making calculations, and writing reminders to others and to yourself. This is a time-tested device. Busy people and good planners consider it a must. Experience will soon determine the type of data to enter on the blank pages at the front and back of the diary, making it your personal "encyclopedia" or miniature "computer" for information retrieval purposes. When the year ends, file the diary in a safe place for future reference.

In summary, the training specialist should be as concerned with marshaling and planning and controlling the use of time as a resource as he is concerned with his other more tangible resource requirements.

Equipment (stEAMMMM)

A modern learning environment is something more than chairs, tables, and a chalkboard. An abundance of training aids exists as a result of a growing emphasis on technology in education and training, which began during World War II. The following paragraphs describe one approach toward organizing, describing, and weighing the several categories of training aids.

CATEGORIES. A training aid is any device or piece of equipment, pertinent to the subject being presented, used to help the participant (trainee) understand and learn. A reproduction or demonstration of a device, process, principle, or situation is vastly superior to a simple word description. Such aids can be divided into the following four major categories.

Visual Training Aids. Aids that make their appeal through the sense of sight are visual training aids. The chalkboard, flat pictures, posters, charts, graphs, diagrams, silent films and filmstrips, transparent slides, material for opaque projection, models (enlarged, miniature, working), actual objects, cutaways, mock-ups, and flannel boards are examples of this category.

Auditory Training Aids. Aids that help the participant learn through hearing only are auditory aids. Phonograph recores, tape recordings, public address systems, telephone, radio, and megaphones are examples.

Audiovisual Training Aids. Aids that make use of both sight and hearing are classified as "audiovisual." Examples include sound motion pictures, videotapes, TV kinescopes, sound filmstrips, slide/tape productions, computer-assisted instruction output units, television, automated simulators, and teaching machines.

Synthetic Training Devices. Aids designed to simulate the action or function of the real device to be operated or used by the participant are synthetic, intended to develop "feel." These include automobile driving simulators, Link trainers for student airplane pilots, simulated keyboard devices, miniature transportation systems with scale model equipment, and the like.

USE CRITERIA. In assembling training aids, one needs to be guided by a number of relevant criteria. Those suggested are:

Economic feasibility of procuring the unit on the scale needed; that is, the unit cost factor.

Appeal to more than one sense.

Ability to focus the attention of all participants on one item at the proper time; ability to pace the instruction at a reasonable speed.

Ability to stimulate the learner's imagination and cause him to interact with the subject matter and possibly the device itself.

Ease and inexpensiveness of maintenance.

Portability and "mailability."
Inherent simplicity.
Durability.

VALUE. The value of each training aid selected or designed can be expected to be in direct proportion to the following characteristics:

Simplicity and Unity. There should be a singleness of ideas, unadorned with irrelevant and distracting material.

Colorfulness. This may be achieved through the use of an attractive design, color, movement, or form.

Flexibility. Trainers use training aids in different ways, depending on their personality, training objectives, individual needs of participants, and other factors.

Timeliness. Training aids must be carefully integrated with the content of a training program. For example, showing a film when the film or projectionist is available is a poor substitute for scheduling it at a time when it is relatable to the subject under consideration.

Visibility. The smallest significant detail produced by a training aid must be large enough for the most distant participant to see.

Acquisition Considerations. Once the decision has been made as to the specific type of training to use, value judgments should be made. One must seriously weigh the pros and cons of renting rather than buying the aids. In weighing this decision, one needs to consider such factors as:

Frequency of use.
Life expectancy of each item.
Frequency of model changes.
Maintenance costs.
Warehousing capability.
Transportation costs in shipping aids to points of use.
Budgetary limitations.
Availability of experienced operators.
Ease of obtaining and stocking spare parts.

Authority (STEAMMMM)

A power or right given to do something is not generally regarded as a "resource" in the training and development community. It is included in the STEAMMMM equation because the absence of proper authorization can be as self-defeating and frustrating as an automobile in the driveway with an expired license plate.

The federal government was without a law sanctioning the use of public money for the training of federal employees from 1776 to 1958. Some agencies, mainly those of the Department of Defense, derived limited authority for training from language inserted in their annual appropriations. Other agencies were constantly in trouble with the General Accounting Office, whose auditors would note and take exception to irregular expenditures for textbooks, training aids, and other related expenses. This lack of explicit authority often was just the excuse needed by some executives to disapprove proposals to conduct training programs that would improve productivity and service. Other, more enlightened executives relied on the "inherent authority of an agency to carry on its operations" as the justification for training, and were able to support at least a limited in-house program.

Some administrators, executives, and managers apparently regard the lack of enabling authority or faulty authority as an unchangeable condition that is "set in concrete." They permit their organizations to continue engaging in sharp practices or doing things inefficiently or ineffectively because of a nonexistent or antiquated law or regulation.

Other organizations have a top drawer of legislative proposals, amendments, and changes working in the offices of their general counsel. This posture is far superior to the practice of trying to do business with a "blunt instrument." Applicable, current, considered, tested needs can be converted into the necessary authority to act through administrative management and legislative processes.

Besides being informed of policy by the head of the agency or business, a director of employee training and career development should be authorized to:

Approve each training and career development program.
Expend funds within budget limitations.
Procure things and services.
Authorize travel by the director, associate staff members, and
    program participants.
Engage consultants and regular and temporary employees.
Use outside training facilities and share those on premise with
    other organizations.
Establish training centers as "delivery systems" for dissemination
    of know-how to a network of points of use.

Manage training and promotion agreements that contemplate variances from established personnel regulations.

The identification of the necessary authorization to accomplish these objectives is as much a part of the planning for the availability of resources as the planning of a budget is. Authority is a resource. The success or failure of employee training and career development programs often turns on the advance planning, finesse, diplomacy, integrity, and initiative that are permissible within the extent of the authority granted.

One personnel management expert once expressed the thought that there are certain "courtesy command channels" through which one can get things done without formalities and without the possibility of having one's authority challenged. For example, the training manager may have a courtesy command connection with the high-speed copy machine supervisor and can get extraordinary service when he is in a bind. He may also be able to get printout information from the computer people as a by-product of their equipment runs for other purposes.

Another type of unwritten authority the training unit may acquire is the authority that comes from knowledge regardless of rank. The unit may have an expert safety-training specialist on its staff whose judgment is so respected that the agency makes no procurements of heavy equipment without having the specialist review and approve technical specifications for the item from a human safety standpoint. Authority vested in knowledge can lead to promotions based on the rank-in-the-person concept. It is an invaluable asset to acquire.

In conclusion, one needs to remember that laws and other manifestations of authority are of the people, by the people, and for the people. They can and should be changed by people of goodwill when it is in the interest of the general welfare to do so.

Money (STEA**M**M**M**M)

It is a sad business when someone rushes off to work in the morning without wallet or purse, or races to the bus stop without having the exact change required by the busdriver. Some training specialists are like that when they have to estimate the costs of operating a program for employee training and career development during the upcoming budget year. Specialists who "guesstimate" never do have the exact change. They are constantly having to "beg, borrow, or steal" money from other sources to cover the cost of a viable program. In the end, their planning is likely to be self-defeating. There is a better way.

There is no better instrument of planning than sound budgeting, which includes budget formulation, budget execution, proper cost accounting and auditing practices, analysis of financial statements, and appropriate follow-through administrative action. Sound budget formulation includes the concept of the Program Planning Budget System (PPBS), which was introduced into the federal service during the Kennedy/Johnson era at the initiative of Robert McNamara, then Secretary of Defense. It requires the projection of fiscal requirements for a five-year period, by program, and the updating of the budget annually. The Carter administration's zero-based budgeting concept is currently being introduced into national government.

Training and career development programs are probably among the most underbudgeted programs in the modern business world. Conservative managements reason that if training saves money by making employees more skilled and efficient, it should pay its own way out of such savings. Obviously, such reasoning is ridiculously false. For example, a thousand dollars spent on updating the training of a safety engineer in one fiscal year may not save a penny that year, but it may save a million dollars over the following five years because less time is lost from accidents and fewer claims are made against the employer for negligence.

Conservative managements also are noted for their contentions that only "fully trained people" should be hired. They have not yet accepted the proposition that education and training are continuing needs of all employees—including themselves. They see training as a form of mollycoddling. When such attitudes prevail in an organization, the training manager is faced with famine with respect to his money needs. He has only one recourse, and it is a good one if he knows how to play his cards. It is not begging, borrowing, or stealing. It is a perfectly respectable alternative, namely, winning the confidence of line operation officials and technicians to the point where they are willing to commit the necessary monies from their budget allotments to plan, produce, and conduct employee training and development programs for the benefit of their own personnel.

For example, in 1966 Postmaster General Lawrence O'Brien, after inspecting postal staff colleges in several European countries, decided that the time had come to establish one in the United States for the training and development of postal supervisors and managers. Unfortunately, no money had been budgeted 18 months in advance for the facility by the small training office in the Post Office Department. Mr. O'Brien went to Capitol Hill and discussed the matter informally with the appropriate committees. The result was that $500,000 was retrieved from contingency funds and operating allotments to operate the Postal Service Institute until flow of the necessary financial resources could be formalized. It is highly doubtful that the Department's controller could have assembled this sum of money if some good spadework had not been done to stimulate the interest among other operating bureaus in having an institute.

A training specialist who associates with, and relates to, operating officials can usually raise enough "venture capital" to run a demonstration program. If it is successful, he establishes his credibility with that client and will probably get more and larger grants with which to solve other training problems in that organizational element. However, there are problems with this approach and it should not be relied on as a permanent solution.

Purse-string controllers are inclined to dictate the content, methods, time, place, faculty, participants, and other important details. They may only be interested in skill training for the here-and-now type of operating problem, with little or no investment in development for foreseeable work assignments. They may have some employees overtrained and others undertrained. They may not be willing to have the training objectively evaluated. They may engulf the training staff to the extent that it has no time left for other organizational elements, where the need may be infinitely greater but where the managements are uncooperative in committing funds. Hence, the total organizational effectiveness is spotty, and employee potential lies dormant or the best talent is lost by turnover because the individuals are not interested in continuing in a work situation that lacks opportunity for career development.

This raises the question as to where authority to allot funds for training and career development should reside in an organization. For the reasons suggested above, and for related reasons, any organization is well advised to assign the people development budget to the director of employee training and career development. In other words, the budget should be a separate "line item" in the organization's budget. It should cover the continuing employee training and career development operations and other human resources development activities of an agency. Further, it should cover the external and internal inputs for special programs. Internal inputs include the costs of a training and career development staff, the purchase of training materials, equipment, courses, and facilities, and travel and transportation expenses associated with these programs. External inputs are the salaries of participants hired to engage in the preliminary career development programs associated with apprenticeship training, recent college graduate hires, disadvantaged and upward mobility program participants, and other individuals hired as reserves to meet expanding future work force requirements.

Expenditures allocated from a centrally held budget must be made within the context of known organizational and individual training and development needs. The money must be spent equitably—in accordance with equal opportunity concepts—expeditiously, and in a timely manner. Essentially, each expenditure should represent a "joint venture" between an organizational element and the director of employee training and career development so as to improve operating efficiency and effectiveness, and indirectly to advance organization development goals and the individual development plans of the employees who become involved.

There are many cautions to observe in budget formulation and execution. Don't plan for more than you need or less than you need during any accounting period. Spend at approved levels to meet program objectives. Balance, flexibility, coordination, participative management, and cost/benefit payback potential are major cornerstones of a well-conceived budget. Long-range projections must face squarely the issues of how best to accomplish the total job of people development. If the judgment of interested executives, after collaboration with the director of employee training and career development, is that the needs can best be met by the establishment of a training center, or by making a major investment in individualized instruction equipment, or by buying training services from outside facilities, then the best option should be introduced into the long-range budget forecast. In this way, the issue remains legitimate over a substantial period, it can be validated as it competes with other "new money" proposals, and the give-and-take process of budget formulation can run its normal course without training and development funds becoming a last minute surprise and hassle.

Manpower (STEAMMMM)

The question of where the manpower comes from to do the people development work is discussed in detail in Chapter 7. That chapter identifies the principal internal and external sources of assistance, and analyzes each source in terms of its advantages and disadvantages. Chapter 7 also deals in depth with the task of recruiting and selecting people developers for the regular staff of the institutional unit of employee training and career development.

The purpose in this chapter with respect to manpower is to underscore its importance to the people development objective and to get it firmly established in the reader's mind as *one* of the resources in the STEAMMMM equation for getting the job done. A naive, inexperienced training person may perceive the primary resource need as one of building as large a staff as possible, and may pay very little attention to the other seven resource elements in the STEAMMMM equation. For example, by neglecting to campaign to obtain adequate space and to have it upgraded into functional, inviting quarters, the training person overlooks one of the strongest cards to play in attracting new members to staff. Pleasant surroundings and efficient tools are rewarding to program participants.

The marshaling of people to serve as people developers should be undertaken in a manner which in itself is a model demonstration (learning experience) of effective personnel management in action. The acquisition phase of good personnel management is not just good recruitment or good selection, or both. It is a cohesive, integrated, balanced process of manpower planning; job analysis; position classification; positive recruitment; careful selection against valid qualification standards; and placement. It requires intelligent use of the probationary period, effective performance appraisal, and counseling as an extension of the initial selection process and as the ultimate test of qualifications for the job. Selection should never be hurried, nor should it result from only a single interview by a single interviewer.

Interviewing is hardly more reliable statistically than the toss of a coin. Careful documenting of opinions from a representative sample of former supervisors, peers, and subordinates is a better measure. The use of a selection panel to pass multiple judgment on the candidate is also useful. In this method, a group oral examination presents problems as a means of studying several candidates around a table, and members of the selection panel serve more as observers than interrogators. Introducing the candidate around to other staff members and explaining some of the work in progress is a good means of observing the quality of a candidate's interaction with others. Having some of the operating officials with whom the candidate will be associated, if selected, serve on the selection panel is sound, and may be the beginning of the liaison relationships that the new staff member will need to have if hired.

As in budgeting for financial resources, the planning for the availability of qualified people at the right place at the right time is a part of management responsibilities that has to be planned and actively pursued on a continuing basis. It is not just a matter of keeping all the bases covered. The staffing questions of who, what, when, where, how, and how much are constantly pressing for answers. The device of a training timetable, discussed previously in this chapter, is a useful "photograph" of the people/job/capability issue at any moment in time.

Materials (STEAMMMM)

Chapter 11 deals in depth with the development of curriculum materials. Of course countless other items of a material nature are essential to a comprehensive training and development program. However, the purpose here is not to describe them, but to outline some cautionary procedures in their procurement and use.

Most organizations have well-established procurement systems that are centrally operated in order to gain economies by quantity purchasing and the use of standardization, quality control, and supply management techniques. They also allow for small purchases in the open market, and may provide petty cash funds to simplify the paperwork and accounting.

The caution is the same as for all other resource requirements in the STEAMMMM equation. Advance planning is needed. For instance, an organization may go to great expense in planning and producing a multimedia instruction program, the end products of which for a given training location need about 3 cubic feet of carton or crate space in which to transport them safely. If the planning overlooked the need for a unique size and shape of carton or crate, a great deal of confusion, delay, damage, and frustration may result. An otherwise excellent program may be recorded as a failure because it showed lack of organization in planning for the dissemination of the training materials and supplies. How many training film failures have you observed because there was no spare bulb with the projector when the bulb in the machine burned out? How many attempts to use chalkboards and easels have you seen end awkwardly because the trainer failed to check in advance on chalk, erasure, or felt pens? How many times have you seen the trainer try to make do without the necessary supplies and materials?

Another caution with respect to materials has to do with quality acceptability. Some procurement systems consistently buy low-bid items, which from a training standpoint may be poor economics. The training and career development unit should make the extra effort, when experience truly dictates that a superior grade of a supply item will make a substantial difference in the result, to justify exceptions from the standard specification. Even the small item of dustless chalk is worth the extra cost if dust contamination of delicate mechanisms is a risk.

Management (STEAMMMM)

Managerial capability is as much a resource as money, space, and equipment. Without it, other resources may be needlessly squandered, misdirected, or left to accumulate and eventually have to be turned back to the budget people for reallocation to other users.

The work of the director of employee training and career development is essentially that of a good manager. He or she needs to be abreast of the state of the art in education and training methodology, in addition to many other qualifications. However, no other qualification surpasses the capability of being an exemplary manager. POSDCORB, a term coined by Luther Gulick, is a classic qualifier that is hard to beat. It embraces planning, organizing, staffing, delegating, controlling, reporting, and budgeting.

In order to get things done through others, the manager must possess not only POSDCORB ability, but must also practice conscientiously the habit of monitoring or overseeing things being done. This requires a check-and-balance system of evaluation—integrally planned as each program is developed—that will systematically report to the manager and higher executives how well the programs are meeting their objectives. This system of evaluation should not be manipulative or subject to influence during or after the training. The vital question to be answered is: What direct or indirect result of the training program advanced organization goals and objectives, and made operating programs run more efficiently and economically than they would have run otherwise?

Conclusion

Leaders of organizations everywhere should take stock of the investment they are making in the development of their human resources, as such resources are no more self-developing and self-maintaining than are machines. The matter of planning for, marshaling, and allocating a fair share of an organization's resources should be assigned a high priority, and should be monitored regularly to ensure their adequate flow to supervisors and managers at all levels.

It is unfortunate that the policy in so many organizations makes the people development function the last to be put in place and the first to be retrenched or eliminated. This shortsighted practice is poor economics and should be abandoned.

7

Finding People Developers

THE discovery of people developers is not an easy task, and is complicated by the fact that they have no natural habitat. They can be
working inside or outside an organization's program for employee
training and career development, or they can be scattered among
other organizations or public service groups. They do not identify
with a particular occupational class or salary level. They may be
supervisors or subordinates. They may be in line or staff positions,
at headquarters or field locations.

This chapter discusses how to conduct the search for individuals
who measure up to the role of people developers. For coherence,
the discussion begins with methods of finding individuals to fill people development positions in institutionalized units. The last section
of this chapter offers suggested criteria for identifying persons who
may qualify for complementary or supportive assignments in the
people development effort.

Definitions of Developer Personnel

Since there are various levels and specialized facets of employee
training and career development work, it is well to begin with a set

of definitions. Those given here are not conclusive, and are not so precise as one would expect to find in a glossary of terms. Each is a summary statement of the burden of a particular position.

Manpower Planner. The person who analyzes the needs of an organization or political entity for the purpose of determining its human resource needs for a discrete period of time, such as a fiscal year or a five-year period, is a manpower planner. The analysis considers such factors as major goals and objectives, technology, state of the economy, labor market, turnover, financial capability, and proficiency achievement time. The data and conclusions may be arranged by occupational class.

Director, Employee Training and Career Development. The director is assigned to take charge of comprehensive planning, organizing, development, and direction of programs to meet the human resource development needs of the organization and its entire staff. The work of this position entails the formulation of goals, objectives, and policies and the necessary planning for resources, methods, records, and reports to meet both the current and the foreseeable needs of the organization and its personnel.

Employee Training and Career Development Officer. The training officer is the one to whom the director delegates a portion of his broad responsibilities, as defined above.

Executive Development Officer or Specialist. This specialist concentrates on the training and development of executives within the context of the director's overall responsibility.

Management Development Officer or Specialist. This specialist concentrates on the training and development of managers within the context of the director's overall responsibility.

Staff Development Specialist. This title is synonomous with employee training and career development officer.

Education Adviser or Specialist. The adviser provides counsel and assistance to employees who wish to strengthen their qualifications through the offerings of outside institutions and groups.

Training Officers. The one who plans, organizes, or conducts specific courses that tend to be of an orientation or skill improvement nature is identified as the training officer.

Audiovisual Presentation Specialist. This specialist plans and technically directs the development of programs and curriculum materials that rely heavily on visual or audiovisual media such as motion pictures, videotape, slide and tape, and sound filmstrip.

Audiovisual Technicians. The person who sets up and operates various items of A/V equipment to facilitate the learning process is a technician, and may also be involved with the preparation, editing, rendering, drawing, and packaging of A/V materials.

Curriculum Development Specialist. The professional who applies the laws of learning and other educational principles to the development of materials required in the conduct of training and development programs is a curriculum specialist. The materials include instructor's guides, participant workbooks, case histories, incidents, outlines, manuals, handbooks, and specifications for illustrative materials and A/V support.

Instructor. The instructor presents an assigned topic or segment thereof and attempts to stimulate learner interaction with fellow participants, with the instructor, and with any device (such as a simulator) that may be employed to facilitate the learning process. Presumably, the instructor operates within the parameters of curriculum objectives set by the curriculum development specialist.

CLASSIFICATION OF PEOPLE DEVELOPERS

The foregoing definitions serve as a backdrop for the discussion on how one goes about finding the talent that forms the heart of the people development function from an institutional standpoint. Titles vary from organization to organization and (to some small degree) between the private and public sectors. The work is more or less the same regardless of where it goes on, but functional classification may vary. In industry, the emphasis tends to be on training for the here and now in such matters as industrial relations, safety, marketing, sales, use of equipment and tools, and customer service. In the public sector, the emphasis is on providing knowledge of regulations, procedures, and continuity of service.

Qualification Standards

Organizations large enough to afford a unit in which to focus the people development function are likely to have published qualification standards. Hopefully, these are the end products of much collaboration between operating officials and appropriate personnel management staff representatives. No one individual can write a realistic qualification standard, and obviously a different standard must be written for each separate position title and for each level (grade) of responsibility within each title category. The purpose here is to offer some general comments that may be useful to persons who (a) merely supervise the writing of standards; (b) collaborate on standards; or (c) actually do the drafting and editing of standards.

NEGATIVE PROFILES

The work of employee training and career development specialists has evolved from that of a classroom instructor to the present, much broader scope. It doubtless will continue to evolve as the function gains recognition by demonstrating tangible cost/benefit results. To get at the heart of what is needed in the most responsible levels of the profession, it is well to establish what *it is not.* Here are some experience-tested *nots,* or negative profiles.

NOT an Old-fashioned Schoolmaster or Schoolmistress. This image suggests a high degree of discipline, rote memory, and other regimented methods of learning and teaching, not to mention the straight rows of hard seats screwed to the floor. The teacher-pupil relationship is distasteful to people who consider that their education and training came to an end when they "finished" high school or college.

NOT a Classroom Lecturer. The lecture method has some advantages when used at the right time and place to present an appropriate subject to a selected audience. It gets low rating as a method of modern training specialists. With the advent of technology and the various methods for stimulating learner interaction, the straight lecture method has become dull and uninteresting. The lecturer or instructor is usually the lowest paid of educators. This method is perhaps more acceptable to advanced students of a subject, for one can probably assume that they are more highly motivated to continue their learning.

NOT a Bureaucrat. The employee training and career development specialist is inundated by flow of numerous documents and items of correspondence. He could spend his entire workday in reading, studying, and routing these papers; in short, he could become the type of bureaucrat who accomplishes little or nothing. The modern specialist in this field deals summarily with his paperwork management responsiblities, keeps abreast of the major changes in laws, regulations, and policies, and leaves to a clerk, secretary, or junior technician the business of keeping this material readily available. The specialist wears out shoe leather, not swivel chairs.

NOT the Author of Decrees. There is a strong temptation for the specialist to draft "decrees" and expect senior officials to ratify and issue them. Nearly any training and development proposal can be made to sound desirable and feasible on paper. Senior people, in their urge to speed production and service, and reduce costs, will sign a high percentage of such proposals in the early stages of their relationship with a people developer. The intelligent people developer knows, however, that operating officials resent having their employees *ordered* off the job for training and development. When it happens, the aftermath is sure to make the people developer regret that he yielded to such shortcuts.

NOT a Merchant in Ready-Made Courses. The people developer has constantly before him the lure of "canned" training courses and faddish approaches to career development. Some manufacturers offer training courses as an incentive to buy their equipment. Research and development groups sometimes develop a novel approach to training and development, or they modify the terminology and make "cosmetic" or semantic changes in the label to enhance its sales appeal. Various types of sensitivity training are one of the most conspicuous examples of this point. A conscientious training and development specialist will not take the bait of such alternatives and allow them to substitute for the hard work required in smoking out the actual training needs and in jointly determining solutions with operating personnel. If the specialist yields, this capitulation may well invite a separation notice.

POSITIVE PROFILES

The other side of the coin bears the question, "What *is* the role of the modern employee training and career development specialist?" I have already attempted to establish the proposition that the people developer is not identified by title, salary, or place in the organizational hierarchy. Instead, the specialist is identified by what he or she *does* and *is* to others. Here are some positive profiles to look for in the people developers of today.

Profile: Manpower Adviser and Counselor. The employee training and development specialist of today advises and consults with the leadership and with operating officials of the organization. He or she advises on such matters as manpower planning problems; the appraisal, selection, and development of managers and executives; agenda planning for high-level conferences and seminars; transfers and reassignments; and related questions of policy; and he or she assists in briefing incoming executives.

Profile: Resource Broker. The employee training and career development specialist is, in effect, a broker who deals in spaces in acceptable facilities where selected employees of the organization can be updated in their technical, professional, and management specialties. He or she negotiates the terms of contracts affecting in-service training and the use of outside facilities, reviews nominations for special programs, and accepts or rejects them. By keeping in close touch with the "training market" by scanning brochures, scouting untapped facilities, and following up to see how much has been gained from certain institutions, the specialist has an up-to-date inventory of current curriculum materials and bibliographies. Thus, the training office is the clearinghouse for knowledge on training aids and equipment, has contact with various subject matter experts who are available as resource people, and can marshal space and other necessary resources with which to stage an approved program.

Profile: Innovator. The specialist is constantly working as a management engineer. Having probably taught such courses as work simplification, job methods training (one of the original "J" programs of World War II vintage), and supervisor training, he or she is skilled in the techniques for streamlining work methods. Service on survey teams, incentive award committees, performance appraisal panels, and similar groups has brought the specialist a wealth of knowledge and the ability to act as a good catalyst of labor-saving ideas. Thus, the career developer is cognizant of technological change, human resistance to change, and the intrinsic value of the nonconforming but creative mind to any progressive organization. Besides the concepts of executive leadership and executive development, the specialist is an innovator, alert to apply new proven ideas in training programs.

Profile: Stage Manager. The specialist is frequently called upon to moderate panels, introduce the leaders of the organization and outside guest speakers, mobilize talent for various occasions, ghost-write speeches and articles, represent superior officers at conferences, and perform other stage management responsibilities. His or her hand is often reflected in policy announcements, special reports, forms design, certificates of recognition, letters of commendation, house organ literature, and the like. Although articulate, the specialist finds that more can be accomplished by staging his objectives and by having a "passion for anonymity."

Profile: Kitchen Cabinet Member. The specialist soon gets to know the senior officers of the organization, and is therefore in position to contribute to their thinking and to influence their conclusions on vital issues.

QUALIFICATION CONSIDERATIONS

Several other suggestions concerning the development of qualification standards are in order at this point. Development work involves a deep commitment to helping solve people problems. The knowledge and experience a specialist must have is not all found in books, and it is not all learned through paid work experience. Countless types of unpaid experience build skill in human interaction, communications, "selling" ideas, problem solving, planning, organizing, and managing things and people. Responsible experience in community development groups such as a parent-teacher association, church, service clubs, youth and senior citizen programs, recreation associations, consumer protection movements, hobby clubs, and the like should therefore be recognized in setting qualification standards. Evidence of creativity and leadership may be manifested in unpaid roles long before employers discover an individual's abilities and potential for developing others.

Qualification standards should be promulgated and issued with the official approval of the director of personnel or the head of the organization. Unauthorized standards serve little or no purpose and generally arouse more suspicion and criticism than serve any good purpose. The approved standards should be available for inspection at every supervisor's desk, or for purchase in a central location at the cost of printing.

Another point about standards is that provision should be built into each standard for exceptions and waivers. Guidelines should be established in the standards for the use of persons authorized to approve waivers. For example, military duty or unpaid experience may have extra weight under certain conditions, or in a situation where the official personnel file of an individual fails to reflect a series of extended details which would have been qualifying had they been officially noted.

Example of Qualification Standards The head of an organization invited me in 1972 to draft a set of criteria against which to judge candidates for the directorship of its newly established national training center. The following "yardstick" was the end product of that effort, and the successful candidate, who responded to an advertisement, was a remarkably close fit to the specification.

DEAN, NATIONAL TRAINING CENTER

I. Professional Competence
With due regard to chronological age, candidate should show a

distinguished record of achievement and currency in a hard academic discipline which is relevant to enlightened _____ management for today and tomorrow. Give preferential consideration to these disciplines:

Social Sciences (Anthropology, Sociology, and History)
Urban Planning
Public Adminstration
Business Administration
Industrial Management
Architecture

It is suggested that the candidate have at least a Master's degree.

II. Leadership Qualities

A conspicuously favorable blend of personality, character, and modus operandi qualities which tend to make him rise quickly to a position of leadership in any circle; more specifically, such qualities as:

Integrity
Strong sense of dedication to the mission of which he or she is a part; radiates enthusiasm for the mission
Charismatic qualities (appearance, poise, mannerisms, dress, voice, etc.)
Just and equitable treatment of others (superiors, peers, subordinates, clients, service groups, etc.)
Self-starting
Effective communicator (listening, speaking, writing, conference leadership, reporting, "selling," etc.)
Does not shrink from the challenge of entrepreneural-type risks
A keen sense of intuitive judgment which functions like a computer—not from an emotional base
Industriousness
Is fired by a strong spark of drive and creativity
Has an accurate perspective on the 20th century, particularly the post-WWII era
Vision into the 1970s and 1980s; an optimistic outlook on life ahead
An awareness of, and respect for, political processes
A natural sense of humor (not forced)

III. Management Effectiveness

Manages essentially by being a successful talent scout, a "people developer," and an encourager of others.
Sets broad goals and objectives, always in collaboration with others affected, and continually reappraises in a posture of flexibility—not abdication.
Conceptualizes well.

Manages time advantageously.

Uses the budget as an instrument of sound planning.

Understands and practices sound cost/benefit concepts.

Maintains continuous and complete accountability.

Fully utilizes all available human resources, identifying persons with potential and developing them to the limit of their practical capabilities.

Smoothly applies the principles of good management which make for a harmoniously orchestrated *group* performance.

Does not let himself/herself become deskbound; through delegation and quality control he/she manages details.

Uses statistics and accounting as decision-making *tools,* never letting them dominate the organization.

Attends to the faithful recording and reporting of events which are significant in the life cycle of programs, as a basis for improving organization development and performance.

IV. Special Qualifications

An individual who is young enough to appreciate the major concerns of at least the generation immediately behind him/her; one who is not so mature that (1) his/her attitudes are "set in concrete" or (2) he/she has exhausted the drives and enterpreneurial spirit which brought him/her to the forefront in days past. *Note:* The 30-to-mid-40s age group is a prime search ground.

An individual whose life reflects a balanced and full schedule of progressively responsible activities in school, job, community, and professional circles.

An individual who has not been insulated from the *real* world all of his/her life; more specifically, one who has traveled extensively in some of the less affluent areas of the U.S. and/or the world at large, or has lived on "the other side of the tracks" or has done some things which routinely associated him/her with such populations.

A socially adjusted individual who is at peace with himself/herself.

An individual who has ample reserves of physical stamina and snapback to withstand the stresses of a bureaucracy.

An individual who has demonstrated a commitment to a program of continuing growth and development through the most appropriate means available at each stage of career development.

An individual who is in a position to give his/her undivided attention to the deanship over a sustained period (minimum of 5 to 10 years), who is free from such stresses as financial pressures and/or spending habits which demand "moonlighting"; domestic relations which are dissipating, militancies, and other employment opportunities for which he/she has been negotiating.

If the individual is married, the spouse should be regarded by the employer as an equally important element on the team. This suggests a home visit before final selection.

An individual who has an established leisure-time activity which is enabling insofar as physical and mental relaxation and the maintenance of healthy perspectives and stability are concerned.

Vacancies and New Positions

Lateral entry is controversial and self-defeating in relation to the objectives of merit plans and good career development systems. Employee organizations, unions, equal employment opportunity coordinators, and individual employees dislike the concept. Occasionally, for the good of the organization, the only reasonable thing to do is to bring in new blood.

POSTINGS

One of the ways to encourage noninstitutional people developers in what they are doing to further employee training and career development objectives is to select one of their number for an institutional job, provided, of course, the person selected has the basic qualifications to satisfy the qualification standard for a specific vacancy. The best way to bring vacancies and new positions to the attention of such people is by posting notices of vacancies. Some organizations detest the policy of posting vacancies. They claim it plays into the hands of perennial promotion-from-within applicants, and therefore generates unnecessary work. As a matter of fact, the reason many organizations fail to post is to avoid the competition generated against a favored individual.

Failure to post is detrimental to all concerned. The organization as a whole suffers because the wider the field of choice, the better the chances of identifying the best qualified person available. The supervisor and management people in the area where the vacancy exists may be "praying" for other candidates so that they can have a choice. The favored individual may be overqualified or underqualified for the vacancy, and his movement into the position could be disastrous to his long-range career goals.

TRAINEE POSITIONS

If posting and other internal publicity methods fail to yield a roster of adequately qualified and interested candidates for a position, and the decision maker is reluctant to go outside for additional candidates, there are several recourses. First, there may be an employee who falls short of the formal qualification standard, but to waive that inadequacy is not the thing to do under the circumstances. It is possible under most, if not all, classification systems to establish formally a trainee position at one or more pay-grade levels lower than the grade of the vacant position. The selected individual who is deemed to have the potential for rapid growth and development into the target positon can be placed under an individual "training agreement."

TRAINING AGREEMENTS. A training agreement is a document that details an intensive program of rotational OJT, selected in-service and outside training courses, tutorial-type help from an adviser, assigned reading, practical observation, communication skills improvement, and the like. It is a high-reward/high-risk agreement for up-or-out utilization of the training avenue to the target position. It is a speeded-up route for the incumbent.

However, it is very important that the merit principle be observed in the selection of the candidate for the individual training agreement. Otherwise, the organization is subject to criticism from its personnel and from any group that may be monitoring its personnel transactions. Further, there should be regular evaluations of the participant's progress, and an adviser should guide the chosen employee in attaining the objectives of the accelerated training and promotion program.

UNDERSTUDIES. Vacancies usually occur as a result of normal retirements, transfers, and resignations, and new positions are created for various reasons. When it is possible to know well in advance of an opening, the understudy method may enable the organization to try out someone for the pending vacancy by moving the individual into place and having the person work with the experienced employee. This method is not a good substitute for an honest effort through vacancy posting, selection panel, and qualifications review against standards. Use of the understudy method too often lets a favored or aggressive individual move into the position when it becomes vacant, and acquire the title and pay by default. Understudy methods can be better implemented by detailing an employee from his regular assignment to the pending vacancy, either with or without additional pay.

SPECIAL CAUTION ON VACANCIES. A special caution needs mention at this point. There are still some administrators and executives, hopefully very few, who have not seen the light with respect to the value of employee training and career development. Such individuals use vacancies and new positions as depositories for "taking care of" some wretched cases. Any given case may be an alcoholic, a low performer who has failed on several other work assignment opportunities, a recipient of personal or political patronage, a superannuated person who needs to serve more time in order to round out his retirement program, or an individual who already has a full-time job such as photographer, speech writer, or house organ editor and who needs desk space and a budget slot in order to be legitimate on the payroll.

Training and development groups have borne this cross of a dumping ground for years, and the burden has been costly. The director of employee training and career development should guard against having these expendables foisted on the staff and should be prepared with work measurement data, program plans, and other solid defenses against the effective loss of productive positions. To the extent that a director is compelled to take marginal workers and nonperformers, the image of the entire program and staff is downgraded in the eyes of consumers who depend on these services.

Outside Searches

The search for persons of ability and potential does not always end happily within an organization, and must resort to outside sources of supply. For this phase to be successful, it is best to engage in some *positive* recruitment, for one cannot expect too much from walk-in traffic during the limited period that a vacancy exists. A number of sources should be investigated before advertising the position.

MERIT SYSTEM REGISTERS. Merit systems maintain registers of qualified individuals who have been examined noncompetitively and found qualified on the basis of verified work experience, academic credentials, and confirming references. Written examinations should seldom be administered to intermediate- or higher-level professionals. "Category ratings" should be used to separate individuals of outstanding qualifications from moderately and minimally qualified ones. By studying a batch of files on eligible employees, and interviewing a representative sample of those who appear to be the best prospects, it is often possible to fill the vacancy without further search.

PROFESSIONAL SOCIETIES. Professional societies usually offer employment referral services as a member benefit. For example, the American Society for Training and Development, the International Personnel Management Association, and the Training Officers Conference are particularly appropriate societies to lend a hand in recruitment.

SPECIAL CAREER DEVELOPMENT PROGRAMS. Special programs such as management intern programs, fellowship programs, executive development programs, and mid-career programs may be useful sources.

WORD-OF-MOUTH ADVERTISING. One should not overlook the merit of placing job vacancy notices in house organs or of distributing desk-to-desk announcements so that word-of-mouth influence of staff on outsiders may bring in some promising candidates. This can be a tremendous help in realizing positive recruitment, but is often overlooked, especially by organizations that tend to vacillate in announcing vacancies until they are desperate.

PERSONAL PATRONAGE. Personal patronage, when used discretely and objectively, can be a productive source. It should be used *after*— not before—merit system sources have been exhausted, in order to keep faith with human resource and career development program commitments. Nothing reflects more negatively on a career system than the practice of *consistently* filling vacancies with friends of friends. Once the preferred sources are checked out and found wanting, it is in order to communicate with a few professional associates in outside organizations and pass the word that a search is under way and that the director would welcome a few referrals of well-qualified candidates. One should follow up by sending a copy of the qualification standard to each point of contact; otherwise, without a precise statement of what is needed, referrals may be poorly matched to qualifications, and this can be frustrating for all concerned.

Personal patronage is a reality in the business world. When used with caution, it can be as fruitful as any other source of supply. Presumably, misfits and marginally qualified persons will be screened out in the final selection processes. However, when an outside supervisor gets an inquiry about a subordinate, especially about one whose career would be furthered by the opportunity, the inquiry must be handled delicately. If the supervisor mentions the vacancy, the subordinate may wonder whether or not the tip is a message to move on, or else.

ADVERTISING. When all other sources have fallen short of the mark, and with time permitting, it may be well to place one or more carefully worded ads in a well-chosen publication. Leading newspapers, journals of professional societies, trade journals, and selected other printed media with substantial circulation should be considered. One advertisement alone for a single run can cost hundreds of dollars. This may seem prohibitive, but it is a small fraction in relation to the salary for the new hire even for one year. Considered in relation to the influence the new hire will have on the employer's total expenditures and salary obligations, the cost is inconsequential. However, advertising fees should be noted early in the dialogue about filling the vacancy and should come as no surprise to officials.

Selection

Selection of qualified persons for full-time people developer positions is a good test of an efficient personnel management system. However, judgment of qualification interlocks with and is dependent upon preselection steps such as job analysis, position classification, qualification standards, and recruitment practices. All the processes that follow selection are test steps for management's efficiency. A weak step, like a weak chain link, can be disastrous.

SELECTION PANELS. Selection should be so arranged that multiple judgments are brought to bear on the decision. Preliminary screening by an employment officer in coordination with the employee training and career development office and the equal opportunity employment officer is essential to conserve the valuable time of higher-paid officials whose participation is needed at critical stages.

A selection panel is distinctly better than a single interviewer. Group orals are a better format than the format of a panel that interviews one candidate at a time. During the group oral, several candidates are introduced to each other and to the members of the selection panel. Then they are invited to cope with a problem that simulates those with which the successful candidate would be coping on the job. Two or three such problems may be submitted to each group of candidates, with up to an hour allotted to each problem, and with members of the selection panel cast principally as observers.

It is well to begin a group oral exercise by having each candidate and each panelist give a brief, personal, thumbnail résumé. The panelists' contributions set the tone and put the candidates at ease. When all candidates have retired from the room, a standardized evaluation sheet should be used to judge each applicant against the qualification standards—not against each other. An overall rating of IN or OUT is given. The panel may spend a few minutes with individual candidates before the evaluation, if information needs to be rounded out or is lacking.

After having seen all candidates in a group oral situation, and after having evaluated them on a standardized form, the panel should then prepare a report to the official who will make the final decision. The report should categorize the candidates into three or more levels of qualification, such as best qualified, well qualified, and qualified. If preliminary screening has narrowed the field to, say, seven finalists, rankings may show two in the top category, three in the middle category, and two in the bottom category. Depending on the instructions from the official making the final choice, he or she may or may not wish to interview the two top candidates, and may or may not wish to receive a single name recommendation from the panel. Ideally, this official should be a member of the panel so that a decision will be the consensus of the conference.

USE OF CONSULTANTS. Instead of the selection panel, some organizations may wish to go the consultant route. This has some definite advantages and possible disadvantages. Presumably, the consulting firm can take a more objective view of the matter. It may be a large firm with a well-established department that concentrates on talent searches, and therefore it is more experienced in discerning clues to strengths and weaknesses in candidates than are persons who perform such responsibilities and may be under heavy, distracting stresses from their own work. Finding the best qualified candidate available *is* the work of the consultant for the duration of each special project. Therefore he or she has the means of making more thorough background investigations, and is experienced in preparing and packaging a report of the findings.

On the other hand, an outside consultant usually knows less about the major goals, objectives, programs, organization, leadership, and internal operations of the organization than a panel of its own experienced personnel. Since the panelists will have to work with the successful candidate, they have a special incentive to make the best possible choice. These are a few of the important considerations in deciding whether or not to use the inside selection panel or an outside consulting firm. Of course it may be feasible to have the best of both worlds by assembling a panel composed of persons from both inside and outside sources.

JUDGMENTAL CONSIDERATIONS. When the panel or the consultant has dismissed the candidates and proceeds to selection, what factors besides the qualification standards should be considered, particularly if the vacancy is in a senior training and career development post or in the director's position? Here are some questions to be answered in making such judgments about each candidate.

—Are any of the candidates fully qualified?
—Are any of the candidates overqualified? Underqualified?
—Of those who are fully qualified, what about their professional competence, leadership, management effectiveness, and special qualifications?

At this point, it might help to do a bit of doodling on paper. For example, the consultant or panel member might try slicing up a circle for candidate A and one for each of the other candidates, to show roughly what each would bring to the job. This exercise may help weight each candidate against the qualification standards. If at least half of what A would bring is solid professional competenence, 50 percent of the circle is given to that strength. The leadership potential of A is low, and worth perhaps only 5 percent, but he is a proven effective program manager, and deserves a solid 30 percent for that. Only 15 percent of the circle is left for such special qualifications as A may have. The exercise is completed by doodling a second circle to depict the weaknesses of A, and even a third circle to focus his potentials.

When this process has been completed for each candidate, it is possible to rank-order all candidates from high to low. Obviously, the percentage estimates cannot possibly be precise. The procedure is merely a graphic scheme to facilitate your judgmental effort.

Here are some more questions to ask:

—Does the philosophy of all the fully qualified candidates square with the organization's current thinking on employee training and career development?
—Should preference be given to candidates who can grow beyond the expectations of the present job? If so, who among the candidates (if any) rates high on this factor?
—Who among the candidates has the greatest capacity to adjust to the dynamics of organizational change? To be a positive change agent?
—Who has the strongest spark of creativity and innovation?
—Who has the greatest awareness of the need for cost-effective programming?
—Whose integrity of purpose makes the clearest reflection?

—Who has the keenest interest in labor/management relations? Community relations?

—Who has the most skill in communicating ideas? In interacting with others intellectually?

—From an all-round standpoint, who will be the most valuable human resource to the organization?

Detecting Potential People Developers in Noninstructional Activities

The employee training and career development offices of an organization would be crowded places if all people developers were to be found there. Many are located in areas not associated with training, and many apply development strategies without realizing the nature of those applications. It is among such employees that management should search for potential people developers.

Where would you, as manager, find such people? Look for supervisors who take the most initiative in nominating subordinates for training and development experiences. Scan performance evaluation reports, particularly the narrative section that supports premium ratings, for evidence. Try to find the path that leads to certain individuals to whom an unusual number of people gravitate for counsel on their problems. Where do people gather on their coffee breaks? Who organizes recreation programs such as bowling leagues, tennis groups, and picnics? Who takes the lead in bringing order out of chaos when there is an emergency or crisis? Who remains the calmest in times of greatest stress from work-load pressures? Whose counsel is most sought and valued by supervisors and managers when they need to adopt new initiatives? Look for people who are accepted on a first-name basis by everyone—regardless of race, creed, color, sex, or status—in the organization. Obviously, this is not a comprehensive list of earmarks, but it may give sufficient clues to help you form your own list as a guide to searching for noninstructional people developers.

Conclusion

The search for individuals to fill institutionalized places in people development work should be conducted systematically on a professional plane, using diverse recruitment sources and relying on careful selection and placement to spot the candidates with the greatest potential for useful service.

The search for people developers who work informally to further the development of human resources should be a continuing one, and appropriate recognition should be given to such people by organization leaders.

8

Designing the
Learning Environment

THE old-fashioned classroom is as obsolete for modern in-service training as the little red schoolhouse, but in actual practice many drab and ineffective classrooms still exist.

The modern classroom is not a formal, uninviting place where the desks and chairs are fastened to the floor in straight rows. Teaching is no longer done exclusively from the front of the room and by the lecture method. Nor is learning a rote process. Rather than a single textbook, an abundant supply of teaching materials and learning aids is available. Education and training have become life-long activities, for members of the labor force must keep pace with the technology of the twentieth century if they are to hold their jobs and receive promotion benefits.

Modernizing the Surroundings

Organized training is still handicapped by inadequately planned and engineered facilities. Although teaching methods and training technological aids are a far cry from what they were a decade or two ago, employers still tend to give low priority to training space.

Uninviting and functionally inefficient training space inhibits the will to learn. So many factors contribute to a conducive learning environment that its design simply cannot be left to amateurs. Among these are location, the overall design concept, physical comfort, acoustics, flexibility, ease of maintenance, and functional furniture.

Some organizations assign any temporarily idle space to training purposes, even though it lacks any of the characteristics that contribute positively to the learning process—such as comfortable chairs in which to sit and work for the required periods. Such lack of foresight diminishes the productive value of the program, and these unfavorable conditions may even be counterproductive.

Before a functionally effective and inviting space for learning and teaching can be designed, it is essential to know the purpose, scope, and trainee capacity of the program. Proximity to other contributive facilities is also desirable. In some respects, an organization's training room ideally resembles a public school layout in which informal teaching methods are used, library materials and audiovisual aids are easily available, and physical design is conducive to learning.

In the consideration of training space, three specific types of training and development facilities are discussed in this chapter: (1) the single-purpose training room, (2) the general-purpose training and development center, and (3) the more sophisticated institute or staff college.

The Single-Purpose Training Room

Dominant Features. There are three fundamental principles to consider in planning a training room. First, it must be safe, comfortable, reasonably shielded from noise, and generally conducive to a high-performance level of learning. Second, the purpose and the method of training should control the design and furnishing of the space. For instance, if the room is to be used principally for orienting new employees, a rectangular space with chairs and tables arranged in a semicircle, or like a theater "in the round," may be the best. Third, the facility must be functionally efficient. Whenever possible, it should have a layout and tone of informality that will put people at ease and stimulate their interaction.

Location. Time away from production costs money. Therefore, the training room should be adjacent to the work area so that participants can reach either location easily and quickly.

The room should be reasonably oriented to minimize traffic and outside noise. Its proximity to rest rooms, elevators, food and beverages, and supply rooms is essential.

Safety. In developing the architectural and engineering specifications to provide safety and comfort for the training room, the following provisions should be made:

—Two or more exits, preferably on opposite sides of the room.

—Panic-bar releases on the doors to ensure quick exit in case of fire, explosion, hurricane, tornado, flood, or violence.

—Ample ventilation and heating and cooling capability. Capacity of the system should allow for unscheduled demands. All equipment systems, either primary or supplemental, should operate quietly.

—Layout that permits easy flow of traffic in and out of the room, and within the room itself.

Structural Features. The following features should be considered in designing or redesigning the room:

—Size and shape, chosen to best serve the room's principal purpose.

—An elevated platform at the front of the room, large enough to accommodate a table that seats a panel of five people and a podium, or a sloped floor, to permit people to see over the heads of others.

—Instructional aids, such as sliding panels of chalkboard, tack board, flannel board, and magnetic board chosen to complement the color scheme of the room.

—Easily maintained floors and walls, with floors preferably carpeted.

—Accordion-fold partitions to provide small areas for group work.

—Detachable wall panels that accept thumbtacked displays.

—A first-quality pull-down or motor-driven projection screen.

—Auxiliary space for film projection, storage, experiential sessions such as role playing, individualized instruction, and related purposes.

—Acoustical treatment to facilitate videotaping and audio recordings.

—Electrical conduits in the floor, walls, and ceiling to expedite availability of A/V aids and to eliminate the safety hazards of extension cords.

Decor. Color dynamics should be employed throughout the room to give it the tone and contrasts necessary to achieve a pleasant environment. An interior decorator's services are a real asset in such planning. The chair is a basic item in the color pattern. The walls, floor, and ceiling should be to harmonize with the chairs, other furniture, and drapes.

Some organizations omit carpeting, but carpets have both educational and economic advantages. Their acoustical properties contribute to a calm educational atmosphere, and management gains favorable attention by implying that management cares enough about its employees to provide an attractively carpeted room for their learning comfort. The economic advantage of carpets is that they are less costly to maintain than floors, which require sweeping, vacuuming, stripping, scrubbing, waxing, and buffing.

Draperies are in the same category as carpeting and should be installed whenever possible. They add a touch of color and livability that nothing else can add, and also have an acoustic effect.

Lighting. Cool fluorescent ceiling lamps are the best source of light, both optically and economically.

In many training rooms the frequency of light-bulb failure is a handicap. This can be avoided by regularly and periodically changing all bulbs or tubes simultaneously shortly before the expiration of their life expectancy.

Master light switches should be located conveniently for rapid access when the room is to be darkened.

Room blackouts are necessary for film and slide showings, and will justify the addition of drapes when total darkness is unobtainable.

Heating. Just any heating system will not do the job. The system has to be scientifically designed with respect to specific conditions: the room population (body heat), outside temperature range, room orientation to the sun, prevailing winds, and the building construction. The thermostat should be factory set and sealed against tampering. In operation, the system must run quietly so as not to disturb the training activities. It may be a self-contained system, such as baseboard panels, or it may be an auxiliary branch of the central plant, so connected that it will operate at irregular hours when special sessions may be in progress.

Cooling. The principles suggested for heating design are equally applicable to cooling. It is inconceivable that any modern training room in the United States would be without air-conditioning capability.

Ventilation. Duct work is exceedingly important in the design of the ventilating system. Many organizations make the mistake of increasing the cooling capacity without changing the size of the ducts. The result is excessive noise and slower change of air, more smoke, more odors, and irregularities in the room temperature. It is also beneficial to install electronic dust-collection units that filter the air and make a more comfortable room environment for persons sensitive to dust particles.

Acoustics. Good acoustics require:
—Cork or other wall covering that will absorb sound.
—Carpeting and draperies.
—Ceiling tile or removable panels with proper acoustical properties.   ˙
—A sound amplification system, with outlets in the ceiling or walls, or built into the podium.
—Hydraulically controlled doors that close quietly. The doors should be thick enough to shut out noises from corridors.
—Floor pedestals or screened booths from which A/V equipment can be operated effectively.

Furnishings. The most important items in a training room are the chairs. If the trainees are uncomfortable, their learning is seriously restricted. Therefore, the type of chair should be the first item of furnishings to be chosen. Chairs come in different colors and in many designs. A good training room chair is one that swivels, rolls, reclines, is properly padded for sitting comfort, is contoured to body shape, has adjustable height and reclining tension control, is attractive, and is durable.

Instead of individual desks, it is well to select modular work-tables. These come in variable lengths, seating from one to four people. A two-place table is a good compromise. However, in some rooms, units of other sizes may help in achieving maximum utilization of floor space. For rooms equipped in theater style, armchairs are sometimes desirable, but as a rule they contribute too little to the flexibility and the informal atmosphere needed in a good training room.

Mobile shelves are convenient for storing participants' reference materials so that they can keep the tops of their worktables clear. Each participant can roll the reference shelf under the table, out of the way. A mobile library cart is useful to accommodate reference materials assigned to the room by the librarian for research.

Art exhibits can be arranged in many communities on a rotating basis, with copies of appropriate art pieces displayed in the room for fixed periods of time without cost. It is well, of course, to have a knowledgeable person make the selections.

Equipment needed depends on the specific purpose of the training room. If the room is primarily for safety training, extensive laboratory equipment may be necessary. If it is for improving or regaining office skills, typewriters and other office equipment will be needed. Learner-paced, individual instruction is best served by carrels, which permit semiprivate study or the use of teaching machines.

Auxiliary Facilities. Regardless of how well its internal facilities are planned, a training room can still be a very isolated and ineffective place unless supported by certain external facilities.

In the immediate vicinity of the training room there should be a lounge area where participants can gather for refreshments, and sit or stand while relaxing from the intensity of the learning activity. Vending machines, lounge furniture, pay telephones for private use and other telephones for official use, local newspapers, and reading lamps are necessities for such an area. Rest rooms should be easily accessible, large enough to serve the traffic, and serviced frequently enough to be clean, free of odors, and properly ventilated.

Reference sources in the library are most valuable when they are readily accessible. Ease of accessibility also enhances clerical, duplicating, quick-copy services, as well as those of audiovisual presentations.

Recreation facilities, whenever possible, should be provided within the instructional space vicinity. Many out-of-town people seek relaxation and enjoyment from table tennis, billiards, and card games. Many training institutes and staff colleges are now incorporating more elaborate facilities, such as a gymnasium or facilities for bowling, swimming, tennis, and archery.

Housing at a nearby apartment house, motel, or hotel, with the participants living together in foursomes, is a good pattern for housing. Much informal communication and incidental learning takes place in such settings.

An extremely important factor in maintaining a learning environment is automobile parking facilities. When a participant knows that his or her car is not on the public streets, is not subject to ticketing by the police, is quickly available, and perhaps is protected from inclement weather, this source of worry and its distracting effect on learning is relieved.

Instructional Aids. Any sizable instructional center will have a central pool of equipment from which items can be borrowed. A single training room may have only a few basic items. However, certain items are now so basic to instruction that they deserve a permanent place in the training room. Here is a list of the basics.

—A *sliding panel assembly* with chalkboard, tack board, flannel board, and magnetic board. This arrangement is the successor to the old blackboard. Also useful is the easel with large-size pads of newsprint paper that is easily written on with grease pencil or with felt-tip pen.

—An *overhead projector.* Projectors offer many advantages: Speakers can face their audiences while working with the projected image on which they draw, erase, or point, or on which they place overlays to present a point at a time—all of this in a fully lighted room. Thus, the trainer can prepare lesson material and illustrations in advance and save much time otherwise spent in laborious use of the chalkboard or easel.

—The *podium* is a preference item for some instructors, but it is a standard fixture for the more formal occasions when training activities are being inaugurated and closed; in this case the podium is a critical item. It is well to get a good podium with a high-quality amplifying system built into it, and a detachable microphone that can be handheld or attached to the clothing. The microphone should have a long cord to give the instructional leader ample range to walk around. The podium should have shielded light to enable him to read his notes and script when the room is darkened.

—*Teaching machines* may be helpful, depending on the subject normally taught in the room and the teaching method. It may be necessary to supply special equipment, such as individual teaching machines and a master console, or input and output units for computer-assisted instruction.

—*Translation equipment* is necessary when instruction is in a second language and has to be channeled through an interpreter. Worktables should be equipped with earphones and with controls that have feedback capability.

—A *television receiving set* is needed for the use of videotape equipment, closed-circuit television, and conventional TV reception.

—*Miscellaneous equipment,* such as maps, globes, chart display racks, flags, insignia, demonstration kits, dictionaries and other reference aids, and safety devices, are among the items that often must be provided.

The General-Purpose Training and Development Center

As the concept of "people development" grows, it may become necessary for the organization to provide physical facilities more extensive than a single training room. In some organizations, training and development continue to be centralized; in others, they tend to be planned and conducted by separate departments of the organization. In such cases, training space tends to be scattered, with none of it of very high quality.

Organizations also differ in their degree of interest in self-education, self-training, and self-improvement on the part of their employees. If there is strong interest in self-help, the organization can contribute to the initiatives of the staff by furnishing an individualized learning environment in which employees pursue subjects at their own pace.

Self-starter programs sometimes alert management to the value of training, and a combination of needs may eventually lead to the establishment of a general-purpose employee training and development center. When this happens, every effort should be made in the design of the center to provide for the full range of needs. The first step should be to secure the services of a consulting architect who is experienced in the design of modern education and training facilities, or, if cost is a problem, to hire a qualified facility planner—one with a multidisciplinary background and experience in rearranging existing space rather than innovating new designs.

A professionally qualified architect or facility planner can convert the most unlikely area into a perfectly acceptable place for learning. Conversion of existing space is usually less costly per cubic foot than a cubic foot of new construction.

It was this author's primary responsibility to develop the conceptual design for a network of 200 U.S. Postal Service employee development centers (PEDC) in the early 1970s. The centers, serving more than 600,000 postal employees, were established at a cost of about $6 million. Each unit of the network is located in an urban post office structure, serving the personnel who work in and out of that building. It also provides certain services for satellite post offices by serving as a repository of standardized programs and aids, which can be sent through the mail system to meet immediate training needs.

The PEDC space design was the joint effort of a cadre of postal training specialists and a teaching architect (David Ward of Cleveland) who is noted for his imaginative designs. The Columbus, Ohio, post office was used for planning a series of space models. Adaptations were made by other post offices in the network. The original model is pictured in Figure 1.

It is necessary to observe all the same basic principles in the design of a center as one needs to consider in the design of a single training room. However, there are many other considerations. The following paragraphs discuss the PEDC design and suggest how the planning factors can be integrated into a multipurpose center.

Library and Self-Paced Learning Area. The combination of library and learning area is the core of the development center. It provides an inviting surrounding and the opportunity for the learner to pursue educational objectives. In it are found reading materials and comfortable furnishings for relaxed study. Study carrels permit use of A/V teaching devices. Films, sound tapes, cassettes, and all other forms of training software are obtainable from a software storage room. This learning area is carpeted and furnished in inviting color combinations to elicit the most positive psychomotor responses from the participant.

Simulator Equipment Area. Most organizations have a variety of operator-controlled equipment. It may be keyboard equipment, such as computer input machines, sorters, manual computers, telephone consoles, and automotive test machines. This area should have simulators, to be used in pretraining and remedial training of operators. Since use of the equipment will make this area noisy, it should be subdivided as necessary, probably with glass, to contain some of the noise. Since a high degree of concentration is required of the trainees, the area should have attractive colors and good light. The weight of the equipment may make carpeting impractical; if so, resilient flooring can be installed.

"Hands-on" Laboratory. The laboratory should permit the participant to gain off-the-job experience in the use of tools and equip-

Figure I. Employee development center space model.
(Courtesy Ward Associates)

1 Distribution and receiving	7 Group instruction
2 Software production	8 Scheme exam
3 Mechanical mail sorting	9 Storage
4 Library	10 Hands-on laboratory
5 Self-paced learning area	11 Software storage
6 Counseling rooms	12 Counselor
	13 Manager

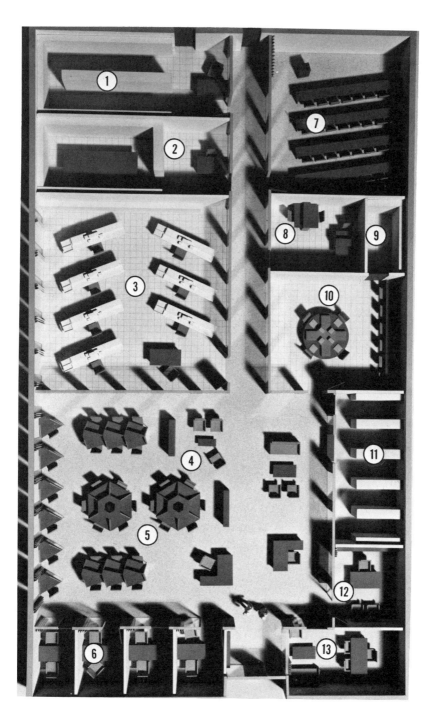

ment. A laborer may want to acquire more skill in the use of hand
tools, in order to upgrade his competency in simple maintenance
work. Another employee may want to try his hand at some simple
electrician's tasks, after studying the theory of them in the self-paced
area.

Counseling Rooms. Several multipurpose rooms for counseling, interviewing, and one-to-one conferences are desirable. A single large
area can be arranged for this purpose by installing portable partitions with glass upper sections. This makes for openness and semiprivate discussion.

Software Storage. A supervised storage room for films, sound
tapes, cassettes, and A/V aids is necessary for issuance and stock accountability. A glass partition allows total visibility of the interior. A
technician maintains records, checks materials out and in, and provides the manager of the center with usage data.

Group Instruction Room. Design of the instruction room provides
an inviting atmosphere, created by using color, attractive lighting,
and modern furnishings. A variety of accommodations is provided
for small "buzz" groups, workshops, or large groups, as the training
objectives dictate. Ample provisions are made for various modes of
visual and A/V presentations.

Production and Distribution Room. In this area subject matter research is done to meet the special needs of the local facility. The
product of this research will be forwarded to satellite offices to serve
as a basis for the design, development, and production of new software to serve the needs of local employee training and development.
It is a work area in which the materials production needs of the
center can largely be met.

Administrative Space. The center staff, directed by a manager,
operates from this space. The services include the following types:

Liaison with all organizational elements using the center
Curriculum planning and materials development
Resources planning and management
Scheduling
Publicity
Space allocations and reservations
Diagnostic testing
Counseling
Registration
Teaching
Progress evaluation

Research and development projects

Records and reports

Maintenance of the area and the center generally, in a manner designed to provide every participant and visitor with an atmosphere that invites participation in the growth opportunities offered.

The Institute or Staff College

PUBLIC INSTITUTIONS

No one questions that West Point, Annapolis, and Colorado Springs are necessary facilities for the development of leadership in the military services of the United States. However, it was not until the 1960s that the U.S. government established a central staff college at Charlottesville, Virginia, for the development of civilian administrators. During the same decade the Postal Service Institute was established at Bethesda, Maryland, for development of leadership in the vast U.S. Postal Service, which is ranked as the third largest industry in the nation. Several decades earlier, facilities such as the Foreign Service Institute at Arlington, Virginia, the FBI Academy at Quantico, Virginia, the IRS Training Center at Arlington, Virginia, the FAA center at Norman, Oklahoma, the Army Management Engineering Training Agency at Rock Island, Illinois, and a few others had been organized. Next to the military academies, probably the oldest (1921) facility instituted by a federal agency is the Graduate School, U.S. Department of Agriculture.

All these facilities show that they have unique sources of technical expertise to convey to participants. All operate on a nonprofit basis, and would strenuously resist any effort of state-funded or privately funded institutions to absorb them and their work.

PRIVATE INSTITUTIONS

Similarly, the larger private companies in the United States have founded company-owned and -operated educational and training institutions. One of the most recent is the Xerox center at Leesburg, Virginia, which is a multimillion-dollar investment with a threefold mission—management training and development, sales training, and maintenance technician training. It is a beautifully designed, functionally efficient complex on a magnificent site near the Potomac River. Xerox could have contracted all this work to some university or community college, or a network of such institutions, but it elected to own and operate its own facility. Numerous other corporations, such as Western Electric of AT&T and General Motors, have gone the same route. Some of the points supportive of ownership and operation of the development facility, and which affect the design of the physical facilities, are worthy of mention here.

Accessibility. Depending on the location of the headquarters of a private enterprise or a major government agency in relation to existing education and training facilities, it may be to the strategic advantage of the organization to select a nearby site. The many advantages of proximity are suggested by the paragraphs that follow.

Economic and Security Benefits. The point has already been made concerning the unique technical knowledge that any organization possesses and which can be disseminated to its own staff. If it has the financial means to do so, it is well advised to establish its own teaching facility, for the knowledge and skills can be transmitted better and cheaper if done directly, rather than through a third party. Further, a certain amount of security must surround the discussion of a company's or a government agency's privileged information in order to protect industrial trade secrets and government intelligence when they legitimately affect security.

Proximity. The facility needs to be within easy commuting distance of the parent organization's headquarters so that officials can readily participate in the teaching program. A taxi ride instead of a cross-country plane trip encroaches less on the time of a busy executive or technical expert. The parent organization has more flexibility in choosing the site than an established institution does. It is a matter of executive time, travel costs, economic investment in the site, and related factors.

Responsiveness. All organizations want the central training and development facility to be responsive to their needs for organization development, management improvement, and the increase of productivity and service to patrons or customers. But a private organization has more control over its own facility than it can ever have over institutions whose faculties teach against the backdrop of "academic freedom" and other institutional guidelines. It wants to have its own philosophy and doctrine communicated in the facility, not the philosophy and doctrine of hired help of institutions over which it has no real control.

Control. Assuming that organizations able to afford their own institutes or staff colleges have made a policy commitment to the concept of career development, rather than to one of lateral entry, then the organization must have the means for more nearly ensuring that its technicians, managers, and executives receive the necessary training and development to perform effectively as they are transferred, reassigned, and promoted to increasingly responsible assignments. It has less assurance when it relinquishes the training and development responsibility to an outside institution.

Auxiliary Roles. In addition to the teaching function, employer-owned and -operated facilities can perform useful related functions. They are ideal places in which to have some research and development work done, for a staff college brings together faculty members, participants, and resource people in a climate conducive to innovation and creativity which is relatively free of the stresses that attend day-to-day operations. The faculty also makes an ideal source of consultative services because its members combine the technical expertise of their discipline with a more intimate knowledge of internal operations, organizational relationships, and other related matters than is possible for most outside consultants.

Flexibility. An organization with its own staff college can enjoy flexibility in scheduling its education and training programs. It may have pronounced seasonal fluctuations in its work load and these may affect the availability of its personnel for off-the-job learning experiences. Academic institutions are, on the whole, more rigid in their scheduling; some publish two-year calendars of course offerings.

Staff Development. In addition to reducing the cost of training to the extent that an organization's staff can conduct the program, the experience of teaching others is in itself a developmental factor. As organizations rotate staff members to the staff college and back to operations, they are improving communications, keeping the curriculum current, and contributing to staff development and organization development generally.

Communication. Educators recognize that the live-in experience of participants in a training tour at an in-house facility is an excellent supplement to the substantive learning phase. Informal channels of communication are established, and racial and ethnic barriers to understanding are minimized, if not eliminated.

BASIC DESIGN OF A STAFF COLLEGE

The overall design and purpose of an institute or staff college are not unlike those of a university. The institution will be a major investment and should endure indefinitely with an ever-expanding influence. Some of the major factors affecting design are discussed below.

Location and Site. The general location and the specific site should be chosen with exceptional care. The rationale of choosing a site with quick access to the headquarters office has already been explained above. Most metropolitan areas now have a circumferential highway encircling the central city. A site just inside or just beyond such a highway is an ideal choice because it facilitates the use of all modes of transportation. Also, it can permit choice of a site less prohibitive in cost and with sufficient acreage to accommodate some open space as well as the essential components that have to be developed.

Preferably, the site should be one that will (1) shield participants from their busy world and encourage self-renewal and the opportunity for reflection as well as learning; (2) lend itself to an imaginative design that will express the parent organization's theme for the future and its traditions of the past; and (3) be as independent as possible of environmental pollution.

Design. A creative architect with experience in the design of educational institutions should be engaged to meet this unusual challenge. The professional should coordinate the design planning by establishing working relations with all organizational elements. Their inputs are exceedingly important. Ideally, headquarters officials will be persuaded to approve site facilities designed for a dual purpose—education and training on the one hand, and research and development on the other. The two functions are natural coordinates, and interchange of selected staff members from one to the other will reinforce both, and broaden and deepen the experience of persons involved.

Comprehensive planning for the education and training function is mandatory and should be a self-contained and self-sustaining operation. Provision should be made for all instructional activities, support services, participant housing, food services, recreation, and general assembly.

Further, the assumption should be made in planning the design that the central facility will serve as the hub of a "delivery system" that will use multimedia methods to permeate the organization with the best known ways of accomplishing the organization's work program. In other words, the design should be expandable, to allow ultimate establishment of branch centers, mobile teams, programmed instruction services, A/V aids and packaged curriculum materials, correspondence courses, computer-assisted instruction, closed-circuit television, and other formats consistent with the state of the art as it evolves.

Production Facilities. Production will need its own units for program development and for planning, developing, and producing graphic, A/V, and printed curriculum materials. This suggests recording studio facilities, planning and layout space, and editing, scripting, duplicating, packaging, mailing, and storage areas.

Teaching Facilities. Space is, of course, the primary requirement of the facility. All the points suggested before for a single-purpose training room and for a general-purpose center are equally applicable in the design planning for this teaching facility. It needs clusters of classrooms, a small auditorium for about a hundred people and a large auditorium for five hundred to six hundred people, a library resource center, and a variety of support space and specialized-purpose space. A studio classroom, individualized study area, computer-assisted instruction, demonstration laboratories, and hands-on workshop space are examples of specialized space needs. In-house advice and assistance to the architect is critical to making adequate provision in the design for all known purposes to be served.

Research and Development. The research and development segment of the total facility must be planned with the same care and user involvement as the teaching space. It will need such resources as an elaborate technical library, laboratories and proving grounds, industrial-type shops for building prototypes, models, and mock-ups, space for exhibits and displays, and adequate storage for heavy equipment and experimental apparatus and vehicles.

Faculty and Research Staff Offices. Private office quarters are essential for the personnel of these groups. The appointments should be of first class, and the decor should be in keeping with the tone of the whole facility. Space should be provided for visiting professionals, fellows, international visitors, and interns.

Administrative Offices. Since it is from the administrative offices that central direction, coordination, and support flow, these offices should be positioned and designed to facilitate their mission. Provision should be made for the office of the facility director, executive officer or comptroller, support services, registrar, and a health unit. These units should be decorated and furnished in good taste, and should provide for sufficient interoffice communication to permit quiet and efficient conduct of business.

Housing. The trend in participant housing is the suite design, planned to accommodate four to six individuals. Four-person group assignment of those with a common interest (division of labor, automobile transportation, and certain recreation activities) is a good practice, with positive educational benefits. A two-bedroom suite with small kitchen, dining area, living room, and two full baths is very functional. The bedrooms should be equipped with study tables and study lamps. Since the live-in experience can be a supplementary learning benefit, the designing architect should bear this in mind when planning the housing element.

Food Services. Institutional food is notoriously bad, or at least that is the reputation it is stuck with. With this in mind, the staff should survey the local scene for specialized advice and technical assistance on food service. Perhaps the final decision will be to contract with a local food-service group to cater the school. This may eliminate the need for an elaborate kitchen, but it does not remove the need for pleasant surroundings in which to enjoy the meal. Again it should be assumed that much informal communication and learning will occur in this area. Maximum efficiency in the flow of traffic and in serving the food is required in order to allow participants a period of relaxation before resuming classroom work.

A special requirement is the availability of beverages during rest breaks. Automated machine beverages are not generally acceptable. They are expensive, and their quality often leaves much to be desired. Many facilities have found that self-service and an honor system of contributing to the replenishment fund is the most satisfactory plan.

Recreation. The cliché "all work and no play makes Jack a dull boy" still holds. If a teaching facility wants to get maximum cost/benefit results, it should provide for recreational facilities. Depending on the acreage available at the site, the architect can plan for activities such as swimming, tennis, bowling, gymnasium sports, golf, horseshoes, archery, badminton, table tennis, billiards, squash, jogging, and bicycling. These facilities need not be developed all at the same time. They can be phased in over a period of years, as experience and funding dictate. They represent a fringe benefit to all employees who are accepted by the facility for a growth and development experience.

Conclusion

The environment for learning is as important in the lives of people as their homes and offices. It deserves and should get a much higher priority in the allocation of prime space and in the design and furnishing of such space. The needs of target audiences and the style of teaching should dictate such decisions as the site, the functional design of the space, the decor, and other dominant features. The services of a specialist (preferably an architect who specializes in educational facilities) should be engaged to develop models and criteria for the development of original and reclaimed space. Large organizations should publish minimum standards for space used for purposes of training and development.

9

Engineering Delivery Systems

A "delivery system" in the people development activity is not much different from a delivery system in a business. It is a matter of moving knowledge, skill, information, and understanding from appropriate sources to points of need. There are diverse ways of making the transfer, but whatever the way chosen, the vehicle and its content should avoid a circumferential route. For example, it would be folly to suggest that all trees in the forest be uprooted and hauled to a forestry school or tree surgeon for examination and treatment. The professional forester monitors the health of the trees, and when he detects that they are beginning to die back at the top or have other symptoms of need for treatment, a tree surgeon or other specialist is called in to treat the trees in their natural habitat.

The Nature and Purpose of Delivery Systems

Unfortunately, many organizations are "uprooting" their employees and sending them hundreds or thousands of miles away to be "examined and treated" by people who are presumed to be training and development specialists. The economics of this practice are

148

often no better than the economics of the preposterous tree procedure would be. Moreover, the people who are shipped off for "treatment" may suffer from shock upon their return to their normal environment just as the trees would suffer if they were replanted. When the economics and shock factors are overlaid by a third factor—the reality of continuing education and training—the case for delivering the system rather than the people can be closed in favor of the system. For good measure, add the fact that most organizations suffer from shortages of dollars for travel of any kind, frozen staffs, attrition, and mounting work loads. Sensible managers are very cautious under such circumstances, and hesitate to separate trainees from the organization for the purpose of outside training.

An example of a delivery system that does *not* work very well is the traditional correspondence course. If one uses the dropout rate as a yardstick which reportedly runs as high as 85 to 90 percent in commercially administered correspondence courses, such a means of transferring knowledge is hardly a commendation for delivery systems in general. Still, correspondence courses continue and may even be proliferating, for one can enumerate several specific advantages that they offer.

The unit cost of correspondence course training is certainly very low in contrast to cost of training that requires the learner to be absent from his work, perhaps travel to a distant place, and receive instruction from an instructor who requires space, audiovisual aids, and other resources. Absolute quality control can be maintained over the technical knowledge contained in the correspondence materials. Despite the high dropout rate, some people do learn something from this mode of instruction. Even if it does nothing more than spot the participants from a sizable audience who have potential for advanced training through other media, it may serve a useful purpose for all concerned, including the dropouts.

From a negative standpoint, correspondence courses represent teaching at its worst. The participants have little or no opportunity to interact with an instructor, with other participants, or with the material. According to educational psychologists, the response from lesson graders tends to be so delayed that it has little impact on learning as compared with the immediate impact of quick determination of right or wrong answers. Correspondence course administration lacks control over the integrity of a participant's lesson preparation and submissions. Actually, all homework could be done in the name of the participant by another member of the family or anyone familiar with the subject matter.

Five case histories are presented in this chapter all of which demonstrate principles of the delivery system concept. They show clearly how technical knowledge can be transferred on a massive scale by various media from a central point to diverse points of use while retaining a considerable degree of quality control and assurance.

Case History 1: Technical Training Program

This case history for Continental Field Operations of the Seventeenth Decennial Census of the United States shows how the training of trainers can quickly produce a multiplier effect and provide an effective delivery system.

The author was assigned the primary responsibility for the conceptual design of a training strategy to deal with the technical training needs of a massive target audience in connection with the 1950 Census of the United States. It was my first major effort in the development of delivery systems. Since the principles and techniques used in that program, 25 years before the origin of this book, are still applicable, the essential facts are presented here as a case history.[1]

BACKGROUND. The social, economic, and political significance of U.S. Census data made the planning and execution of the Seventeenth Decennial Census of the United States a distinct challenge to the Bureau of the Census. Operationally, the 1950 Census involved visits to 45.7 million dwelling units and 5.6 million farms to obtain the necessary information about each of the nation's 150.5 million inhabitants and the condition of their housing accommodations, and about the country's farm economy. Of the many problems inherent in a national undertaking of this magnitude, the technical training of field personnel was particularly important. Certain factors common to all censuses made this problem unusually difficult.

THE PROBLEM. The broad aim was to develop a system of technical training that would telescopically convey, with reasonable quality control and assurance, more than 1,000 bits and pieces of information from the Census headquarters in Washington, D.C., to approximately 150,000 temporary field employees at some 5,000 locations, over a four-month time span, within a fixed budget, using a plan of organization, methods, materials, and devices that were compatible with the then-current state of the art in training.

DEVELOPMENT OF THE TRAINING PROGRAM. All decennial censuses

[1] This case history is fully documented in a Master's thesis on file in the library of The American University, Washington, D.C., and entitled, "A Study of the Technical Training Program for Continental Field Operations of the 17th Decennial Census of the United States," June 1951.

taken prior to the 1950 Census were handicapped by the fact that no special training materials were prepared for those responsible for gathering the raw census data. For example, a large part of such training as there was for the Sixteenth Decennial Census in 1940 was accomplished in very large classes (as many as 1,000 enumerators) conducted by district supervisors who were also responsible for many administrative matters.

In 1944, therefore, the Bureau appointed a full-time training director (this author), and by 1946 had begun to experiment with new field-training methods. Out of these experiments evolved certain methods and devices, such as training guides and sound filmstrips, which were used advantageously in the 1950 Census program. The Census of Business in 1949 and a series of pretests of the 1950 Census served as additional proving grounds for training organization and methods. In June 1949, a training committee headed by the training director assumed responsibility for shaping the final training plan and coordinating the development of the basic training materials. Expert advice from outside the Bureau was obtained at several points to check the plan for any possible defects. In October 1949, a dress rehearsal was held in North Carolina under controlled conditions. This resulted in minor refinements and a signal from management to proceed with the mass printing and production of training materials and audiovisual aids.

ADMINISTRATION OF THE TRAINING PROGRAM. The implementation of the technical training program presented a challenging problem in logistics—a problem of getting the necessary manpower, material, and equipment, in the proper proportions, to the proper places at the proper time. The preparatory work involved the printing of training manuals and guides, the commercial production of A/V aids, the assembly and shipment of training materials to the field, the development of public relations tools, and the organization for field operations. The field structure for continental field operations consisted of 14 area supervisors, 451 district supervisors, 8,300 crew leaders, and 134,000 enumerators. A corps of 20 chief instructors and 330 technical instructors substituted for area and district supervisors, respectively, in relaying technical instructions from Washington to the crew leaders. This "short circuit" delivery system is illustrated in Figure 2.

Chief Instructor Training. The training of 20 regular and 6 auxiliary chief instructors was conducted in Washington from December 12, 1949, to December 23, 1949. The chief instructors were self-instructed in the work of enumerators, crew leaders, and technical instructors.

Figure 2. 1950 census delivery system for technical training.

Administrative Channels	Technical Training Channels	Training Locations	Number Trained
Director			
Chief, field division	Chief instructors	1 (Washington)	26
Area supervisors	Technical instructors	3 (Washington, St. Louis, San Francisco)	330
District supervisors			
Crew leaders		500 district offices	8,300 crew leaders
Enumerators		5,000 misc. places	134,000 enumerators

Technical Instructor Training. Five teams of four chief instructors each trained 16 classes of technical instructors in Washington, St. Louis, and San Francisco during the period January 9, 1950, to March 3, 1950. Five cycles of this training were conducted. The pattern of training for technical instructors simulated the crew leader and enumerator training. Of the ten days allotted for each technical instructor class, one was devoted to practice presentation. This permitted training specialists from Washington headquarters to pretest each instructor's teaching performance.

Crew Leader Training. Two cycles of crew leader training were conducted. Some of the technical instructors trained at one location during the week of March 8 and at a second location during the week of March 15, while others trained at only one location. An average of 16 crew leaders were assigned to each class, and there was a total of 508 training locations. The crew leader training simulated enumerator training, and in addition provided instruction in methods of training and supervising enumerators. Practice presentation was also used at this level to measure the potential effectiveness of crew leaders as instructors.

Enumerator Training. The 134,000 enumerators were trained by the crew leaders at 5,000 locations between March 27, 1950, and March 31, 1950. At this, as at all other levels of the training, the size of the classes was kept as small as possible (14 to 17 trainees per group), and the use of the lecture method was minimized. A pamphlet was given to applicants for motivation and pretraining purposes.

A standardized and uniform approach to the training was adopted from the *Crew Leader's Guide* (a comprehensive lesson plan); the *Enumerator's Workbook,* which contained practice exercises for laboratory periods; a series of 12 sound filmstrips, which served as motivation and instruction in basic concepts; and a series of recorded narratives and test interviews. An *Enumerator's Reference Manual* served as an encyclopedia of terms, definitions, and field procedures.

The training materials were prepackaged and regionalized to facilitate their distribution and use in urban and rural areas. Urban enumerators received 16 hours of training spread over 4 days at the rate of 4 hours daily. Mixed urban and rural crews generally received 24 hours of training spread over 5 days on a 5–4–5–5–5-hour basis.

Several types of training media were used, including question-and-answer discussions, sound filmstrips, written exercises, role playing, chalkboard demonstration, sample forms, practice enumeration, and lecture. Crew leaders did as much on-the-job follow-up in the early stages of enumeration as time permitted.

Evaluation. There was no scientific evaluation of the Census training effort. However, there are several strong indicators of its success. First, senior management officials supported the idea of upgrading the end product of the huge statistical undertaking by improving the input raw data through the training of the field force. Senior statisticians and economists in charge of Census operations willingly diverted several million dollars from projected monographs and other by-product publications to the training investment.

Second, these same officials approved the idea I advanced to short-circuit the field administrative channels with an ad hoc set of technical training channels (delivery system). This was done on the premise that administrative channels during a major census are clogged with countless nontraining types of official business—political liaison, organization, space procurement, employment, public relations, administrative policy and procedure articulation, and finance. It would be impossible for managers and supervisors in the administrative channels to take time out from everything else to conduct adequate technical training. Moreover, the considerations in selecting the people for the administrative hierarchy were entirely different from the considerations used to select the ad hoc training cadres.

Third, the statistical results of questionnaires returned by 287 technical instructors and 355 district supervisors, as well as subjective evaluations submitted by various observers, indicated that the training program was generally effective, particularly at the enumerator level. Finally, perhaps the best evidence that senior executives at the Census Bureau were pleased with the cost/benefit results is the fact that the Bureau ordered the same strategy repeated a decade later for the 1960 Census. Incidentally, I had accepted a transfer and promotion from Census to General Services Administration in 1953, and was therefore not at Census to promote a repetition of the delivery system described above.

Case History 2: TEAM Program

This case history shows how mobile teams can serve as an effective delivery system.

BACKGROUND. Early in the history of its reorganization, an enterprise, herein designated "Enterprise X," decided to do some management development. The key to its program was in the convening of some vertically drawn samples of managers instead of the traditional, horizontally drawn samples. The decision was made to build and implement a standardized version of the program, to be known as Team Effectiveness Approach for Management (TEAM).

TEAM was given its trial run in one of Enterprise X's field offices. It peaked with a staff of 37 two years later, after TEAM had been in X's offices in 28 major United States cities. The objective then was to have it reach a total of 150 cities.

PROGRAM DEVELOPMENT. A contract was made with an outside group that could devote the uninterrupted time of an experienced course development staff to the task of adapting the substantive material and building a delivery system strategy. The developmental effort moved along expeditiously. The contractor's representatives were oriented to the problems of X's management through briefings and visits to selected field offices. It can be safely assumed that they reviewed the writings of social scientists who have been associated with relevant significant studies of recent decades.

The TEAM program was described in the Record of Training, which goes to the official personnel folder of each participant, as:

> A comprehensive vertical management training program for the development and encouragement of problem solving and decision making capabilities.

Its ultimate goal, continued the statement, was "the organizational development necessary to meet the management challenges posed by the technical and social demands of the changing work environment."

The TEAM program of instruction was conducted in three phases:

Phase I: 40 hours of lecturettes and participant practice in a group dynamic situation; 8 hours of reading and research.

Phase II: 32 hours of application of the techniques, principles, and concepts learned in Phase I.

Phase III: Continuation of Phase II under its own impetus as supported and utilized by the local field-office manager in shared decision making.

Staffing. The TEAM program was powered by people with the title of management instruction specialist (mobile), working as members of teams, each of which had a team chief. A typical team consisted of one team chief (mobile), two senior management instruction specialists (mobile), and one management instruction specialist (mobile).

The TEAM staff was carefully recruited. The individual who coordinated the recruitment effort recalls that only about one of 100 applicants was selected. In other words, the first 25 TEAM staff members came from a field of 2,500 candidates. The level of unemployment at the time (about 6 percent) within the labor force favored the recruitment. Retired military, ex-churchmen, former consulting firm personnel, dislocated aerospace personnel, and many other groups were well represented in the applications. Several paid advertisements were used to stimulate the flow of applications.

The position description for the team chief shows that experienced and well-rounded persons were sought for this program, specifically, with a background of education and/or experience in such subject areas as general management, work analysis, oral and written communication, morale and motivation, individual behavior, organizational and group behavior, leadership, racial sensitivity, and labor relations.

Structuring of Participant Groups. The structuring of groups of participating managers from field offices evolved from the original concept of a vertically drawn sample to a more sophisticated concept. If *operational improvement* was desired, a functional or *family* group, representating at least three management levels, was established whenever possible. When improvement in *interdepartmental* coordination was sought, a group composed of managers taken from a diagonal cut across departments was attempted. If there was a specific task with a defined end point or goal, the *task group* made up of individuals having the necessary experience and ability to find a solution was the structural objective. These three variations in concept are illustrated in Figure 3.

Phases II and III were essentially problem-solving activities under the guidance of TEAM members, who provided expertise in the problem-solving *process* and not in field operations as such. Phase III was a series of eight 4-hour sessions spread over an eight-week

Figure 3. TEAM program participant structuring scheme.

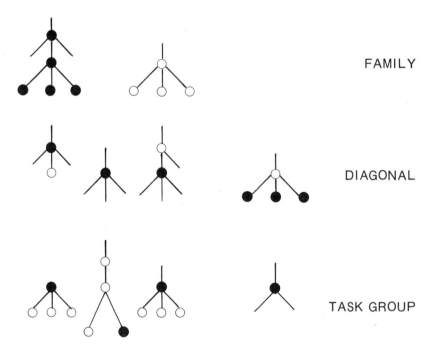

FAMILY

DIAGONAL

TASK GROUP

period to allow for reflection, fact finding, and interpersonal communication.

At any one time, TEAM drew out not more than 20 percent of the managers from participating smaller field offices, and not more than 40 managers at a time from the larger field offices. The sessions were consistently conducted at a place away from the field office in order to minimize the distractions and press of work in the usual environment.

Results. Tangible results are not easily measured in a program such as TEAM. They may show up in the form of better service, better management, or a better working environment. Savings up to $400,000 have been claimed for specific improvements attributed to TEAM, but there was no program incentive for managers to claim tangible savings because regions and headquarters recaptured proven savings and reduced the next budget allocation proportionately. TEAM spokesmen took the position that the program gave back to the manager at least some money he could use to do other things that needed doing. An Enterprise X official liked to say that TEAM was paying "12 to 1" on the investment. As a delivery system, it was definitely moving know-how in modern management and problem solving to the point of need in the enterprise, and it did this a great deal faster and cheaper than would be possible by shipping managers and their staffs to a central place for eight-week training programs.

Case History 3: Regional Training and Development Centers

BACKGROUND. This case history illustrates how a network of regional centers can serve as a delivery system to facilitate the transfer of knowledge, skill, and understanding from a central point to field personnel.

Educational systems in the United States have historically kept a presence near the people to be served. Public schools and church schools have provided a "neighborhood facility." Controversy always tends to ensue when a threat to this concept arises, as in the current issue over busing to achieve racial balance, or when rural schools are "consolidated" with schools at larger places in the name of better education. It is also true that as the child matures and is ready for junior high school, high school, junior college, or community college and university, the parent's tolerance for distances increases. There is also, of course, the economic and convenience factors for students (particularly graduate students) who divide their day between school and paid employment.

Even at the state university level, educators have discovered that a single campus, centrally located, is not a satisfactory response to popular demand for educational services. For example, The University of Texas began operations at the State Capitol in Austin. It now has a continually expanding network of branches at Galveston, Houston, El Paso, Arlington, Dallas, San Antonio, and elsewhere in the state. In several of these cities, it has an intracity network of campuses.

I took this phenomenon into account when I was assigned the task of planning the establishment of the Institute. Figure 4 depicts

Figure 4. Regional center delivery system.

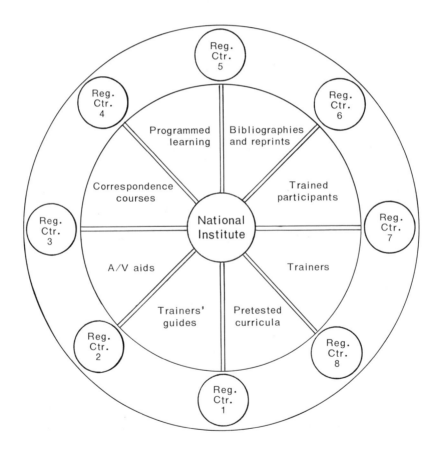

the extension center network then projected, and its anticipated relationship to the Institute headquarters.

THE EXTENSION SERVICES DIVISION. The Institute began its operations, in January 1968, with a commitment to carry training services to the field. One of its four operating divisions in the initial organization was called the Extension Services Division. The first opportunity the Institute had for making good on its commitment arose when a mobile team operation began delivering a two-day safety course in larger cities. The course, known as Safety for Supervisors, was packaged and taught by a contractor under the general direction of, and with logistical backup from, the Extension Services Division. This instruction reached thousands of field supervisors within a period of approximately one year. Instructors were trained and the course was pretested under the supervision of the Extension Services Division. During the same period, thousands of first- and second-line supervisors at or near their duty station were receiving a one-week prepackaged course in modern supervision.

Since these first two courses were of an ad hoc nature and only partially supported by the Institute, they cannot be categorized as delivery systems, in my judgment. However, they did serve to kindle further interest of both the Institute and the field in the idea of carrying the training to participants instead of transporting them to a resident school.

The Institute's field centers are more than just a place from which to conduct a particular program more conveniently. As originally intended, they were to represent a fundamental decentralization of the management school's activities. The Institute's comprehensive catalog system of training and development systems and opportunities once described the Institute field centers thus:

> Many of the programs offered at the Institute are also offered at the Field Centers . . . .
>
> Along with the present development programs, the Field Centers will also provide each region with the advantage of "in residence" development consultants who will be able to assist in meeting problems and needs specific to the region or any of its subordinate units. Field Center consultants will work with top management in local field offices and at higher organizational levels in the region, aiding them in identifying and solving problems. Centers will assist in the conduct of management conferences in regional, area, and district locations. Such conferences will familiarize field managers with current management concepts in the areas of communication,

motivation, problem solving, and organizational improvement. These meetings will also offer managers the opportunity to share experiences and insights through group discussion and idea exchange, and afford the opportunity to brief managers on new field operational techniques and procedures.

ADVANTAGES OF THE REGIONAL CENTER DELIVERY SYSTEM. The field center is a multipurpose unit. It radiates teaching services and consultative services to its clients. For the parent institute, it serves as a conduit through which needed information can be obtained for the development, refinement, and evaluation of instructional materials. For example, as Center personnel move about within a region, they may discover some outstanding and innovative management or field operations practices. These can be fed back to faculty members for their use in the enrichment of instructional programs. Arrangements can be made on the spot for faculty members or contract personnel engaged in developmental work to visit such establishments.

The Center is in a distinctly better position than a central institution is to take soundings with respect to current and future training and development needs. It is also in a better position to observe the impact of Institute programs on the development of individuals and organizational effectiveness. The Center can perform an important personnel management function by spotting field employees who merit consideration for a tour of duty at the Institute headquarters.

Case History 4: Employee Development Center Network

BACKGROUND. This case history is a study of a delivery system that involves a multimedia approach to the transfer of technical knowledge on one of the most massive scales ever attempted in the United States. The delivery system is a major effort involving an initial expenditure of over $6 million to move technical know-how from a central point to, or near, the thousands of points of use throughout the United States.

The system is in the form of a master plan for a continuing program of employee training and development in a vast network of field offices. The system described here is referred to as the Employee Development Center (EDC) network.

ORIGINS AND BASIC GOALS OF EDC CONCEPT. The EDC proposal recognized four fundamental goals of supervisors and managers with respect to their large work forces:

1. To train new employees quickly and correctly so that they would be initially productive.
2. To initiate a system of upward movement to higher skill levels, a plan for continued training and development to provide continuity in quality service at all levels of responsibility.
3. To be in position to respond flexibly to special circumstances that arise in the service.
4. To adopt a policy of improved retention of personnel.

The plan phased in the use of a network of EDCs as the system for delivering standardized, pretested, quality controlled, and semi-automated training to meet *initial* and *continuing* training and development needs of field personnel. The delivery system designer (this author) also advocated the development, at appropriate locations, of consolidated physical facilities to serve as modern learning environments for target audiences. Detailed characteristics and functions of the EDCs were listed, and a division of labor was suggested for the field manager and the parent training center.

The EDC plan was a broadside assault on the employee training and development problem in the field. It endeavored to correct *everything* that seemed to be wrong with such training in the past, but it might have been better restricted to the many glaring weaknesses of the old system, such as instructional method, space, hardware, or staffing.

Specific Objectives of the EDC Network. EDC was directed specifically to a variety of field training needs. It changed the *instructional method* by substituting self-pacing systems and materials, and machines built on the teaching machine principle, and eliminated the conventional classroom and job instructor.

EDC approached the need for a *delivery system* from several angles. It advocated a network of architect-designed, attractive, functional facilities to be strategically located in the United States so as to maximize the possibilities for serving the personnel of large host field offices and neighboring smaller field offices. These facilities were to be called EDCs and were to operate on the principle that employees should be "trained in place" by training facilities owned and operated by the local managers.

The delivery system was reinforced by the proposal to develop a small sound filmstrip machine with standard magnetic tape playback capability and an accessory that could convert it into a viable teaching machine. The small machine was to have been produced against technical specifications that were developed by a qualified research group. The objective of buying the machine at a substantial reduction from the price of commercially available machines was realized.

This unique machine, with features specifically engineered for the enterprise, was to serve as a "receiving set" in smaller field offices where thousands of employees are employed, and who traditionally have been deprived of training opportunities.

Another facet of the delivery system was the idea of using the local community's academic facilities (night high schools, junior colleges, community colleges, trade schools, and the like) as auxiliaries of the EDC manpower development capability. Standardized courses in the community, related to field operations and career development objectives, were to have been tapped, and field employees were authorized to attend (at subsidized expense) and take, for example, a course in drafting. Unfortunately, this objective was not approved.

EDC responded to the need for *timely training content* by offering a rapid-response packaging system, the output of which would be units of standardized, pretested, quality-assured material in programmed instruction format. Each unit would contain the *best known way* of doing a field task or set of tasks.

In order to encourage *upward mobility* EDC offered a self-instructional system in basic education and skills improvement units. This material and the instructional hardware supporting it can be, and is being, used to support both on-the-clock and off-the-clock training. Some dramatic examples on record show how unskilled employees with as little as a third- or fourth-grade education have used EDC facilities to master reading, simple mathematics, and other basic education essentials. Thus, they advanced themselves to the readiness level required for entrance examinations and training leading to reassignment to mechanic positions. Under special circumstances, on-the-clock time for basic education units of instruction in the EDC is justifiable.

The *testing and counseling dimension* in the employee training situation was considered by providing such facilities in the architectural design of EDC space, and by including counselors in the staffing pattern.

A more *systematic approach* to employee training, backed by readily available (preferably computerized) data, was realized by including a codified scheme for foreseeable offerings and by projecting the development of a data bank.

EDC documented the existing and future *state of the art in educational technology* by listing, in the inventory of equipment to be placed in the EDC, a battery of modern training aids, the most sophisticated of which was the videotape replay device. Computer-assisted instruction and computer-managed instruction, and perhaps closed-circuit television, will be added at appropriate stages of development.

The search for *professionally qualified managers and supporting staffs* was supported by a set of qualification standards that would guide the recruitment, selection, and placement programs.

Especially important was the EDC stress on the concept of *continuing education and training* by offering a system with maximum flexibility that would serve new employees, reassigned employees, employees given new tasks to do, employees dislocated by technology, and others in either a pre-resident school or a post-resident school, or both.

The need for training and development as a *cohesive, integrated, organizationally coordinated management function* was satisfied by the proposal to merge all employee training functions under strong leadership and technical direction. In the past, the function had been fragmented and was dispersed among diverse jurisdictions.

Cost Question. The cost question inevitably arose in discussions of EDC. A cost analyst of the finance department investigated this issue in 1971 and, after studies in five major cities, reported that "savings resulting from the installation of EDCs at Chicago, San Francisco, Memphis, New York City, and Philadelphia would result in an Internal Rate of Return of approximately 210% (150% if research and development costs are included)." The cost of energizing one EDC to serve 5,000 employees was estimated at $108,000. The cost of operating an EDC of the same size was estimated at $129,000. Both figures were exclusive of the rental value of space and the cost of space maintenance—presumably constants in the comparative cost study.

FORMAL COMMITMENT TO THE EDC DELIVERY SYSTEMS. In 1973, a major metropolitan newspaper in the United States carried a seven-column article reporting a $6.5 million self-help investment in the EDC system. Excerpts are quoted here from the article to indicate how fully it is formally committed to the EDC delivery system.

> The [_____] is spending $6.5 million on prepackaged education to train employees, provide better service and win back customers lost to its competitors.

> Mr. _____ officially dedicated the nationwide program today at the new . . . Employee Development Center.

The [_____] plans to set up 200 of these centers across the country. They will use film strips and viewing machines, tapes and earphones, rather than classroom teachers. . . .

Paralleling mandatory courses in new . . . technology are self-development courses which employees can take on their own time around the clock to improve their reading, learn mathematics from fractions to algebra, make themselves 60-word-a-minute typists or 100-a-minute shorthand stenographers. In the Philadelphia center alone, 900 employees have signed up for the self-development programs. . . .

Mr. _____, manager of this district, sees the program not only as a landmark for the [_____] but as something the rest of industry will follow "if we do it successfully."

Case History 5: A Problem in the Training of Foreign Nationals from Underdeveloped Countries

BACKGROUND. Since World War II, the United States has been engaged, under authority of the Mutual Assistance Act, in sharing technical assistance with as many as 80 underdeveloped countries at any particular time. As an integral part of the foreign aid program, the technical assistance part suffers from a lack of public understanding. Taxpayers tend to see all aspects—capital and technical assistance aspects alike—as a "giveaway" scheme. While many of the notions about the program are quite inaccurate, there is an element of merit in the taxpayers' claim that foreign aid is wasted effort.

Typically, one overseas mission of the Agency for International Development (AID) will spot some people who are already employed in their government, but who are lacking in sufficient technical knowledge to carry out a program to which their country has committed itself. For example, a foreign country may have committed itself to tax reform, but it lacks the necessary expertise in tax assessment and tax collection methods to ensure the success of the program. Then the host government identifies cadre to receive training in the United States, the AID mission administers tests for English language proficiency, and then prepares the paperwork for those who pass the English test. The AID provides funds for the training, which may vary from short courses to an academic program leading to a degree.

Unfortunately, the success of this system depends heavily on the quality of selection, and the selection system consists essentially in

AID's accepting those the host country nominates, provided the nominees pass the English test. Sometimes the test is compromised and the participants arrive with only enough English to say, "Thank you very much!" and a few other basics.

Any nomination system, regardless of whether it is being used by a less or a more fully developed country, leaves much to be desired. Political, ethnic, racial, sex, age, seniority, rank, and other extraneous factors too often influence the nomination process. The foreign country's nominee may be (1) the son, daughter, or other relative of an affluent family who has great influence with a political leader; (2) someone with a physical condition that can be better treated medically in the United States; (3) someone who is not sufficiently self-disciplined to adjust to the fact that education in the United States is not politically controlled but that grades must be earned, not bought or commanded; or (4) someone whose main objective is to emigrate.

Much of the wasted effort and other resources consumed by the technical assistance program could be saved if a more intelligent delivery system were used and made to serve as a quality control on the participant selection system. I once proposed, but failed to gain, full acceptance of a multifaceted delivery system that I believed would greatly strengthen the selection process and be in the general interest of both the United States and all less developed countries. It had four phases, each of which is briefly described below.

PHASE I: CORRESPONDENCE PROGRAM. Through the auspices of the overseas mission of AID in any particular country, or in a regional cluster of underdeveloped countries, interest in a correspondence program would be promoted. Programmed instruction would be a superior mode for this phase, but the conventional correspondence system is much cheaper and perhaps more appropriate for an AID recipient, since programmed instruction often involves teaching machines and that means electricity and other complicating demands. Perhaps as many as one to two hundred participants could be enlisted to participate in this phase.

The objective of Phase I would be to stimulate interest among a universe of employees who work in some specialized field in the public sector or in private enterprise. It might be tax work, supply management, education, public health, or agriculture. The course development and administration would most likely be contracted by AID to a university or private firm. The lesson responses would be collected by the AID mission and forwarded to the contractor in the United States for grading and return through channels. A major goal of this phase would be to gather sufficient evidence about the

motivation, self-discipline, and industry of the entire body of participants to identify those who would be most appropriate participants
in the next phase. After Phase I had run its course to a logical
conclusion, it would be terminated and Phase II would begin.

PHASE II: OVERSEAS WORKSHOP. Assume that a hundred participants in Phase I engaged in the correspondence program and that
20 were selected to participate in Phase II. A mobile team of specialists (minimum of two members) would then travel to an overseas
location, to be arranged in advance by the AID mission. The AID-
sponsored team, probably employees of the original Phase I contractor, would conduct a workshop of appropriate duration at the designated location. They would have two major objectives: (1) to teach
all participants as much as possible, and (2) to identify one or more
participants who showed the most promise for becoming trainers.
While in the local area the team would, of course, visit local offices to
familiarize themselves with the culture and the state of the art in
their field of specialization. Perhaps a reconnaissance trip in advance
of the workshop would be a good investment if funding were sufficient to support it. Upon their return to the United States, they
would be in a position to modify the material for both Phase I and
Phase II.

PHASE III: TRAINING OF TRAINERS. Assume that two or three participants in the workshop program were supported for this phase.
They would then be funded for a program of study and practical
observation in the United States, tailored to their individual needs.
Obviously, since they had survived two stages of competition, both
their own government and the AID mission would know more about
their qualifications for training in the United States. Therefore, their
government would be in an infinitely better position to resist pressures internally to accept Phase I and Phase II participants who did
poorly (e.g., those who submitted no correspondence course lessons
or who were dropouts from the workshop). Also, the AID mission
would have evidence on which to support or reject individual nominees. This procedure would assure opportunity for qualified trainees, regardless of economic or political status. Furthermore, it would
guarantee that AID funds would be used productively and to the
benefit of the recipient. It is also possible that those persons rejected
would have learned something by participating in the workshop.

PHASE IV: GETTING THE MULTIPLIER EFFECT THROUGH INDIGE-
NOUS TRAINERS. When Phase III participants had completed their
program of study and observation in the United States, including
special training in how to train others, they would return to their

own country to begin a series of workshops patterned after the original one conducted by the AID team. Perhaps an AID team member would monitor the initial run of the recipient's workshop and tutor its members to the desired proficiency level. The workshops would continue until needs of the underdeveloped country in that particular subject-matter field had been adequately met. In the meantime, the four-phase cycle could be in progress in other fields.

FUTURE OF THE MODEL. As the United States taxpayer becomes even more stubborn in resisting the traditional pattern of technical assistance, the model suggested in this case study, or some variation of it, will have to be adopted. Although it was proposed a decade ago, when bringing foreign nationals to the United States was enthusiastically promoted by foreign aid administrators, changing economic conditions may now make it a viable program for foreign assistance. The need for AID still exists, but taxpayers' doubts and their concern with rising federal expenditures have curtailed the funds to support it. Therefore, administrators are searching for other alternatives. Perhaps the time has come to implement this model.

Guidelines for Designing Effective Delivery Systems

The five foregoing case studies collectively reflect a set of guidelines that can be useful to the people developer. The art of delivery system design and development lies in the choices one makes under a particular set of circumstances. Any professional—architect, urban planner, scientist, medical practitioner, and others—starts with fact finding, methodically works out a solution step by step, applies it, and analyzes the results. This process is repeated as often as necessary until an acceptable solution has emerged. The process is no different in the design of an effective training and development delivery system. The essential steps are discussed in detail below.

Analysis. The logical first step, after the need for a delivery system has been determined, is to do some careful analyses. These include systems analysis, job analysis, and task analysis. The objective is to find the best known way of accomplishing a given operation or series of operations. This may require travel and observation in more than one location where the work is normally done. If it is a projected operation that has never been done, or one that has not been done in a relatively long time, the analysis may have to be made on paper, using some of the available charting techniques such as

PERT, lattices, process charts, work distribution charts, and work measurement. A simple excursion in the job area for the purpose of interviewing or watching individuals who now perform the work is another way. It is best to use the services of an experienced systems analyst, methods analyst, or industrial engineer to make the analysis.

Instructional Units. Once the basic data have been assembled from on-site analysis or other methods, it is well to arrange the raw material in logical instructional units, at least in outline form. The question is: "What is there to be taught?" A topical list of units to be taught, with a rough estimate of the number of instructional hours required, is critical to subsequent steps. In other words, are there ten logical units of instruction requiring an estimated total of 40 hours of instruction, or should there be 40 units requiring in the aggregate about 80 hours of instruction time?

Economic Analysis. The next step could be in the form of some economic analysis to determine the comparative costs of transferring the technical knowledge by several different media. What is the unit cost (cost per participant) of transferring the knowledge from a central point to the points of use by options A, B, C, and D? The analyst must know whether or not the delivery system is needed on a one-time or a continuing basis. Also to be considered are all cost elements—such as space, equipment, travel of participants, travel of instructors, and shipping costs—the typical participant's learning capacity, the size and location of the ultimate target audience, curriculum materials and production cost, and storage requirements. Having the economic data well in hand is essential to the objective of selling the soundest training strategy to decision makers.

Scheduling. The time frame for the first cycle of know-how delivery has to be firmly set at some point. As a minimum, the optimum time span for a cycle should be established by the program planner. The reader may have noted that the time span in Case Study 1, the 1950 Census case, was approximately four months. In another situation, a cycle might be finished in a few weeks.

Formulating the Budget. It is nearly impossible to sell any training program or delivery system that has no price tag or for which no one seems to know its cost. There are no blank checks for training. Therefore, program planners must draw up a detailed and realistic budget, including contingency allowances. The economic data gathered in the previous analysis will be useful in formulating a persuasive budget presentation. The inputs of operating officials should be solicited for this budget, since it will be their personnel who will ultimately receive the training. For example, they may insist on including in the budget the cost of temporary replacements for participants assigned to training. They may also wish to include the salaries of all participants as a cost of program operations.

Quality Assurance. During the planning of the delivery system, one needs to build in a method of ensuring quality control at all stages of the knowledge transfer. If the technical knowledge must filter through three levels of trainers, quality controls have to be in place at all three levels. The objective may be to prepackage, test, and disseminate standardized technical knowledge, using semiautomated methods and devices such as through programmed instruction. If mobile teams are to be used, all teams should receive their training from a common source so that one team is not teaching one version while another team is teaching something else. Dry runs, or practice teaching, is an excellent means of quality assurance. Monitoring actual training, at least on a sample basis, is another means.

Management Commitment. If the installation of a delivery system represents a new initiative for an organization, the program planners should allow a generous amount of time to obtain the necessary authorizations and commitments. Executives do not always look kindly upon strange new moves, especially when considerable risk may be inherent in the first-time use of a new method on a massive scale. One way to ease the distress that such decisions generate is to suggest that the delivery system be pretested on a small scale. This takes time and may add to the total cost, but it may also make the difference between a "go" and "no-go" posture.

Materials Development and Packaging. Once a commitment has been secured, a production schedule for curriculum materials has to be set and executed. Equally good arguments can be made for doing the developmental work with in-house talent or contracting the job out to a qualified curriculum materials development contractor. A combination of the two approaches is also a viable option. Again, the quality controls should be in place and functioning. If a multimedia delivery system has been sold to management, more than one contractor may be required. The time frame may determine whether one or more contractors are needed. The objective is to produce, or have produced, quality materials suitable for the media to be used.

Training of Trainers. If the strategy calls for the use of trainers, it is essential that they be trained not only in the subject matter but also in the subtleties of how best to teach the material. If, in the practice teaching phase of their preparation, some instructors are colorless and lacking in motivation for the assignment, they should be withdrawn from the trainer role before it is too late.

Equipment. If training equipment is required to make the delivery system function as conceived, the program planners should try to arrange to have an impartial laboratory or a procurement specialist make a careful study of the equipment possibilities already on the market. If products available cannot be bought on the scale needed at a unit cost consistent with the economic analysis, technical specifications should be drawn up for having manufacturers bid on a modified design. Standardized equipment is a practical necessity in a sizable delivery system requiring equipment. Having assorted equipment complicates the task of training operators, stocking replacement parts, shipping equipment units, and maintaining the necessary quality control.

Space. If the delivery system requires accommodation beyond the conventional training room, a space design project should be conducted, using if possible the services of an architect or facilities planner who is experienced in modern education techniques and the design of training facilities. A series of models can be developed to guide local offices in the alteration of existing space. This, too, is an essential element of the overall objective of quality control because the learning environment is truly a vital part of the picture.

Trainee Population. In linking together the delivery system network, it is advisable to plot the points at which the greatest densities of target audience individuals live and work. The purpose is to minimize travel time and distance traveled. Time is money, and money is always scarce in most organizations.

Testing and Counseling Dimension. Some provision should be made in every delivery system, whenever possible, to provide for testing and counseling. It is a serious mistake to "spray on" training to a whole class of personnel. It is an exception rather than the rule when performance appraisal systems identify specific training needs. A more recent concept, the individual development plan, is beginning to be accepted as the preferred system. The idea is to provide the employee with whatever guidance and assistance he or she needs in identifying those training experiences that can be immediately related to the job or can be rationally fitted into the long-range development goals and objectives of the employee.

Evaluation of Results. No system is acceptable as a delivery system until some professional has observed it function during one or more complete cycles and has compared the results against the original training objectives set by the program planners. Ideally, professional evaluators should be persons other than the program planners.

Otherwise, management may continue to hold whatever reservations it had at the start.

Provision for Completed Loop. Delivery systems can be self-repairing and self-improving if sufficient provision is built in to signal malfunctioning. Further, provision must be made for spotting what appear to be innovative approaches in the work program so that each new approach can be checked out and, if found advantageous, can be packaged and disseminated through the delivery system channels.

Conclusion

Organization leaders should candidly examine their policies and practices in the light of the delivery system concept and guidelines presented in this chapter. In considering a delivery system tailored to transfer knowledge and skill at relatively low unit costs, these leaders should not yield to the shallow argument that it is impossible to conduct training because of the expense of travel.

10

Selecting Training and Development Methods

PEOPLE development work is still an art, and it is unlikely to ever become a precise science. If the transfer of knowledge, skill, and understanding from people to people were as simple as boiling water or following a recipe to bake a cake, life might be much less complicated. Since the attainment of the best results is largely left to the creative imagination and expertise of the training and development specialist, who has a wide variety of methods to choose from, the experience of seasoned practitioners should be useful to executives and personnel who participate in, and approve, a training program. The following basic guidelines may be helpful in analyzing both philosophical and technical approaches.

Some Basic Guidelines

The choice of training and development methods *should:*

—Recognize individual differences in participants, and the training approach should accommodate such differences.

—Encourage a full response of the participants in the instructor/participant relationship. Ideally, the participant should be stimulated to interact with the instructor, the program content, and other participants.

—Introduce a balanced (multimedia) approach to teaching, since people learn through different media and one medium reinforces another.

—Correlate with the practices of technically qualified instructors, each of whom is part scholar, part showman, and part missionary.

—Facilitate the use of the training program as a catalytic agent to disseminate the most current knowledge and the best known ways of performing the particular work methods and systems.

—Encourage each participant to supplement the employer-sponsored training and development activity with self-education and self-training.

—Call for the use of master craftsmen and "old Turks" in the ongoing processes of training, evaluation, and utilization of younger, high-potential participants.

—Include provision for upgrading communication skills, which are critical to career development.

—Treat each training and development experience as a building block—not as an isolated happening—in a total, continuing, soundly conceived system of human resource development and utilization.

PITFALLS IN METHOD SELECTION

Equally important in the choice of methods is knowing the conditions to avoid. Weigh each choice carefully and:

—Don't let the "MC" approach of a TV variety show become the pattern for training; that is, avoid an uncoordinated, disjointed string of guest artists who talk *at* the participants.

—Don't be misled by participant feedback that usually tells the instructor and the program director what they want to hear.

—Don't assume that the training is penetrating the philosophy and behavioral habit pattern of the participant.

—Don't assume that the participant is in position to practice his newly acquired skills, for he may be layered by people whose policies and practices are in conflict with what he is learning.

—Don't assume a faculty member or resource person is still current and that his or her inputs will be relevant.

—Don't assume that all participants have the same readiness for learning, or that they learn and retain knowledge and skills at the same rate.

—Don't accept the outmoded conclusion that reluctant or slow learners are destined to be failures on the job.

—Don't place too wide a range of learning capabilities and experience levels in the same group. Try for this good mix:

Assessed Rank of Candidate	Groupings
1 (highest)	I = 1s, 2s, and 3s
2	II = 2s, 3s, and 4s
3	III = 3s, 4s, and 5s
4	
5 (lowest)	

—Don't fail to follow through with OJT assistance of an informed, constructive and timely kind.

—Don't let the constructive approach to the training program be diluted by teaching fads that have little or no relevance to the work of the organization.

CATEGORIES OF TRAINING METHODS

In the following inventory of accepted training methods, an attempt is made to distinguish between methods that tend to be most useful in the immediate job situation or on-job training (OJT), and those that usually require the release of the employee to engage in learning experiences away from the job (off-job training). The latter category is subdivided three ways to show differences in the approach to training. In summary, the inventory of methods has four classifications:

1. On-the-job training: individually oriented.
2. Off-the-job training: group oriented and conventional.
3. Off-the-job training: experiential; group or individually oriented.
4. Off-the-job training: self-paced and individually oriented.

A brief description is given in the remainder of the chapter for each of the methods possible within these four classifications, together with comments, such as a principal advantage or disadvantage, and something of the best condition for use. The subcategories in each classification are arranged alphabetically.

This inventory of methods is by no means exhaustive, but it is certainly representative and does reflect the state of the art at this time. Many of the methods described may be partially or completely mediated with appropriate equipment.

On-the-Job Training: Individually Oriented

Apprenticeship. Parents began to apprentice, or "bind out," their sons during the Middle Ages in Europe, where apprenticeship was an essential part of the craft guild system. At that time, a person was bound by agreement or contract to work a certain period of time in order to learn an art or trade. Today, a senior craftsman takes charge of the apprentice's practical experience, which may be supplemented by specified amounts of formal education. In the federal government, standards are coordinated by the Bureau of Apprenticeship, U.S. Department of Labor. This one-to-one relationship of apprentice and trainer is still a viable method in the trades, and people who learn through it eventually master the necessary skills. However, more modern methods of training bring individuals to the desired proficiency level faster and more economically, but fail to recognize individual differences, which the apprenticeship system did.

Audiovisual Aids. Numerous visual, audio, and audiovisual aids can be used in the work situation to reinforce the indoctrination and training of an individual. The wide choice includes such items as chalkboard, easel, overhead projectors, opaque projectors, microscopes, audio tapes, slides, videotapes, motion pictures, filmstrips, stereo slides, charts, globes, maps, blueprints, photographs, and sketches. These aids can be used to illustrate goals, objectives, organizational relationships, policies, procedures, systems, strategies, conditions, and the like. Audiovisual aids alone are not sufficient instruction, and do not replace but are only supportive of good supervision and training.

Bulletin Boards. Bulletin boards are not managed properly in most places. Usually, they are a poorly used and often abused method of conveying new information. They become cluttered, disorganized, and unattractive. There are several ways to add more appeal to make them a meaningful and continuing source of useful information.

Boards can be compartmentalized, so that people know specifically where to look for items of special interest. They can be used dramatically at times to convey a concept by having everything else removed so that a single item will be the focus of attention. An organization would be well advised to place its employee training and development unit in charge of the bulletin board service so that it can be programmed to accomplish certain objectives that are consistent with the organization's broad goals and objectives.

Briefings. The briefing method is popular at the executive and administrative levels. For example, when a new political figure is appointed to a public agency, it is customary to arrange for a series of briefings to help him absorb quickly the necessary background for his assignment. Upper-echelon military officers practice the policy of getting frequent briefings on such matters as the latest foreign intelligence, the status of military campaigns, and the capability of proposed new weapon systems.

Committee Assignments. The supervisor or manager is in position to orchestrate committee assignments in a way that should enable each employee to have progressively more responsible and diversified experience. The interdisciplinary team approach to problem solving is unsurpassed as a management strategy for people development and for getting things done. Individuals who have the committee exposure gain new perspectives and motivation for new initiatives.

Computer-Assisted Instruction. Organizations that have computer-assisted instruction (CAI) available can employ the input and output devices to further the development of individuals. CAI is a sophisticated form of instruction requiring some orientation to the computer language and the mechanical operations. The computer is centrally programmed, and therefore the material is quality controlled and designed with particular target audiences in view. For example, a maintenance crew may keep its technicians updated through a remotely located computer.

Consultations. In the course of one's work it is frequently possible to learn by consulting with others in allied organizational elements, at higher echelons, and even at lower levels. This need for consultation is particularly present in the case of complex organizations, those that are decentralized, and those that rely on a vast array of suppliers, subcontractors, or outlets for their goods and services.

Demonstrations. The act of showing someone how a machine, process, system, or procedure functions can be good instruction, provided it is accompanied by proper interpretation and interaction to ensure comprehension. These demonstrations can take place as a normal part of supervision, on or near the work place.

Detailing. Not much growth takes place as long as an individual does the same set of tasks day in and day out. A well-rounded picture of each step in the larger operation can only be obtained by finding opportunities for the employee to actually perform related steps for temporary periods. Informal detail for up to 90 days is a feasible way to do this, even under merit systems that require strict accounting of all variances from the approved position description.

Field Trips. Nothing is more stimulating or enriching from a learning standpoint than for a headquarters employee to visit a field office, or vice versa. Supervisors can use field trips as a broadening experience by varying the pattern of investigation done by subordinates on field assignments. Instead of having a subordinate go on a single mission, the supervisor can make up a multimission itinerary by letting the traveler investigate some questions raised by other employees who need to communicate with the field.

Follow-up Coaching. While a good instructor will permit the employee to work without supervision at some point and let him or her perform as well as possible on the job, an effective supervisor knows that a certain amount of follow-up is good insurance against the development of bad work habits and attitudes. Coaching is a subtle form of follow-up. It may be done with a question or two, a commendation followed by a suggestion of an alternate approach, the sharing of some reference material, or in any other way most comfortable for the supervisor.

Four-Step Method. Industrial training specialists publicized the four-step method in the early stages of World War II through the facilities of the Training within Industry Service, War Manpower Commission. The method was packaged as one of a series of 10-hour courses for factory foremen and civilian government supervisors. The four steps in good person-to-person instruction, according to this method, are (1) prepare the employee, (2) present the job, (3) try out performance, and (4) follow up. The method is reliable, if faithfully followed, in teaching any person to do a routine job quickly, correctly, and conscientiously. It also has significant implications for the planning and administration of more sophisticated forms of training and development.

House Organ. Many organizations use internal house organs to disseminate official policy information, personnel changes, new program developments, beneficial suggestions for which awards have been made, and the like. The house organ can be anything from a slick-print newspaper or magazine to a "memorandum to staff" from the supervisor or manager of a given unit. Employees like to receive information or comments from the person in charge, something that informs, interprets, commends, encourages, or lends a measure of security and understanding. Tremendous value can accrue from skillful use of this medium to build healthy attitudes and a common language of understanding.

Issuances. As an organization grows in volume of business and number of employees, it is essential to good organization and management that a system of official issuances be established to guide the decisions and conduct of its officers and other employees. Otherwise, the head of the organization has to make countless repetitive decisions, many of which may be relatively unimportant. A good issuance system is compartmentalized into such categories as orders, official notices, policies, procedures, and forms control.

Job Analysis. An unsurpassed way to learn the intricacies of a job is by following it through, step by step, from a logical beginning to a logical end. There are many useful applications of job analysis in supervision and management. Therefore, a supervisor can utilize the services of junior personnel in making new job analyses periodically. It is especially good training for the analyst to chart each operation that advances the work, the delays, reviews, distances, time factors, physical conditions, and related factors. By asking such questions as why, who, what, where, when, and how, the analyst gains detailed insight into the nature of the job.

Job Rotation. The detail of an employee to a special assignment is similar to job rotation, but rotation usually results in a permanent shifting of employees about, from one assignment to another. Some organizations choose selected employees to switch jobs within a given organizational element. Others move employees progressively, both laterally and vertically, within their entire field service, shifting them from field to headquarters, and vice versa. The U.S. Foreign Service and the national defense agencies of the federal government make extensive use of this principle. Investigative agencies such as the FBI and IRS also move their employees about in order to enrich their experience or to serve other administrative purposes. Such a system requires a reliable appraisal/counseling plan in order that both management officials and the employee get the necessary feedback and develop their growth potential.

Observation. Practical observation is a relatively inexpensive method of training. Again, the observation technique must be orchestrated wisely by the supervisor. For a young draftsman or a young engineer with an architectural firm, a few hours of observation at a construction site where the foundation work is in progress can be very meaningful as a learning experience. It is best when the observer is given an opportunity to report his observations and check them against the experience of senior specialists.

Public Address System. A public address (PA) system can be both a curse and an asset, depending on how skillfully management uses it to convey meaningful and timely information. Organizational changes are among the types of information. People should not get any surprises in their daily newspaper about their own place of employment. The PA system is the fastest possible way to advise employees that a big contract has been won or lost; that profits are up or down; that new products, designs, or services are being introduced; or that the manager of the place has just resigned. Obviously, no skills can be taught over a PA system, but greater confidence in management and a sense of security can be cultivated, and changes in attitude can be subtly directed.

Reference Materials. Training directors should encourage the employee to build a reference shelf of books about his or her trade. This is another source of security—having readily available a few books on the current best thinking in the field as well as official issuances of the organization. These books should include a good unabridged dictionary, atlases, technical manuals and handbooks, source books, schedules, directories, economic and demographic data, or whatever the specialized requirements may be. At the least, the employee should have a list of these books and know where ready access to them is available.

Research Assignments. A genuine learning experience is realized by searching out previously recorded knowledge about a given subject and preparing a position paper, report, strategy plan, or a proposal for alternative courses of action. It is humbling to find that one's notions are not supported by the literature in one's field, but it is reassuring to find that they are. Familiarization with research tools is the formation of a good work habit that can lead to self-propelled growth long after a single research assignment has been completed.

Speakers Bureau. From time to time, many organizations designate selected members of their staffs as their representatives at community gatherings to discuss such community development matters as public schools, parks and recreation facilities, transportation, planning, regional coordination, and the like. Organizations with enlightened management respond to invitations to cooperate with such community groups. Individual employees who respond to such opportunities, either on their own initiative or as representatives of their employers, inevitably derive much benefit and experience, some of which may be applied on their bread-and-butter job. The organization usually builds a better image from its policy of encouraging employees to be active in the community.

Supervision. Normal day-to-day supervision probably accounts for about 90 percent of all the on-the-job training one receives. This is why it is so pathetic when supervision is weak and no example of performance is on the job for the subordinate to imitate. Every supervisor has his or her own style. Some supervisors supervise exceedingly well, merely by encouraging subordinates and by challenging them to give the best of their talents and abilities. Other supervisors are natural teachers, and radiate enthusiasm for what they are doing. Patience, going the extra mile to help a slow learner over the rough spots, making just the right assignment to each employee, as in casting for a play, shrewd use of incentives, all these are some of the ways in which supervisors encourage people development.

Task Groups. Task groups are generally superior to committees as a means of people development, provided they are disbanded as each problem is solved and a new task group is formed when another problem needs attention. Standing committees permit talent to become dormant and disillusioned. The supervisor can test each employee in a variety of roles through task groups. Task group action diversifies an individual's experience.

Tutoring. Individual tutoring is a private, one-to-one relationship somewhat like the apprenticeship method of training. An experienced employee takes under his wing someone who has pronounced performance weakness and provides intensive assistance directed to the specific weaknesses; for example, an employee may have a language deficiency. This method may also benefit the tutor, if it is necessary for him or her to review subject theory as well as the practical aspects of the subject in order to help the learner.

Work/Study Methods. A combination of work and study assignments is advisable for individuals who need a bridge from school to the business or industrial world. Cooperative relationships between universities and both public and private employers in the United States began around the turn of the twentieth century and have grown steadily in number ever since. In some communities, the work/study format is an interchange experience between community college and employer and even between high school and employer. Depending on the distances between school and work place, the student may apportion day attendance time; in other cases, school and work days may alternate during the term period.

Off-the-Job Training: Group Oriented and Conventional

Conferences. Training conferences are prevalent in all organizations. They are probably the easiest form of group training activity to organize, but not much is accomplished in the great majority of them. Planning, the choice of a conference leader, and follow-through are all vital in the success of a conference. There is a fine line between a conference that is convened solely for the exchange of information and one that is intended to teach people something. The cost/benefit results of a one-week conference for training purposes are only a small fraction of the cost/benefit results of a one-week workshop.

Courses, In-service. Regular courses on a wide variety of subjects exist in many organizations. Some are offered after official hours and others are given during working hours. For example, in some organizations, refresher training courses for typists and stenographers may be run during office hours, and a course in business economics may be run after hours. Such courses are generally taught by employees of the organization, and the courses are tuition free. A record of each course taken is entered in the employee's official personnel folder.

Courses: Manufacturers and Suppliers. Many manufacturers and suppliers offer (usually as a sales incentive) training in the use of their commodities at little or no cost to the buyer. This is particularly true of complex mechanical or electronic equipment. Consuming organizations that take advantage of such offers can then claim "factory-trained mechanics" as an incentive for their own customers to buy their merchandise or services. It is well for using organizations to look carefully at courses of this kind to make sure that they are something more than sales promotion.

Courses: Outside Academic. It is standard practice for most employers to encourage their employees to take outside courses that are job-related. Most employers are willing to subsidize the tuition and fees, in whole or in part, if the employee submits evidence of a passing grade. Since such courses are normally taken after hours, the employee is making an investment—time and effort. Many institutions cater to this group by maintaining a college of general studies with off-campus meeting places, a convenience factor designed to attract employee students.

Courses: Trade Union. Unions have traditionally emphasized upgrading the skills of their members in order to enhance the bargaining power of the unions. Union-sponsored courses provide the employee with still another training and development opportunity.

Fairs and Exhibits. Every industry stages fairs and exhibits from time to time. Employees are therefore obliged to avail themselves of opportunities to keep themselves informed of the latest technological innovations by attending such activities. Attendance is customarily at the employer's expense.

Films and Other Audiovisual Aids. Some employers make a practice of showing motion pictures as a continuing education activity, even though all audiovisual aids are intended as supportive material rather than the principal vehicle of instruction. Films move so rapidly that it is difficult for people to gain anything other than some general knowledge from them. Sound filmstrips and slide/tape media are among the finest teaching aids, since they cover one point at a time at a pace conducive to learning.

Institutes. An institute is a gathering of people with common interests in a particular field of specialization. Resource people are usually there to enrich the exchange of knowledge. The larger group may subdivide at intervals to discuss tangential aspects of the broader field. Reports of proceedings provide a good follow-through means. Attendance tends to be large, often a hundred or more.

Meetings. A meeting is a less formal gathering of people, usually called for the primary purpose of discussing specific aspects of their work program. Training is a secondary or incidental objective. The meeting is often held in the office of an operating official who has overall program direction responsibility. Changes in policy or objectives frequently prompt such meetings.

Orientation. Most employers provide an orientation program for new employees. It generally begins on the day on which new employees are inducted. If more than one session is held, subsequent sessions are given daily or at intervals that will interfere minimally with ongoing operations. Such sessions are usually conducted by the training staff, and cover such matters as the organization's history, objectives, organization, and employee benefits and responsibilities. At present, no aspect of most employee training and development programs needs more improvement than orientation programs.

Seminars. A seminar is a gathering of a relatively small group of people who have common professional interests in a specialized field. Ideally, the group is limited to 10 to 15 people. Provision should be made for ample interaction and informal discussion by all participants.

Symposia. The difference between institutes, seminars, and symposia can be imperceptible, depending on the style of the coordinator. At a symposium, participants usually read prepared papers as a basis for intellectual discussion.

Television. Closed-circuit television is an expensive medium unless large numbers of people can tune in and participate in the training activity. This TV system requires cable connections to send the image from transmitter to receiving sets. It has the great advantage of being able to capitalize on the presence of a single expert to ensure quality control, but it does not allow easy feedback and interaction between participant and instructor.

Workshops. An assembly of people whose learning is acquired basically by performance under expert guidance is a workshop in which lectures and straight presentations are reduced to a minimum. Participants are required to engage in exercises and produce end products, which may be reviewed by other participants or critiqued by the workshop conductor.

Off-the-Job Training: Experiential; Group or Individually Oriented

Experiential methods afford the participant more of an opportunity to "get inside" a given set of circumstances and react as if he or she were on the scene of action. The following methods are representative of this excellent approach to training.

Case Study. Harvard University made the case study method famous by its successful application in teaching law. Each case is the recorded reconstruction of a set of circumstances with definite starting and ending points. The issues are pointed up and the personalities are as vivid as the characters in a theatrical production. The learning takes place as participants interact with the material, with the instructor, and with each other. The case is analyzed in terms of what participants think was done correctly and what mistakes they think were made relative to the context of accepted practice within their field of specialization.

In-basket Analysis. A method often used to train managers and executives is the in-basket procedure. The participant is permitted to study the contents of a senior official's "in" basket prior to the beginning of the day's work. The trainee studies each document and meditates about the action he or she would take as an occupant of the official's chair. After the day's business is finished, the participant caucuses with the official to get a post facto interpretation of what actually happened to each document and why. In this way the trainee comes to appreciate the impact that judgmental and decision-making processes have on the outcome of each transaction.

Incident Process. The incident analysis method of training is a derivative of case study, and concentrates on a small fragment of a more complex set of human relationships. It may be an explosive type of circumstance in which smoldering emotions erupt and cause a critical incident to occur. The method was introduced by Dr. Paul Pigors while he was active as a professor of psychology at M.I.T. It has tremendous impact on participants, who may become so embroiled in deciding what they would have done had they been in the situation that the moderator is compelled to have them role-play the parts, cluster around certain solutions, caucus, and have spokesmen argue their respective positions. It is an exercise in decision making because the facts are dealt out piecemeal by the moderator and therefore participants recognize the need for more information. The incident method can also be a good leadership and communications training experience if the moderator role is rotated. Prepared kits of incident process material can be purchased.

Live-in Experience. Off-the-job training that has the added feature of providing a live-in experience for participants is doubly enriching. Residential quarters, such as a suite for four participants, establishes informal communication channels that may continue to function long after a particular training activity terminates. Participants will spend a great deal of time eating together and participating in recreational activities. They will also do their home study assignments together, discuss office practices, and exchange information on work in general.

Models. Working models and prototypes enable the participant to understand the makeup of machines, housing project designs, land use schemes, transportation systems, architectural designs, and the like. Models are far superior to drawings. Although they may be expensive, they can serve as valuable training tools, and help planners and decision makers spot imperfections before costly change orders have to be written.

Retreats. The "retreat" from job surroundings was developed by the executive class out of practical necessity. Executives are constantly under such stress that they have little time to back off and get the necessary perspective on the issues they face. They find a place at a safe distance away from the work area where they can hole up for a few days or (usually) a weekend and concentrate on forward planning, budget issues, organizational planning, merchandising strategies, or whatever the current issues happen to be. Participants dress informally, are fed on site, and usually have available some built-in recreation facilities such as swimming, golf, or tennis. The retreat is a very productive practice.

Role Playing. The method of role playing grew out of psycho-drama, which is a form of cathartic therapy in which a patient acts out spontaneously some improvised situations related to his or her problem, often with the aid of others who assume the roles of other persons involved in the problem. It is an excellent means by which a participant can fully express an uninhibited appraisal of a situational condition. By videotaping and replaying the role action, the participants can study their behavioral patterns and collect constructive critiques from each other and from specialists.

Sensitivity Training. A system of sensitivity training is another contribution by behavioral scientists to the state of the art. It originated as a method in the 1940s and 1950s, when experiments were conducted over a decade or so by social researchers at one of the most reputable universities in the United States. A group of participants, usually 10 to 12 in number, engage in a week-long critique of each other, with the leader often remaining silent or merely sparking the interaction. Participants "take each other apart" by making the most caustic, biting, and stinging comments they are capable of aiming. This training is "packaged" under various faddish names by commercialists, and each appearance of the retitled basic system is loudly acclaimed by its distributors as the ultimate in leadership training. In this author's considered judgment, sensitivity training is better left on the shelf. When only a nonprofessional person is available either on or off premises to conduct sensitivity training sessions, it amounts to the blind leading the blind. The effects on some individuals can be emotionally devastating and may leave permanent scars. The method is dangerous when amateurs attempt to practice the skills of behavioral scientists and psychiatrists.

Simulation. Simulation first became popular with the introduction of the Link trainer, a device used on the ground for training aircraft pilots. This device consisted of a capsule that resembled the cockpit of an airplane. The instructor sat at a console connected to the capsule by electrical circuitry, and was able to confront the student pilot with flightlike problems to which he had to respond within the same time frame as he would encounter in flight. Noise, feel, stress, crisis, equilibrium, and other flight conditions were simulated. Common use is now being made of simulators in training for the operation of planes, automotive equipment, keyboard devices, and numerous other things. They have extraordinary value as teaching tools.

Training of Trainers. Most systems of training that require a rapid multiplier effect on a massive scale involve the training of trainers. A dry run of the training materials, used in the manner that program developers expect them to be presented on the training scene, is a good way to begin. Seasoned practitioners should be present to observe the dry run and to assist in evaluating the practice demonstrations. A few resource people can help by reviewing the laws of learning and related educational psychology concepts. A laboratory kind of checkout on audiovisual devices is also an essential part of the training of trainers. Subject-matter experts should be on call to answer questions on content.

Understudy. The understudy method is similar in objective and method to apprenticeship training, except that it tends to be used for higher-rank positions. An individual is given a semipermanent assignment to work alongside a more senior person, usually with the prospect of having the understudy grow into the position when it is vacated by the senior person's retirement, transfer, or promotion. It is expected that the close association of the two individuals will effect a transfer of knowledge, skills, and attitudes.

Vestibule Training. The term "vestibule" is said to have originated during World War I when machine workers were taught the best methods of operating the machines in a separate part of a plant before being put on the production line. Courses were intensive and given by specially qualified instructors. Although the term is not so common now, the principle has great merit and should be used by more organizations. For example, this author has long advocated that clerical and secretarial personnel should receive vestibule training before being delivered up to demanding supervisors who expect beginners to be errorproof and to know the organization's policies and practices from the outset.

An empathetic, seasoned craftsperson should run a vestibule shop, producing real work on call to offices awaiting the assignment of proficient personnel. In this way, all interested parties gain—participants, who will be graduated from the vestibule unit as they individually reach the desired proficiency level; the receiving offices where vestibule graduates are placed; and the personnel office.

Videotape. One of the most marvelous inventions of this age, from the trainer's standpoint, is videotape. The camera, tape deck, and television set as a package have the capability of capturing and instantly recreating before the eyes of the participants a scene such as the role play of a critical incident. It is especially valuable in the third-person type of instruction, such as training for selling, investigative work, public relations, counseling, and interviewing. An organization can also use videotape as a means of two-way communication between its headquarters and field personnel.

Off-the-Job Training: Self-Paced and Individually Oriented

Correspondence Courses. Comments are made in Chapter 5 on correspondence courses. They have limited utility, but under certain conditions can be made to serve a useful purpose.

Internships. In many respects the internship form of training is just another variation of apprenticeship training in the crafts. For example, medical interns are "interned" for a fixed period of time in a hospital to observe and to participate in medical practice that is supervised by senior medical practitioners. Management interns perform rotating work assignments under the supervision of a series of senior managers over a projected period of time. Young professionals in all disciplines know and generally like the pattern because it serves as a transitional period, and helps to eliminate the trial-and-error/sink-or-swim element in acquiring recognized professionalism. Modern internships are enriched by many other types of experience besides work assignment, including in-house seminars with other interns, attendance at high-level meetings, access to privileged items of official business, subsidized courses at local institutions, guided reading, leadership opportunities, communications exercises, field trips, more frequent appraisal/counseling, assignment of an advisor, and an accelerated promotion schedule. The internship form of training is exceedingly valuable as a people developer.

Journals: Trade Union and Professional Society. The mouthpiece of all employee organizations, unions, and professional societies is the newsletter or journal they publish and distribute to members. Many organizations subscribe to such publications and either place them in their library or circulate them among interested staff members. Such literature tends to pile up on desks, and only the genuinely interested employee is likely to pluck a journal from the stream, stuff it in his briefcase, and read a few selected articles at home or on the way to and from work. Some system is badly needed for expertly digesting professional society and trade union literature so that members can get the message without having to plow through the whole body of available material. Libraries might do the job if their staffs included specialists in the various disciplines. A number of journals require contributors to provide a brief summary or abstract as a preface to each article accepted for publication. A universal adoption of this policy would be a practical solution.

Practice. The cliché "practice makes perfect" has merit. Young executives might have a better record as they approach the top if their early training afforded them more practice in decision making. Teachers, actors, athletes, musicians, typists, and countless others— and their teachers and coaches—all accept this principle. Still, many training programs continue to be planned and executed without any opportunity for the participants to *practice* the new knowledge or skill under expert supervision. Training and development specialists should give preferential consideration to methods that include a practice or interaction element. Workshops are better than meetings. Internships are better than straight course work. Programmed instruction in the classroom is better than traditional correspondence courses.

Professional Societies. Young professionals accelerate their growth and development by becoming active in a professional society. This affiliation affords them continuing opportunities for associating with other professionals, hearing guest experts speak, reading the literature, making informal contacts, accepting assignments on committees, and contributing articles for possible publication. Everyone, regardless of the type of work in which one is engaged, feels the need to get together with others of similar interests to see how they approach the same type of problems.

Programmed (Self-Paced) Instruction. Programmed instruction is an outgrowth of the work of B. F. Skinner, Harvard psychologist. Its basic principle is that one learns quickest and retains the most by learning one thing at a time, systematically, with sufficient repetition and reinforcement through immediate confirmation of the accuracy of the learner's response to test questions. The programmed instruction (PI) format on the written or printed page is different from that of conventional textbook presentation. PI may also be presented to the participant by various machines, which are called "teaching machines." A teaching machine may be a device with a filmstrip projection attachment, tape cartridge with playback capability, and a responder attachment with keys. Computer-assisted instruction is essentially an application of PI.

The simplest form of programmed instruction is an unconventionally printed page with the answer strip concealed. The subject is fragmented into bits and pieces of information, each of which is presented to the learner as a "frame." After a sequence of frames, usually five or six, the student is self-tested. If his or her comprehension checks with the programmed answers, the next group of frames is attempted. If not, then the sequence is repeated until all key points are mastered.

The terms "programmed instruction" and "self-paced instruction" are practically synonymous. The latter term has become popular as the name of the method adopted at Arizona State University in 1965 and which is now established in the Center for Personalized Instruction at Georgetown University. Regardless of title or accoutrements, self-instruction has had remarkable success—in university, high school, and even lower levels. It has tremendous possibilities and is destined to make group instruction as obsolete as the horse and buggy. Resistance to change and the initial capital investment in curriculum materials development are the principal obstacles.

Reading. Guided reading is unsurpassed for people who can master how to do something merely by reading about it. Random reference to newspapers, magazines, books, and professional journals that inundate offices and homes is futile as a learning process. The people developer is highly selective in what he or she suggests for another's reading consideration. A slim book containing specific information, a reprint of a single article, a newspaper clipping, mention of an upcoming special television program, a position paper on a controversial issue—these are a few examples of the selection technique used to gather training media.

Sabbatical Leave. Progressive organizations offer sabbatical leave as a fringe benefit to their professional personnel, as a means of self-renewal. This special form of leave may afford full or partial pay. The employee, after the specified number of years of uninterrupted service (usually 6 to 8), must show intent and good faith by advancing a plan to show how the time will be used to acquire new knowledge and accomplish the self-renewal objective. When properly planned and coordinated with the other commitments and intra-family responsibilities, the sabbatical leave can be mutually rewarding for the employee, immediate family members, and the employer.

Teaching Assignments. One of the finest ways to learn, grow, and reap a full measure of self-fulfillment is to teach. Organizations with in-service training facilities would be well advised to promote teaching tours as a prestige assignment, and to rotate selected staff and line operations people through such facilities. If there is no in-service training facility, the next best move would be to arrange for employees to take long-range leaves of absence to accept a teaching assignment elsewhere. This is also an excellent way to spend a sabbatical leave. Some employees in metropolitan areas are able to have the best of both worlds by combining their bread-and-butter work with an after-hours teaching assignment, which usually requires several hours of one evening a week.

Tests. A good way to trigger the motivation to learn more about a subject is to begin with a test experience. It can be self-administering or it can be built into the design of a training program. Obviously, tests need to be valid, practical measures of useful knowledge and skill. Quiz-kid types of tests are counterproductive. Training programs in general would yield far better cost/benefit results if more provision were made for pretesting, post-testing, and OJT follow-through.

Conclusion

The leaders of organizations should take a hard look at how employees of their organizations are trained and developed. They should support studies to determine to what extent individualized instruction methods are transplanting conventional *group* methods, which so often condone the erroneous assumption that the needs of a selected group of individuals are exactly alike at the time a given course or program is to be run. Managements should make sure that enough people developers are present and capable of selecting methods that will produce the greatest cost-effective results.

11

Producing
Curriculum Materials

CURRICULUM materials do not just evolve spontaneously. They have to be produced and planned in a deliberate manner. The proverbial professor who talks "off the cuff" may well have used the same ideas and clichés for so many years that he has committed his subject matter to memory and needs no props or cues.

The surest way for a program coordinator to lose control of the content of training programs is to have a series of guest artists appear, like guests on a TV "talk show," and perform without benefit of curriculum materials designed to balance and time the presentation, adhere to sequence and priority of subjects, illustrate and stimulate participant interaction, and provide cohesion and integration with other elements of the curriculum.

One of the primary responsibilities of a director of employee training is curriculum development, which in this book means the process of conceptualizing and making ready for use the necessary curriculum materials of the desired quality by whatever process is economically and administratively the most practicable. This chapter discusses the several basic strategies of producing curriculum materials, including both written and audiovisual aids. It also suggests a few cost yardsticks and reminds the reader of quality assurance considerations.

Strategies for Producing Curriculum Materials

Of course some hard decisions have to be made before one can cross the bridge to curriculum production work. What organizational and individual training and development needs are to be met by the curriculum materials? What are the qualification requirements necessary to teach such material? What is the nature of the learning environment? What socioeconomic and political factors will influence the learning situation? How can the new knowledge, skills, and attitudes be applied in order to support management's philosophy and objectives?

With these and other related questions settled in advance, one can begin to come to terms with the strategy problem. However, another good preliminary step in approaching the strategy decision is to do some simple research to find what materials exist already and in what modality for the particular subject to be taught. There may be a clearinghouse or library collection with sample curricula worth scanning. A large public or private agency with an active training structure may have a program that could serve with minor modification. There may even be some possibilities within your own organization. Professional people tend to squirrel away outlines for talks, articles, and papers they have written or collected, or notes they have made at conferences and professional meetings. They are often generous in sharing such material, particularly when a credit by-line is given to their material in the end product. The strategies discussed below are arranged in this author's order of preference, based on many years of experience in directing the production of curriculum materials.

BEG OR BORROW. The first and perhaps the cheapest strategy is to beg or borrow from any reliable source available, either in-house or off-premise. Obviously, there are no absolutely free sources of curriculum materials, and one should not let oneself conclude that there is. If there are, they are likely to be "canned" curriculum materials, which are nearly always available in any field. Quality suffers when one takes and uses such material on an as-is basis without necessary modification. One must adapt, not adopt. And the cost of adapting is one of the costs of curriculum development, for it takes time and human effort. There is also the inevitable possibility that any source willing to lend or give away curriculum materials will expect either some similar goods or services in return. Therefore, acceptance of gratuitous offers probably only defers the cost of your own curriculum materials production. Beg or borrow discretely and make the necessary advance calculation on what that strategy will ultimately cost your organization.

PURCHASE. Increasingly, curriculum materials are being produced commercially to fit certain instructional modes. For example, there is a wide choice of programmed instruction material in the basic education field. Programs in reading improvement, mathematics, English, general science, electricity, and electronics and related fields are relatively inexpensive and need no modification. A comprehensive catalog of such materials is available in large libraries. One university is reported to have abandoned the teaching of statistics in conventional form with professors and has converted to teaching machines and programmed (self-paced) instruction. Some of the larger publishers offer instructional guides, textbooks, and audiovisual (A/V) aids as a package.

In weighing this choice, one needs to consider how many cycles of the course will eventually be run. Commercially available materials are copyrighted and normally cannot be reproduced without the express permission of the copyright holder. Therefore, the initial purchase may be only the beginning of the cost. If it is a field that is subject to dynamic changes, the material will be revised frequently and may require updating the material holdings of the entire target audience from time to time. As already suggested, one curriculum item is sometimes interlocked with other items, so that the purchase of a $10 textbook may end up as a $35 investment per participant counting workbooks, instructor's guide, A/V aids, and supplementary handout materials.

The great advantage of the purchase plan is that it can be a swift solution to the need for curriculum materials. The caution is to check by telephone or letter in advance to make sure the materials are available in the quantity needed and that a purchase order will be honored upon receipt. Many a training coordinator has been sorely disappointed when outside orders of materials failed to arrive by the scheduled date of use.

PRODUCE MATERIALS WITH IN-HOUSE CAPABILITY. There are several means of producing perfectly satisfactory curriculum materials on the premises. It is this author's judgment that materials can be provided better, cheaper, and faster inside than by contracting with outside organizations. There are four specific approaches to accomplishing the job inside. These are discussed briefly below.

Using Nucleus Staff. Many organizations have a training and development staff of sufficient size to include a nucleus curriculum development unit. Such a unit presumably has one or more persons who are already well oriented to the mission, goals, policies, objectives, and methodology of the parent organization. They can move expeditiously into the heart of the curriculum development problem. They have well-established channels of communication, and they can tap auxiliary support service groups for background materials, graphics, printing and duplicating, and other support. Their work will require fewer reviews, since it is of a known level of reliability.

Such a group enjoys the confidence of the director and the senior staff, and can respond to priorities without the pressure of the profit motive, which may pull a private group off your job at a critical juncture and deploy it to the job of a regular customer or a larger customer. In other words, when the director elects to go the in-house route, the responsibility for attaining a reasonable completion date target is a concomitant of that decision. This is true because failure to provide materials to a particular project may require the director to reassign a curriculum unit from another project that had expected to finish on time, but which would be delayed as a result of material transfer.

Using Task Groups. Every organization, public or private, has a domain of technical know-how that it has developed from its beginning, and there is no better source of curriculum material development help than the practitioners who handle that technical expertise. The director of training and career development is advised to draw on that bank of knowledge and experience. Even though the training office staff may consist of only a secretary, a task group of in-house experts can be marshaled to help organize a program. The group can help set behavioral objectives, make the basic outline, identify reference materials, do rough scripts, collect photographs and other visual materials, and describe case histories and incidents worthy of use for experiential purposes. If the subject is one that lends itself to unitization, more than one task group may be formed.

In the composition of task groups, it is well to provide a balance of talent. Technical experts naturally have a tendency to emphasize their technical specialties. A visual presentation specialist can see ways to illustrate the material to facilitate learning. A training specialist has a sense of timing that dictates a change of pace and the use of multimedia methods to present a topic. An executive-level person may want to interject some policy considerations to counterbalance the technical minutia. A field person has the practical operator's view, and the headquarters official may be more interested in the economic or political issues. Hence, it is well to subject the developmental process to the scrutiny of persons who individually bring different perceptions to the worktable and who collectively inject balance into the program.

A distinct advantage of the task group approach is that it involves the very interests that will ultimately profit most from a successful training and development venture. Joint venture is a key to consensual acceptance and adoption of the program.

Using a Temporarily Expanded In-house Staff. The early retirement options of the federal civil service and a considerable number of private industries are making available to the training specialist a wealth of talent for temporary duty. This talent is available on short call, and retired individuals welcome an invitation to lend a hand on an interesting new project. Because they require minimal orientation to the curriculum development work, and are experienced in working against deadlines, they can serve as team members, or individually, with wide latitude for independent judgment.

The recruitment and selection of temporary staff for curriculum development is something that can be accomplished expeditiously if "personal patronage" is used as a means of spotting qualified and available persons. Merit system registers may be useful if one has sufficient time to run reference checks and await the often time-consuming procedures for certifying eligibles. Presumably, such registers are largely made up of persons who are seeking long-term appointments on which to base careers. Seasoned retired people usually do not wish to have their names on registers, since they already have an established source of income. It is well, therefore, to check around among a few professional contacts, identify a group of people with outstanding recommendations, and then establish a selection panel and conduct interviews. Over a month's time it is possible to assemble a corps of able curriculum development specialists and have the project under way.

It is reasonable to assign specific project responsibility to the temporary staff members, particularly if they have technical specialties as well as curriculum development experience. For example, an individual with an engineering background and curriculum experience would be a logical candidate to take the lead on any aspect of the curriculum that has engineering implications. A person with a specialty in creative writing might be assigned to the script work that supports the audiovisual aid productions.

Temporary staff members can easily develop a pioneering spirit if they can be motivated to see the importance and urgency of the curriculum project. They will work long hours, without regard to the clock, to meet self-imposed commitments on quality and quantity of production. Their pride of authorship and creativity is a strong inner drive, and they need minimal supervision and coordination. Financial independence does a great deal to relieve the stresses and tensions that beset people who were once competing for their place in the sun.

Contracting for Outside Assistance. A last, but by no means inadequate, resort is to contract with an outside group to produce the necessary curriculum materials. The federal government has specific procurement regulations, which have to be faithfully observed in reaching for external sources of talent. These regulations provide a model for organizations in the private sector and may be adopted in toto or modified.

The federal regulations are time consuming and do not necessarily result in an award going to the best qualified firm. Competitive bidding usually determines what price you pay for outside help. The best procedure is to obtain at least three bids from qualified firms. A representative of each firm should be interviewed in depth to assess the capability of the firm to respond by the target completion date with an end product that meets your quality standards. It is even better to visit each of the firms to whom serious consideration is being given after sealed bids are opened. Reference checks with previous clients is good insurance. Regional or local firms are generally more satisfactory than remotely based firms.

A system for monitoring progress should be clearly established in the contract specifications. Preferably, the invitation to bid should include a penalty clause for failure to complete the work on schedule. Without this, there is less incentive to reach interim target dates. Every effort should be made to meet the customer organization's obligations under the contract, such as making installment payments on schedule, completing the review of interim curriculum materials submissions promptly, and acting on contract amendments decisively.

Development of Written Materials

Certain categories of curriculum materials recur repeatedly in the work of training and development staffs. Each of these deserves some comment in a book like this. The guidelines suggested below are applicable, regardless of the strategy chosen to produce a given set of curriculum materials. A typical specification is given in Appendix III.

EXPERIENTIAL EXERCISE MATERIALS. One of the best tests of a set of curriculum materials besides the fundamental requirement of content validity, balance, and change of pace, is the provision for participant interaction with the material itself, with the instructor, and with other participants. There are many ways to ensure interaction, including: role playing, critical incidents, case study, lecture/discussion, problem-solving workshops, videotaping, panels, buzz sessions, tests, practice performances with self-critiquing, practice teaching, use of teaching machines, computer-assisted instruction, programmed instruction, participant demonstrations, team projects, management games, and others.

The development of materials for experiential forms of training should be a cooperative venture between the curriculum staff and operating officials. The material needs to be grounded in realistic operations methodology and terminology. Canned materials make it difficult for reluctant learners to adapt such materials to their work environment. For instance, a critical incident that actually occurred in the past is superior to an imaginary one, especially if the actual disposition of the incident can be reconstructed and used for post-mortem discussion purposes. A series of decisions with which the organization's administrators were confronted in the past is better role-playing material than are hypothetical issues. Workshop problems involving some actual fiscal data of the organization are preferable to those based on contrived figures.

Such materials should be carefully labeled and coordinated as a package so that each exercise can proceed smoothly and without confusion. The instructional leader needs special guidelines to cue emphasis on the dominant principles and key points of each exercise.

Since the cost of curriculum materials can be a substantial factor in the budget when the program is run on a continuing cycle basis, it may be feasible to reclaim some of the experiential exercise materials.

REFERENCE MANUALS. Many programs of a continuing nature, such as orientation manuals for new employees, may be compiled as separate projects by the technicians of the organization who have the best available knowledge. Many such manuals are difficult to use from the learner's standpoint. The writer has to resolve the dilemma of whether the manual should be organized as a reference tool or as a self-teaching text as the reader works his way through it.

A reference manual is a poor substitute for a training program, although some organizations limit their training effort to it. Ideally, it should *supplement* a well-organized program of presentation, practice, A/V aids, discussion, home study, and follow-up activities. A compromise between an encyclopedia format and one that permits the material to flow in the sequence in which an employee performs the work is possible.

A well-planned table of contents and a comprehensive index are necessary. Appendixes with such material as flow charts, process charts, completed facsimile forms, maps, and the like are useful. A list of answers to commonly asked questions is also helpful.

HANDOUT MATERIAL. Materials that are worth distribution in training and development programs are deserving of special attention by those who prepare them. Every handout item should preferably be

> Printed or duplicated by a process that renders it legible and easily read.
> Identified with an appropriate heading.
> Dated.
> Prepunched neatly and precisely with a three-hole punch.
> Coordinated with the sequence of events in the program.
> Accompanied, if possible, by a loose-leaf notebook with the name of the organization and training program embossed on the cover.

Development of Audiovisual Materials

The same strategies as those for written material are open to the training and career development director with respect to the development of audiovisual materials. Again the choice is between the use of in-house or off-premise facilities. More capital outlay is usually required for A/V materials because of the equipment needed to produce film in quantity. The following guidelines are suggested.

MOTION PICTURES. Motion pictures are one of the poorest forms of training aids, perhaps even the poorest, because people are accustomed to watching motion pictures and television as entertainment. They often fall asleep in doing so unless the action is very exciting. The film will not slow down, stop, or back up for difficult points, unlike videotape cameras that can furnish "instant replay" service to viewers. Moreover, they run too long and cover too much for convenient learning purposes.

Motion pictures are quite expensive and they are not easy to update. The equipment is harder to operate than most other A/V aids and the unit cost of equipping all work stations is usually prohibitive. If one has a compelling reason for the use of motion pictures in training and development work, all possible sources of loan and rental should be exhausted before considering original production. If production is the choice, it is best to contract with a firm that has full production capability, rather than deal separately with a series of contractors as production progresses. A panel representing all in-house interests should be chosen in advance of the contract award so that timely decisions can be reached on questions referred by the contractor. It is important to stipulate in the contract all mutual agreements with respect to copyrights, credits, cost of prints, and relevant post-production distribution.

SOUND FILMSTRIPS. The use of 35 mm filmstrips with synchronized magnetic tape for sound is unsurpassed as an economical and effective means of A/V support for training programs, particularly where the work force is widely scattered and many copies of the material are needed. It is much easier to make, or contribute to the making of, sound filmstrips than it is to make motion pictures.

A task group can develop the outline of content. Someone with even a slight artistic touch can do rough sketches of the proposed visual prints. An in-house photographer or anyone handy with a camera can collect prints from which usable scenes can be culled and retouched and cropped. Persons with a clear, pleasant voice usually can be found within the organization to do the audio portion if a low budget is a consideration. If one can afford the cost of a professional, such as an experienced radio or television personality who "moonlights," it is well worth the extra cost. A professional's pacing, emphasis, and tonal qualities add authenticity to the end product. A sound filmstrip should not exceed 15 to 20 minutes in length.

SLIDES. Slides are the ultimate in flexibility. They can be replaced easily and inexpensively as changes occur, and synchronized tapes can be recut or oral scripts can be rewritten. Slides are the most practicable when the requirement is for a relatively small number of slide sets. When hundreds or thousands of sets are needed, the sound filmstrip is by far the best choice.

Equipment for handling slides and tape together is considerably more expensive than sound filmstrip equipment. Moreover, a trainer has better control of the learning situation with sound filmstrips than he has with slides, as participants are less likely to interrupt while the subject is being presented in a 15 to 20 minute sequence.

VIDEOTAPE. The most useful teaching tool ever made, from the trainer's standpoint, is videotape. It is particularly valuable for "third person" training; that is, when someone needs direction by a trainer in how to deal with a third person, such as in interviews, investigations, and public relations. There are some cautions.

For example, if one is establishing a "delivery system" for technical know-how throughout the organization, and playback equipment is needed at a number of locations, a careful cost analysis is essential. The width of the videotape is critical; half-inch tape is much cheaper, but it has limitations. Compatibility is also a big factor, since videotape depositories that lend and rent tapes are now standardizing. If an organization intends to do much videotape recording for distribution to its field locations, it would be better to have a small studio constructed with relatively soundproof features, good lighting, and a few basic "sets" for staging purposes. This assures uniformity of material for general distribution.

PROJECTOR MATERIAL. Glossy prints, 8 x 10 inches in size, are an excellent means of illustrating instructional material. They can be projected with an opaque projector, arranged on tack boards, or circulated among participants. They are inexpensive and easy to manage. A commentator can interpret them one at a time as appropriate.

An overhead projector, the successor to the chalkboard, is another great aid. The trouble is that too many trainers lack the initiative to prepare their material in advance. With this equipment, one can project overhead transparencies, point, erase, use hinged overlays—all in a lighted room while facing the participants—and pace the material to suit the learners' grasp of the content. These are advantages over motion pictures, which are run from the back of the room, with the lights out or dimmed, full speed from start to finish. In contrast, overhead projector transparencies are presentable one at a time and lend themselves beautifully to a question-and-answer period. The visuals can easily be filed in ordinary folders and used repeatedly. They can be produced inexpensively in-house on several types of duplicating equipment, and operation is much faster and cleaner than the laborious chalkboard exercise. With a chalkboard, one's back is to the audience and visibility may not be nearly so good, depending on the quality of the writing surface and room conditions.

HOOK-AND-LOOP BOARDS AND MAGNETIC BOARDS. These media have waned in popularity as overhead projectors and videotape have been introduced. There are still situations in which they can be very useful and they are faster and more economical than nearly any other device save the chalkboard. The great advantage is in the psychology of being able to focus the learner's attention on one point at a time, and the ease of flashback or repetition.

Hook-and-loop material, a fascinating system, is even used in wearing apparel. One strip of fabric surface has a vast number of tiny hooks, and the opposite surface to be "fastened" consists of an equal number of tiny loops that interlock as one surface is pressed against the other. They can be easily pulled apart without damage to either surface. The original version of this device was known as the "flannel board" because the fibers of the flannel provided a surface to which the material with hooks could adhere. Flannel boards became obsolete because the hook backing sometimes fell off and spoiled the presentation.

EASELS. An easel serves somewhere between the chalkboard and the overhead projector. Presentations can be prepared in advance, done easily with grease pencils or felt pens in multicolor, and saved for future use. Two or more easels can be used during a presentation to enlarge the viewing surface and provide flexibility in sequencing the points to be covered. A pad of blank paper can be used to record participant inputs. Pages can be torn off and laid aside, or taped to other room surfaces. Easels are collapsible for ease in carrying from one place to another, whereas chalkboards are usually stationary.

EXHIBITS. Good libraries and museums are skilled in the use of exhibits for educational purposes. Training specialists do not use them nearly enough. An exhibit is an excellent means, for example, of providing continuing orientation to both employees or clients and customers. They afford opportunities for the involvement of key members of the organization. They can be made mobile. They can be constructed in ways to be semiautomatic for use in lobbies, cafeterias, and other public places. Outside exhibitors are often interested in contributing to an exhibit in appropriate ways.

MODELS. Many organizations have a shop in which industrial art skills are practiced. The training and development staff can make good use of such skills in the design and development of working models to simulate actual operations of the organization. For example, the Federal Highway Administration uses models to illustrate complex interstate highway designs. The Federal Aviation Administration uses them to illustrate airport traffic control patterns. Local fire-fighter and police schools use them in countless ways. This author once used a professionally made model to advance a proposal for the establishment of a network of employee development centers in which optimum space layout, decor, and space utilization were salient features.

Some Cost Yardsticks

The production of curriculum materials cannot be ignored as a budget item, regardless of whether the work is done in-house or contracted out to private firms. A training staff is advised to compare the cost of both approaches—time, if done inside, and contract dollars if done outside. Unfortunately, there are no rigid formulas for measuring cost because of such things as competitive bidding, fluctuating economies, variances in scope of work among similar projects, production deadlines, and varying amounts of in-house input.

There has long been a rule-of-thumb yardstick for having 16mm motion pictures commercially produced. The cost begins at $1,000 per running minute of film-in-the-can ready for viewing, and increases as other expenses are added, such as filming at a remote locale, extra cast, script changes, background music, and service. The production of 35mm slide or filmstrip programs is less expensive. One can count on having them cost about one-third as much as the 16mm motion picture film, or a range of $3,000 to $6,000 for a 15-minute presentation ready for use.

In the development of written curriculum materials, a fairly reliable measure is to calculate the cost of creative effort on the basis of 3 man-hours of time for each hour of classroom instruction. In other words, the compiler of a 1-hour presentation will have to work an average of 3 hours in researching the topic, outlining, sequencing, specifying A/V aids, and doing other related curriculum development tasks. It may take much longer, and in some instances may take less. This ratio suggests that a last-minute substitution in a chain of guest lecturers for a training program may be costly.

In planning for classroom manpower, one should estimate a minimum of 2 man-hours of staff for each hour of instruction. Manpower may consist of the classroom principal plus an aide for most of the time, or an instructional coordinator plus a roster of part-time resource people, audiovisual technicians, and guest appearances of organization officials.

Quality Assurance

The production of curriculum materials—as does the production of shoes, automobiles, or anything else—needs strict control for quality assurance purposes. This applies to both in-house productions and off-premise contracts. The scope-of-work clause in the contract, together with careful monitoring, is the best insurance against faulty end products. A loose, ambiguous specification can result in curriculum materials that completely miss the mark.

The trainer's guide is another excellent means of quality control. It sets the parameters for the curriculum development specialist (provided it contains a good outline prepared and approved in advance), and it sequences, paces, times, and orchestrates the subject matter in the most effective manner that can be conceived by the development specialist.

One can, by experience, develop a set of good quality standards for A/V aids to illustrate the program operations of an organization. As in writing, simplicity and clarity are paramount requisites. The span of a viewer's attention has long been regarded by commercial media specialists to be about 15 minutes, so change of pace and sequencing are important attributes. Any visual frame that stays on the screen longer than 45 seconds loses the audience. Color is essential. Clearly articulated script by a pleasant voice is a must.

The quality of any curriculum material depends on its being the result of a successful joint venture between, on the one hand, one or more subject-matter experts and, on the other hand, one or more training specialists who also have A/V support. Quality of instruction, then, is the blend of knowledge and talent and a multimedia approach that yields the most useful vehicle for people development.

Conclusion

Top management of organizations should have the quality of curriculum materials examined periodically to make sure that training and development programs are not being run on a "talk show" basis by in-house and outside "guest artists." They should establish a priority system such as the four-option plan suggested by this chapter to control the strategy used when curriculum materials must be provided for a program. They should require that all group instruction be conducted with a trainer's guide. They should make sure that contracts for outside assistance contain a tightly worded scope-of-work element to assure the quality of curriculum materials produced and careful monitoring of contractor performance. They should monitor the choice of audiovisual aids and reject those that cannot be mass-produced economically and which cannot serve widely scattered employees efficiently.

12

Assembling and Controlling Training Aids

$\mathbf{T}$RAINING aids support people development programs, but no aid alone can substitute for even the simplest type of training program. As audiovisual (A/V) technology has grown in complexity and diversity of choice, the training and development specialist has had to assume much greater responsibility for knowing the market, for the management of the procurement process, for reflecting the state of A/V aid technology in curriculum design, and for good property management and accountability.

The Challenge

Take, for example, the position of the director of employee training and career development of a large public service or private organization. The director may have substantive and property accountability for thousands of units of equipment scattered widely throughout national or world branches. Equipment that is obsolete, undependable, hard to transport, or difficult to use is an expensive asset of questionable value. The best of equipment is a liability if the organization lacks the ability to provide it economically, or if usage over its reasonable life expectancy is not sufficient to justify its purchase.

The assembly and control of a practical and productive set of training aids, whether used by a small one-person training office or a chain of instruction centers, should be undertaken and carried forward as skillfully as the planning of the curriculum content.

Basic Set of Aids

When a buildings maintenance technician is assigned to service a building, what tools should he keep on hand? When does he rent or borrow tools instead of buy tools? How does he keep track of what he owns? When called by a tenant to solve a specific problem, what tools does he select from his entire collection and take to the work site? What about maintenance and updating of his tools?

These same questions apply to the people developer. As in so many human equations, the best answer is some form of compromise between the extremes. A buildings maintenance technician would be extravagant, to say the least, to buy one of every tool in existence. It would be even more ridiculous if he were to insist on having the latest model of every tool made. Obviously, he has to make some choices. A basic set of tools for the buildings maintenance technician and a basic set of training aids for the people developer makes good sense.

At this point, the items that comprise a "basic set" will be identified.

Chapter 11 categorized commonly needed training aids. From those categories, one might begin a small-scale training and development operation with a basic set that contains the following items:

1. Several easels
2. Several pull-down screens
3. Overhead projector
4. Opaque projector
5. Slide projector
6. Filmstrip projector
7. Sound/filmstrip projector
8. Tape recorder
9. 16mm motion picture projector, with audio-input capability for synchronizing a speaker's commentary with the visual presentation

10. A still camera for producing negatives for 8 x 10 inch glossy prints

11. A battery of simple teaching machines for learner-paced programs such as basic education and specialized programs relevant to the organization

12. A set of individual study carrels

13. A basic set of videotape equipment, including camera, tape deck, TV playback unit, and essential accessories

These items will cost $12,000 to $15,000, depending on models and makes selected and the number of units of learner-paced equipment and individual study carrels. If one needs to phase in holdings of this magnitude, the order in which the items are listed above is not a bad one for sequencing their purchase over whatever period one's budget dictates.

How to Acquire Audiovisual Aids

Interestingly, the options for meeting A/V aid requirements are not much different from those for meeting the curriculum materials requirements discussed in Chapter 11: beg or borrow (transfer or loan), purchase commercially available units (off-the-shelf purchase), produce with in-house capability (in-house construction), and contract outside for units built to your specifications.

This section will discuss these elements of materials applications in relation to their acquisition possibilities, and the principal advantages or disadvantages of each method.

TRANSFERS AND LOANS. Transfer or loan of equipment is a perfectly viable option under limited circumstances. For example, the training office may operate within an organization that has invested heavily in A/V equipment to support its public or customer relations effort. It makes sense to borrow equipment from another department in the company if it is accessible and available for a given period of time.

Another source is a nonprofit film library. It makes sense to borrow, and even pay a modest rental if necessary, rather than buy.

There are situations, however, in which this option is unsatisfactory. If a training requirement involves the development and continuing use of a massive delivery system, hundreds or perhaps even thousands of A/V units will be needed. Granted that it might be feasible to borrow (from schools, churches, and local government agencies) enough to stage the program each time, it would be foolish to attempt it because the conglomerate of diverse makes, models, and states of repair, in addition to the intricate spare parts problem, would soon bring training to a standstill. Moreover, operator competence would be impossible to assure because of the distance from the sources and communications factors. No competent training director will attempt to conduct a program when its success might be completely nullified by equipment unreliability.

OFF-THE-SHELF PURCHASE. It may be cheaper from an economic standpoint, and smarter program administration, to buy audiovisual equipment, even though the budget may force the director to settle for less units at the outset than will be eventually needed. The essence of a master-plan approach is to plan intelligently, know where the program is supposed to go, and make progress at a comfortable pace. This assumes that there are readily available items of hardware, at reasonable unit prices, to meet current and foreseeable needs. Competitive bidding among suppliers should squeeze out excessive profits.

For example, a videotape system may be needed for headquarters and regional offices, and finally for district and a few of the larger local offices. The important thing is to research the state of the art, check comparative prices in the marketplace, and decide what is in the best interest of the training program for the next five to ten years. If a half-inch system is chosen hurriedly because it is cheaper, the choice may be self-defeating because videotape libraries may be changing to wider tape. It may be that the system is cheap because it is obsolete and is being dumped on the market.

Before making a hard decision, ask several distributors to leave a demonstrator model for trial and to demonstrate to interested officials of the organization. Also ask for opinions of other users of the makes and models to which serious consideration is being given. Their experience may tip the choice. The budget office should be a party to the decision, since it is in effect the departmental banker. The contract officer should act as agent, of course, in effecting any large-scale or open-ended procurement transactions.

The availability of preventive maintenance is a vital part of the decision to buy, for the organization's investment can be depreciated unless expensive repairs can be avoided. Meticulous record keeping, suspense systems for maintenance scheduling, and taking advantage of equipment guarantees are critical in realizing the full and useful life expectancy of audiovisual aids.

IN-HOUSE CONSTRUCTION. Homemade A/V aids can be most effective and they are economical. For example, suppose the requirement is for a mobile exhibit for use in various cities to interpret a new activity of the organization. A good industrial arts shop may be accessible on the premises, one maintained to serve objectives other than employee training and development. Such shops generally have plenty of expertise and are usually very much interested and eager when asked to apply their skills and tools to a project that is different from routine work. Even if a few components must be bought, such as audio items, the shop still feels a sense of pride of craftsmanship and will go out of its way to make a superior product.

Chapter 9 described my experience in directing the production of a series of sound filmstrips as a part of the A/V aid productions for a Census of the United States. The art work, scripts, photography, and design were all done by in-house staff members. Commercial laboratories were used to make the master print of each filmstrip, record the audio commentary, and mass-produce prints and phonograph records. It takes careful coordination between in-house groups and any outside auxiliary suppliers, but this is not difficult if sufficient time is allowed for the production schedule. It is far better to have control over the substantive portions of A/V aid productions, and leave to industry the task of reproducing masters, than it is to farm out all production.

Using the in-house staff can itself be a development experience for employees who become involved in A/V aid productions. Such work may uncover a secondary skill, such as photography or cartooning, and enable an employee in a dead-end job to discover dormant talents and eventually enjoy upward mobility. The flexibility with which an organization authorizes overtime adds additional assurance to the production coordinator's commitment to finish the in-house project by the scheduled target date.

A training staff with a nucleus A/V capability will, in time, accumulate a number of devices that are useful in putting a professional touch on in-house products. For example, the devices and materials that simplify the tasks of titling, labeling, spiral binding, collation, film editing, legends, chart symbols, hole punching, stapling laminations, and the like are great time savers.

Admittedly, it is difficult to assess the true costs of in-house A/V productions. A custom-built house costs more than a mass-produced house, and the same may be true of A/V aids made on the premises as a one-time product. Therefore, it may be better to use in-house talents when there is no pressing deadline. By making use of these talents when employees have valleys in their work load, it may be considerably cheaper to do the job inside than to farm it out to commercial firms.

CONTRACTING FOR OUTSIDE ASSISTANCE. Throughout my experience I have had several opportunities to test the thesis I have advanced in this chapter; namely, that when an organization has an audiovisual requirement for a relatively large number of equipment units, it should take the initiative and expect the market to meet its specifications, rather than go shopping and buy on an "as is" basis.

A recent example of this policy occurred in 1972 when an organization had a large requirement (15,000 to 20,000 units) for sound/filmstrip devices in order to establish a delivery system that would communicate the best known ways of doing certain tasks to thousands of nonurban employees. On request, a qualified research group developed a highly sophisticated set of technical specifications to control the competitive bidding process. An outline of these specifications is included below to show the comprehensiveness of the specification. Interestingly, equipment meeting these specifications was available for roughly half of what other sound/filmstrip devices cost, and the cheaper model had many desirable features that others lacked.

If a company elects to contract for outside assistance, it is absolutely essential that several steps be taken, to safeguard a major investment. First, expert assistance in devising the technical specifications for bidding purposes will be needed. Obviously, this includes an impartial expert who has no vested interests in the products of any supplier. Government agencies have government laboratories to call on for help. Many private organizations have scientific laboratories or research and development facilities, and use their personnel or engage expert consultants.

Another precaution is that every step in a sound procurement system must be observed. For example, the purchase contract should be studied and approved by an attorney. A good bidder list should be developed before the request for procurement (RFP) is circulated. An on-site plant inspection should be made of several of the more promising bidders. During production, on-site inspections should be made periodically to ensure that the target delivery date will in fact be met by the contractor. A quality control procedure should be followed faithfully in receiving and accepting the merchandise. A good history of the procurement project should be kept for future reference.

A Technical Specification for Procurement of a Sound/Filmstrip Projector

OBJECTIVES OF PROCUREMENT

The procurement is to obtain audiovisual education devices meeting the following:
1. Multimedia capability employing audio and visual media.
2. Synchronized A/V capability.
3. Portable and mailable.
4. Durable.
5. Easy, low-cost maintenance.
6. Individually viewable.
7. Usable in home environment for self-study.
8. Possible to connect some type of simple operator response (or feedback control) to the audiovisual device to indicate a right or wrong answer.

FUNCTIONAL REQUIREMENTS

A. *Optical Performance*
　　1. Film size and image format
　　2. Screen size
　　3. Magnification
　　4. Viewing angle
　　5. Screen-area luminance
　　6. Screen contrast
　　7. Effects of glare
　　8. Resolution across screen
　　9. Distortion across screen
　　10. Color rendition
　　11. Focus control
　　12. Length of filmstrip
　　13. Projection lenses
　　14. Mirrors
　　15. Condenser lenses and heat-absorbing glass
　　16. Projection lamp
　　17. Ease of cleaning

B. *Audio Performance*
　　1. Type of cassette
　　2. Tape configuration
　　3. Stepping/cueing system
　　4. Length of reproducing time
　　5. Audio quality
　　6. Reproduce amp. output
　　7. Reproduce system response

C. *Mechanical Performance*
　　1. Size, weight, and shape
　　2. Sturdy construction
　　3. Lubrication
　　4. Maintenance and operational convenience
　　5. Drop resistance
　　6. Noise
　　7. Filmstrip advance
　　8. Wear of filmstrips and magnetic tapes
　　9. Ambient temperature control
　　10. Filmstrip temperature rise
　　11. Vibration
　　12. Safety
　　13. General life test

D. *Electrical Performance*
　　1. Power
　　2. Power-cable assembly
　　3. Circuit control
　　4. Components, wiring, connectors, and print boards
　　5. Safety

E. *Human Factors*
　　1. Portability
　　2. Convenience in loading filmstrips and magnetic tape cassettes
　　3. Style and appearance
　　4. Ease of operation
　　5. Labeling of controls and connections
　　6. Ease of maintenance
　　7. Training necessary to permit use of audiovisual device

F. *Miscellaneous*
　　1. Interactive response
　　2. Headphone jack
　　3. Cartridge loading, operation, and storage of 35mm filmstrips
　　4. Carrying and storage case
　　5. "Mailable" case
　　6. Warranty and service
　　7. User operating manual
　　8. Service manual

Standardization and Interchangeability

Standardization and interchangeability of training hardware is an area on which both public and private sectors need to concentrate and make some real progress. All the necessary machinery for coordinating standardization and interchangeability is in place: the General Services Administration for federal units and trade associations and professional societies for the private sector.

The federal government and large private organizations need to reconsider their procurement policies. The tendency is nearly always to buy what the marketplace is featuring, rather than take the initiative, develop a set of technical specifications, and contract with the lowest responsible bidder to produce items that meet the precise requirements of training and development programs. By buying higher-priced existing models, rather than lower-priced special models, organizations with large and scattered target audiences are likely to end up with too few units to serve their networks of decentralized organizational elements.

Training-aid supply systems do not usually *ask* training and development practitioners what they need. Instead, they stage fairs and exhibits to promote the sale of existing hardware. Too often, these promotional efforts result in imbalances between curriculum software and the readily available hardware.

The Bureau of the Census, U.S. Department of Commerce, has on several occasions demonstrated the feasibility of the proposition that the buyer can make his own market, from inception of a hardware need to the delivery of the end product. By collaborating with the National Bureau of Standards in the development of technical specifications for the production of 5,000 small filmstrip projectors and 5,000 small phonograph record players for training a civilian army of enumerators, vast savings for the taxpayers were realized. The projector and record player together cost $31 for each of the 5,000 training locations, and the same projector alone began immediately to sell commercially for $65.

The universal interchangeability of training software in standardized equipment should be another important objective of both the public and private sectors. This applies to such items as filmstrips, audiotapes, videotapes, slides, teaching machine materials used in programmed instruction, computer-assisted materials, and other items. Repositories are being established, but they cannot be of maximum service to their user publics unless they can stock fully interchangeable software items.

An ongoing problem is the failure of large "single" employers to join in centralizing and maintaining standardization and interchangeability of training aids and equipment. When one major organizational element in the federal government (department or agency) designates an A/V item as surplus, it often ends up being given away or being sold at a fraction of its intrinsic worth. Without a policy of standardizing and procuring only interchangeable equipment, no training unit can anticipate what the surplus market of the parent enterprise may yield.

All user departments should be required to inventory and periodically publish their holdings in A/V equipment, together with a projected replacement date for each major item.

Control of Audiovisual Aids

Suppose there is a problem of shipping a package of A/V items to a network of field locations. The choice is between using some make-do cartons that are in stock or can be bought, and having a carton manufacturer make some containers to accommodate the shipment precisely. By all means, plan to have them made. It may take a little longer and cost pennies more, but it will pay nice dividends in terms of reduced breakage and storage problems. The know-how and materials now available in the packaging industry can be put to good use, and should not be ignored.

Another work-simplification example pertains to the assembly of a series of A/V aids for outgoing shipment. The items may be received in quantity from a variety of suppliers and have to be repackaged for transshipment. Here, again, industrial experience can be used to great advantage. The shipping unit can set up a temporary assembly line by renting the necessary conveyor track equipment. This allows a quality control over the collation of the assorted items, and eliminates the problems arising in the field because items are missing from omnibus cartons.

Preventive maintenance is a valid concept and should be observed in the care and operation of A/V equipment. Centralized accountability and record-keeping systems should be set up and should work with zero error reliability. Whether or not an organization pays service contract add-on charges or relies on in-house maintenance capability will vary from one organization to another. Cost/benefit studies will soon determine the most economical course of action to take. Such studies will also spread light on the question of how long to use an item before trading it in on a new model. Normally, an administrative services group, rather than the training and development office, operates the preventive maintenance system and advises procurement people on optimum trade-in schedules.

Audiovisual aids are in some ways comparable to the rental car business in that they get shuffled about frequently from user to user. This suggests that they are more susceptible to minor impairments and malfunction than equipment that serves a single owner exclusively. The custodians of loan-service equipment should, without fail, practice a policy of having each item of equipment inspected against an experience-tested check list immediately upon its return to the shelf. This prolongs the useful life of the equipment and saves much needless delay and embarrassment in the training situation. Thoughtful custodians will keep a ready supply of spare parts on hand and try to have the equipment carrying case include an extra set of parts that commonly fail, such as bulbs.

A simple control, sometimes overlooked, is the identification plate or engraved serial number, which reduces the possibility of misplacement, and confirms ownership if items are stolen and recovered. Incidentally, a favorite time for thieves to strike seems to be just after an organization has occupied new quarters and before building security measures have become operative.

Some training and development people are not the best housekeepers, not because of personal laxity but because the marginal space in which they often have to operate leaves little choice. For example, a makeshift training room may have no lockable storage cabinet or inner room in which to store the A/V equipment when it is not in use. The A/V equipment either has to be carried from its secure storage place to the training room and returned after each training session, or it has to be left in unprotected areas in hopes that no misfortune will befall it. Some training specialists are not physically able to serve as pack animals, but in some organizations a request for transport service, even from one corridor to another of the same building, is a bureaucratic project of much magnitude.

This housekeeping problem accentuates the need for better planning with respect to the A/V aids that support training and development activities, and on which the learner and trainer are so dependent. A large auditorium or a multipurpose room in the training center needs a lockable projection booth that has built-in storage facilities for the equipment. Even a single training room can have a lockable metal cabinet in which a few pieces of basic equipment can be safely stored.

Conclusion

Top management of organizations should review practices in the procurement, production, and use of audiovisual aids to determine whether or not maximum, practicable use is being made of such aids in meeting large-scale operations needs. Together with individualized instruction, these aids can save tremendous sums of travel money and productive time.

Training directors should require their staff to follow a priority system, such as the four-option plan proposed in Chapter 11, in procuring audiovisual program materials. They should advocate a goal of standardization and interchangeability of these aids within industry and government, and their staff should be requested to verbalize that objective wherever and however possible. Having an audiovisual device made in quantity to an organization's specifications is often the best course of action from both a functional and an economic standpoint.

PART THREE

Delivering
New Knowledge and Skill

$\mathbf{P}_{\text{ARTS}}$ One and Two have attempted to answer the "why-what-where" questions of the news reporter's traditional formula, as applied to an efficient job training and career development program. The six chapters in this Part III round out the remainder of that formula by presenting the "when-who-how" of the delivery system. Overviews of Chapters 13 through 18 follow.

Chapter 13. Organizing and Conducting a Program

Some hard decisions have to be made prior to setting in motion any employee training and development program. Funding has to be authorized and provision made for publicity, records, and reports. Dates, content, faculty, eligibility, and a seemingly endless list of miscellanea must be decided. At this point in the development program it will be the *system,* rather than people, that directs the new development experience. With an indiscriminate nomination procedure, trainee selection becomes nothing more than personal patronage and only makes the "rich richer and the poor poorer." "Upward mobility" is still a cliché in many organizations.

The little red schoolhouse with its lone teacher has passed into limbo. Instructional teams are the preferred way of conducting programs now. This interdisciplinary approach provides a change of pace for the participants and dispenses wider and deeper substantive knowledge.

Appreciation sessions for the benefit of top management are a good investment, since training is more effective when filtered down than when flushed up from first-line work levels. Management is more likely to support programs into which it has some insight and has had an opportunity to make some input than it would be if programs were merely perfunctorily authorized.

A great deal of experience goes into preparation and presentation of modern training and development programs. First of all, perhaps the most important of all preparatory materials, is the trainer's guide, which controls the substance, the manner of presentation, and the participants' interaction. The guide may have a multiplier effect, a series of steps taken to ensure quality control and to make sure that its coverage is fully adequate.

Chapter 14. Developing the Art of Supervision

Upon the effectiveness of supervisors, at all levels, rests the success of the entire organization, but too often the supervisor's training is nonexistent or inadequate. Developing the art of supervision begins with the art of selection. The substance of supervisory training should concentrate on four fundamental requirements: knowledge of the work, knowledge of responsibilities, teachable skills, and certain desirable personal attributes. Models should be plausible experiential simulations of conditions that supervisors normally encounter on the job.

Training and development is properly a joint venture between employer and supervisor. It is the employer's responsibility to cultivate and sustain the supervisor's need for a feeling of pride in the organization by good public relations and by providing distribution of employee information and reports. The supervisor responds by his dedication to the job, the productiveness of which may be further rewarded by extra pay in the form of bonuses and group awards.

Chapter 15. Design for Executive Growth and Development

From among all the theories on what "management" is, one must decide what constitutes the fundamentals of a design for executive growth and development. First, an acceptable definition of management assumes (1) that it is the art of performing a series of *specific processes* required to get work done effectively through others; (2) that individuals with potential for executive leadership are more likely to emerge from a manpower pipeline that is systematically loaded with an integrated, soundly administered personnel management system; (3) that the accelerated growth and development of any particular individual for executive leadership is best accomplished through a joint-venture relationship between the employer and the employee, and (4) that executive leadership abilities are the cumulative total of all inputs to one's work experience, education, training, and development.

Second, no short-term "quickie" courses can open the doors to executive development.

Third, a really sound design for executive growth and development *must* provide substantive knowledge, spiral-staircase progression, people/production orientation, participative management practice, fusion of inside and outside talent, and rotating tours of duty. Execution of the design requires specified types of inputs to accelerate the formative years, specialist and middle-management years, and the executive leadership years.

This model for accelerated growth and development of executives has as its objective the movement of high-potential individuals from entry level to the earliest retirement option in the minimum number of years consistent with working conditions. In periods of national emergency, severe economic crisis, calamity, or other abnormal circumstances, models like this should obviously be suspended. The faster the upward mobility of all capable elements of our society, the greater the opportunity to compete and fill places of responsibility and meaningful, productive careers. If promotion channels are impeded by poor personnel management and poor executive development, both employees and employers are deprived. It is argued that the model described in this chapter will save great waste of national human resources.

Chapter 16. Choice Strategies for Dealing with Target Audiences

No standardized list of target audiences is applicable throughout industry or government. The configuration varies considerably from group to group because the objectives of each group are unique. A representative sample consisting of 13 target audiences is discussed in this chapter, with choice strategies for dealing with each. The list includes new employees, blue-collar employees, clerical employees, secretaries, supervisors, supporting services staffs, middle managers, subprofessionals, professional and scientific personnel, field employees, executives, administrators, and international visitors.

Some common threads of purpose run through all strategies. Earlier chapters have dealt with these in detail; for example, making a careful analysis of training needs, and assuring that training and development is a continuing experience rather than a one-time process. Another is the idea that "vestibule" training reduces learning time and elevates individuals to their comfortable proficiency level more efficiently and with less frustration. Tailored training is superior to "canned" training, and should present the best-known ways of doing each task rather than force learners to rely on the "buddy" system for necessary knowledge, skills, and understanding.

Chapter 17. Instructing Large and Scattered Target Audiences

Phenomenal developments in technology generally have had significant impact on training methodology. This strongly suggests that media-directed instruction will predominate and that the explosion in training technology will continue.

When target audiences are concentrated, the learning center complex has an assortment of learner-paced, media-related equipment, and possibly tailored space. When target audiences are scattered, the sound filmstrip, overhead projectors, videotape equipment, and television are very practicable and economically feasible modes of instruction. Even better may be the methods that offer learners an immediate verification of their answers; namely, the teaching machine, written programmed instruction, computer-assisted instruction, and selected sound filmstrip machines.

Chapter 18. Developing Developers and the State of the Art

People developers are found by identifying those people who (1) demonstrate a potential for development in institutionalized units, and (2) contribute significantly, wherever they work, to the people development process in their own way.

The U.S. Civil Service Commission has identified four roles that persons in training and development units perform: learning specialist, administrator, program manager, and consultant. This chapter identifies 11 types of training and development positions in which these four roles and others are performed. A minimum staffing pattern is suggested for typical small, medium, and large training and development operations. These types are examined from three standpoints (activities, competencies required, and the developmental needs of occupants) and applies the analyses to a variety of position classifications.

The state of the art in training and development is subject to continuing improvement, as in any other profession. It takes good communication and strict self-discipline on the part of practitioners. Some of the measures deserving of serious consideration include: a formal system of certification; liaison with educational facilities that can generate a supply of practitioners; a system for recognition and reward for organizations that excel in people development, or even for censure of those that exploit human resources; and improved employment service assistance to outstanding training and development practitioners.

13

Organizing and Conducting a Program

THE decision to install a training and development program sets in motion a series of steps that can be logically labeled as belonging to one of two groups: preparation and implementation, or more simply as organizing and conducting. Within each group, the steps are ranked sequentially, and it is in this way that they are discussed here.

Organizing the Program

ADMINISTRATIVE CONSIDERATIONS

Starting Date. Coordination in the early stages of any significant event is a mandatory step toward its management. Organizing a people development program is no exception to the rule. One of the first things the program must have is a firm starting date, and the setting of that date requires careful coordination with other activities. A critical step in organizing and conducting a program is to check the calendar to coordinate the timing with the availability of all resources needed, confer with official spokesmen for client organizations that will furnish the participants to be trained, confirm the readiness of curriculum materials and equipment, and fix the date.

The importance of many factors must be evaluated before setting the date. These include seasonal work-load trends, vacation schedules, availability of resource people, climate, competing events, the feasibility of securing executive-level inputs, pretraining and posttraining possibilities, and the like.

The Place. Another matter that deserves administrative attention in the early stages is the place. With the convenience and speed of national and intercontinental travel, the choice of places has been greatly expanded. Some training enterprises are now booking training space by computer, and the schedule is built around transportation schedules in and out of major cities. Once the place has been determined, there are other questions. For example, should the program be staged as an in-house operation, or in a campus environment, or at a retreat within easy commuting distance? Should the training facility be self-sufficient with lodging, food service, and recreation facilities, or should it be restricted to classroom space?

Objectives. The objectives of the specific program may need review from an administrative standpoint. Presumably, the curriculum development team will have had some understanding of the broad objectives of the program, if not the specific objectives of this particular presentation of the course. On the other hand, there may have been some exception that affects a particular group of participants. What they *need to know* and what they *need to be able to do* are the two basic questions that must be answered from both a programmatic and policy point of view. New systems, new technology, new budget considerations, new staffing limitations, new consumer implications, all these are examples of variables to which a training program may have to respond or accommodate.

Content. As objectives change, content may have to be changed. Again, it is obvious that effective coordination between those who are responsible for organizing a program and those who are producing the curriculum materials is essential. Additional curriculum research, writing, printing and duplicating, and production of audiovisual (A/V) aids may be needed. It is seldom possible to run two cycles of the same program in exactly the same way and use identical curriculum materials. As target audiences change, some modification of the program content may be needed.

Participants. Next comes the administrative deliberations about the composition of the participant group. Shall it be homogeneous or heterogeneous in composition? In other words, should the group be a horizontal slice of employees in a given occupational line of work, or should it be a vertical array of persons representing several levels of responsibility? Normally, the horizontal sample is more appropriate for training purposes because it ensures better participant interaction and common understanding of issues and problems. This question deserves an answer early in the organizational process. The answer will have a direct effect on choice of faculty resources, place, instructional methods, evaluation, and follow-through.

Faculty Resources. The next step is to choose trainers or faculty resources. Will the program be adequately run by in-house staff alone? If the staff needs to be supplemented, from what sources should the guest faculty be selected? If outside instructors are brought in, then an administrative decision about the means of compensation must be made—contract, consultant, or short-term appointment.

Funding. Most ventures require capital, and training and development programs are no exception. The "banker" in this case is the official in charge of the expense budget. Money has to be allocated to the various categories of expenses that the program will entail, such as compensation of outside resource people, travel, procurement of materials and services, printing and duplicating, and many other items. Every organization has its own special procedure for reserving funds, and preliminary procedures for their authorization can be time-consuming and frustrating because they must be justified, not only when they are first allocated, but also when they are periodically reviewed. Whenever possible, it is well to "walk" the requisition for funds through the clearance channels. Unconscionable delays may upset the timetable arranged for preliminary steps in the program.

Publicity. After all elements of the program have been stabilized, the next step is to provide for internal and external publicity. This is critical within the context of a career system concept. Some managers and supervisors still believe in the "let 'em learn" school and are not receptive to people development. They will actually destroy rather than distribute program announcements. This negative practice is pernicious, and can be countered only by publicity systems over which such managers and supervisors have no control. For example, the training and development office can use house organs, bulletin boards, local newspapers, literature racks in the personnel office, lunchrooms, and, perhaps, mailings to the homes of selected employees.

It may be well to prepare a simple brochure for this selective distribution. A piece of heavy paper or light cardboard stock, approximately 8½ x 11 inches, can be folded into three panels and inserted in a business envelope. A logo can be designed for quick recognition of these brochures, and they can be color-coded to distinguish among different series of programs. The brochures can also be mailed in appropriate quantities to field offices for local distribution. The message of each brochure will provide essential details about a particular program. Selection standards should be set forth very clearly in such brochures, to avoid misunderstandings and applications of persons who are overqualified or underqualified for the program.

Incentives. During administrative deliberations about the new program, it may be advisable to decide what, if any, incentives will be available to the participants. These may be one or more of a variety of things: certificates, plaques, social events such as a banquet, letters of commendation for the official personnel file of participants who distinguish themselves, a copy of the certificate to the file of all participants who successfully complete the program, local newspaper publicity, group photographs, individual photographs of participants receiving their certificates from an executive, and souvenirs. Incentives may also include special forms of recognition for regular faculty members and outside resource people.

Records and Reports. Records and reports are basic to administrative planning. Some organizations have discarded traditional record keeping in favor of computerized records. This means that precisely designed input forms have to be completed for each participant; such forms should be combinable with the application-nomination form so that the clerical work can be decentralized, but they are not easy to design. It usually takes several revisions of the form, and experience in collecting data and responding to demands on the data bank, before an optimum format can evolve. Obviously, without basic records, the training and development office will have little of a statistical nature in its regular and special reports to management on its activities. The annual report can be rewarding for all concerned if it is laced with meaningful statistics. It can also be devastating, especially for managers and supervisors who have practiced a negative position on training and development.

SELECTION OF PARTICIPANTS

As organizations move closer to career system concepts that justify a vested interest in the development and proper utilization of human resources as an asset with intrinsic worth, it will become less of a burden on the training staff to run a positive selection campaign every time it senses the need for a specific program. In other words, the *system* will identify individuals who are ready for, and deserving of, a new development experience. The system, not people, will be the initiative exercised by management, and its adoption will result in a substantial change in personnel duties and responsibilities, or will involve new technology, systems, locale, policy objectives, demographic factors, and the like. The initiative for assembling the participant group will shift from the training and development office to another arm of management, such as an employee utilization office, or to a line official in charge of some major segment of operations.

The indiscriminate nomination system that functions in most organizations without regard for any guiding career system is too often a personal patronage scheme, enabling supervisors and managers to reward the faithful and withhold from those who are qualified but out of favor. Therefore, in *system* selection, products of nomination systems will consistently get close scrutiny, and their basic qualifications and the objectives of the nominators will be explored.

If the program announcement has been well conceived and explicitly worded, selection is made easier. Official personnel folders may be helpful, but unfortunately many folders may be mere skeletons. Since the range of program possibilities is so great, it is impossible to set down any hard and fast rules on selection. For example, if a typing or shorthand refresher course is announced, and the eligibility standard is a basic, previous course to learn the fundamentals, simple pretests can be administered to screen out those who failed to master the touch system at any speed in typewriting training, and those who failed to learn shorthand characters.

Selection for relatively long-term training such as apprenticeship or internship training cannot be handled by simple mechanical tests. Some vocational counseling may be required as a supplement to screening tests. Use of a selection panel is a well-recognized technique when subjective judgments have to be made about an individual's potential for certain lines of work. Members of the panel use various techniques to study the candidates. One that never fails to evoke the interest of both panelists and candidates is the group oral session. This places several candidates in an informal situation, with panelists cast as observers, where candidates are asked to deal with simulated problems requiring judgmental choices. The degree and quality of candidate participation in the problem-solving exercises suggest many useful clues to the philosophy, resourcefulness, style, initiative, communication skills, and other qualifications of the candidates.

There is no substitute in selection for having a seriously conceived set of criteria that is compatible with job requirements and the needs of individuals at the time of the announced training. Such criteria should be established, if possible, with the mutual advice and consent of interested line and staff officials. Further, rating and evaluation sheets should be used by persons charged with selection responsibility, and their recorded notations should be made a part of the file history.

The nomination/application form will be of some help in comparing the qualifications of the candidate against the selection criteria. It may be advisable in some programs to supplement the data on the form with statements from present and former supervisors. Data from any interview held will also be useful in the final selection process.

After selections have been made, it is good management/employee relations to notify both the successful and the unsuccessful candidates. Nothing can cause more agonizing than the suspense of a candidate's long wait for a management decision on selection for a prime training opportunity, only to learn elsewhere that he or she has not been chosen. It is equally traumatic if no official advice is received regarding the disposition of the candidate's application.

DEVELOPMENT OF INSTRUCTIONAL TEAMS

Teaching is hard work. It takes long hours of preparation, and it draws deeply from a teacher's energy reserves. It has been said that the most effective teacher is part scholar, part showman, and part missionary. Any one of these roles requires persons who are dedicated to perfection and to the conscientious and effective use of their skills in people situations.

Effective instruction is best conducted by a team, the members of which complement each other. Participants, like television audiences, seem to prefer a change of pace and personalities rather than face the same individual hour after hour. Therefore, in preparation for a program of considerable duration (probably in excess of a day), the training and development staff needs to put together a well-balanced team. A good combination is a team leader, assistant team leader, and project aide. The aide concentrates on arrangements for space, equipment, supplies, and the necessary paperwork transactions. The aide also must collate handout materials into kits, notebooks, or packages, and keep up with requests for duplicating service as the program advances.

The team leader is in charge of the program from the time he or she is introduced to the participants until the program ends. The leader starts and stops sessions, makes presentations, presents resource people, leads question-and-answer discussions, manages small-group activity, coordinates home assignments and extracurricular events, evaluates the feedback he gets during the program, and directs other staff members who are assisting. He or she endeavors to establish rapport with each participant and to see that all participants become actively involved in the instructional activities. A team leader should have charisma, stage management skills, and the ability to orchestrate the program effectively within the framework of the curriculum developer's instructional strategy.

Presumably, there is a trainer's guide or instructional outline that sequences, times, and controls the flow of subject matter and the use of media. The team leader can enrich this scheme with his/her own personality, but must not stray substantially from the guide. To ensure this, the instructional team should be given at least an abbreviated dry run of the program or selected sessions of it. During this dry run, the team can be exposed to any in-house subject matter experts who have contributed to the program materials development. This gives the team members more depth of knowledge and more self-confidence to handle the classroom dialogue.

In selecting teams, thought should be given to building them around people with identifiable, contributive characteristics. The prestige and background of certain individuals may qualify them to perform better as team members for certain programs than for others. Curriculum developers should not be overlooked in forming teams, for they have the advantage of knowing the material intimately. It is unusual to find a person who is equally effective as a team member and as a curriculum materials development specialist, but one cannot arbitrarily dismiss the possibility.

An aide is normally a clerical or junior administrative type of employee, and is not a substitute for the team leader and assistant team leader. The assistant team leader, however, should be capable of taking over and relieving the team leader of all duties in and out of the classroom. Some teams prefer to specialize the duties of the two professionals; for example, the leader always starts and stops sessions, and the assistant leader manages the workshop type of activity, which is less formal and requires the leader to move about the room and counsel informally where porblems exist.

The team is essentially a task group, put together for the purpose of carrying out a specific mission. Members may travel together, eat together, and confer before, during, and after each day's activities. When the program ends, the team may be disbanded and the members may never work together as a team again. The team concept is an excellent device by which management can engage in some people development on its own. Each member should be assessed by someone who has overview competence. The members should be encouraged to assess each other in terms of their individual performance and their support of other team members.

Conducting the Program

APPRECIATION SESSIONS

Effective training starts at the top and filters down to the point of use. It is as difficult to "flush" training up from the lower levels to the upper levels of an organization as it is to flush water uphill. Therefore, a sound principle to guide the introduction of any training and development program is that of holding "appreciation" sessions for senior officials before taking the program into the lower levels of the organization.

For example, a one-week program for first- or second-line supervisors might well begin with a 1-hour appreciation session for the senior staff of activities from which candidates are to be accepted. It is good strategy to conduct the appreciation session before the final touches have been put on the program content. The senior staff's reaction to, and suggestions for further refinement in, the program can honestly be invited. Hence, they feel some pride of authorship and they are knowledgeable when subordinates try to discuss the program with them. It may also secure their firm support for a specific program and for training and career development generally. The principle is that "people are generally *down* on what they are not *up* on." Another cliché that seems to fit is that people had rather be "sold than told."

The appreciation session is a collapsed version of the full program. It should include the objectives, a brief participatory exercise in which the participants do something rather than merely listen, and perhaps a sequence from one of the A/V aids. The master trainer or team leader may also want to preview the plan for evaluation and follow-through, project the cost/benefit results of the program, and respond to questions. The team leader may also find in the appreciation session some opportunities to enlist executives for brief appearances during selected portions of the program; for example, executives to role-play judgmental situations. It is also a good occasion on which to collect some quotes from executives, which can be used to show management support at appropriate intervals as the program is conducted.

PREPARING FOR EACH TRAINING SESSION

A seasoned training specialist approaches each session with the same care and preparation as a master chef shows toward a delicious meal. He or she has the right equipment, materials, and supplies on hand at the right place at the right time—no makeshifts, no fumbles, no excuses. For example, the trainer doesn't have to use a handkerchief to wipe the chalkboard. He has an eraser. He doesn't have to interrupt the session to go for another pad of easel paper; he has a reserve pad on hand. A good instructor prepares. The projector has a spare bulb. The blackout drapes are in place, and they work when the cord is pulled.

This training specialist does not arrive in the classroom at the last moment to find the furniture in a disorganized mess and have to enlist the participants to help him shove the furniture into the arrangement he wants. Broken or uncomfortable chairs have been already isolated or removed from the room and replaced by comfortable chairs.

In advance of the first session, place cards are available at a convenient spot in the room where participants can locate them as they arrive and take the seats of their choice. Lapel labels and felt pens are available for individuals to use in identifying themselves and to establish the name by which they would like to be known by the instructional team and other participants during the program. In advance of subsequent sessions, the aide or another member of the team will tidy up the place cards, rearrange the furniture, and place new handouts and reference materials at work places that will be used in the next session. Ash trays will be empty if smoking is permitted in the room, and minor office devices, such as staplers, hole punchers, and rulers, will be in place.

The team will be checked out on any A/V device they intend to operate, and they will have made advance arrangements with A/V technicians to be at the classroom at a designated time to operate more sophisticated equipment. The team will have in hand the telephone numbers of such technicians to call at the last moment if it appears that they are not going to keep their commitment; it will have fallback alternatives if the committed technicians fail to appear.

The instructional team should avoid a regimented seating arrangement. Experience in training has shown that informal arrangements produce more participant interaction, with each other and with the faculty. If there are no tables, a semicircle chair arrangement is a good plan. If there is a set of tables, a T-shape pattern is satisfactory for general presentation and discussion sessions. A round table for 10 to 12 participants is ideal for a seminar. Tables are critical to workshop activity. Experiential material suggests the need for flexibility in changing the furniture arrangement so that small groups can quickly be formed for problem solving, role-playing preparation, buzz sessions on issues, review of the circumstances set forth in critical incidents, and the like. Small breakout rooms are also a valuable addition to a single classroom so that small groups may be completely isolated for activities such as management game exercises requiring innovative responses to fast-breaking developments that would affect organization policy.

Another item that any good instructional team will prepare in advance is a lockable cabinet for the classroom or teaching station. This is necessary in order to secure accountable property items when the room is not in use by the training group. The team leader should make an issue of this item if the administrative people drag their feet on supplying a cabinet. There is a need to secure such items as tests, textbooks, A/V equipment, spare parts, supplies, and handout materials. A pull-down or tripod screen, electrical conduits, and extension cords should also be safeguarded.

The team should check out all environmental support systems of the classroom area in advance. This includes heating, lighting, air conditioning, ventilation, noise factors, and blackout curtains.

Finally, the team should scout the auxiliary support facilities to make sure that they are adequate for the size of the group expected. Coat racks, rest rooms, library, transportation, food service, rest-break refreshments, and parking and lounge space are among the support facilities that contribute to the success of a total training complex. Pay telephones and one or more "house phones" are also a necessary provision, particularly to serve managers and executives who feel that they must keep in touch with their offices and with their homes.

All these advance preparations will pay big dividends in terms of maintaining a harmonious working relationship with participants. If items to which they are accustomed at their own places of work are not present and working in the training situation, morale will soon deteriorate and the malaise will spread throughout the group of participants. This makes the program counterproductive, despite the quality of its content and presentation style.

THE INITIAL SESSION

Introduction. If the instructor is introduced to the group by some member of the organization, it would be best to arrange for that introduction by a representative of top management, who might make appropriate reference to the fact that the program has been approved and is endorsed by the head of the organization. The choice of top-level officers has an element of risk because some executives are inclined to ignore the time schedule or may preach a "sermon." Nevertheless, it is worth the risk. If the instructor is lucky, the introducer will ask the team leader to prepare some notes for his/her use in making the introduction.

Establishing an Informal Atmosphere. Establishing an informal atmosphere and putting a group of people at ease cannot be accomplished by simply asking them to be at ease. The instructor should set an example, and this is not difficult if he or she knows exactly what is to be said and how it will be said. Pitfalls to be avoided are "talking down" to the group, "preaching," and setting a "schoolroom" atmosphere.

Getting Acquainted. The trainer's own experience can be established briefly by relating present work assignments and making reference to previous activities that have made a significant contribution to his or her background. As the brief résumé of background is concluded, it may be a good idea to exhibit a name card made from a piece of folded cardboard 8 to 11 inches long and with the name clearly printed on both sides. This sets the pattern in case the instructor asks the participants to print their own place cards and exhibit them where participants on either side can read the cards.

As soon as the members complete the printing of their name cards, ask each member to interview the person to his left and to be prepared to introduce him/her. The purpose of this is not so much to get the information but rather to set each member at ease and to begin to break down the communication barriers among them. The background pattern set by the instructor helps in this exercise. The introductions should proceed spontaneously and haphazardly without any specified order.

Establishing Objectives. The instructor may want to begin this phase by minimizing his or her expertise, pointing out that the collective experience and individual backgrounds of the group members would soon detect anyone who bluffed and tried to pose as an expert. The only purpose of this kind of introduction is to help them make better use of what they *now know* by sharing their knowledge and skills with each other. They were selected because of their own skill and experience; they presumably are the best qualified persons available for the particular jobs they hold.

The next step is to establish some mutual interests. The trainer makes clear that the participants were brought together to accomplish several objectives. These objectives are enumerated and perhaps supplemented by a handout, if necessary, or written on the chalkboard or easel. Each is briefly explained.

Finally, the instructor stresses his/her own confidence in the program, assuming he/she has been sold on the program and is convinced of its value. The instructor's manner of delivery, attitude, and tone of voice clearly show his/her sincerity, strong belief in the importance of the objectives of the organization, and confidence that the participants will absorb the content and apply it meaningfully in their work.

Concluding the First Session. At the close of the first session the schedule is reviewed and an overview of the agenda is given. If possible, a handout containing this information should be distributed. Finally, trainees should be informed of the awards (certificate or service pin) they can receive if they complete the program satisfactorily. A description of the awards may also be included in the handout together with a list of eligibility standards and an announcement of the place and time of the presentation ceremony.

Using the Trainer's Guide

Basic outlines of training presentations are contained in the guide. The wording or language can be changed to suit the audience and the trainer's own personality, but every point must be stressed and all subject matter must be covered. No instructor should rely on his/her memory, regardless of how well the session has been prepared in advance. A guide permits the trainer to "orchestrate" the material, properly sequenced, timed, and related to organization objectives. It will usually contain suggestions for sparking participant interaction, for making home assignments, and for developing experiential situations in the classroom. It will also contain cues for the use of A/V aids and may exhibit sample handouts.

Effectiveness of the Trainer. The trainer can do much to enrich the guide. Personality and style often provide a change of pace. Special efforts should be made to draw the attention of poorly motivated participants and incite their interest, for their lackadaisical attitudes may affect other trainees and diminish the general effectiveness of the learning atmosphere. Trainers practice accepted teaching techniques such as repetition and recency, summarizing frequently or asking others to do so, and similar approaches. They should watch for participants who "catch fire" as the subject matter unfolds. These trainees may be the natural leaders in the group, or they may even be the more reticent members for whom this is a dramatic new experience that has brought them out of their shell. Such individuals may be prospects for future trainers, or people developers in the finest sense of the term. At the least, they increase the instructor's effectiveness by an infusion of enthusiasm. They can also assist in the public relations effort to publicize the program and attract people for whom the program can be a truly good developmental experience.

CONTRIBUTIONS OF TEAM LEADERS

The senior team leader should make a special effort to counsel junior members of the instructional team as the program progresses. The more they communicate with each other, the better they can support each other and the participant group.

The team leader should make relations with subordinate team members a model example of supervision. He/she should delegate authority commensurate with responsibility, and maintain effective communication with the team members. Informal modes of address should probably be used by members, regardless of age or sex differences. Appraisal and counseling can be done informally after each session rather than as a formal procedure. A minimum number of formal meetings of the team should be held because they tend to be time consuming and accomplish very little. Each member is accountable for results and should be left reasonably free to exercise resourcefulness to get things done as required.

Meal periods may sometimes be used as an extension of the classroom. People may wish to eat together, especially when they have work assignments in progress and when they can take some useful information back to their duty stations by conferring with participants at the "home office" or at a field station, as the case may be.

The team leader may wish to adopt some simple means of communication for advising management and other interested persons of the progress of the program. This may be, for example, a daily or weekly memorandum that mentions highlights and gives praises to all who have made a conspicuous contribution to the success of the program. Such a medium enhances the reputation of the training

and development staff, the team members, and others who contributed in one way or another to the development and conduct of the
program. Such communications, if issued periodically, serve as a
useful chronology of the training program when it later becomes
necessary to submit an annual report or special reports. They are
also useful in publicizing the program at field stations or other scattered offices.

MONITORING FOR QUALITY ASSURANCE

Knowing what to do has only one acceptable outcome—the quality of what has been done. Quality control has general application,
but it is especially important when concurrent cycles of the program
are being conducted at different locations. The training and development director has to have a system for monitoring the programs.
This may consist of personal unannounced visits, or the appointment of observers to oversee runs of the program. These reviews are
easily coordinated if a common check list of criteria is used. All draft
reports are to be discussed with the local team before they are made
a matter of official record.

The only way to ensure the highest quality in training administration is to insist that teams work from officially approved trainers'
guides, using all the media and other supportive materials and devices prescribed by the guide. When it is found that performance is
clearly below established standards, the only solution is to coach and
work with weaker team members until they bring their performance
up to expectations, or fail and have to be relieved of their program
responsibilities.

Organizing and conducting a professionally prepared training
and development program is a challenging task. To do the task
superbly is to experience one of the most self-fulfilling experiences
of one's life.

Conclusion

Organization leaders should review the performance of their
training and development staffs periodically to make sure that employee training and development programs are conceptually well
organized and conducted, for a good message can escape the ears
and minds of the audience unless it is well organized, properly
timed, and effectively presented. They should reexamine the partici-

pant selection policy in relation to the organization's goals and objectives and within the context of career system concepts. They should compare the substance, methodology, and learning environment provided for each program with the known state of the art in employee training and development. They should check to determine how quality assurance measures are integrated with program plans.

14

Developing the Art
of Supervision

Throughout an organization, people are being supervised by other people. Without this supervision, groups of individuals would work without a common purpose. That is, the individual employee would have no organized goals and objectives, priorities, direction, resources, technical knowledge, information, training, performance standards, or rewards for accomplishment. There would be no referee to settle disputes, no one to fill vacancies, and no one to discipline members who disrupted the group or the flow of the work program.

The Nature of Supervision

The head of a large organization, working alone without supervisors, would soon be submerged in a morass of details. Regardless of their titles or the level at which they try to furnish leadership to subordinates, supervisors are the pivotal members of organization and management. Every decision formulated, every policy established, every program or objective initiated centrally in an organization must filter through the supervisory channel—subject always to the hazards of misrepresentation, misunderstanding, and ineffective execution.

Too often, a supervisor's training is nonexistent or inadequate. Yet, he or she must be the buffer between management, the union, and employees, and must rate, initiate penalty actions, and handle promotions. Whatever the supervisor does in this role is subject to resentment, suspicion, and hostility from employees. Therefore, upon the effectiveness of supervisors, at all levels, rests the success of the entire organization. Incompetent supervisors can literally paralyze the functioning of group members, and cause havoc in the organization.

Nicholas Butler, a former president of Columbia University, is credited with having observed that there are three kinds of people: Those who make things happen, those who watch things happen, and those who don't know what's happening. To be effective, supervisors must be of the first type—those that make things happen. However, the manner in which they make things happen is probably as important as knowing what their role is. Rather than react to problems, they must act to correct conditions at the work scene and to neutralize external factors that threaten to affect morale and productivity negatively. They must concentrate on the things they *should be* doing rather than the things they are best at and the things they prefer to do.

Similarities between Supervision and Management. A three-day conference of a group of high-level managers in the early 1940s reached a consensus on a definition of "management," which is equally relevant to supervision. Management (supervision) is, according to that group, the act of

> Guiding human and physical resources into dynamic organization units that attain their objectives with satisfaction of those whom we serve with a high degree of morale and sense of attainment on the part of those rendering the service.

A simplified definition is, "the art of getting things done through others." Lawrence A. Appley, retired president of the American Management Associations, popularized within professional management circles his own definition: "Management is the development of people and not the direction of things."

Fundamental Requirements of Supervision

KNOWLEDGE OF THE WORK

There is no substitute for a thorough knowledge of the work one supervises. The supervisor needs to know every facet of the work and to keep abreast of changes in it. He or she needs a thorough background in why the work is being done and what purpose the results will serve.

Suppose, for example, that the supervisor is in charge of a unit that edits and codes survey documents, compiled by the field representatives of a marketing research group, so that data can be computerized, analyzed, and published. Obviously the supervisor should know something about subjects such as the objectives of market research, cost factors, survey instrument design, computer capability, techniques of the field representatives when they make direct contact with prospective respondents, mail survey methods, implications of callbacks for clarifying or supplementing data, and types of decisions made by clients on the bases of survey data.

The supervisor is severely handicapped without previous face-to-face communication with specialists in the organization who contribute in one way or another to the end product. For example, the senior specialists in planning, procurement, finance, personnel, public relations, and operations may be just names on an organization chart or numbers in the phone book. If the supervisor regards these specialists as people to be avoided, he or she may be denied a fuller measure of their support when help is needed.

The supervisor is at a disadvantage if he/she has never done the work being supervised, or if experience gained years ago has not been updated by learning new methods and technology, and by issues in labor/management relations that affect employees' outlook and attitudes.

The supervisor must, of course, be expert in the work systems, methods, and technology that will achieve the best cost/benefit ratio results.

KNOWLEDGE OF RESPONSIBILITIES

The supervisor may view the job as shirt-sleeve, working supervision that requires him to turn out as much work as any other employee in the group. He or she may work 10 to 12 hours daily and take a briefcase home in order to do a "share" of the paperwork and meet the demands imposed by top management and other superiors. Such demands may seem to be nuisances, and may be so expressed to his subordinates. This type of supervisor may believe the best way to get a piece of work done well is to do it himself—in other words, "delegation to dummies is for the birds." Obviously, this type of supervisor does not understand the nature of supervision.

A supervisor who never gives any thought to the way his staff is organized or to the distribution of work needs insights into the concept of management by objectives, and needs to practice the concept regularly. Most organizations strive for management improvement, and the supervisor is in an ideal position to help by gathering and keeping an upward flow of beneficial suggestions to decision makers. Organization development needs the united efforts of supervisors.

The supervisor has a myriad of responsibilities. They begin with the obligation of being an active member of the management team, one who thinks ahead with top management and contributes to the long-range planning. He or she should know that budget formulation is an excellent tool for planning, and should be able to contribute intelligent estimates and narrative justification. A supervisor without this capability is a liability to the senior staff.

An important area of supervision is the development of human resources. If the development of people is the way to get things done, the supervisor must realize the importance of training, education, and development of career employees. His or her responsibility is to practice enlightened personnel management, which involves manpower planning, recruitment, selection, placement, utilization, training, and development, employee relations, wage and salary administration, performance standards, grievances, records, performance appraisal, and counseling.

Further, the supervisor needs to use persuasive tactics to influence personnel policy and procedure when the evidence supports change. Supervisors who accept the rigidity of laws, regulations, policies, and procedures lack leadership. There are methods of analyzing regulations, policies (and the laws that sustain them), and labor/management contracts, and the supervisor should learn them. A working knowledge of equal employment opportunity, upward mobility, the physically handicapped, veterans, mentally retarded, and other special groups in the labor force is essential in maintaining untroubled human relations.

The supervisor is responsible for various reports, for this is management's way of drawing information from supervisory channels on which to base new program initiatives, organizational realignments, staffing, priorities, and commitments. Recurring reports have an established cycle, such as annual, quarterly, monthly, weekly, or daily, and all have filing deadlines. Each type of report usually is accompanied by instructions that dictate the content and format. Special reports can be very troublesome, especially if they are originated by policy and planning groups that are whimsical in their demands as a result of their own insecurity or incompetence of their creators. Supervisors may become a bit cynical and callous toward their reporting responsibilities if these types turn up frequently.

The supervisor has responsibility for coordinating the activities of his or her group with those of other groups having related goals and objectives. In a sense, the supervisor is the connecting link, and must coordinate intergroup activities by direct contact, in the early stages of developments, and on a continuing basis. Failure to coordinate can be as damaging to human relations and production as the failure of gears in mechanical devices.

INTERACTION WITH SOCIAL ISSUES

Morality has become a lively issue since Watergate and the scandals that were headlined about prominent Congressmen in the mid-1970s. Paul H. Appleby, former Assistant Secretary, U.S. Department of Agriculture and former Dean, School of Citizenship and Public Affairs, Syracuse University, once said: "Endurance of organization depends upon the quality of leadership; and that quality derives from the breadth of morality upon which it rests." First-line supervisors and their subordinates form the broadest base of the organizational pyramid. Appleby's statement, therefore, seems to imply that supervisors, too (and by inference supervisors at higher levels), need a strong sense of morality.

In Senator George D. Aiken's (R-Vt.) farewell remarks to the Senate of the United States, on December 11, 1974, he read a statement that he actually had written in 1937:

> A party may be simply a political organization before election. Yet if it is successful, it becomes the government itself. Therefore, government can be no better than the party in control or about to acquire it. While "government official" is a more dignified-sounding term than "party politician," yet it does not necessarily follow that a person becomes more scrupulous, more efficient, more wise or more tolerant simply because he has been elected or appointed to a position of authority.

Senator Aiken said it was just as applicable in 1974 as it was in 1937.

The citizen is beset with all kinds of developments that leave him bewildered and wondering just who can be trusted. These doubts arise in a broad spectrum of our society and are accentuated by special-interest groups, research findings, and even restrictive legislation. For example:

"White collar" crime
Scandals among high officials in national, state, and local governments
Disclosures in connection with food-processing investigations
Ralph Nader's work
The ecology movement
Common Cause
Truth-in-lending laws
Freedom of Information Act ("Sunshine" laws)
Test results of public water supplies
Bond referenda failures
Central city decay and redeveloper scandals
Religious body mandates
Lobbies
Marches
Labor leader behavior

Inevitably, the supervisor is drawn into discussions of these and related topics by subordinates. As in political campaigns, he or she can take a middle-of-the-road posture, or veer to the conservative right or the liberal left, but the strength and integrity of that conviction is constantly being tested. Essentially, the supervisor is both the "political" and the "spiritual" leader of his small constituency, regardless of personal preference. Whatever the ideological issue, the respect of the staff is best retained by respecting employees' right of free choice in their own views on the vital issues of the times. The more a supervisor listens or asks questions instead of expressing opinions, the more followership he is likely to have. The more he or she practices the philosophy of justice and equity in the lives of individuals—regardless of race, creed, color, sex, age group, or other extraneous considerations—the sounder his or her ground. The supervisor has two choices: to mock those who live by such a philosophy or to live it by being an example to others. Only the latter will radiate a sense of fair play to fellow human beings.

SKILL REQUIREMENTS

The supervisor needs almost an unlimited repertoire of skills in order to cope effectively with his responsibilities and the problems that arise. One survey found that the individual holding the ultimate authority in the organization must (ideally) exhibit the initiative and willingness to take risks while applying the judgment and administrative skills of a good manager. More specifically, a manager should

—Be a doer, active, dynamic, and innovative.
—Have an unusual degree of self-reliance, as distinct from the compensatory, overaggressive boastfulness of the basically insecure (that is, take calculated risks with a minimum of anxiety).
—Have empathy and intuitive judgment of a high order.

If all this is true for the top leader, it has to hold to a lesser degree for supervisors.

There are at least three fundamental skills that an effective supervisor is known to need: teaching, methods improvement, and job relations. Each of these skills deserves a bit of amplification.

Teaching Skill. The skill of teaching or instructing is the ability to train a person to do a job quickly, correctly, and conscientiously in the way the organization wants it done. The necessity to instruct is constantly present as objectives, program, organization, methods, technology, staff, and other circumstances change. Whether or not the supervisor attends to the individual instruction needs of each employee as they occur is not the question. Even if this responsibility is delegated to an experienced peer of the trainee, the supervisor cannot evade the final responsibility. He or she needs to monitor the performance of the person who accepts the delegated responsibility to instruct, and needs to be able to discern acceptable instruction from ineffective instruction. The supervisor is constantly teaching, though it may be by example only. Expressed attitudes, strategies in dealing with production problems and with difficult human relations episodes, personal conduct and stature, work habits, and interpersonal relations with people of all races, creeds, and colors—all these are supervisory expressions that teach by example and beget either followership and loyalty or disrespect and passive resistance.

A central thesis of this book is that people developers are found in every organization from top to bottom, that no occupational category is without them, and that their titles may bear no clue to their capabilities for the development of human resources. Therefore, the supervisor who is gifted with this ability may not be perceived by his subordinates as a teacher or instructor. All they know is that they are constantly learning from him, that they admire his traits, and that they regard him in much the same way as people admire their spiritual leaders. Further, they willingly give their best efforts in helping to meet the goals and objectives set by such a supervisor.

Methods Improvement Skills. To have the skill of making methods improvements is to have some of the skill of the industrial engineer or the management analyst. The supervisor shows this ability by finding ways to help the unit get more and better work done in less time and with less effort by making the best use of the available manpower, materials, and equipment. There are many techniques for making methods improvement, but there is no substitute for innovation and creativity. The stopwatch was the symbol of an efficiency expert during the industrial revolution and for many years thereafter. Frederick W. Taylor, sometimes referred to as the "Father of Scientific Management," is credited with making work methods more efficient at industrial workbenches. Taylor's methods were forced to give way to more subtle approaches with the advent of the labor movement and behavioral science research.

The supervisor needs to have an open mind in considering existing methods, willingness to try promising innovations, and proficiency in the use of certain data-gathering devices such as task lists, process charts, work distribution charts, and work counts. He or she must be skilled in

Using the standard questions of why, what, where, when, who, and how.

Eliminating, modifying, and rearranging.

Pretesting prototype systems and working hypotheses.

Analyzing statistical and accounting data.

Presenting and selling demonstrably better ways.

Applying the concept of participative management in smoking out ideas for improvement.

Tirelessly following through with changes that have already been approved.

Giving credit where credit is due for help received.

Above all, the supervisor should have the integrity and courage to admit failure when attempts at methods improvement fail.

Job Relations Skills. The skill in preventing or solving people problems at the work scene is the ability to establish foundations for good relations in order to get results through people. This skill must be accompanied by the skill of handling a problem in human relations in a manner that will help production and service. Job-relations skills probably deserve the heaviest weight on the skill scale because it is through people that the supervisor aims to discharge his or her total responsibility to the organization. If job relationships are agreeable for subordinates, they will support the supervisor by finding better ways and means of accomplishing the work, and they will absorb much of the instructional load by helping each other. They will be more interested in self-education, self-training, and self-improvement, and exercise of responsibility and skill in that area will be less burdensome. Each employee will become an aide and assist the supervisor within the limits of that person's capacity.

In resolving problems, the supervisor should get the whole story, not jump to conclusions or pass the buck, and check results. When a new machine is installed in the supervisor's unit, the accompanying handbook gives directions on how to keep it in good operating condition, or tells what to do when it breaks down or fails to operate properly. A skilled mechanic should be called to adjust, repair, and maintain it. Supervisors also get new employees, but no handbooks come with them. Even with experienced new employees, it is often necessary to make adjustments, eliminate frictions, or repair human breakdowns. How is the supervisor to keep subordinates working together harmoniously and productively? What will he or she do if a subordinate fails?

The supervisor cannot take on the responsibility of solving all personal problems of his employees, which cover a broad spectrum: family, health, finances, domestic relations, legal affairs, investments, and educational, recreational, and other interests. Any human relationship in which the supervisor has to take action is a problem. The supervisor has to be alert to changes in the outside affairs of an individual that indirectly begin to affect the worker's job relations and create problems. If the supervisor has an understanding relationship with the employee, the trouble will not go undetected very long. Some problems are well beyond the supervisor's capacity to solve. Again, the supervisor may, by expressing sincere concern and asking a few questions without expecting answers, reassure the employee, and give him confidence to resolve his difficulties. For example, say the supervisor knows an employee has a child graduating from high school and requires financial assistance for higher education. The employee does not know how to raise the money, so the supervisor suggests several sources such as a loan through the Credit Union. Should the employee follow through on the suggestion, the supervisor may give further help by speaking to a member of the Credit Union committee on behalf of the employee.

Behavioral science studies are constantly proposing new theories of supervision. Research by the Survey Research Center, University of Michigan, shows that people-oriented supervisors tend to get better results than production-oriented supervisors, and that the principle of supportive relationships within a work group is one on which supervisors can build better relations.

Douglas McGregor[1] advanced theories X and Y as choices of supervisory style, with Y being a set of positive assumptions about the employee's capacities and interest in the work. Frederick Herzberg[2] advanced the theory that job enrichment is a key to effective supervision. Abraham Maslow[3] constructed a hierarchy of human needs that established self-fulfillment as the ultimate need. All these theories appear to have merit and should provide useful guidelines to any supervisor who wants to improve his effectiveness.

Communication Skills. The various communication skills are definitely interrelated with supervision and their mastery is critical to the supervisor's success. The interest of people generally in improving their communication skills is attested to by the tremendous sales volume of three books written by Dr. Rudolph Flesch: *The Art of Clear Thinking,*[4] *The Art of Plain Talk,*[5] and *The Art of Readable Writing.*[6]

Since the supervisor is communicating all day long, he or she should strive to be an efficient reader, writer, listener, conference leader, telephone user, and public speaker. Consider for a moment the implications of weakness in interrelated communication skills. In conferences, the supervisor may overparticipate or underparticipate. His writing may be verbose and confusing to the reader. He may talk in legalistic phrases or jargon. His reading may be slow, halting, and with poor comprehension. He may mumble on the telephone and become very long-winded. He may be colorless and dull as a public speaker. He may lack the art of listening and consequently fail to hear properly when his subordinates, peers, or immediate supervisor try to communicate with him. Fundamentally, his deficiency in these communication skills may be caused by fuzzy thinking and his fuzzy thinking may be rooted in a shallow knowledge of his work.

Problem-Solving Skills. Mary Parker Follet wrote in *Dynamic Ad-*

---

[1] Douglas McGregor, *The Human Side of Enterprise* (New York: McGraw-Hill, 1960).

[2] Frederick Herzberg *et al., The Motivation to Work* (New York: Wiley (Interscience), 1959).

[3] Abraham H. Maslow, *Motivation and Personality* (New York: Harper & Row, 1970).

[4] Rudolph F. Flesch, *The Art of Clear Thinking* (New York: Harper & Row, 1951).

[5] Rudolph F. Flesch, *The Art of Plain Talk* (New York: Harper & Row, 1946).

[6] Rudolph F. Flesch, *The Art of Readable Writing* (New York: Harper & Row, 1949).

ministration [7] that there are three ways of dealing with conflict: domination, victory for one side; compromise, each side gives up a little; and integration. Consistently, Follett sought to force home a realization of the fact that the democratic way of life, implemented by intelligent organization and administration of government and of industry, is to work toward an honest *integration* of all points of view. Thus, every individual may be mobilized and made to count both as a person and as an effective part of his group and of the society as a whole. She saw four fundamental principles of coordination to be of paramount importance: Coordination by direct contact of the responsible people concerned, in the early stages, as the reciprocal relation of all factors in a situation (for example, extra sales cost may account for extra sales), and as a continuing process. A simple example of her integration theory would be this: A library student wants the window open. The librarian wants it closed. The integration solution would be to open a window in another office where the student could study.

There are many other approaches to problem solving, depending on the nature of the problem, and ardent advocates of methods such as these:

Brainstorming	Work measurement
Work simplification	Committees
PERT	Experimentation
Operations research	Consultants
Computerization	Fact-finding surveys
Visual control methods*	Investigative reporting
Task groups	Audits

The supervisor cannot abdicate responsibility for problem solving, and must have a strategy with which he or she feels comfortable. It is one of the most exciting and self-fulfilling challenges faced—to achieve a high batting average as a problem solver.

Decision-Making Skill. The late Dr. Cathryn Seckler-Hudson of the American University, Washington, D.C., defined leadership as "the influencing and energizing of people to work together in a common effort to achieve the purposes of the enterprise." This means that the leader (supervisor) does not make all the decisions, but with a high degree of finesse and diplomacy is able to get subordinates to

[7] Henry C. Metcalf and L. Urwick, Editors, *Dynamic Administration: The Collected Papers of Mary Parker Follett* (New York: Harper & Row, 1940).
*Including closed-circuit television, floor walkers, control boards, observation towers, aerial observation, space satellites, and others.

identify with, and feel a part of, each decision, and this in turn motivates them to help in carrying out the decision. One company has cleverly managed to create the impression in its ranks that the supervisor or foreman is present as an "assistant to" the employees, who are actually in a subordinate relationship. Participative supervision and management, collaboration, advise and consent, all these seem to make up a master key to decisions that will advance the organization's goals in the most expeditious manner possible—and with satisfaction and self-fulfillment for those rendering the service.

Skill in Managing Time. The management of time is generally perceived to be of concern only to busy executives. This is a mistake because supervisors do need just as much counsel on time management. Americans are noted for their restlessness, mobility, and ability to organize and get things done efficiently. They seem to have very little difficulty in precise time management when it comes to such events as keeping appointments, overseas travel, marriage, funerals, getting dinner ready for guests, moving from one place of residence to another, and space launches. There are "countdowns" for these and many other events. Unfortunately, supervisors are not nearly so time conscious in their day-to-day work.

In the usual busy office are three mail trays: "In," "Out," and "Hold." "Hold" should be a "No. 1" on the "Ten Most Wanted" list of public enemies. Much of the contents of such boxes could be delegated, disposed of with a phone call instead of a memorandum or letter, or made an agenda item at the first opportunity to meet with one's staff. Instead, many supervisors tend to "squirrel away" the most complex of their in-coming communications, put them at the bottom of the heap, and procrastinate until the senders agitate for a response.

The first step in effective time management is *prevention*—as in fire protection. It matters not too much what the system is for preventing time loss and wastage, as long as it works for the individual and he uses it faithfully.

We are accustomed to shopping lists, lists of bills to pay monthly . . . lists, lists, lists. Supervisors do not use this technique enough. They fail to inventory the things they need to do today, this week, this month, and plan accordingly. A list for each period would help.

The calendar is a marvelous, readily available time-planning guide. Again, we seem to think only top executives need a good calendar, so they receive a nice, large calendar as a status symbol to blend with the appointments of their office. But supervisors are given inexpensive little things with postage-stamp-size pages. Perhaps this saves a few dollars, but hundreds or thousands may be lost by depriving the supervisor of the most natural and convenient planning workbook he could have at hand. This is bad economics. A diary-calendar kept in one's pocket during waking hours is an excellent system for managing extra-duty appointments and chores, and for jotting down ideas as they occur.

Some supervisors operate a "suspense" system in a file drawer, with a tab for each day of the month and one for each month of the year. This may be an excellent system if it is kept current, but currency takes effort and making notations is usually a delegated responsibility.

When time seems to be crowding the supervisor, a time-use survey may help. This is done by meticulously recording a series of randomly selected days or a representative week and noting the time spent on each item. After analysis, the weak spots are identified and are corrected by elimination, consolidation, rearrangement, and perhaps a new system for time management.

Skill in Managing Change. The effective supervisor encourages innovation and creativity, and practices it to the extent possible. Creativity inevitably involves conflict. Therefore, the supervisor really needs to consider the conflict as the normal state of affairs, try to reconcile conflict over any particular issue, and accept its minimization as a distinct challenge and achievement. The foundations for good relations, including the participative management concept and the techniques of problem solving discussed above, hold the best promise for resolving conflict from change. A model supervisor is not an autocrat or benevolent autocrat. He leads and guides.

Skill in Doing Staff Work. An additional skill that a supervisor should acquire early in his experience, which is often reserved for higher-level officials, is the completion of documents necessary to implement a particular action or decision. Assuming that the supervisor has been privy to the decision-making process and knows the outcomes, he or she takes the initiative (reverses manager and supervisor roles) and prepares all documents required to authorize and execute the directive. The manager is not asked to answer questions or solve problems in framing the document. The supervisor works out the courses of action and presents them to the manager, with details attached separately to the main document.

This operation is primarily a time-saver, for the order does not have to make its way down the line before the supervisor can act on it. Moreover, since the supervisor has closer understanding of conditions at his level and can formulate the document to conform with those conditions, much time need not be lost by appealing to management for modifications.

PERSONAL ATTRIBUTES

Over and above the knowledge and skills needed by a supervisor, certain personal attributes are desirable. Several of the more important ones are discussed briefly below.

Sustaining Strengths. The supervisor needs stamina and energy reserves to handle the daily demands of people control and development. Physical and mental systems for self-renewal include athletics, hobbies, reading, or silent meditation, but whatever the recreative activity adopted, it has to work for the individual.

Balance. The supervisor needs equanimity in his or her surroundings and should avoid conflict with the social, economic, and political "climate" by adopting a neutral stance.

Conviction and Dedication. The supervisor needs to believe in and be dedicated to the purposes of his or her organization and of the narrower confines of the work assignment. If the job, whether in a private or public organization, is disliked or seems inconsequential, he or she will not contribute to the limits of capability.

Flexibility. The supervisor needs a high degree of flexibility, a temperament for comfortable adjustment to changing conditions, and the capacity to see the humor in situations that might otherwise be distorted and become serious problems.

Outside Interests. It is doubtful that a supervisor, regardless of knowledge and skill in the work itself, can long retain the full respect and admiration of subordinates, peers, and superiors if his or her private life is known to be unsavory. Strangely enough, the opposite is not always true—good works on the outside may not earn good marks among associates on the bread-and-butter job. However, the able, industrious, dedicated, and generally effective supervisor is likely to assume comparable roles in his or her community. Whatever the community project, the supervisor is convinced that it needs doing and that things don't get done without effort and leadership. Successful participation in such events is not likely to be ignored by management, since the current public relations objective is to emphasize the contributions made by private and public organizations to the populace.

Presentability. One other attribute, which is not usually found on many lists of qualification requirements for supervisors, is personal hygiene and appearance; that is, good grooming, good taste in selecting clothes, and self-discipline to avoid obesity, excessive use of alcohol and tobacco, neglect of one's health in general, and excessive fatigue.

It is amazing that these factors influence a person's acceptance to the extent that they apparently do. There is even evidence that tall people and handsome men and beautiful women are more likely to be popular choices for leadership roles. Note, for example, the talent searches of 1976 in the television industry for women in lead roles. Premium money went to women who met the program requirements and possessed the plus factor of sheer beauty.

Selecting the Best Candidate

The art of selection is complex. One should proceed on the assumption that the best candidate is not necessarily the person who:

Does best in the interview.
Has the greatest depth and breadth of technical knowledge.
Has a superior formal education.
Has seniority over other inside candidates.
Already works for the organization.
Is of the preferred sex, race, age group, and marital status for the job.
Will have to come from outside the organization.
Has the best references.
Presents the neatest and fullest application form.

According to the *Washington Star* of December 20, 1976, two management experts (Herbert M. Greenberg and his wife Jeanne, who operate the Marketing Survey & Research Corporation, Princeton, N.J.) disclosed an interesting research finding through the December *Personnel Journal* magazine. According to their research findings, 80 percent of the workers in the western world are in the wrong jobs because they were hired for education, age, experience, race, and sex, and not for what really counts—personality desirable for the particular job. Their study reportedly covered 350,000 job applicants of 7,000 corporations in the United States, Canada, and western Europe.

One should also proceed on the assumption that no single individual is fully capable of selecting the best qualified candidate from a group of candidates. In the fall of 1976, when the National Broadcasting Company needed to replace its "Today" program star, Barbara Walters, management set about finding her successor in a manner analogous to the days when David O. Selznick searched for a "Scarlett O'Hara" to play in *Gone With the Wind*. But NBC did not make it simply a matter of private screen tests or an interview. The "Today" show gave its public five live try-out performances before it picked a winner. Readings were probably taken on viewer reaction to the candidates by the TV rating people, so that, in a sense, the "Today" audience had a strong voice in selecting the new female member of the "Today" team.

The point made here is that multiple judgments rather than a single judgment should be used in choosing supervisors. A selection panel could be composed of a representative from nonapplicant members of the staff where the vacancy exists, from the management level immediately above, and from a group the head of which will be a peer of the individual selected. The panel's judgment will still need ratification by the chain of command, but diffusing responsibility for narrowing the field to the single best choice is a good move.

As in the NBC example, it is good to see one or more of the leading candidates in action on an ad hoc basis before final selection. This can usually be arranged by details or other special arrangements. The only sure-fire test is the performance test. Unfortunately, any brief try-out performance will not measure the candidate's potential for sustained high-level performance or for meeting the full range of problems to be encountered.

Short versus Long Job Tenure

Very few posts in public service or in free private enterprise are filled on an "appointment for life during good behavior" basis. Supreme Court justices enjoy this status, but the President of the United States is limited to eight years in office. Football coaches, regardless of their coaching record, get a fixed-term contract. Mayors, superintendents of public schools, and governors of states serve fixed terms. However, supervisors are likely to be appointed for *life during good behavior,* and this is a mistake, for no work could be more stressful. The supervisor's image and effectiveness, like those of political leaders in arenas at all levels, gradually erode away or settle down into a static pattern. In the military and foreign service ranks, the fixed tour-of-duty concept is practiced. Some church associations rotate their ministers from community to community, and this seems to work better than having a congregation go through the divisive and traumatic experience of firing an ineffective or misbehaving minister or of tolerating the minister until he or she retires, quits, or dies.

A scheme for rotating supervisors in and out of supervisory posts is suggested. Sabbatical leaves from the hard, grinding work of supervision would provide the needed pause for creativity and self-renewal.

Continuing Training, Education, and Career Development Components

The agenda for the growth and development of the supervisor, which should be a *joint venture* between employer and employee, is carefully outlined in the five sections of the previous heading, "Fundamental Requirements of Supervision." The fifth of these, personal attributes, is probably entirely within the control of the employee, but even this area can be modified by the employer in such ways as:

Counseling
Encouragement
Support of in-house recreational programs
A more flexible policy toward shifts, hours of duty, holiday leave, and community involvement
In-house medical facilities; or absorption of a major share of the employee's health insurance costs

SUBSTANCE OF SUBJECT MATTER

Inputs of training and subsidized outside educational courses should be career related. Each training and development experience should be a purposeful building block rather than an isolated, random event that will make no contribution to what the employee needs to *know* and needs to *do* on the job. There are whole families of courses, both in-house and outside, to advance the supervisor's knowledge of his or her work, knowledge of responsibilities, and the requisite skills needed to perform to the limit of a person's capability. For example, personnel management is supported by a family of courses in functions and processes. Next to training in the work itself, the development of the post of supervisors as the vanguard of sound personnel management or industrial relations may well be the most important.

Some of our largest and most successful companies in the United

States, and certain elements of our public service at the national level, owe their generally acknowledged effectiveness to a history of continuous emphasis on enlightened practices in the acquisition, development, and utilization of human resources. Similarly, there are whole families of courses supporting financial management, methods improvement, and communication arts.

The mistake of many organizations is to try to cram all lessons to be learned from course work into the supervisor's behavioral pattern at the outset. They do not provide sufficient refresher opportunities or opportunities to acquire advanced knowledge and skill. Spaced learning is generally more effective than intensive learning. A blend of alternating theory and practice is the way in which doctors and military leadership are developed. This method should be used more in the development of effective supervisors.

The sequencing and timing of developmental experiences are key points. There is no substitute for expertise in the work itself, so proficiency should continue to have the highest priority. Inputs to improve the supervisor's knowledge of responsibilities and special skills needed can be interwoven or sequenced in such a way as to be more meaningful in relation to supervisory work requirements. For example, in advance of a period during which the individual will be participating actively in budget formulation, a workshop in budget processing could be offered. In anticipation of a new budget allotment that would require a major expansion in the regular staff, the supervisor could be authorized to take a basic course in personnel management which would emphasize recruitment, selection, and placement. If the unit's resources were being cut back, the supervisor might profit from a course in management improvement or work simplification. This kind of sequencing provides some theoretical introduction to each major on-the-job learning experience. If inservice training staffs could publish long-range (one- to two-year) schedules of their offerings, as outside educational institutions do, managers could better mesh the theory and practical experience learning needs of their staffs.

Another key point is that all supervisors do not need the same amount of training in all subject-matter areas. A supervisor who is already noted for skill in plain letter writing certainly should not be assigned to such an elementary course. Rather, the proper assignment would be as an instructor of the art.

No organization should expect either OJT or organized training and development courses to cure bad selection or to do the whole job of development alone. The supervisor has a manager, and the climate created by the latter is critical to the supervisor's continuing growth. If, for example, he or she returns from a course eager to apply some lessons learned, but soon gets the "wet blanket" treatment from the boss, the enthusiasm is damped, and it may take a long time for the supervisor's interest to regenerate. Therefore, the organization has to commit itself to training and development at all supervisory and management levels. It has to have the courage to include in the performance appraisal of upper-echelon supervisors and managers some indication of the extent to which they apply— and encourage subordinate supervisors to apply—modern management practices. When the evidence supports reassignments, transfers, downgrades, or removals, management also must have the courage to follow through with appropriate action. Otherwise, the organization invites a compounding of problems in production and morale, and its customers or patrons will feel the effects.

METHODS

Basically, the methods used in training supervisors need to be experiential; that is, they should simulate the conditions that supervisors can expect to encounter on the job. Experiential methods include role playing, management games, case studies, critical incidents, workshops, videotape feedback and critiques, and motion picture episodes—all of which end with the open-ended question, "What would you do under these circumstances?" The experiential methods are far more effective than highly theoretical lectures.

One of the finest approaches is the "incident process," originally advocated by Dr. Paul Pigors.[8] This system uses a series of specific incidents, rather than a more involved case history, as the vehicle for learning supervision and management. Participants are taught to select and bring to the classroom a list of incidents that class members can discuss. The instructor is trained to identify supervisory principles expressed in the lively discussions that inevitably develop around the presentation of each incident. Participants acquainted with the basic facts of an incident may rotate as moderators. This helps in sharpening skills such as conference leadership, problem solving, decision making, and interpersonal relations.

Cultivating Pride in the Organization

Supervisors, perhaps even more than the newest of employees in an organization, have a special need for a sense of ownership in

[8] J. W. Williams, *Case Methods in Human Relations: The Incident Process* (New York: McGraw-Hill, 1961).

their organization. They need to have pride in the place where they work. A supervisor can be severely "bruised" in efforts to become a faithful servant in carrying out management's objectives and in being acceptd by subordinates and peers, but this risk is insignificant when he or she can report good things that the organization is doing for immediate family members or close friends. How does an organization meet this normal need?

The authority of a line supervisor is narrowly circumscribed. He or she cannot hire, fire, promote, or discipline; cannot procure materials; cannot modify the organization or change basic systems and procedures; cannot commit funds. Nor can the supervisor pursue outside contacts, since these are the special province of liaison and public relations officers. Yet, despite these limits of authority, the supervisor is held responsible for operation stalls or money losses.

COMMUNICATION

A first step in cultivating pride is to identify those employees having highest priority as the target audience to be informed of public relations activities. An inflexible rule of the organization should be that employees will first learn from management about developments that affect them, rather than through the news media. Supervisory channels should be used to inform employees of impending major developments. This means that an organization might have to produce its own in-house periodical and produce and distribute special notices quickly. Whenever possible, the organization should have a simple newsletter for the specific benefit of supervisors.

The positive value of periodicals, newsletters, and special announcements is dependent on the expertise with which they are composed, organized, and produced. Their content should be approved by a senior executive, not by the training staff or the personnel or industrial relations office. These groups can contribute, and should, but the supervisors need to get the Hawthorne effect of knowing that top management is taking a special interest in them.

If the corporate practice of sending annual reports to stockholders is sound practice, so is a periodic (not necessarily annual) report to supervisors. The content will be different, but the purpose is the same—to make the recipients feel wanted, proud, and informed with respect to progress and future goals.

Another way of developing pride and a sense of belonging is the typical American picnic. This can be a fun-filled event for all members of the organizational family group. It can also set the tone of management's feeling toward its supervisors by arranging a special occasion when executives mingle and enjoy food and recreation with employees. An annual banquet may also be a possibility in some organizations.

RECOGNITION

Organizations that have a bonus system may well be ahead of organizations that don't, provided their system of pay and fringe benefits, opportunity, and working conditions is just and equitably administered. The federal civil service has no authorization for bonuses, but it does have authorization for making group awards. Such authority should be used a great deal more as a challenge to team effort and improved productivity and service. For example, professional sports certainly makes use of this tactic.

The psychology of granting bonuses and group awards is sound, and can trigger dramatic improvements if it is used imaginatively. Highly efficient performers, when highly and publicly rewarded, exert social pressure on laggard members of a team. They also provide more incentive for a supervisor to act as a change agent by introducing better systems, methods, and technology—some of which could, of course, be gleaned from subordinates' suggestions and duly acknowledged.

Regardless of the definitions of supervision and management, there still remains the issue of *how to develop* the art of supervision. That is the primary intent of this chapter.

Conclusion

Organization leaders should make an objective study to determine the real effectiveness of their supervisory selection and development systems. To the extent that such systems are found deficient in meeting the fundamental requirements of supervision, as detailed in this chapter, the systems should be redesigned and reinforced. The prevailing policy of leaving supervisory employees in positions of responsibility indefinitely should be reevaluated. Management should take positive steps so that supervisors can derive a continuing good measure of pride from their association with the organization.

15

Design for Executive
Growth and Development

T_{HE} organization of the federal civilian service is entirely different
from that of private enterprises. In a department store in an urban
area, one may find a "department" to be a corner of one floor where
men's shoes, automobile tires, or pet foods are sold. In the federal
establishment, a "department" is a major chunk of national government, such as the State Department or the Department of Agriculture. Federal departments are headed by members of the President's
Cabinet. Federal entities of lesser rank, such as boards and commissions, are classified as "independent agencies." The Civil Service
Commission, the National Labor Relations Board, and the Railroad
Retirement Board are examples of independent agencies.

Organizational Hierarchies

Typically, the organization and leadership of a department or
agency in the federal government look about the way Figure 5 shows
them. The purpose of this chapter is to set forth a formula or design
for producing, in the shortest feasible time, a continuing supply of

259

Figure 5. Organizational hierarchy in a federal establishment.

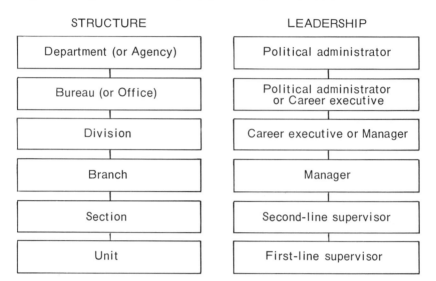

STRUCTURE	LEADERSHIP
Department (or Agency)	Political administrator
Bureau (or Office)	Political administrator or Career executive
Division	Career executive or Manager
Branch	Manager
Section	Second-line supervisor
Unit	First-line supervisor

career executives who have consistently high performance capability. Able and effective leadership at the executive level counts heavily in any enterprise, private or public, for executives continue to function even if top leaders come or go. These executives need the vision, the conceptual and managerial skills, and the substantive knowledge to inspire confidence in top administrators, subordinates, and the general public.

There is no secret about how political administrative jobs are filled. To be sure, their holders are not subjected to the civil service merit system. Partisan politics, nepotism, and personal patronage are three of the prime means of staffing high-level federal jobs, and the arguments in support of this method are persuasive. Citizens look to the political party of their choice for results. They hold the victorious party accountable only to the extent that it has the latitude for filling the top jobs with individuals in whom it has complete confidence. The electorate will not interfere unless the choices are people of questionable ethics, or people who are known to be insensitive to specific segments of the electorate.

This truth is confirmed by the fact that the general public raised no serious objection when President John F. Kennedy practiced nepotism by appointing one of his brothers, Robert F. Kennedy, as attorney general. The electorate raises none when a President practices partisan politics by appointing a preponderance of people from his own party to Cabinet posts, and none when personal patronage is practiced by appointing long-standing personal friends and associates to other key positions.

The Management Theory Carnival

Ever since the industrial revolution spread to the United States in the late nineteenth century, a carnival of theories has swirled around management, each claiming to be the last word in how to get things done through and with people. John G. Hutchinson quoted in *Readings in Management Strategy & Tactics* [1] an excellent analysis of this movement by Harold D. Koontz, who described the theories somewhat more realistically as a "jungle," although the word "carnival" seems more appropriate because of the accompanying fanfare and tremendous profit taking of the promoters. Koontz started his analysis with Frederick Taylor, called "the father of scientific management" by some, and worked his way through Henry Fayol, the Hawthorne Plant (Western Electric) experiments of the 1930s and 1940s, Chester Barnard, and many others, including some of the better known behavioral scientists. He identified six major "schools" of management theory: human behavior, decision theory, management process, mathematical projection, social system, and empirical observation. He referred to the advocates of each school as "intellectual cults" and compared them to the widely differing and often contentious denominations of the Christian religion. The sources of mental entanglement, he said, include semantics, faulty premises and assumptions, misunderstandings of principles, and inability or unwillingness of management theorists to understand each other.

Lawrence A. Appley, retired president of the American Management Associations, endorsed a definition developed in 1939 or 1940 by a three-day conference of high-level managers in the American economy, as follows:

> Management is guiding human and physical resources into dynamic organization units that attain their objectives with satisfaction of those whom we serve with a high degree of morale and sense of attainment on the part of those rendering the service. [2]

[1] Harold D. Koontz, *Journal of the Academy of Management,* Dec. 1961, pp. 174–188, cited in John G. Hutchinson (New York: Holt, Rinehart, and Winston, 1971).
[2] Lawrence A. Appley, *What Is Management?* AMA film library, 1939, rev. ed. 1950.

This and other definitions of management are not too far apart, but there are subtle differences. For example, the Appley definition emphasizes customer satisfaction and the worker's sense of attainment, while other definitions put a heavy value on efficiency.

Early thinking in the evolution of a truth or body of useful knowledge such as the art of management is often very sound. Therefore, it is difficult to dismiss Luther Gulick's POSDCORB formula for good management. He had apparently adapted this label from the Frenchman Henri Fayol's *General and Industrial Management,*[3] and defined it as follows:

—*Planning:* working out in broad outline the things that need to be done and the methods for doing them to accomplish the purpose set for the enterprise (or public service organization)

—*Organizing:* establishing the formal structure of authority through which work subdivisions are arranged, defined, and coordinated for the defined objectives

—*Staffing:* the whole personnel function of bringing in and training the staff and maintaining favorable conditions of work

—*Directing:* the continuous task of making decisions and embodying them in specific and general orders and instructions, and serving as the leader of the enterprise

—*Coordinating:* the all-important duty of interrelating the various parts of the work

—*Reporting:* informing the executive's superiors of what is going on, which also means keeping himself and his subordinates informed through records, research, and inspection

—*Budgeting:* all that goes on with respect to fiscal planning, accounting, and control.

In *New Patterns of Management,* Rensis Likert[4] of the University of Michigan suggested a beautiful definition of management by identifying a list of two dozen properties and performance characteristics of a highly effective group

PREMISES OF THIS TEXT

Management Is a Series of Processes. There is obviously some merit in each of the definitions proposed above, but many of the schools of management, as Koontz so clearly showed, are based on wrong premises. At its best, management is an art, not a science. This

[3] Henry Fayol, *General and Industrial Management* (Management Classic Series) (New York: Pitman, 1949).
[4] Rensis Likert, *New Patterns of Management* (New York: McGraw-Hill, 1961).

leaves in serious doubt the validity of the math model disciples. Personality characteristics have never been validated as a true measure of effective leadership. Since human behavior is volatile and variable, it is doubtful that the behavioral scientists have any sure-fire formulas for leader development.

This leaves us with Luther Gulick's POSDCORB as a good place to anchor because it identifies a *series of processes,* the existence of which no one can deny. Certainly, by now, there is a body of reasonably reliable knowledge and experience about these processes, which can be reduced to strategies, tactics, and even principles. For example, Mary Parker Follett,[5] a profound thinker and seasoned practitioner, spoke with great clarity in 1942 in *Dynamic Administration,* her book on the process of coordination. The renowned late Cathryn Seckler-Hudson,[6] a distinguished professor and head of the Political Science and Public Administration School at The American University in the 1940s and 1950s, articulated precise meanings of a series of "principles and processes" of public administration.

Integrated Personnel Management Is a Cornerstone. Another management premise adopted in this text is that integrated personnel management, soundly and equitably administered, is a vital requisite to executive development. Integrated personnel management is a series of carefully conducted processes: manpower planning, recruitment, selection, placement, utilization, training and development, qualification standards, salary and wage administration, labor/management relations, incentives, performance standards, performance appraisal, career counseling, grievance settlement, equal employment opportunity, upward mobility, career development systems, records, and reports. Without the functioning of integrated personnel management, there is limited opportunity for the manpower pipeline in any organization to be loaded with the kind of material that will systematically deliver attractive choices of talent with potential for executive leadership. Executive development takes time—like good cooking, lawn maintenance, forestry, or community development. The "climate," the ingredients, an informed approach, and many other things are very important to its lasting success.

Joint-Venture Investments Necessary. It cannot be emphasized too strongly that executive development, like any other form of training and development, is best done when it is done as a "joint venture" between the developers and those who are being developed. Any

[5] Mary P. Follett, cited in Likert, p. 313.
[6] Cathryn Seckler-Hudson, *Organization and Management: Theory and Practice* (Washington, D.C.: American University Press, 1955).

form of investment, capital or human, requires full commitment and considerable risk and sacrifice. Executive development is no exception. The employer invests productive time and tangible resources. The individual may need to invest leisure time and even match his or her employer's dollar investment in part or dollar for dollar.

End Products Reflect Cumulative Inputs. The premise here also holds that executive development is not realized by a single episode in an individual's career. Rather, it is the sum total of all inputs made by all concerned parties—as in the development and maintenance of good health and one's education and specialized knowledge. Therefore, the better conceived and controlled the growth and experiences are under the joint-venture arrangement, the more likely the participant is to achieve the target goal in an optimum time span.

A key point is that this chapter does not deal with what *management* is but with what *managers* should be. Enough is known on this subject, perhaps more than enough. More is known than is being practiced. What is needed now is better performance from present executives and a framework for developing executives of the future. This chapter aims to influence organizational leaders, educators, students, and the citizenry at large on the issue of how best to prepare people for advancing to positions of executive leadership.

Pitfalls to Avoid

The retiring oil company official who spoke so eloquently when talking about "people development" may have reacted simplistically when asked how his company was developing executives. "We hire field hands," he answered. This may have been true, but the official ignored the hiatus between field hand and executive. He might have explained that field hands were selected very carefully, that all persons selected as high-potential material for future executive posts were started as field hands, or that the company had a screening process that periodically spotted among field hands the few who had the earmarks of an executive. Had the official meant literally what he said, it would imply that the company followed a "let 'em learn" procedure, on the premise that "cream rises in the bottle." This is one of the pitfalls to be avoided.

Quickie Courses. An equally hazardous pitfall is the "quickie course" approach in attempting to mature executive talent or recondition individuals whose leadership leaves something to be desired.

Courses, seminars, and institutes offered by the commercial market and by in-service training facilities of federal organizations usually last from one to three weeks. Many are based on the wrong premise; for example, that the primary need of executives is problem-solving and decision-making ability. The organizers may assume that executive development is synonymous with human relations training, and therefore concentrate on sensitivity training and other highlights of behavioral science that have invaded the market and ignited the carnival atmosphere. Unfortunately for executive development, this carnival has brought huge profits to the faddists who introduced each new "brand" of the commodity.

Quickie leadership training does little or no good, and may well be counterproductive in its net effect. Sensitivity training can be crude, sadistic, and unsettling for its subjects, for habits and attitudes cannot be changed abruptly. They form at an early age and tend to solidify, like wet cement mixtures. Like hardened cement, they can be crushed, but the pieces can never be fitted together again into a meaningful whole. People subjected to the crushing blows of their peers in a sensitivity session may hurt inside for years. It is a most unprofessional approach to leadership development. Development of any kind takes time. Accelerated courses spoil it.

The Seniority Trap. Another pitfall is the seniority trap. The originates in the idea that "anybody can do it" if he has been around longer than any of his peers. This belief probably enmeshes more organization administrators than any other. The course of least resistance is to pick the senior person in the competing group. This is just as ridiculous as it would be to always pick the oldest male for the executive role, or the tallest, or the fairest. The seniority qualification has a stifling effect on talented young people who demonstrate more brains, more management ability, more creativity, more acceptance, and more productive capability. Further, policy continuity suffers from natural attrition, which is less frequent among younger candidates, who have longer life expectancy.

The Specialty Delusion. Selecting and trying to develop as an executive the individual with the greatest technical ability (the best engineer in the group or the best anything else) is frequently a mistake. Engineering abilities alone do not make an executive. They may form a sound foundation on which to build leadership in an engineering organization, but it may take years of continuing development to recast the engineer in an executive role. The same is true, of course, of any professional field, such as medicine, law, accounting, or banking.

The Gruff-and-Tough Hurdle. Basic personality traits and social outlook of a person certainly affect an executive's performance. Since leadership inevitably must build willing followership and depend on teamwork for results, it is difficult to see how an arrogant, authoritarian, self-admiring egomaniac can be transformed into an effective leader. Therefore, while an outgoing personality is not the sole requisite for leadership, much care needs to be given to this factor in selecting individuals for executive leadership roles.

The Greener-Side-of-the-Fence Fallacy. Some organizations make the mistake of nearly always going outside for executives. This is another path of least resistance. To select from among a sizable number of competing candidates from inside the organization takes courage and conviction that the selection methods are fair and effective. Some organizations, however, tend to go outside rather than draw on internal resources. They never introduce "new blood," and this dilution of the candidate pool weakens the organization, for new blood enriches and diversifies the experience reservoir.

The Brain-Trust Pool. No argument can prove that "leaders are born, not made." It is a notion of no merit and deserves no discussion. We can also dispose summarily of the proposition that a particular university or cluster of universities in the nation has a monopoly on leadership selection and building capabilities. Nor is this true of any trade association or professional society. Individuals coming from such sources may have the inside track in being selected for leadership positions because of personal patronage considerations, but their need for continuing training and education remains virtually unaffected by their "pedigree." Actually, they may be at a substantial performance disadvantage because their peers and subordinates may test them in countless ways to try to find flaws in their makeup.

Sound Design for Executive Growth and Development

Four premises have been set forth in this text with respect to management, and they are worth repeating: (1) management is the *art* of accomplishing a series of processes required to get work done through others; (2) individuals with potential for executive leadership are more likely to emerge from a manpower pipeline that is systematically loaded with an integrated, soundly administered personnel management system; (3) the accelerated growth and development of any particular individual for executive leadership is best accomplished through a joint-venture relationship between the employer and the employee; and (4) executive leadership abilities are the cumulative total of all inputs to an individual's work experience, education, training, and development.

Other significant factors or elements include knowledge, progression, orientation, participation, fusion of available talent, and job rotation, all of which are discussed below.

Substantive Knowledge. At the *executive* level, substantive knowledge should not be compromised. The "jack of all trades and master of none" is not the best choice for an executive position. For example, the budget officer for a federal agency needs to know a good deal about budget formulation and budget execution processes; ideally, the officer should have an accounting background. A division chief in a statistical bureau needs a foundation in statistics and survey techniques. A housing management executive needs background in housing and in management methods.

Generalists may be all right as political administrators at the top or as administrative officers at much lower levels where they have a wide assortment of administrative management activities to oversee.

Spiral Staircase Progression. Executives who reach their positions by a narrow, elevator-shaft type of avenue—the desk-to-desk approach—often arrive with inflexible notions and without the necessary perspective to integrate and properly manage closely related activities. In other words, the executive in charge of financial management operations will probably be a more effective leader if he or she has progressed vertically through several of the allied fields, such as systems, budget, accounting, auditing, and contracts, rather than having moved up through any one field.

People-Production Orientation. Some "merchants" of management philosophy belabor the issue of whether effective leaders are more people oriented or more production oriented. Experience has shown that leaders need *both* types of orientation. The mix is not so important. It may be 50:50 or 90:1, but the ratio doesn't matter as long as the staff knows that the executive accepts and respects them as individuals. Nor does it matter how he or she allocates the hours in a day. Obviously, some problems, whether people or production connected, take longer than others to solve; skill rather than time is the crucial element.

Participative Management. The effective leader does not bark commands, send down written orders, and expect servile obedience from subordinates. The group is closer to the scene of action than the executive is. Executives in federal organizations and in most private firms usually have private offices and may have to work behind closed doors in order to regulate the traffic at their desks. They may even be quartered on a different floor or in another building. Quick sessions with working supervisors, the exchange of notes, intercom talk, walk-throughs, regular staff meetings, circulation of reading files and other media can be used to maintain the two-way flow of information.

The use of certain incentive systems facilitates the participative management theme. Work simplification programs are one of the best systems ever devised. Employees are encouraged to do process charts, work-distribution charts, and work counts and to make proposals for accomplishing more work with less effort through rearrangement, simplification, or elimination of tasks. By tying work simplification to cash award incentive schemes, the federal government could save huge amounts of money. From time to time, departments and agencies go "all out" on one or the other plan, but they never manage to tie the two together. Yet, Texas Instruments, which has long encouraged work simplification from the top down in its company, reportedly attributes about 10 percent of its net profits to work simplification methods originated by employees.

Fusion of In-house and Outside Talent. Strict adherence to the promotion-from-within concept can be as deadly and debilitating to an organization as the seniority system of selection. Similarly, steady use of outside sources to fill executive posts can be demoralizing to career people. No other merit system proposed has ever been superior to that of selecting the best-qualified person available. When a federal or private organization can buy better experience and talent than it can find in the organizational entity where the vacancy exists, it should go elsewhere—*every time.* This does not mean that because a single department lacks candidates to fill a given vacancy, the departmental or personnel director should bypass other departments. From a human relations viewpoint, qualified persons in other units of an organization should be given first preference.

Rotating Tours of Duty. Success of the tour-of-duty rotation in the United States military services has convinced both federal and private executives that the system accelerates growth and development of command capability. The system has been long practiced in the foreign service, in investigative agencies such as the FBI, IRS, and the Postal Inspection Service, and in some of the genuine career systems of the federal establishment, such as the Forest Service. Some public school systems in urban areas rotate their principals. The rotational tour is not an original idea, but it deserves greater recognition. The Hoover Commission endorsed it in 1955, and the Civil Service Commission has tried it from time to time, but it always fails. As far as federal officials are concerned, there may be underlying reasons for hesitating to adopt this system, such as rosters tainted by political influence or implications of its use as a dumping ground, that is, a "lemon exchange." Therefore, they avoid it. In other words, federal people trust each other no more and no less in executive talent searches than they do on security investigations. One agency can do a "full field" security investigation of an individual, but the minute the person is transferred to another agency—if not before—the whole investigation process starts over from point zero and covers the same ground.

A good case can be made for rotating persons of executive rank on cycles of about every five to eight years. Federal civil servants usually work in four or five departments and agencies during their career. How to manage a rotational tour system and preserve the sovereignty of departments and agencies is a tough question. One way would be to establish citizen panels to review periodically the total past performance of executive-level personnel of each department and agency. This would be accompanied by freeze orders severely limiting the right of any department or agency to hire from any source other than the federal establishment.

Execution of the Design

We have to assume in the federal civilian service that the executive branch—from the top down, administration after administration, backed by the legislative branch—has a genuine and enduring commitment to top-quality public service and to such measures as may be needed to ensure the continuing supply of capable career executives. We can safely make a comparable assumption for the private sector. If such assumptions are shaky, so is the quality of service to their future respective publics.

It must also be assumed that the four criteria set forth for management development in the preceding section will be acceptable to all concerned—top administrators, their line and staff officials, and potential candidates for executive growth and development. For example, if an organization is staffed with employees who have no interest in contributing to their own growth and development by some self-help measures, that organization is in trouble for an indefinite time, though not necessarily forever.

THE SHAPE OF THE OVERALL DESIGN

Coincidentally, the design favored by this author for the accelerated growth and development of individuals with high potential for positions of executive rank resembles a cross section of a piece of steel known in the trade as an "I-beam." It has, as Figure 6 shows, a broad base, a relatively narrow vertical column, and a superstructure similar to the base. This symbolic representation suggests careful design, strength, and great utilitarian value, all of which can be translated into the principal characteristics of an able executive and his development. Each stage of the executive's development is described below in terms of this model.

THE FORMATIVE YEARS

The initial stage is represented by the base of the I-beam section (see Figure 6). This model assumes that the candidate for executive rank enters upon duty directly from an institution of higher learning. He or she may be knowledgeable in the arts and sciences or a specialized field such as business administration, enginering, journalism, or law.

This is the stage during which orientation to an organization's laws, objectives, programs, policies, and procedures needs to be intensive and recurring. Many federal agencies sadly neglect this opportunity to orient and indoctrinate the new employee properly. They may superficially cover the obvious, which any new employee can easily learn for himself, such as paydays, time and leave procedures, special privileges, and the formal organization. They completely neglect such matters as political issues affecting the agency's work, impending budget actions, technological changes, the status of labor/management relations, import of the consumer and environmentalist movements, the status of women and minorities in the agency, and a host of other questions affecting its daily operations.

Training Agreements. Many federal departments and agencies enter into "training agreements" under which they are committed to do a series of things—all good. The training agreement is one of the finest strategies ever devised for the training and development of people, provided it is lived up to by all parties concerned. The agreement is an outcome of the Whitten Amendment, which was a World War II control measure invoked by the Congress against the Executive Branch. The latter was inclined at times, during the excitement of waging war, to promote some federal employees faster than their record could justify under the merit system. The Whitten Amendment slammed on the brakes by stipulating that federal civil

Figure 6. Symbolic design for executive development model.

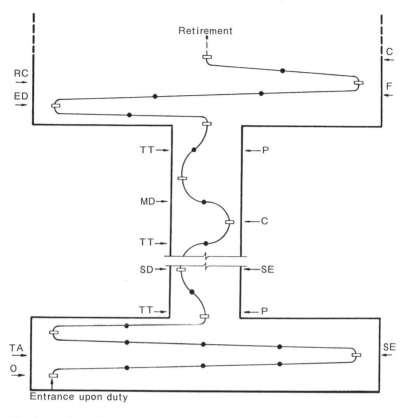

Employer Contribution

  O — Orientation
TA — Training agreement
TT — Technical training
SD — Supervisory development
MD — Management development
ED — Executive development
RC — Retirement counseling

Employee Contribution

SE — Self-Education
  P — Professional societies
  C — Community activities
  F — Foreign assignment

Assignments
  ⊏⊐ Regular   ● Special

servants could not be promoted in grade oftener than annually, or before earning the time in grade required by the published qualification standards, whichever was the longer.

    The exception provided by the Whitten Amendment was the training agreement, for which the Civil Service Commission was to issue guidelines to control the development and administration of such agreements. The guidelines were to provide a means of accelerating growth and development by collapsing time, so to speak, through a more intensive schedule of training, education, and work experience.

The agreement honors the open competitive principle at the outset, then locks in the participants for the duration set by the agreement. An agency may have parallel programs, one of which introduces new trainees from civil service registers; the other broadcasts internally within the federal organization for interested candidates. Agreements usually call for such things as rotating job assignments, a few selected outside courses and some in-service training, periodic performance appraisal and counseling, assigned reading, and an up-or-out promotion arrangement from a specific entry grade to the target position grade. For example, an employee may enter at GS-5 and exit from the agreement 30 months later at GS-11. If performance appraisal is judged unsatisfactory or marginal at any stage by a panel, promotions are suspended and may or may not be resumed. When the participant completes all requirements stipulated in the agreement, he or she reverts to the ranks and competes with peers for further advancement opportunities. Each participant has an adviser to guide in the selection of rotating work assignments, courses, the preparation of reports, and the search for an appropriate career field.

Work Assignments. During this formative stage, which may last for several years, the objective should be to expose the participant to several specialized career fields in which he already has some subject-matter grounding or definite interest. For example, if the participant comes to work with an educational foundation in business administration, his or her schedule of rotating work assignments may be in such specialities as procurement, contract management, internal audit, and financial systems design.

Each work assignment will presumably expose the participant to a different supervisor, and each supervisor will be asked to make an independent performance appraisal. The appraisals will tell the participant more—and management more—about his strengths, weaknesses, and interests than would the judgment of a single supervisor over a longer period. This record becomes valuable benchmark information when the participant and management are ready to make a choice of a career field where the participant can settle in for a sustained period of time, perhaps years. A good term to apply to this job rotation system is *planned mobility*. It hastens growth. It collapses time. At the same time it builds a broader base of experience for the participant than would be possible by a straight-track move from desk to desk.

Continuing Education. During the formative stage the participant should also be expected to begin making inputs to personal growth and self-development. It is possible in every urban area (through universities that offer extensive evening curricula) and in rural areas (through educational television and individualized instruction methods) for any employee to continue his education. Even for individuals who were terribly disadvantaged in their early educational opportunities and perhaps finished only a few grades of schooling, it is possible to compensate for this deficiency by high school equivalency courses and basic education skill improvement with individualized, programmed instruction materials and teaching machines. People with serious intentions of establishing a career therefore have virtually no excuse for not pursuing an educational program on their own initiative.

THE SPECIALIST AND MIDDLE-MANAGEMENT YEARS

The intermediate period is represented by the vertical column of the I-beam section (see Chapter 4 and Figure 6 in this chapter). The illustration shows a break in the column to represent time. The candidate remains in this phase of growth and development for a substantial number of years. Several control factors will be operating including turnover, promotion policy, the candidate's performance, the level of continuing demand for the organization's services, and its success in defending budgetary requests.

Assume that the formal training plan covers an employee's training and promotion only until he or she enters the career path symbolized by the column in the I-beam. This suggests that management officials—with the advice of several supervisors and the performance rating panels, and the expressed interest of the candidate too—have settled on a specialized field of work for the candidate. For example, it may be the work of an economic analyst in the Department of Commerce, or that of a facilities planner in the General Services Administration. Regardless of what it is, the duties and responsibilities require the incumbent to devote time and attention to a substantive field without having supervisory responsibilities.

There are many joint-venture inputs of a continuing nature to be made during this period. The employer's inputs include in-service and outside training and education experiences, and the employee's preparation for responsibilities assumed upon moving into supervisory and middle-manager roles. It is likely that there will continue to be some changes in work assignment and position title, but these will not be so many as the rotating work assignments during the formative years. The changes will be more subtle. The participant will be tapering off a journeyman type of work requiring little or no supervision over others, and will be emerging as a leader with increasing amounts of time devoted to planning, organizing, and directing the work of former peers.

The employer is obliged to increase amounts of technical training commensurate with the candidate's actual needs for current duties and preparatory to expanded duties. Much of this will be demanded by changes in technology, shifts in the direction of official programs, and organizational adjustments. Most of the training should occur within the organization, but some can be better done at the plants of suppliers, at research centers, educational institutions, or professional society facilities. The objective should be to build and retain a permanent cadre of skilled and efficient employees who are well abreast of scientific, professional, technical, and management developments in their specialized fields.

Many federal departments and agencies traditionally let employees drift into supervisory roles without benefit of any specialized training until the Civil Service Commission (CSC) ordered a minimum of 80 hours of such training for all new supervisors. This development of the past decade is the second major move by the CSC to strengthen federal supervision. The first significant effort was made during World War II when the Commission introduced the "J" programs. These programs consisted of a series of three 10-hour packaged courses in the fundamentals of supervision—job instruction, job methods, and job relations. The Commission now offers courses of its own, through its Bureau of Training, to agencies having inadequate means to meet the minimum supervisory training requirement. It features a course called "Supervision and Group Performance."

To be any good, supervisory training, like orientation, needs to be of a continuing nature. No 10-, 80-, or 800-hour course given as a slug of training at a given point in an individual's life and work experience can make a permanent change in his behavioral tendencies. Even if the course is perfect and accomplishes its purpose, the participant's superiors may downgrade his efforts the first time he tries to use the prescribed method of handling a problem in supervision. The best training he will ever receive is the coaching given by people developers with whom he associates on the job. These associates may be superiors, peers, or subordinates. They may have no license to teach, and might feel very uncomfortable doing so in a classroom. The most successful is probably that which is conducted in a workshop format using simulated real work situations.

In 1955 the Hoover Commission said: "We have done little to improve the presently haphazard manner in which we train and equip middle and lower management to do their present jobs and identify and develop future candidates for top management positions." The Commission in its final report observed with respect to management training:

> As the employee advances in his field, there comes a time when he needs either advanced knowledge of his occupation, skill in supervision of others, or both. He also needs diversified working experience so that he becomes a more valuable employee, available for more flexible assignments. It seems logical that his agency should provide him opportunity and positive encouragement to acquire this type of advance knowledge, skill, and diversified experience.

The passage of two decades and the Government Employees Training Act of 1958 has brought substantial improvement in this area of the federal service, but a great deal more has to be done. Performance appraisal and career counseling are critically needed, for it is at this stage that the candidate for executive rank either makes it or is sidetracked. In the military service, failure means early retirement. In the civilian agencies, it spells wastage of lost opportunity and a long, dull period of working out one's retirement.

The same things can be said about the training for middle-management responsibilities as have been said about first-line supervisor training. The content of such training should obviously deal with more sophisticated problems such as those encountered when directing the work of first- and second-line supervisors. The principles and processes of middle management are essentially the same as those at the first-line supervision level and those at the executive level. The difference is in emphasis—how one allocates one's time, and the level of skill required. To repeat: Management training like supervisory training should be a continuing experience punctuated by periods of elapsed time and supplemented by wise counseling that any alert manager can get on the job from individuals who have the knack for people development and a genuine, unselfish desire to help others along the way.

During the specialist and middle-manager years, the candidate's contributions can be many, and he has as much obligation as his employer for continuing to make inputs into his growth and development. It begins with an obligation, soon after he finds himself in a specialized field and on his way, to join a relevant professional society and to take an active part in its program. The professional societies could and should have a much greater impact than they do. This might be the case if young professionals were more inclined to affiliate and become active participants. This would dilute the influence of seniors who capture leadership spots in such societies and pass them around among their factional allies for prestige-building purposes. Professional societies can offer rich opportunities for young professionals to update their thinking, meet distinguished personalities, hear issues discussed, cast their votes, and form friendships in a particular industry or throughout the federal establishment which can last a lifetime.

Another obligation of the executive rank candidate is to engage in self-education, self-training, and self-improvement programs on his own time and at his own expense. Even if there are no course needs immediately relevant to his official duties, there may well be a need for a course to build or strengthen a hobby, recreational, or citizen interest. The sooner such interests are cultivated, the more balanced will be the life of the candidate. It is a well-known fact that executives suffer from great stress, which can lead to physical and mental disorders unless the stress is offset by activities that bring a change of pace, new perspectives, and physical renewal.

A third measure that all executive potential candidates can take during this intermediate phase of their career growth and development pertains to the community in which they live. This model holds that they should, under their own initiative, find a place of responsibility in their respective communities and work at it—hard. There are countless ways in which this can be done. Some of the better known avenues include nonpartisan political affairs, the PTA, civic associations, citizen task groups, consumer and environmentalist movements, community development projects, the League of Women Voters, local government boards and commissions, charitable causes, church-sponsored programs that aim to improve human welfare for selected segments of the population with a conspicuous need, and others. A practitioner's experience in this field of service can instill many lessons. It can increase awareness of the processes of democratic government and his or her responsibilities as a citizen. It can sharpen his or her communication skills and interpersonal relations abilities. It can supply a feeling of self-fulfillment, which the bread-and-butter job may at times not provide. In brief, it can be a tremendous growth experience.

THE EXECUTIVE LEADERSHIP YEARS

Again quoting the Hoover Commission's report: "As the employee enters executive ranks he needs to gain a working knowledge of Government programs outside of his own, a more thorough insight into public attitudes and legislative issues, and a more comprehensive view of the techniques of management." This was a shrewd observation of a citizen body with good staff assistance over two decades ago. It makes the recommendation for citizen participation in community affairs a meaningful one, for if the executive candidate begins early to explore issues among people at the grass roots level, and to work cooperatively toward the solution of common problems, he or she will need less grooming when arriving in an executive position. Further, there should be an earlier arrival at that level. The whole idea of the I-beam model is to accelerate growth and development.

The employer's obligations during this period are to continue the individual's development and to begin the process of preparing the employee for retirement. The I-beam illustration shows an open-ended number of years to be devoted to executive leadership. It may vary from a few years to many years, depending on the age at which the individual arrives at that level and what his or her objectives are for a second career. The federal retirement system has a series of early retirement options. The most popular one is retirement at age 55 with 30 or more years of creditable service. Hazardous work or general reductions in force in a department or agency can qualify a person for retirement at age 50 with 20 years of creditable service. People may work on until compulsory retirement at age 70. Again, the individual can take steps in his formative and intermediate years to build outside interests and a sound system of investing his savings so that he can be freed from his regimented first career much earlier and be able to pursue other interests.

There is a wide choice of executive development activities to which the employer can subscribe. These generally tend to be better conceived than training opportunities at the supervisor and middle-management levels, with the exception of certain offerings that stem from behavioral science creations for the fad market. Again I express a preference for *substance* over style for executives. The more current an executive is in the fields of specialization over which he presides, the more secure he is and the more acceptable he is to the practitioners for whom he must provide intellectual leadership.

One of the soundest investments the employer can make in its executive is travel—travel to observe, confer, or inspect. The destinations should not be limited to operations under the executive's direction. Selected visits to other federal organizations, to state and local governments, to the private sector, and even to other nations could pay nice dividends.

Periodic counseling and literature can spark the individual's interest in such aspects of his future retirement as finance, legal, occupational, recreation, health, housing, and travel. The employee's inputs should continue throughout this phase of his career. It may be appropriate to begin an evening teaching assignment, or to take a leave of absence to work for an international organization—a measure encouraged under a federal statute and by the International Recruitment staff of the State Department. He may be ready to compete in local elections for certain posts, such as the school board, or city or county government. To the extent that he has a travel program for vacation purposes, this can contribute regardless of where he goes.

Conclusion

This model for accelerated growth and development of executives in any organization has as its objective the movement of high-potential individuals from entry level to the earliest retirement option in the minimum number of years consistent with conditions of employment. In periods of national emergency, severe economic crisis, calamity, or other abnormal circumstances, models like this should obviously be set aside. The more upward mobility the capable as well as the disadvantaged elements of our society can achieve, the greater the opportunity for the maximum number of those who wish to compete for places of responsibility and meaningful, productive careers. When promotion channels become clogged from poor personnel management and poor executive development, or from sluggishness of public servants themselves, everyone in the equation loses. Use of this model could save great wastage of the nation's human resources.

Organizational leaders should take stock of their sources of trainables and of their methods for selecting and developing individuals for positions of executive leadership, using the standards suggested in this chapter as guidelines. They should critically reexamine the real effectiveness of their personnel management programs and drastically reorganize and revitalize them where necessary, since a soundly conceived and smoothly functioning, integrated personnel management program is a cornerstone of successful executive development.

They should put in place systems that will, in the long run, encourage a greater degree of "joint-venture" participation by both employer and employee with the aim of providing a continuing, richer choice of talent for executive leadership posts.

16

Choice Strategies for Dealing with Target Audiences

The skilled diagnostician in any trade or profession makes invaluable contributions. The problem may be in medicine, machine or systems maintenance, forest management, or people development. This is the specialist who can relate the symptoms or known needs in a given situation to the available remedies, quickly and correctly, and prescribe a feasible course of action.

Expediting Individual Training and Development

This chapter has a different objective for each of several classes of readers. Each objective tries to reduce drastically the learning time for all training and development (T&D) practitioners who are reading this book. Trial-and-error learning is a slow and hazardous process, and there are not too many schools in which the subtleties of T&D can be learned. For experienced practitioners, the objective is to examine the benchmarks that I have established for my own guidance, and invite comparison. It is hoped that there may be a few new ideas to challenge the thinking of this group.

For executives and administrators who may lack the necessary in-house capability with which to come to grips with their people development problems, this chapter should be a quick kaleidoscopic view of the kinds of activities one should expect to see going on in their organizations after they institute the T&D function. Students in search of a career and individuals who may be considering a switch from their present lines of endeavor should also gain good insight into the many opportunities for creativity and service by studying this chapter.

The material applicable to each target audience is not at all exhaustive. One or more choice strategies are discussed to stimulate the reader's thinking; in some cases the purpose is to destroy some of the myths that have grown up around conventional training methods before the state of the art became so advanced.

Further, the inventory of target audiences is not comprehensive. Those discussed are the more common types that a practitioner of T&D confronts. There are countless combinations too numerous to mention. And, of course, there are the "rare bird" groups that need an occasional T&D experience. For example, the occupation of a security policeman may not fit any of the categories discussed below, but these officers definitely need initial and continuing training. Safety training is excluded because it involves complex, interrelated disciplines that are not amenable to rhetorical presentation. It is a special kind of training done by persons who have made a life-long career of that unique occupation. Discussions of 13 target audiences follow.

Identifying Target Audiences

New Employees

Traditionally, the larger organizations in the public and private sectors have conducted "orientation" programs for new employees. This is one of the poorest examples of T&D, especially when organizations conduct it as a one-time, first-day event of one or more hours in the lives of their new employees. Too many trainers rely on the lecture method or a package of printed materials to convey the most exciting story the organization has to tell—what it does for society.

Orientation can *inform* a new employee of many things, including his benefits and responsibilities. It can *motivate* by demonstrating dramatically what the organization is doing and essentially how it does it. It can *challenge* by portraying the career opportunities that lie ahead and by appealing to the new employee to give a full measure of his or her talents and abilities, and thus become a contributing member of the staff.

The first concept that a trainer has to accept is that orientation is a *continuing process*. It literally begins before the new employee reports for duty, and it continues until the day of separation from the organization. The house organ, the bulletin boards, the pay envelope inserts, the press releases, management's posture in individual grievances and organized labor disputes, and preretirement counseling—all contribute to some degree to the employee's orientation as his or her career develops. The richness of both content and method in the initial and continuing orientation experiences is limited only by the imagination of the T&D specialists.

If top management and operating officials are sufficiently enlightened to authorize a first-quality orientation program, it should be presented in installments. The installments should introduce information in sequences arranged in accordance with the "need to know" for performance reasons. One session can be done through audiovisual aids. Another may be in the form of a guided tour to points of interest where products or services can be demonstrated. Another can be simulation of some kind, such as role playing to show how decisions are made or customer relations problems are approached.

Another thing to remember is that orientation is not an activity peculiar to the personnel office alone. The responsibility should be shared by all levels of supervision and management. Perhaps the individual who can make it most meaningful is the first-line supervisor, since it is he or she who must lend credence to the policies and practices that the new employee first hears.

BLUE-COLLAR EMPLOYEES

The traditional way to develop employees for a "trade" in the crafts—such as carpentry, masonry, electricity, plumbing, and welding—has been through apprenticeship programs. The Bureau of Apprenticeship, U.S. Department of Labor, Washington, D.C., coordinates the development of standards and authorizes the certification of individuals who take this career route. The method grew out of the father/son artisan relations of early history, and is highly successful in perpetuating the knowledge and skill held by the trades. From a cost/benefit ratio standpoint, however, it has to be rated slow, inefficient, and economically poor.

The best way to train people in the crafts is probably by computer-assisted instruction (CAI), if an organization is large enough to afford a computer system for other purposes. First graders at age 6 are learning by this method in schools with experimental teaching capabilities. The method assumes for apprentice training the feasibility of having input-output terminals at or near the duty stations of the participants. Another strategy is that of learner-paced, individualized instruction in a programmed instruction (PI) format with simple teaching machines that have a learner response mechanism to enable the participant to track his progress and immediately restudy sequences he has not grasped the first time. Correspondence courses can, for some individuals, accomplish the same results as CAI and PI, but participants must have an exceedingly high degree of self-reliance and determination to finish correspondence courses.

The four-step "J Program" method discussed in Chapter 10 is superior to the old apprenticeship method, but its success is highly dependent on the patience and skill of the participant's immediate supervisor. Manufacturers' courses and trade union courses may have value, the key again being the skill of instructors.

All the modern methods mentioned presuppose several other dimensions besides pure instruction. The first is counseling capability, and the second is the ability to administer tests that indicate where the participant should begin learning. If counseling and testing demonstrate that the participant requires certain remedial basic education as a starter, then there has to be the in-house or external services available to meet this need.

Ideally, a certain amount of planned mobility or job rotation can accelerate the blue-collar participant's progress regardless of what strategy is used. Work/study arrangements that alternate the theory and practice are also good. The designation of a resource person to meet at appropriate intervals with a group of blue-collar participants who are roughly at the same point in their development is also an excellent ingredient. This person helps clarify troublesome points, and (together with the counselor) provides the encouragement that is so critical to continued progress.

CLERICAL EMPLOYEES
Customarily, a new clerk is introduced to his or her desk and left to figure out the routines from a pile of reference manuals. In other circumstances, he or she may learn by the "buddy" system—a system

that transmits the bad practices as well as the good. Essentially, the clerk gets on-the-job training and that is about all.

A superior method for training clerical personnel, described in Chapter 10, is called "vestibule" training, which can be used on an individual or group basis. When used on an individual basis, the new clerk should not be assigned to the unit to which permanent assignment is intended, but rather to a vestibule entry unit where the supervisor is known to be capable of skillful, patient, and efficient pretraining of individuals in the best known work methods, using actual work assignments comparable to those to be faced by the participant after permanent assignment. The group approach, which may involve the intake of substantial numbers of new clerical employees over a fairly brief period, requires the establishment of ad hoc work units, which exist solely for the purpose of presenting standardized, quality assured training on productive work assignments drawn from the line operations.

If the target audience is scattered geographically, an excellent method is the use of trainers who operate from standardized and pretested training materials, including a trainer's guide, practice exercises, and supporting A/V aids. Another possibility in the case of a large metropolitan area or region is that of closed-circuit television, using either the employee's time or the organization's time, or a share of each.

Assuming an effective supervisor training program, the "J Program" (the four-step method) can be successful. Ideally, in all these plans some job analysis should be done by skilled systems engineers who can identify the steps and key points that need to be transferred in the teaching of each task, regardless of what training strategy is used.

SECRETARIES

A prevalent misunderstanding of the secretarial function is that proficiency in shorthand and typewriting is the main requirement. It is doubtful that the world champion in these mechanical skills would contribute much to an office as a secretary if they were the individual's only qualification. Any office that restricts its secretaries to shorthand and typewriting is misguided. It really wants a "stenographer," for whom the pay is a great deal less, according to the standard wage and classification system.

A secretary, in the true sense of the term, is an individual who must exercise much latitude in judgment as well as a wide range of other qualities, such as resourcefulness, diplomacy, planning, office management skills, communications skills, and integrity. For maximum effectiveness, the secretary needs exposure in depth to the laws, regulations, policies, program goals and objectives, and procedures and practices of the immediate organization for which he or she works and of any parent organization that may be involved. The need for continuing orientation is particularly acute in this position.

Maximum effectiveness in the secretary/supervisor relationship is not instantly achieved. It takes some tolerance and candid appraisal/counseling in both directions. A coaching or tutorial approach is needed by the supervising official to convey his or her standards and level of expectations. This is not done by harshly or sarcastically returning work heavily marked to denote personal preferences in expression. It is not done by retaining all responsibility rather than progressively delegating it. It is not done by fault finding when things go wrong, nor is it done by expecting less than the secretary is capable of doing.

It may be a good investment to have the secretary sit in occasionally on the interview of an applicant, attend a conference of field representatives, "walk" a document through clearance channels, attend a human relations course, draft a letter, or sign his or her name to correspondence. These departures from routine incite pride in the organization and develop self-confidence.

SUPERVISORS

Authorities on the science of management agree that supervisors are the backbone of any organization and that top management is heavily dependent upon them for the proper execution of program plans and objectives. What, therefore, must management do to train these key people so that they will behave on the job as if they were the organization head? Again, the answer is not just OJT (on-the-job training) or anything like it. It is an overall approach to a system of continuing training, education, and development.

I must again endorse the World War II "J Program" as one of the most reliable components of a supervisor training program. These 10-hour programs in their original format covered the skills of instructing others (JIT), improving work methods (JMT), and building and maintaining good relations with others (JRT). Another excellent component of the program, which is an expansion of JMT, is called "work simplification." It has great potential value, particularly when it is used to support the idea that every employee is potentially a part of the team for simplifying the work and making it more rewarding for all concerned. A standardized course presented by a skilled trainer in supervision is probably the best building block to put in place initially.

Many of the newer approaches to T&D are applicable to supervisors. The experiential training techniques are particularly effective in simulating problems in interpersonal relations. Programs in programmed instruction format can be meaningful to many supervisors. Details, field trips, and rotational assignments can broaden the supervisor's perspective.

The supervisor in reality has a twofold job—to deal with production problems and to deal with people problems. Management experts carry on endless dialogues among themselves and with others over whether the production or the people problem is more important. The answer is *neither* because both people and production are involved in every problem. Granted that balance between the two and the treatment of each employee as an individual are essential, one dare not be production-oriented or people-oriented in the approach to supervision. What is suggested is that the supervisor's continuing program of training, education, and development needs to be double-tracked. He or she must build and maintain breadth and depth of knowledge in the substantive program aspects of the work. This means a diversified program of meetings, conferences, courses, reading, observation, committee assignments, and the like. It also means that one must continue to sharpen the skills for dealing effectively with people as individuals through such means as may be individually appropriate. Appraisal/counseling is an essential element of the supervisor's growth and development.

SUPPORT-SERVICE STAFF

It is on the heads of support-service staffs that the charge of "bureaucracy!" is often hurled, and with some justification. To their lot falls the responsibility for interpreting the organization's regulations and for trying to make its systems, procedures, and forms meet their intended need. A problem arises if these practitioners become calloused, negative, impatient, procrastinating, and intolerant in their application of the bureaucratic modus operandi. They lose perspective if they apply a law, regulation, policy, procedure, or form in a literal manner and consider it inviolable. They do not see the demonstrated awkwardness of a form as an opportunity for work improvement. They do not see an outmoded policy as an agenda item at a future meeting of decision makers.

Further, each of the support-service staff groups is inclined to be highly suspicious of other groups, and each operates as if it were isolated from all other staffs. Referral, consultation, and cross-line communication are not terms in their vocabulary. Many of the individual practitioners are insecure because they started in a clerical capacity and advanced by sheer seniority and a mastery of the "book." They hide behind the book, and, as a last resort, throw it at the client to corroborate what is too often a conservative interpretation of a rule.

How does one divest people of these work habits and attitudes, which admittedly do not apply in every case? One of the best ways is through the proved method of internship training (Chapter 10). Actual exposure to the several lines of support-service work is unsurpassed as a means of penetrating the barriers and establishing working understanding. These individuals should be encouraged to become active in professional societies, to avail themselves of opportunities to attend workshops, institutes, and seminars, and to attend fairs and exhibits of current systems and devices. They should also be encouraged to build a shelf of professional literature so that some tools will be at their fingertips to help build self-confidence and the courage to try new approaches. Case histories and critical incident materials are especially good for this purpose.

Practical observation and opportunities to be present at meetings and conferences where major issues and program plans are discussed should help build a broader perspective. The idea is to help these people develop sufficient flexibility to seek solutions rather than become an extension of the original problem.

MIDDLE MANAGERS
Persons who supervise supervisors (normally first-line supervisors) are categorized as middle managers. They have survived the first round of elimination and are bound for the executive ranks if things continue to go well for them. In the federal government, they are the Branch Chiefs within the divisions that constitute bureaus, which in turn are the major elements of departments and agencies. When they reach middle-management rank, they need some detraining as well as training, education, and development. For example, as supervisors of supervisors they have to learn that they can no longer make work assignments directly to individual employees. To do so would create the awkward two-boss conflict. They have to learn the fundamental principle that administration is the art of getting things done through people—in their case, through supervisors. They have to master the functions of management and become skilled in their use—functions that include planning, organizing,

staffing, delegating, coordinating, controlling, budgeting, and reporting.

There is no substitute for formal T&D activities in meeting these needs. Training may include in-service activities such as seminars, institutes and workshops, or academic courses in a college or university. Preference should be given, in selecting the facilities, to those that feature modern methods such as case study, in-basket, critical incidents, gaming, and the use of videotape equipment and other high-quality A/V aids. The accelerated development of this group also depends on a steady input of good performance appraisal and counseling, with an appropriate amount of diversification in assignments to build self-confidence and perspective. This is accomplished through such methods as job rotation, details, committee and task-group work, practical observation, and understudy assignment.

SUBPROFESSIONAL PERSONNEL

Individuals whose skills complement those of the professionals with whom they form work teams are categorized as subprofessionals; for example, the nurse who teams with the doctor; the draftsman who supports the engineer or architect; the law clerk who serves the jurist. The performance of the professional obviously depends heavily on the knowledge, skill, and diligence of the subprofessional. How, then, does one best develop the subprofessional?

The first concept to be applied is the same as that for all other target-audience categories—the need for continuing education, which cannot be met through a single T&D experience because technology and the state of the art in the subprofessional's work is constantly changing. One of the best solutions in this case is the work/study arrangement at strategic intervals in the subprofessional's work history. Perhaps the nurse begins with the conventional duties and responsibilities. After several years of demonstrated performance and motivation, he or she may be selected to train for the "nurse/practitioner" role. In this mode, the doctor in effect supports the nurse by performing those tasks assigned by the nurse; that is, those that require greater knowledge and skill. However, the nurse takes charge of the situation and relieves the doctor of many of the tasks heretofore done by the doctor and which the upgraded nurse, through special training, can now perform. The nurse may work part-time as she receives the advanced training.

There are many other approaches to subprofessional T&D. Programmed instruction, simulation, working models, tutoring, practical observation, briefings, demonstrations, and A/V aids can all be used to advantage for selected portions of the training. The four-step method, which is the foundation of the "J Program" approach to instruction, is unsurpassed in teaching a specific skill—preparation, presentation, tryout performance, and follow-through.

The ideal approach is essentially the apprenticeship method, or a one-to-one relationship between expert and protégé, except that the protégé is not expected to master and execute the more sophisticated concepts and procedures of the profession. An organization can improve its operating efficiency by "deskilling" its professional positions and using properly trained subprofessionals to do much of the work for which a full professional is really not needed.

PROFESSIONAL AND SCIENTIFIC PERSONNEL

Perhaps it is safe to generalize here by saying that the higher one climbs on the pay scale, the more refresher and advanced training, education, and development become necessary to keep one in a viable position in relation to the state of the art in the specialized field of work. This suggests that the means of providing the necessary changes and improvements in knowledge, skill, and understandings become more complex and sophisticated as one grows. For example, the ultimate in our concept of training reached its peak as the astronauts were being prepared for the moon flights. They were already aeronautical engineers, experienced test pilots, and other specialists at the time of their selection. Countless other disciplines were overlaid on their basic qualifications during the long, tedious, and grueling training process.

First, it is probably best to divide the professional category into subcategories of junior and senior specialists. The approach is somewhat different for each subcategory. The junior professional or junior scientist can best be developed (after receiving foundation theory through formal education) by such methods as internships, observation, research assignments, symposia, job rotation, assigned reading, and teaching. For example, medical doctors are still required to do an internship in which they work under the guidance of senior specialists. Teaching and research assignments are excellent methods for stimulating the thinking and growth of young specialists. The young highway engineer doesn't grow as fast as he is capable of growing by sitting at the same desk for 5, 10, or 15 years. But he grows rapidly when a series of rotating job assignments expose him to a succession of problems with technical, economic, geographic, and demographic implications. The young forester doesn't gain a fast mastery of forestry by sitting in a lookout tower or by riding a specified route in the same forest for years.

With respect to the senior professional or scientist, it takes a myriad of things to enlarge one's capacities, and the method in each individual case may be entirely different. For example, the State Department reportedly discovered that career diplomats who were drawn from the specialized field of economics were able to improve their performance substantially when they were exposed to the principles and processes of administration. The interdisciplinary approach to education is gaining momentum in many educational institutions. Underdeveloped countries ask sponsors to supplement the technical training of their nominees with an element on modern management. Engineers also have a branch of their discipline, called "engineering administration."

Sabbatical leaves of absence are one of the finest means of stretching an individual in a professional or scientific field. More organizations should adopt this idea as a fringe benefit and as a means of organization development. The professional societies continue to perform a valuable service to members by publishing journals and by staging conventions and symposia. Educational institutions with schools of continuing adult education perform a great service by offering teaching assignments to senior specialists who are regularly employed outside the academic setting but who enjoy a part-time teaching role. Closed-circuit television has great possibilities for expanding the learning opportunities, both for teacher and student. Fairs, exhibitions, and demonstration projects contribute. Exchange programs between governments and between the public and private sectors can be of tremendous value.

Organizations need to continually reexamine their policies with respect to the development and utilization of seniors in the professional and scientific ranks. Do such people have the proper tools with which to work? Do they have the proper climate and encouragement for growth? Are their work schedules sufficiently relaxed to permit both pure and applied research; that is, do they have time for creativity or is the organization compelling them to be bureaucrats? Are they given adequate incentive and due recognition for their achievements? Is their voice heard when new objectives and programs are formulated? Does the organization have positive and equitably run recruitment, selection, and promotion-from-within programs to systematically replace them with deserving candidates as they leave the ranks? These senior specialists are the brains and the future of the organization, so the answers to these and related questions are very important.

The personnel in field offices generally view the personnel in headquarters offices as dull, confused, incoherent, and procrastinating human beings. The feeling is mutual at headquarters. In other words, communication is weak or nonexistent. The objective of the T&D program obviously needs to attack this root condition.

This means that, in the case of field personnel, there is a need for all the training that the employees normally require in their respective roles *plus* the additive needed to close the communications gap and build mutual respect and cooperative relationships between field and the central office staffs. To do the latter, there is no better way than to have the field representatives trade "shoes and hats" with central office employees from time to time. For example, the Forest Service has long had a policy of rotating professional foresters into Washington, D.C., to do tours of duty there. They are certain to return to the field with a more accurate perspective on the issues, problems, and personalities that have to be dealt with at headquarters. The rotational system works in reverse, too, and presumably with comparable results.

Another very intelligent approach to the development of field personnel is through the use of a well-designed issuance system that incorporates a table of organization, functional statements, policies and objectives, regulations, systems, and procedures. An issuance system that operates on an authoritarian basis, emanating arrogance and illogical reasoning, is worse than no system at all. It generates hostility and passive resistance. On the other hand, a system of participative management in which field task groups are set in motion to write discussion drafts of new policies and methods, or to supply the background material for a new A/V production, can excite the interest of field personnel, damp their negativism, and convert them into active supporters of reforms. The constructive use of their ideas and comments becomes a building block for their own development.

There are many other methods for building field personnel into a full partnership role. These include briefings, videotape mailings (two-way), house organs, conferences, details, committee assignments, conference hookups by telephone, and the use of field personnel in speakers' bureau roles to further community relations objectives.

EXECUTIVES

Recall the example (Chapter 15) of a major oil company official who, when asked how his company chose executives, said that it hired field hands. This may not have been the whole story in that particular company, but it suggests that the process of executive development is not a simple matter to be negotiated in a single, "quickie" encounter between the aspiring executive and some facility that claims to have expertise in molding executive capability. It takes time. It takes some planning. It is a cooperative undertaking between a number of interested individuals, including the target person, who must of course have the potential for executive development.

Executives are the end product of a carefully laid system that includes all the recognized elements of human resources development. This means manpower planning, equal employment opportunity policies, qualification standards, recruitment, selection, placement, performance appraisal, counseling, orientation, merit promotions, incentives, equitable compensation, recognition, and effective personnel supervision and management. With all these internal management systems in place and working as intended, not all persons who enter the "pipeline" will make it to the executive ranks. The tapering effect of the pyramid or diamond-shaped career cone (see Appendix II) means that some will be passed over or lost through attrition as time passes.

In other words, if the people development systems in the organization have been in place and working over a period of years from the time that the executive development candidate first entered the organization, much of his or her development will have already taken place before an executive position becomes available. The individual's self-education, self-training, and self-improvement efforts will have been matched by strategically timed and selected developmental experiences provided on the organization's initiative. The latter may have been an internship at the outset to help speed up the exposure to career-ladder opportunities and to gather multiple-judgment appraisals on the individual's potential for growth and development. Job rotation and outside involvements in community affairs will also have contributed to the total development process.

What further development does this leave? It leaves the need for continuing briefings on program goals and objectives, field trips, conferences, occasional seminars, institutes and workshops, teaching assignments, sabbatical leaves, professional society involvement, and understudy relationships. It leaves performance appraisal and counseling by organizational leaders. It requires "management by encouragement," that is, the executive is encouraged to take some controlled risks in finding more efficient and economical ways of doing business. It means having the executive play an active part in organizational renewal. In other words, the individual in an executive position who feels comfortable with the status quo, with being a spectator as change occurs instead of being the change agent, with avoiding risks rather than taking risks—such an individual is atrophying!

Intensive institutes, or a semester or an academic year away from one's place of work, while attending special programs of study for executives may be all right about once in a decade, provided there is a heavy mix of subject-matter knowledge and a very light mix of such fads as sensitivity training and the countless other gimmicks that have been on the market for the past 25 years. Facilities that emphasize these fads and gimmicks make no contribution at all; in fact, they are counterproductive because the sending agencies expect more of their candidates than these facilities are able to deliver.

In this author's judgment and experience, there is no substitute for steadily building the executive's substantive knowledge of the field in which he or she is at work. An executive tends to procrastinate, not because he is an unwilling "problem solver" (many fad courses feature topics on problem solving) but because he simply is not abreast of the technical field in which a decision is needed. In other words, an executive in a statistical research organization probably can be helped more by a one-day seminar on "What's New in Sampling Methodology" than he can by a whole week of such topics as "Problem Solving" and "Decision Making" in a seminar labeled "Executive Development for Statisticians."

ADMINISTRATORS

Incoming administrators to top positions in an organization are often from an outside source. In public service agencies they may be political appointees, and in private organizations they may be transfers from other companies. In some instances they will be genuine products of a long-standing career system. The comment here is directed toward the problem of dealing with the first two categories—political appointees and "transplants."

These incoming administrators, particularly the political appointees, almost invariably arrive with the notion that the staff of the organization in which they are to assume high-level administrative duties is more or less incompetent and needs "shaking up." In fact, their political forces may have campaigned for office on the proposition that a drastic shake-up of governmental agencies is essential to the public interest. Not until the individual has spent about two years in the organization does he or she realize that the staff is not nearly so bad as it had been represented. And, at the end of the term, the outgoing administrator will often commend the staff for its dedication and competence. Unfortunately, this may occur after the administrator has disrupted the organization and, as promised, has "shaken up" the staff.

If an organization is lucky, the incoming administrator can be prevailed upon by influential friends of the organization not to make hasty changes. It is during this armistice that some constructive things can be done to orient the individual to the facts of life in his or her new home. The T&D director should have a well-conceived plan and be ready to outline it to an aide of the new official or to the official himself at the first opportunity, preferably even before the official enters upon duty. The plan should include an imaginative and diverse program of activities that will provide an intensive orientation to such vital matters as the mission, organization, staff resources, products and services, network of duty stations or service outlets, technology, and financial condition. The plan could be implemented by

Briefings by a team from each major organizational element.
A walking tour of the headquarters facility.
Field visits to selected facilities.
Consultation with the industrial relations or personnel staff and labor leaders to sense the reaction of employees.
A sampling of customer complaints, and talks with the public relations staff.
Viewing recent A/V productions about production systems and processes.
Examining the annual reports for the past few years.
A truly open-door policy for a limited time each day or week for the first few months so that employees, regardless of rank or title, may drop in and discuss their concerns; solicitation of letters from field personnel.

The new administrator, like other employees, needs a continuing program of orientation. Too often such officials soon become surrounded by a "palace guard" and are insulated from the realities of the organization to which they are expected to give leadership. The T&D staff can break down the effects of this insulation by arranging retreats, social and recreational events, breakfast and luncheon roundtables, institutes, seminars, symposia, and other activities in which the administrator is requested to participate in some way that invites two-way communication.

INTERNATIONAL PARTICIPANTS

Many organizations, both public and private, are called upon from time to time to assist in the orientation or training and development of foreign administrators, technicians, fellows, and students. Some organizations are reluctant to get involved with such activities because they apparently see them as a time-consuming, profitless endeavor, if not a money loser, and a possible source of trade-secret leaks. This is seldom if ever the case.

The federal government has, since World War II, under the foreign aid program, sponsored and partially subsidized the training of foreign nationals from the underdeveloped countries with which the United States has had friendly relations. Participating countries usually continue the trainee's salary and pay transportation costs. The number of students in the United States under this program now runs from 3,000 to 5,000 and was considerably higher in the years immediately after World War II when the Marshall Plan aid was given to West Germany and Japan. The participants fall either in the category of persons who need academic programs or those who require a series of special programs, consisting principally of practical observation and on-the-job training. The Agency for International Development (AID) operates the program through its Office of International Training.

The AID participants are a small percentage of the total of foreign persons in the United States, which may be as high as 100,000 at any time. There are numerous sponsors, including such international organizations as the United Nations, the foundations, many large business and industrial firms with international operations, educational institutions that offer fellowships to foreign students, and public or privately sponsored individuals from the sending countries.

Since any government agency or private firm in the United States may be approached by foreign visitors or their advisers for observation or OJT assignments, it is advisable to adopt a specific policy with regard to acception or rejection of these individuals and how they will be accommodated if accepted for training. There are many advantages to accepting foreign nationals, but this is not the place to present the case for or against such a policy. The best approach is to accept a few and let the results speak for themselves.

Assuming that only an occasional international visitor must be dealt with, the T&D director should designate one of his or her staff members to plan and coordinate the visitor's program. If it is to be an extended stay, the program coordinator should ask an appropriate subject-matter specialist in the individual's field of interest to serve as adviser to the participant. After each OJT assignment or other learning experience, the adviser can help interpret the situation. In the meantime, the coordinator may have made arrangements in the community for home hospitality, which can greatly reduce cultural shock and enrich the visitor's understanding of American family life. Most metropolitan areas have scores of families who are actively participating in home hospitality for foreign nationals.

If considerable numbers of participants are expected, there may be other alternatives rather than having all come to the United States. Not all who come are able to profit from the experience. Therefore, selection of those who are ultimately chosen could be refined by a plan I have long advocated. The state of the art in T&D now is such that the first phase of a group's indoctrination to the concepts of a given field of specialization could be accomplished by some form of programmed (learner-paced) instruction. After this first phase, which might be offered to a hundred or more participants in their own country or region, the sponsor could select a smaller number consisting of those who show the greatest potential. The next phase would be conducted in a workshop located in the host country or region and accommodating a manageable size of group. A mobile team, perhaps supplemented by local resource people, would conduct the workshop. Selection would then be made of those whose demonstrated performance in the first two phases clearly showed their qualifications (including English proficiency) and motivation for making the most of T&D opportunities in the United States. A rapid multiplier effect can be gained by training those who come to the United States to train their fellow countrymen.

Conclusion

Organization leaders should insist that their training and development staffs identify a list of logical target audiences and propose a strategy for dealing with each audience. A staff paper containing such information is certainly worthy of review and approval at the highest decision levels. The strategies should be reviewed periodically (at least annually) to update them with respect to advances in the state of the art and in relation to organization development changes, new goals, fiscal factors, and conditions in the marketplace or public service area.

17

Instructing
Large and Scattered
Target Audiences

Training and development specialists have seen a tremendous advance in training technology since the beginning of the World War II era. There have been significant improvements in electronics, sound systems, optics, and manufacturing capability for producing audiovisual hardware.

We have experienced the introduction of commercial and educational television media. The equally amazing device of videotape, which can provide an entire library of reel-type material in full color with animation that can be reproduced on a conventional television screen and a tape deck playback mechanism, has made its advent.

The long history of computer development reached a climax with completion of the first automatic computers. Subsequent models were the forerunners of machines used in computer-assisted instruction (CAI) and computer-managed instruction.

298

Dynamics of Training Technology

Research experiments by B. F. Skinner at Harvard formed the basis of his theories of learning, and these theories were applied in the development of teaching machines and individualized, learner-paced instruction as a viable means of teaching.

Finally, space travel, satellites, and interplanetary probes became possible through a phenomenal proliferation of electronic and computerized devices. This tremendous array of technological capabilities inevitably invaded the province of training methodology and will continue to have impact on it for years to come.

In view of all this, there is no doubt that mediated instruction is the trend of the future and that expansion of this type of training will continue. Certainly, the pressing need in every professional, scientific, technical, and management field is for media to keep practitioners abreast of developments that affect what they do and how they do it. It is out of the quesion, financially, to move people from duty stations to a central location or even to regional locations as often as they need training under the continuing education concept. For example, doctors from all over the nation cannot be running to the National Institutes of Health at Bethesda, Maryland, to learn a newly developed technique for medical diagnosis or treatment. Moreover, since the written word is often confusing and people are already inundated with things to read, the transfer of knowledge must be accomplished in other ways.

Among the delivery systems discussed elsewhere in this book, mediated instruction offers as much quality assurance as, if not more than, any other. It is almost impossible to visualize what the twenty-first century will bring in training technology to cope with advances in our civilization generally. It seems a safe bet that mediated instruction will be in the forefront of the means for coping.

All this is not to say that the need for the training specialist to plan, organize, and direct programs of training and development has been or, in the foreseeable future, will be eliminated. Neither are we about to see the end of the classroom instructor. The new technology merely provides more versatile tools for such people. The ways in which the technology can be used effectively are limited only by the imagination of the training and development staff of any organization.

The training specialist is, increasingly, obliged to orchestrate the multimedia systems of instruction. This is especially true in organizations with large and scattered target audiences. Travel dollars are being scrutinized and training does not enjoy as high a priority in many places as it deserves. Therefore, the challenge is to turn to, and use to the maximum feasible extent possible, a self-administering system of mediated instruction.

Mediated Instruction for Concentrated Target Audiences

The "learning center" concept is gaining in popularity. A learning center is the name given to space that can accommodate the use of a diverse battery of mediated instruction devices for individualized training purposes. The space has to be functionally designed, comfortable, inviting, and easily accessible. Preferably, an architect who knows training and educational requirements should be consulted in the design stage. Part of the space needs to be equipped with individual study carrels into which a variety of individualized learning devices can be placed, depending on the desired program of study for a particular individual.

In the same learning center, one can find employees engaging in self-training activities ranging from the basic 3-R skills, refresher typing, and blue-collar trade topics to highly sophisticated subjects such as mathematical sampling, electronics, and executive leadership styles. The merits of the learning center idea are described more fully in Chapter 9 of this book.

Mediated Instruction for Scattered Target Audiences

Audiovisual Devices without a Teaching Machine

Audiovisual (A/V) devices are those by which a group or an individual may receive instruction through visual and/or auditory media. Examples include motion picture projectors, tape recorders, 35mm slide projectors, 35mm filmstrip projectors, combination slide/tape machines, combination filmstrip/tape machines, overhead transparency projectors, opaque projectors, videotape equipment, and closed-circuit television.

We know that people learn through different media, and it is doubtless true that some can learn satisfactorily without teaching machines or any audiovisual means whatsoever. Some people can read a complicated technical manual and figure out what to do and how to do it. For others, it takes a reliable four-step method and a great deal of follow-through. The latter may be served best by a combination of A/V and teaching machines, the subject of the next section.

35mm Sound Filmstrips. One of the A/V tools with the greatest potential for delivering knowledge to large, scattered target audiences is the 35mm sound filmstrip. In the beginning, sound was recorded on wire and later on long-playing phonograph records. Eventually these were replaced by cartridge tape, which needs no threading and is not subject to the accidental breakage that befell the recording wire. The cartridge tape can, of course, be synchronized with the visuals on a continuous strip of 35mm filmstrip. Relatively inexpensive machines in the $100 to $200 range can be purchased in quantity on the commercial market for the use of sound filmstrip.

Sound filmstrip machines today are almost as portable as a book. Training and development specialists should capitalize on that factor by encouraging employees to check out small units for home or office use to increase their knowledge and skill. Some offices make the mistake of buying luxury models of such equipment, which are good only for stationary use in a classroom. Portability is a prime requisite. That not only makes the machine useful at the home office of an organization, but also gives it potential for being packaged in a carton of made-to-order design and shipped to and among field offices.

This system of mediated instruction can achieve an extremely low unit-cost ratio. *No other system of instruction involving an A/V dimension can compete economically with it.* I have always found it a favorite and have used it successfully on a massive scale on many occasions. In the hope that readers of this book will be encouraged to adopt it as an integral part of their delivery system, this chapter includes a step-by-step approach to the in-house production of sound filmstrips. The procedure was developed years ago, and is still as good today as it was then. Perhaps it is a solution for underdeveloped countries, especially since battery-powered machines are now commonplace in the technology.

Overhead Projectors. Overhead projectors have a tremendous advantage in the learning situation where an instructor or group leader is present. They are essentially the successor to the old-fashioned blackboard and even the more modern (green-surfaced) chalkboard. They are vast time-saving devices because the instructor can do his lesson planning in advance and have his illustrations and key points produced as transparencies. A transparency is a clear acetate substance similar to film positives such as motion picture and 35mm filmstrip materials. When an organization can afford to equip its field offices with an overhead projector, the central office can develop a series of transparencies on any or all subjects for which mediated instruction is appropriate. Each series of transparencies may be accompanied by a guide or outline to facilitate use of the series by instructors or by trainees themselves.

Transparencies are easily stored for subsequent use. Overlays can be hinged to them to add additional dimensions. An individual can assemble a group in a lighted room and face the audience as he projects the image over his shoulder. He can point by placing a finger or object on the transparency. With a grease pencil, he can add notations, which can be easily erased. Amazingly, transparencies can be made right in the office by any employee using a burncopy machine, thus saving the time and added expense it takes to send things out to commercial facilities. With special acetate color overlays, the transparencies can be produced in color, to show, for example, progressively, the systems of a unit (organization) or changes under varying conditions.

Overhead projectors and transparencies cannot approach the low unit cost of sound filmstrips, but they have their place in any well-equipped organization. The fuss and bother of (frequently missing) chalk and erasers, and the tedious wait of an audience while an instructor or conference leader laboriously does his chalkboard work, justify the additional expenditure. However, like all aids in the classroom, there is an occasional need for a chalkboard that no other tool can satisfy. Certain techniques make it the only feasible device because it has become a part of the teaching "act," and thus it becomes a significant factor in the transfer of information.

Videotape Equipment. Videotape is another among the marvelous inventions, each of which seems to have some magic that others lack. It has largely supplanted the motion picture as a training tool because the video camera can capture a scene and give an instant playback, without the complicated business of sending the tape out to a commercial laboratory to have the audio and video material integrated and synchronized on a single piece of film stock negative and positive. Whole libraries of such videotape can be accumulated very quickly, and can be sent back and forth between various offices in an organization.

Videotape is an exceedingly flexible tool. It can be combined with other training methods, such as role playing and the use of case studies and critical incidents. It is unsurpassed as a means of "third person" training, such as sales, interviewing, counseling, bargaining, grievance settlement, and instructing itself. The videotape camera can record a simulated sequence, using the learner to role-play the part of the future practitioner. Another person can role-play the client or respondent with whom the learner will, supposedly, have a relationship when the learner is fully trained. The resource person can, after the role playing and instant playback of the videotape, critique the learner's performance and invite the learner to do some self-appraisal. The vivid mirroring of an individual's own performance is usually more convincing than anything the resource person or others might say.

Videotape comes in several sizes. The smaller the width of the tape, the less expensive it is to acquire and operate a system, but the more limitations it has. In other words, 1-inch videotape yields a great deal more resolution and quality than half-inch tape. The cost of equipment rises sharply as the size of the tape increases. Organizations should weigh very carefully the decision as to the width of the tape they will use, and then *standardize* on that size. A critical input to the information they need for an intelligent decision is what is being used in videotape depositories from which they are most likely to draw materials for training purposes. The National Archives Service, General Services Administration, Washington, D.C., is assembling a bank of A/V materials that have been produced by and for federal departments and agencies.

Videotape is a superior means of linking an organization's offices through a common language or understanding of a subject-matter area. Take, for example, an organization that has a national or worldwide network of offices. Its scientific, professional, and technical staffs are faced with the problem of keeping abreast of their respective fields. Travel funds are limited. Time is short. Coordination is needed between the central policy and executive staffs and the line and staff groups in the field. Local experience is needed at headquarters, and headquarters policy needs interpretation in the field. If it has videotape capability, headquarters can convene a panel, videotape the policy position and rationale for current thinking on a given issue, and fire it off to the field offices. Concurrently, these offices or a representative one can be gathering local opinions on one or more videotape reels, and dispatching them to headquarters. Field offices can communicate with each other similarly. Headquarters can then identify and publicize outstanding examples of the vital processes such as space utilization, system design, mechanization, marketing, planning, production, organization, management improvement, and money management.

Television Media. Closed-circuit and educational channel television are other media for reaching large target audiences with quality-as-

sured instruction at relatively low unit cost. This medium offers the
possibility of placing before a television camera the individual(s) who
is the acknowledged expert in his field, and having his performance
fed live into countless places where the target audience is distributed. A kinescope (previously recorded) performance can also be
used to give the expert more flexibility with respect to the time when
he records his performance.

Educational facilities in some communities are making considerable use of this medium to reach their markets. In one case, it may
be housewives who want to update their knowledge in some field or
acquire a hobby. In another, it may be an organization with a network of outlets where personnel require continuing training in
order to keep up with technology or customer relations dialogue. An
institution in the Washington (D.C.) area has used an educational
TV channel to teach first-line supervision. As early as 1949, the
Bureau of the Census conducted an experiment to test the feasibility
of training its enumerators through closed-circuit television channels. It was learned that television-trained enumerators were no better or worse prepared then enumerators who received their training
in conventional classroom format.

Audiovisual Devices with a Teaching Machine

Studies of learning-center populations suggest that the teaching
machine may be the most efficient of all methods. It permits the
learner to test himself as he progresses through the subject matter.
It is probably the most reliable method of individualized instruction.
Even at the elementary school level, one can now find children
operating simple A/V devices to gather information about a subject.
They may be using such equipment individually or in small clusters,
depending on how the teacher manages the learning situation. The
teacher is accessible but she is not dominating the learners. She is
guiding the learning activities and leaving to mediated instructional
tools the burden of *showing and telling* the student what he needs to
know or wants to know in order to advance his knowledge.

Types of Teaching Machines. There is a whole family of what are
called "teaching machines." Functional illiterates can learn to read
and improve comprehension on such machines. They are also useful
for refresher courses such as basic science and mathematics, or for
learning a foreign language. The opportunity to learn and record
one's progress without the stress of competing with a group of people under the watchful eye of a teacher can be a strong incentive for
a "late blooming" individual. For those who learn quickly and do not

wish to be held back by slow learners, the teaching machine is a boon. Perhaps our society would not be so cluttered by discouraged dropouts if educators themselves had been given this advantage in past generations.

Programmed Instruction. Programmed instruction has made extensive use of teaching-machine equipment because it focuses the learner's attention on the significant points *while he learns.* After he answers an item correctly, he receives immediate confirmation that he has mastered the relevant information. This allows him to proceed with confidence to other items.

A separate professional society of practitioners has grown up on a national scale to promulgate the principles and methods applied in programmed instruction. "PI" is a far cry from correspondence programs, although the latter have merit under selected circumstances. They have always had a feedback feature, but the trouble is that the correspondence system of learning may require days or weeks to return to the learner a confirmation of his scores on a given lesson. Instant feedback of machines, according to psychologists, is decidedly better from a learning and motivation standpoint. In fact, some experts estimate that PI can cut learning time by 30 to 50 percent, since it eliminates wasted time caused by confusion, attention to irrelevant detail, and getting "stuck." The PI specialist organizes the material in a psychologically sound sequence.

PI materials are pretested and modified during production until all test subjects attain high scores, thus more nearly assuring high levels of achievement when the PI materials are released for mediated instruction purposes. Better retention is also claimed for PI.

More than a decade ago, advocates were forecasting that PI would have impact on the schools by allowing teachers to spend less time lecturing and more time with individual students; on industry by combating human obsolescence from changing technology; and on overseas countries by helping underdeveloped countries catch up with highly industrialized countries.

Computer-Assisted Instruction (CAI). Computer-assisted instruction is a sophisticated example of the audiovisual device with a teaching machine feature. The computer can be based hundreds or thousands of miles away from a single learning situation or a network of teaching stations. For example, a class of elementary students can be in Phoenix, Arizona, and the computer can be in Los Angeles, California. The students enter their answers to problems at 10:00 A.M. on one day and almost instantly, as if an airline reservation clerk were querying the space availability on a specific plane flight, the computer will respond with definitive information. If the school system is buying less expensive time on the computer, it may request an overnight computer response.

The classroom may have several response media, including an audiovisual device such as a small TV-like screen. If it happens to be a class in plane geometry, the response may be a printout supporting the student's findings, or it may be a negative response saying something like, "Your answer is incorrect; recheck your figures and the theorem on _____." The system has the fascination of a game-room machine, forcing the student to work harder and harder to outwit the machine or, in effect, to measure up to the expectations of the central programming station.

Sound Filmstrip Machines. Some sound filmstrip machines can be equipped with an inexpensive responder unit with several buttons. This unit enables the learner to press a button to indicate his answer to a question posed by the A/V material. If his or her answer is wrong, the machine may force backtracking and repeating a sequence of frames.

The foregoing examples are intended to be illustrative only. One need only to visit an A/V fair or exhibition reflecting the state of the art to be impressed, and perhaps overwhelmed, with the wide assortment of sophisticated possibilities for mediated instruction.

A Guide for the Production and Use of 35mm Sound Filmstrips

PURPOSE AND ADVANTAGES OF SOUND FILMSTRIPS

The 35mm sound filmstrip is a practical training aid. It combines the advantages of words and pictures, thus appealing simultaneously to the senses of sound and sight. When used as a "prop" by an instructor, supervisor, or any person seeking to teach other people *why* or *how* to do something, the sound filmstrip serves a very valuable purpose.

A motion picture cost yardstick has traditionally been $1,000 per running minute, or $15,000 for a 15-minute film. Many entertainment motion pictures that run 1½ hours cost the producer $1 million or more. A good sound filmstrip can be produced for $500 to $1,500 at government facilities, or 3 to 10 percent of the cost of motion pictures.

The projection of sound filmstrips is much simpler than the projection of motion pictures. Equipment for their projection costs only a small fraction of the cost of motion picture equipment, is more readily available and less apt to break down, and spare parts can be stocked and interchanged with more ease.

CHARACTERISTICS OF A GOOD SOUND FILMSTRIP

A good sound filmstrip is neither too long nor too short. Here is a summary of the characteristics of a good sound filmstrip.

Length and Scope. The running time of the filmstrip should be from 10 to 15 minutes. Its content must definitely teach something or at least be a motivating influence on the audience. Unless it teaches or motivates, the filmstrip has no value. There must be a sharp beginning and ending to the filmstrip. It should not attempt to cover too much ground. Five or six major points, and five or six minor points per major point, are all that any filmstrip should attempt. The filmstrip content may consist of either concepts or techniques. An example of a concept is this: "What is Records Management?" An example of a technique is the statement, "How to Clean, Wax, and Polish Floors."

Action and Number of Frames. A sound filmstrip should seek to achieve the action of a motion picture. It must be more than a series of still pictures, such as those an individual would show as a series of still photographs of his wife and children to a friend. There should be sequences of "almost animated" action, and each sequence should be related to the preceding sequence by some transitional clue.

The sound filmstrip should range from a minimum of 60 frames to a maximum of 100 frames—the more frames (separate images), the more possibility of action; and the more frames, the shorter the audio with each frame. No frame should have audio of more than 45 words.

Organization of Script. The script should hang on a good outline. Like a story, the script should begin with a brief introduction of what the filmstrip is all about. It should then move into the body or main part of the filmstrip. At the end, there should be a "summing up" or review of the main points presented. Repetition is one of the laws of learning. The pattern, "Tell 'Em What You Are Going to Tell 'Em—Tell 'Em—Tell 'Em What You've Told 'Em," has been used successfully countless times in film production. There are many clever techniques for doing the summary. A flashback of key frames is often a simple, effective method.

Audio and Video. Casting for the voices, or voice, will depend upon the nature of the subject matter. A single voice or narrator is appropriate in some instances. In other situations, several voices are needed. This is particularly desirable when each sequence involves a different locale and the possibility of different people. Male and female voices are needed in some filmstrips.

There is sometimes the "third person" situation that necessitates having a commentator cut in at spots to explain an action. The voices should be professional, if possible, and well matched with the visuals they support—that is, the voice of an older person would obviously not be suitable if the employee shown on the film is young. Enunciation and articulation should be sharp and crystal clear. Pace should be a little faster than normal conversation, to keep the audience alert and on its toes.

Variety is the "spice" of filmstrip production. Perhaps this is why variety shows on television are the popular choice of commercial sponsors. This suggests the use of several media—photographs, cartoons, sketches, charts, illustrations, and other material.

The backgrounds should be ultra simple so as not to distract from the idea or teaching point in each frame. There should be one point and *only one* in each frame. Simple word-picture presentations are needed. Complex, obscure, hard-to-get graphics have no place in sound filmstrips. The art work must not be gaudy or overdone. Manikins, stick figures, or other neutral illustrations are usually more effective than human portraits that reveal racial and body features.

An illustrator can paint out distracting elements of the background by skillfully retouching with opaque paints or by air brushing.

A split frame is permissible occasionally, but too much of this slows down the pace and confuses the learner.

Legends (superposed words) over a frame are necessary in spots, but, like split frames, should not be overdone. Legends should be concise, large, legible, and conspicuous.

Black and White or Color? Most subjects can be treated effectively in black and white. Color should be used only when it is essential to proper teaching. A good illustrator can use shades of gray to achieve variation. Black and white is a much cheaper medium than color when it comes to the mass reproduction of prints. If only a few prints are needed (dozen or less), it would be feasible to work in color. Color is usually more appealing to the eye and sparks attention.

Music. It is good to begin and end each sound filmstrip with a brief musical strain. This gets attention at the start and sets the tone for the film. It should be faded in or out at the point where narration begins or ends. The Army, Navy, and Air Force bands have recorded a great deal of music which can be used. One must be careful not to select music that is copyrighted unless given permission by ASCAP, the musician's union.

Audience Participation. It is possible to build into a sound filmstrip the provision for audience participation. This can be done by the use of a few "trailer" frames with which the supervisor or trainer primes discussion. Question-and-answer response patterns can be set up, and various other devices can be used.

Records, Tape, and Storage. The audio part of the filmstrip should be recorded on one side of a 12-inch, microgroove, vinyl plastic (unbreakable) disc, at 33⅓ revolutions per minute, *or* on a cartridge of tape. A 15-minute commentary can easily be put on one side of such a record or on a cartridge of tape. A second commentary, for another filmstrip, can go on the reverse side of the same record or on a second track of the tape cartridge. The use of 78-rpm and standard-groove records should be avoided. Such records involve one or more interruptions during each showing when the projectionist turns over the record. It also involves more packing, shipping weight, and risk of loss and confusion.

Each filmstrip should be packaged in a metal can with lid and printed label. The record should be labeled to correspond with the label on the film can. The tape cartridge should also be clearly identified.

Instructor's Guide. Each filmstrip should be accompanied by a guide containing instructions for mechanical projection; an outline for the instructor to use in introducing the filmstrip; suggestions for use in conducting the discussion after the filmstrip is shown; and follow-up tips of things to look for after the employees are back on the job.

ORGANIZATION FOR PRODUCING THE SOUND FILMSTRIP

A sound filmstrip just does not happen. Like any worthwhile accomplishment, it takes some organization, manpower, ideas, materials, time, and money. Fortunately, money is not a prohibitive item, since the other requisite items are in ample supply in most organizations. The important thing is to mobilize the talents, knowledge, and resources that already exist and bring them to bear on a training problem.

One of the best known strategies for doing this is a "task group." A subject-matter technician working alone would be handicapped. He might be tempted to overload the filmstrip with fine points that the learner would seldom need in his day-to-day operations. He might depend too much on words to carry the message. A training specialist would be even less qualified to produce the filmstrip because he lacks the fundamental knowledge of the subject. Even if working together, these two persons would still be inadequate. They need the skills of the photographer, the artist, the writer, and the practical experience of the operating official or his representative. A team or task group on which all these skills are represented and coordinated is the best approach to filmstrip production.

Other skills are needed in the final stages of the filmstrip production (narrators, sound engineers, film developers, and printers), but these are not needed on the task group.

The task group should meet frequently enough to assure that agreement is reached at all significant stages of the filmstrip production. On the average, the task group will meet at least six times. Material will be circulating among the members of the task groups between meetings.

The task group is the vehicle for implementing the production of the filmstrip. It should not assume responsibility for deciding whether or not to produce a particular filmstrip. Overall policy matters must be left to the conventional channels of official business. It is a good practice for the task group to submit its final script product to a policy-making (administrative) official or review board for official sanction.

In general, the more staff and line people (ultimate consumers) involved in the production process, the better the filmstrip will be and the more complete the acceptance will be. Make it a "community effort."

PRODUCTION STEPS

The following steps are the principal ones to be taken after a training need has been identified and the sound filmstrip is selected as an appropriate training aid. The steps are listed in sequence.

1. Establish task group.
2. Analyze potential audience.
3. Select specific subject to be covered.
4. Establish the objectives of the filmstrip.
5. Enumerate the main points to be made.
6. Prepare an outline of main points and subpoints to establish the skeleton on which to hang the script. This may require research, a job analysis, or having one or more employees perform a job under observation.

7. Shape the outline into several action sequences, as if a play were being written with several acts and scenes.

8. Using a two-column format, with outline of audio on the left side, develop a concise description of the video for each frame. Video works better on the right because the audio is usually developed first and it is more logical to make the first entries on the left-hand side of a page. A sample "frame" would then look like this:

Audio	Video
Applicant is interviewed.	Photo of interview scene.

9. Develop the first draft of the script. (At least six drafts of the script will probably be necessary before it reaches the state of final approval.) The audio side of the scenario then begins to take shape, as indicated in the same sample frame:

Audio	Video
A critical step in the selection process is the personal interview.	Photo of interview scene.

10. Develop pencil sketches and specifications for final rendition of visuals. These can be very small (2 by 2 inches) and rough.

11. Mount each sketch on a separate sheet of paper. Type or write the script for each picture underneath it. If paper about 5 by 8 inches in size is used, the mounted sketches can then be stapled together, book style, into a neat little presentation.

12. Polish script and sketches.

13. Practice recording of script on tape. Voices may be nonprofessional for this.

14. Make a larger set of pencil visuals (9 by 11 inches), with script under each, and tack up around the room for critical review. Play back tape recording. This gives proper perspective and permits a good check for continuity, action, transition, and the like.

15. Resolve controversial and doubtful spots in the audio and video. Get the task group's final approval before proceeding beyond this point in the filmstrip production.

16. Select locale for each sequence.

17. Have the photographer shoot for photographic frames.

18. Have visual presentation specialists do necessary art work, illustrations, legends, transparent overlays, retouching, airbrushing, and other details.

19. Mount all finished frames on 9 by 11 inch cardboard stock of

uniform thickness (about ⅛ inch). Number frames consecutively in pencil.

20. Try out tentative version of sound filmstrip on lay audience, preferably at level of ultimate use.

21. Refine script and visuals. (Changes should be very minor at this point if previous steps have been skillfully done.)

22. Obtain final administrative approval of script at appropriate level (the higher the level, the better). It is not essential to clear visuals unless the task group is unable to resolve doubtful frames. For purposes of clearance, it is suggested that the ribbon copy of the task group's final version of the scenario—audio and video—be mounted in a folder, using metal fasteners, with a clearance sheet on top. The clearance sheet should be signed by members of the task group and the administrator who is giving final approval.

23. Type several copies of the finally approved script, double-spaced, extra large type. Number the frames. Let each page contain several complete frames of script. Don't break a frame at the bottom of the page, as this will handicap the voice artists. Proofread very carefully.

24. Have a photographic laboratory convert the mounted frames (story board) into a master negative, 35mm continuous filmstrip, and make a positive print for proof purposes.

25. Have the script recorded in a soundproof studio or room. The audio for each frame should be punctuated by an inaudible, high-frequency signal in order to synchronize the tape with the filmstrip. Professional voice artists should be used if possible. A radio technician can operate the equipment to insert the signals. He holds a copy of the script as the voice artist reads it. Since the recording will be on tape, it can be erased and modified if changes are required. If the ultimate product for the audio is to be phonograph records, they can be made from the tape.

26. Review the tape proof against the officially approved script.

27. Review the filmstrip proof against the story board.

28. Get new proofs if corrections are extensive.

29. Give OK to filmstrip and tape producers. Number of filmstrip prints and tapes will be administratively determined. Factors to consider include number and location of training places, timetable, availability of funds, and the like. The cost of a print and a copy of the tape should not be more than about $1.00 each.

30. If several filmstrips are done as a series, it may be desirable to procure an album or other suitable container for the filmstrip ma-

terials. An omnibus "kit" for the filmstrips (in cans), tapes, guides, and other material is a good plan.

31. Distribute filmstrip kits for operational use.

32. File copies of filmstrip kits for archival purposes.

33. Conduct evaluation study to determine usefulness of film-strip materials. This study should be designed to improve future filmstrip productions.

USING THE SOUND FILMSTRIP

If a sound filmstrip has been skillfully produced, and if a guide or instructor's manual accompanies it, nearly any supervisor or fore-man can use the filmstrip as an effective training aid. Under no cir-cumstances should the filmstrip be shown without some before-and-after comment from a person familiar with it. If presented alone, the filmstrip may do more damage than good. The stage has to be set, then the filmstrip, then the interpretation.

If the supervisor is resourceful, he can relate the filmstrip to cur-rent operating problems with which the group is confronted. If all members see in it the possibility of gleaning some new ideas that will help them *do more work with less effort,* they will most likely accept it enthusiastically and participate in the showing with a much more co-operative attitude.

The filmstrip should be introduced whenever possible by an operating official. He can relate it to the practical world of work in the organization better than a training specialist can.

It is good practice to use an evaluation sheet to collect anony-mous evaluations of the filmstrip and any suggestions for improving the present or future productions.

Conclusion

Training practitioners and organization leaders should look beyond the character and quality of training in a few of their classrooms. They should explore the numerous possibilities (using existing technology) for disseminating technical knowledge and in-formation on a continuing basis, with quality assurance, and at eco-nomically tolerable unit costs to large and scattered target audiences. In some circumstances, the technology could be adapted to cus-tomers or clients as well as employees.

18

Developing Developers
and the State of the Art

THE development of people developers, like the development of any other group of specialists, starts with selection. This definitely does not mean that people who specialize in training and development are born, not made. The task of development is simplified if one can begin the development with individuals who have some commitment to the field, and some of the skills, technical knowledge, and personality attributes that seem to enhance one's chances of success.

This chapter deals with the assorted categories of work in the training and development field, the basic competencies required, and some measures that an organization can take to accelerate the development of developers. It also offers some suggestions on how organizations can contribute to the growing state of the art in people development. And it is the judgment of this author that there is scarcely a better way to ensure a dividend on an organization's investment in the future than to advance the art of developing human resources.

Readers will note that this author has a strong preference for certain competencies in people developers, such as communication

314

skills, and for certain measures to assure their development, such as continuing education, training, and appraisal/counseling.

Someone once observed that the most effective classroom performance is given by a person who is skilled in teaching, showmanship, and missionary techniques. That observation showed a clear understanding of the tremendous challenge encountered in the art of people development.

Federal Civil Service Categories of People Developers

As one surveys the scene of adult education and training in the business world beyond traditional institutional lines (principally consisting of high schools, business colleges, community colleges, junior colleges, colleges, and universities), one will note wide variances in the size and scope of people development programs. Chapter 6, which deals with space requirements, gives a clue to these variances. Literally, the size and scope of programs vary all the way from one-person units to sophisticated institutes and staff colleges that employ hundreds of persons.

The U.S. Civil Service Commission has identified four roles in the training and development function as follows:

Learning Specialist: concerned with designing, developing, conducting, and evaluating learning experiences

Administrator: concerned with arranging, coordinating, and maintaining the support services of the various development programs

Program Manager: concerned with setting policy, planning, controlling, and managing the various programs individually or collectively

Consultant: concerned with research and development, and providing management and employees with advice and assistance

This is one way of describing the function, but it does divide the work into four rather arbitrary and artificial roles. Take, for example, the one-person training and development office in a relatively small organization, or in a larger one that is just beginning to introduce the function into its operations bloodstream. It has no "learning specialist," "administrator," "program manager," or "consultant." The one person it does have may simply be conducting a standardized orientation program for new employees, or a packaged course for supervisors, or a safety course for plant personnel.

Proposed Categories of People Developers

It is better to start with a set of assumptions about the size and scope of training and development (T&D) activities in an organization, and then examine the roles that *should* exist in each of the typical scenes. While there can be many variations of each format, four will suffice for demonstration purposes. These are:

Small T&D Office: one to three professionals and one clerical employee

Medium-Size T&D Office: 5 to 15 employees serving a major organizational element such as a bureau in the federal government or a large department in a private concern of national or international trade territory

Large T&D Office: up to 100 or more employees serving a large private company or public agency

Institute or Staff College: up to several hundred employees.

SUGGESTED STAFFING PATTERNS

One should find a minimum of the following types of T&D personnel in the several categories of offices:

Small T&D Office: one T&D specialist, one trainer (instructor), and one clerk.

Medium-Size T&D Office: one or more T&D specialists, one or more trainers, one curriculum materials development specialist, one audiovisual (A/V) presentation specialist, and clerical support.

Large T&D Office: one director of employee training and career development; one or more program plans and standards officers; a staff of employee T&D specialists, some of whom are specialized in such areas as supervisor development, management development, executive development, and professional and scientific staff development; staff of curriculum materials development specialists; staff of trainers; staff of audiovisual presentation specialists; research and development staff support; and administrative and clerical support.

Institute or Staff College: one director and one deputy director, one executive officer, one registrar, a faculty of subject-matter experts, staff of curriculum materials development specialists, staff of audiovisual presentation specialists, research and development staff support, and administrative and clerical support

Activities, Competencies, and Developmental Needs of People Developers

The four categories established earlier are repeated below, in about the same order in which such personnel would be added in a large organization from the time a T&D program is first launched until it reaches its ultimate size and scope. A large organization might well have all four of the categories, depending on its degree of decentralization and a variety of administrative factors.

TRAINING AND DEVELOPMENT SPECIALIST

The specialist is expected to:

—Identify T&D needs.
—Determine specific T&D objectives.
—Design courses and programs (including evaluation schemes), fitting the most appropriate methods and devices to subject matter, participants, and trainers.
—Prepare curriculum materials.
—Prepare specifications for outside production of curriculum materials, including ones of an A/V nature; oversee production.
—Identify trainer possibilities from within the organization and on the outside.
—Establish criteria for participant selection and coordinate the publicity and selection processes.
—Teach.
—Consult with management officials on organization goals, program plans, and fiscal matters.
—Consult with operating officials on problems of production; respond with T&D program proposals and estimates of resources needed.
—Counsel with supervisors and individual employees on their career development objectives and available opportunities, both inside and outside.
—Develop T&D policies and procedures.
—Keep records and prepare interpretive reports.
—Perform managerial and administrative functions as required.

Basic Competency Requirements. The education of the training and development specialist should be earned in one or more institutions of higher learning, preferably culminating in the Master's degree in a specialized field such as pedagogy, English literature, science, agriculture, business administration, or the social sciences. The specialist background should have produced a degree of competency in the following skills:

Communication	Positive customer (client) relations
Analytical	Creativity
Teaching	Counseling
Managerial	Problem solving

In addition, the specialist should be familiar with the current state of the art in T&D work and be fully committed to people development. He or she should exhibit vision, perceptivity, and awareness of the forces influencing the organization climate, and should display initiative and energy in conducting a training program.

Developmental Needs. Competency weaknesses may be corrected by assignments in a trainer (instructor) training facility, or in a small T&D office as a generalist, or in a medium T&D office as a specialist. Other options include continuing education and training experiences, self-education and self-training through involvements in appropriate professional societies and community organizations, and special assignments to task groups for sharpening analytical and problem-solving skills.

TRAINER

A trainer is expected to conduct courses using standardized lesson plans and curriculum resource materials; counsel individual participants; and compile, summarize, analyze, and submit evaluation data.

Basic Competency Requirements. Obviously, a trainer must possess teaching and counseling skills. A rich background in the objectives, policies, practices, products, and services of the organization enhances competency.

Developmental Needs. Weaknesses in skills or knowledge may be corrected or compensated by assignment in a trainer (instructor) training facility, special training in counseling methods, continuing orientation to the parent organization's objectives, policies, practices, products, and services, or updating of appraisal/counseling methods. Attendance at fairs and exhibits relevant to the T&D field is also helpful.

CURRICULUM MATERIALS DEVELOPMENT SPECIALIST

Working closely with subject-matter specialists, the materials development specialist prepares for group-instruction programs such material as trainers' guides, practice exercises, case studies, critical incidents, handouts, reference manuals, scripts, and other appropriate curriculum materials. In close association with subject-matter specialists, he or she prepares material in proper format for the several kinds of individualized instruction, including programmed instruction, computer-assisted instruction, correspondence courses, and teaching machines.

As an ongoing activity, the specialist observes operations with a view to recommending modification of operating procedures that are ambiguous and difficult to teach, observes the training process and studies feedback from participants and trainers in order to refine the curriculum materials, and participates in learning experiences that upgrade one's background in relevant subject-matter fields and coordinate one's skills and knowledge in T&D methodology.

Basic Competency Requirements. The materials development specialist must have a background in relevant subject-matter fields sufficient to absorb the essentials of what a participant needs to *know* and needs to *do* in order to perform in a fully satisfactory manner. He must be thorough and conscientious in applying the requisite skills of communication, analysis, and problem solving, and be well informed with regard to current methods for teaching adults.

Developmental Needs. A materials development specialist is expected to have the same educational background as the training and development specialist. In addition, he or she will have attended special institutes and schools to acquire technical skills compatible with the current state of the art in adult education and training, engaged in continuing education and training, and expanded appraisal/counseling skills. Diversified and progressively more sophisticated assignments will build background in the subject matter of the organization for which curriculum development work is done.

AUDIOVISUAL PRESENTATION SPECIALIST

The A/V specialist engages in the following activities:

—Develops conceptual designs for A/V presentations.
—Prepares story board roughs for 35mm filmstrip and slide presentations.
—Supervises photographic aspects of A/V projects at various locales and in studio.
—Sketches and renders portraits, cartoons, posters, animation material, and assorted other items.
—Supervises development of motion picture and videotape productions.
—Works from scenarios and scripts to develop individualized instruction materials for use in teaching machines.
—Directs production of workbooks and handout materials, using appropriate visuals to illustrate the printed word.

Basic Competency Requirements. Competency is reflected in communication skills, artistic abilities, creativeness, currency in the state of the art in A/V presentation media, and background in relevant subject matter fields.

Developmental Needs. The specialist may attend special institutes and schools to fill any gaps in technical knowledge (for example, design, graphics, photography, sound, lighting, animation simulation, videotape systems, publications layout, exhibits). He or she may visit fairs and exhibits, or observe at other facilities with more advanced A/V technology. Continuing education and training, and development of appraisal/counseling skills, will be ongoing pursuits.

DIRECTOR OF EMPLOYEE TRAINING AND CAREER DEVELOPMENT

The activities of the director are numerous. Among other duties, he or she:

—Plans, organizes, and directs the development and administration of a comprehensive program of employee training and career development.

—Collaborates with administrators in matters of executive development and utilization.

—Coordinates development of plans, standards, physical facilities, faculties, curricula, participant selection standards, and other matters relevant to the activation of institutes and staff colleges.

—Consults with operating officials on significant studies that inquire into matters of morale, productivity, and labor/management relations.

—Keeps abreast of the state of the art in employee training and career development through work in professional societies.

—Maintains an awareness of the outside activities of educational institutions, coordinating the in-service T&D programs of his organization with such institutions.

—Contributes to the field of professional literature.

—Observes the national and international scene for social, economic, and political developments that may have impact on his program activities.

—Provides the necessary representation of the director function and reports progress and problems through established channels.

—Oversees the development of budgets to meet fiscal requirements.

—Takes charge of developing a staff to carry on the activities of the organizational function.

Basic Competency Requirements. The director must have demonstrated professional competence in a hard academic discipline, preferably in social science, urban planning, public administration, business administration, or industrial management. His or her leadership qualities must be demonstrated at a high level. Management effectiveness and special qualifications, such as those discussed in earlier chapters, are interdependent.

Developmental Needs. The director's educational background must be at least comparable to that of the training and development specialist. He or she should advance through job rotation in the early stages, as for the T&D specialist, and should engage in continuing education and training to gain experience in teaching and in curriculum development. This objective can be achieved by attending institutes and schools to improve management effectiveness and executive capability, by self-education and self-training in appropriate professional societies and community activities, by attendance at high-level conferences of both line and staff groups, and by courses to develop appraisal/counseling skills.

Program Plans and Standards Officer

Within the framework of organization goals and objectives, the plans and standards officer develops comprehensive curriculum plans, calendars, fiscal requirements, facility needs, faculty needs, and qualification standards, and engages in other appropriate planning activities. He or she keeps abreast of the state of the art in employee training and development, and relates program plans as required.

Formulation of standards affecting participant selection, trainer qualifications, program evaluation and follow-through, cost/benefit ratios, use of outside training and education facilities, and physical environment for learning is a primary function of the position. In addition, the standards officer proposes doctrinal standards for the guidance of curriculum development specialists and trainers engaged in in-house T&D work.

Basic Competency Requirements. The educational and experience background of the standards officer must be necessarily diverse and expansive. The standards officer must have sound perspective of the people development function in relation to organization goals and objectives. Competency is reflected in the ability to analyze specific T&D needs, as determined by individual employee development specialists; to shape comprehensive curricula for future development; to translate such curricula into staff, facility, fiscal, material and equipment, travel, and other needs; and to communicate in precisely written formal language.

He or she must have a general awareness of social, economic, and political issues that have impact on the T&D function and must be able to articulate and gain acceptance of doctrines that accurately reflect whatever course seems most appropriate for the organization to pursue in the interest of the general welfare. Central to the officer's competency is the ability to draft and gain acceptance of policies and procedures that enable the organization to operate its T&D activities with a high degree of uniformity and coordination.

Developmental Needs. The development requirements of the standards officer parallel those of other specialists: job rotation; special institutes and schools for program planning, and policy and procedure development; continuing orientation to the organization's objectives, policies, practices, products, services, and customer (client) complaints; continuing education and training; fairs and exhibits; self-education and self-training in appropriate professional societies and community activities; appraisal/counseling skills.

RESEARCH AND DEVELOPMENT STAFF

The R&D staff is responsible for:

—Conducting special studies of pretraining and post-training performance of various occupational groups to establish cost/benefit ratios and curriculum planning benchmark data.
—Planning and directing experimental projects to test the comparative effectiveness of alternative teaching methods.
—Developing designs for improving the physical environment for learning; consulting with educationally oriented architects and engineers.
—Developing specifications for unique designs of audiovisual aids and equipment to enhance teaching effectiveness; working with scientific laboratories and contractors to perfect and reproduce such designs.
—Cooperating with research groups in studying broader issues of morale and productivity in the organization.
—Analyzing turnover data, recruitment trends, upward mobility rates, and other relevant material for evidence of career-ladder defects and need for better career system planning; presenting its findings and recommendations.
—Studying the findings of major R&D projects in the human resource development area, as reported to national reposi-

tories and clearinghouses; gleaning pertinent ideas for use in the organization.

—Compiling information useful to other T&D staff members on outside T&D facilities; making spot checks on the performance capabilities of such facilities. Maintaining a roster of resource persons who are competent, reliable, and reasonable.

Basic Competency Requirements. Each staff member must be properly qualified as an educational psychologist, using such tools as statistics, scientific sampling, graphic presentation, and research methodology. He or she should have an analytical mind and a compelling curiosity to seek answers to questions through logical approaches and the use of modern technology, including computers. This involves complete objectivity in the examination of one's own findings and those of contemporary groups, as well as a willingness to admit failures in the R&D effort. An interest in exploring new frontiers while preserving the best of old ones is a necessary preliminary to advancing the state of the art in T&D work.

These requirements are best expressed in an ability to organize and present research findings in readable formats for lay readers.

Developmental Needs. The developmental needs of a staff member are similar to those of the T&D specialist: continuing education, orientation, and honing of skills.

ADMINISTRATIVE AND CLERICAL SUPPORT

Support of the various activities is provided by central programs of space utilization, communications, transportations, procurement and contracting, fiscal controls, property accounting, time and leave, payroll, personnel management, library administration, records management, printing and duplicating, furniture and fixtures and A/V equipment maintenance, travel, administrative reporting, and related assignments.

Basic Competency Requirements. Administration of these various components of support requires specialized knowledge and experience in one or more of the areas, such as procurement and personnel management. Effective interpersonal relations with operating personnel depends on cooperative attitudes and sense of responsibility and diligence in meeting deadlines, thus providing positive (not passive) support to the T&D operations, and vital cost conscientiousness and communication skills.

Developmental Needs. Dedicated institutes and schools provide technical skill development in specialties such as contracting, procurement, personnel management, budgeting, and library science.

Other needs are served best by continuing in-service training courses to keep abreast of new policies and procedures of the parent organization, or by self-education and self-training programs compatible with duties and responsibilities, including appraisal/counseling.

Director of Institute or Staff College

The activities of a staff or institute director are similar to those listed for the director of employee training and career development. This, of course, assumes that the basic competency requirements are also similar.

Developmental Needs. A director of an institute or college certainly must be acquainted with the work of the specialties under his or her direction, in order to supervise program plans and standards, curriculum development, or the faculty. Weakness in any facet of his competencies may be helped by practical observation in other institutes and staff colleges, or by the usual means recommended for high-level administrators.

Executive Officer for Institute or Staff College

The executive officer generally heads the administrative and clerical support staff when the institute or staff is large enough to warrant his or her appointment. This executive usually serves as a member of the director's senior staff, participating in the disposition of policy issues and the overall administration of the college, and may also serve as the comptroller, having substantial delegation of authority and responsibility over funds available to the facility.

Basic Competency Requirements. The hallmarks of a competent executive officer include:

—Effectiveness in applying the principles and processes of modern management.
—Sound judgment, unwavering integrity, and accountability in the use of financial resources.
—Awareness and day-to-day practice of such concepts as value engineering, quality control, preventive maintenance, program planning budgets, cost/benefit ratio analysis, work simplification, work measurement, economic order quantity, and pretesting.
—Service attitude toward operating groups to which support is expected.
—Ability to project plans and to translate these into requirements.
—Communication skills.

—Physical stamina to meet pressing deadlines and untold contingencies.

Developmental Needs. The educational background of an executive officer should offer a Master's degree in educational administration, social science, business administration, or public administration. Deficiencies in any of these areas may be compensated by attendance at institutes and special schools to acquire the necessary technical knowledge in such fields as computer applications, forms design, records management, counseling, and human relations. Of course continuing education and training, orientation to the organization's objectives and services, and appraisal/counseling are recommended.

REGISTRAR FOR INSTITUTE OR STAFF COLLEGE
The following activities are assigned to the registrar:

—Designs and administers systems controlling admission to specific courses and programs, data gathering, space reservations, housing accommodations, recreational activities, emergency care of participants, certification of program completion, reporting, field communications, travel requirements, and associated activities.
—Advises the executive officer on the need for new policies and procedures to make the facility run with maximum efficiency.
—Counsels with individual participants and their supervisors with respect to special problems and their career development objectives.
—Collaborates with program plans and standards officers, R&D staff, curriculum materials development specialists, and others concerning prerequisites for particular courses and programs.

Basic Competency Requirements. Competency of the registrar is centered in the following capabilities:

—Effective interpersonal relations with participants, faculty members, and T&D staff.
—Thorough application and understanding of the programmatic goals and objectives of the institute or college.
—Acceptance of and full commitment to modern concepts of people development, with attention to equal opportunity, upward mobility, and career development.
—Effective office management and supervision.
—Building a favorable image of the organization through good public and customer (client) relations.

Developmental Needs. The developmental needs for the registrar are very similar to those listed for the executive officer. The role of the registrar, when well conducted, is an excellent stepping stone to a higher-level appointment. Unfortunately, in many institutes and staff colleges the status of the registrar may not be given deserved recognition, and his or her capabilities may not be exploited.

Developing the State of the Art

When people begin to work together, they soon recognize the interdependence of their respective functions. People in many professions, such as law and medicine, actively exchange technical knowledge and experience, and apparently rely on such exchanges to advance their professional practice. They also appreciate the security offered by membership in a professional association with influence and resources. People developers, too, can and do profit from professional associations. If some of the existing societies do not measure up to their charter objectives, the fault may lie in the neglect and inertia of their members.

If one were to take an impartial look at T&D professional societies, most likely the results would include a negative report, with such specifics as:

—Inbred leadership
—Stagnation; lack of an active program
—Squabbling among the small group that comprises the hard core of the membership or between its factions
—Undue emphasis on the formalities of keeping the organization alive
—Bland literature
—Superficial programming for main events
—Ineffective involvement of members and people who should be members
—A bankruptcy of resources needed to exploit professional issues
—Preoccupation of members with high-priority interests.

The rationale for demanding stronger professional societies that will spearhead dissemination of the state of the art is clearly based on the need to enlighten professionals now unresponsive to dynamic innovations in methods of people development.

Emerging patterns of organization and management spell out more than decentralization, mobility, realignment, mission change, and technology. There are deepening and widening relationships between a complex federal government and the state and local governments. Public concern over the cost of government at all levels and the need to restore credibility through greater efficiency, economy, productivity, and general effectiveness lend impetus to the pressures created by citizen reactions. These reactions of the general public have been legitimatized by civil rights legislation, equal opportunity measures, and other public policy initiatives, but still the pressure increases on legislators to guarantee minorities and women their rightful place in the social, economic, and political life of the nation.

The most successful reform movements are those in which there is maximum citizen (member) participation at all stages. For instance, the rise of consumerism illustrates the effect of mass influence. Therefore, if people development is the key to a better, more fruitful life, the societal constituencies must get to work to improve and standardize the state of the art. A positive plan of action is sketched below for the serious consideration of interested professional societies.

Certification. Develop qualification standards that are sharply defined. Certificate members for a fee. Develop and police a code of ethics.

Education. Hold indoctrination sessions for new members. Conduct institutes of the one- to two-day "all meat" type. Have forums in suburbia in which contemporary philosophies may be exchanged, and elder statesmen and junior members can meet each other in a relaxed atmosphere away from stressful offices. Select from the ranks of the profession individuals those who should be writing (but aren't), and encourage them to contribute to the flow of literature. Find a solution to the self-defeating trend of escalating prices for formal luncheons and dinner meetings; consider breakfasts, picnics, retreats, coffee hours, and other less expensive and bothersome formats.

Introduce more learner-paced materials and teaching machines for self-improvement purposes. Sponsor travel plans to domestic and international centers of training where educational objectives can be furthered.

Institute Remedies and Reforms. Encourage the societies to become counsel for the defense in selected cases of alleged inequity, discrimination, or malpractice imposed by employers on individual members of the profession. Examples of malpractice would cover such episodes as:

—Launching certain types of employees (new supervisors, operators of complex machines, sales people) in their work without prior or adequate training.

—Exploiting the T&D staff by imposing on it burdensome non-T&D work, underpaying it in relation to other facets of personnel management, not giving serious consideration to its members for promotion-from-within opportunities, and so forth.

—Consistent failures to allocate a fair share of resources available for personnel management (industrial relations) programs to the T&D effort.

—Blaming operational failure on lack of T&D success when the facts show that the T&D staff has never been allowed to function in the area in which failures have occurred.

—Justifying certain monies in the name of T&D, but immediately capturing such monies and diverting them to non-T&D purposes.

Press such cases, with the aid of qualified attorneys, until a reasonable solution is reached, or all remedies (administrative and legal) are exhausted. Formulate and promote acceptance of draft legislation and regulations as appropriate.

Rewards and penalties. Grant a few attractive cash awards annually. Establish a program of national recognition, comparable to the "Oscar" and "Tony" programs of the entertainment industry. Institute a plan of censure and decertification to penalize malpractice.

Talent market. Operate an active placement service for persons entering the profession or new to a given geographic area. Have an active out-placement service for the displaced. Counsel members on the preparation of résumés (fee basis).

Service for hire. The professional society should furnish a consulting service to private and public-sector organizations. This service can easily be staffed with retired persons and others who can arrange to take short leaves of absence. Operate a programming service for international organizations and private companies sponsoring foreign nationals for study and practical observation assignments in the United States.

The plan of action outlined above will take full measure of three ingredients: money, discipline, and politics. Public school teachers and administrators have learned how to levy the necessary charge against their energies and resources in order to upgrade their lot and their opportunities and become a full partner at the labor/management table. People developers out in the real world of work need to take a leaf from the public educators' book of experience.

The easiest way to start anything is to start. In this case the thing to start is a group of T&D professionals dedicated to the creation of an entity completely and purposefully designed to centralize the instruments for people development, a national resource too long neglected.

Conclusion

The future of this vital corps of people in our society, whose job it is to maintain and further develop the labor force, depends on two factors: how well we develop people developers and to what extent the state of the art of people development is allowed to keep pace with advancing science, technology, and management. Therefore, organization leaders must lend encouragement and tangible support to recommendations that have great promise for contributing to these two factors. For example, an occasional experimental program that promises to break new ground should be supported by all professionals, and the results should be appropriately publicized. Exchange programs that offer growth opportunities to individuals engaged in employee training and development work—opportunities that will take them to other sectors of the American society, to other nations, or even to very different roles in their own organizations for a change of perspective—should be encouraged. There are countless ways in which top management can make constructive investments in the future by guiding the continuing growth and development of individuals who are dedicated to helping others realize what is possibly the ultimate in the hierarchy of human needs—self-fulfillment through helping others achieve self-fulfillment.

PART FOUR

Examining Results and Determining Future Course of Action

ALL the ingredients of a successful career development and job training program have been discussed in the preceding parts of this text. In this part it will be assumed that the program basics have been organized and are ready to be put into operation. The question is: What other steps should be taken now and later to make sure that the program is operating successfully? For the present, an overall assessment can be made, and the same measurements can be made periodically when the program becomes active. That is the subject of Chapter 19. To monitor the program, management must adopt a follow-through procedure so that weak spots can be identified and so that new developments can be added. Follow-through is discussed in Chapter 20.

Finally, the text concludes with Chapter 21, "Establishing a Training Center or Institute," which is not only a real-life description of a successful program, but is also a summation of all elements in this text.

Overviews of these chapters follow.

Chapter 19. Measuring Results

There are many valid reasons for measuring the results of people development programs. To gather before and after performance data and to determine the impact of training and development is the scientific way. To expect the support of top management and the continuing motivation and best efforts of the people development staff without feedback information on results is expecting too much. To try to enlist learners in training and education activities without knowing how the results will benefit them is futile.

Existing evaluation efforts have many serious limitations. Typi-

332

cally, programs are self-evaluated by the same people who plan and administer them. This method lacks objectivity, professionalism, and credibility. Because resources for proper evaluation have not been committed by most organizations, a full return on investment in employee training and development may never be realized.

The first principle of evaluation is "check and balance." Outsiders are more likely to correctly appraise training and development activities than is the organization's own staff. Evaluation within the context of career system concepts poses questions about each employee's case: "How were his or her training experiences related to the organization's goals and objectives?" and "Were such experiences purposeful building blocks in his or her career development?"

Evaluation should not be overdone. The need is to make sure that it is an integral part of every training and development program, and that its design has top quality.

Chapter 20. Following Through

A training and development experience may well be counterproductive if the participants are not informed of the concepts, methods, and techniques offered. The "loop" is not complete until the T&D director or his assistants can accurately answer the question as to whether or not the specific program advanced organization goals and contributed to the participants' career development in a purposeful way. Since behavioral changes take time, this question obviously cannot be answered at the instant the training ends.

Diverse follow-through methods can be used to gather evidence. These include the use of such groups as the management improvement staff, internal auditors, budget analysts, supervisors and managers, and the training and development staff. Remedial work, such as coaching weak participants, will need to be done. To this end, former participants can sometimes be enlisted.

Follow-through should not be viewed solely as a checkup of former participants to verify their application of classroom lessons. It is also an opportunity to introduce advanced ideas, to build on to basic knowledge and skill already acquired.

Follow-through is a two-way street. It informs the training and development staff of possible weaknesses in the training program, and it encourages participants to continue their training through advanced reading, involvement in professional societies, and other means of self-education, self-training, and self-improvement.

Without follow-through, the practical test of on-the-job performance is not available for evaluating the current program or for discovering the desirability of further modifying it.

Chapter 21. Establishing a Training Center or Institute

Both public and private organizations in the United States have several decades of experience in the establishment and administration of training centers and institutes and have supplemented it by drawing on a century or more of western European experience in this area.

The present trend is toward establishing local training centers and institutes rather than sending professional, technical, managerial, and executive employees away to universities and other sponsors of leadership training. The theme of "anything (an *institution or company*) can do for us, we can do better" is defended more on ideological grounds than on cost/benefit grounds. As a definitive example, or model, this chapter develops the case history of the U.S. Postal Service Institute at Bethesda, Maryland, in 1968. A number of federal agencies have established their own centers, and many large companies have adopted this plan.

19

Measuring Results

ONE can argue with a fair amount of success that the cost of evaluating the T&D effort would be better invested in developing human resources because training, education, and development activities are self-evaluating. In other words, the results of good T&D are self-evident, and bad T&D self-destructs. If a merchant can know when a product or service is not moving, why does an organization need to measure the results of its T&D program?

Theoretically, the argument can be supported, but realistically it is invalid because no well-managed organization will allow a program to run indefinitely without close scrutiny to see if it is paying its way.

Objectives of Measuring Results

The more data available to decision makers about even their most successful programs, the more progress they can make toward their major organization development goals. More specifically, a good set of objectives in measuring results of T&D programs would include the following eight elements.

Gathering Before-and-After Performance Data. Objectively measurable performance in many jobs, particularly in the crafts and office skills areas, can be observed before training commences and periodically as it continues. Quantitative, qualitative, and manner-of-performance data can be converted to graphic form to show each participant's progress or lack of progress. Learning curves can be plotted to determine the plateaus where learning slows and where performance peaks as a result of the impact of the training. These before-and-after data can become an indispensable tool both for the T&D staff and for supervisors and managers.

Providing Budget Data. Organizations cannot project their budget requirements without solid data on which to base their production estimates. For example, turnover experience enables a budget analyst to predict the approximate number of new employees who will be needed in specific occupational categories in order to maintain customer or patron service at the desired level. This analyst must know how long it takes for a new employee to complete basic training and reach a reasonable proficiency level. The cost of providing the basic training is a known. However, if new training methods are introduced and evaluation data show that the training cycle can be substantially shortened, this can translate into a budget saving. Cost/benefit data can be used to strengthen budget justifications and as a budgetary consideration in many decisions that have to be made from an overall agency-planning standpoint.

Gaining Management Support. It is a well-known fact that the T&D function is one of the last, if not the last, management function to be funded by many organizations, and it is the first function to be pared down or eliminated when retrenchment is necessary. Top management tends to have serious doubts about staff services for which there is no tangible proof of need. Hard data from evaluation studies are therefore usual in alleviating such doubts and in gaining management's active support of new initiatives in T&D beyond the straightforward activities such as orientation for new employees and basic skill courses. Management may in turn find evaluation data useful in convincing owners, taxpayers, customers, or other vested interest groups that revenues are being efficiently and economically used as a result of T&D programs.

Gaining the Operating Official's Support. T&D is normally not budgeted as a separate department. Its costs are charged to operating funds over which operating officials usually have full control, once the funds have been allocated by senior management officials and administrators. The T&D specialist may be the one who identifies an operating problem that can be solved by training, but the operating official holds the purse strings. Therefore, he or she is not likely to let go unless the T&D specialist can present objective evidence that training is the solution to that problem. Evaluation data may mean the difference between a Go and No-Go decision.

T&D Staff Guidance. Evaluation data are vital to the work of curriculum development specialists and the T&D director. They may signal the need to add, alter, or drop whole courses and programs or components. They may suggest new initiatives in the use of training media, materials, and equipment. They may indicate new sequencing, new selection standards, or more precise forms of tests and measurements. Evaluation data can obviously affect T&D cost benchmarks. Such data may, in fact, change the direction of the whole T&D effort.

Recruitment and Utilization Staff Guidance. One of the most attractive benefits the recruiter has to offer the prospective recruit is the organization's T&D program. The Navy has for years used training as an enlistment incentive. Why don't civilian government agencies and private employers use the same incentive? Individuals in search of career opportunities are not always just interested in the starting salary; they may want to know how the career promotion system works and what it takes to advance. Case histories of before-and-after training results are helpful. Placement officers can see ways to fill hard-to-fill vacancies when they have evaluation data to show the impact of training. This is particularly true in areas where performance is objectively measurable.

Aids to Career Counselors. Counselors cannot work in the dark. They need objective data on how employees of varying backgrounds and occupational pursuits are responding to training. As they deal with individual problems, they have to know both the limitations of training and the growth potential that can be expected from its use. The counselor assists the employee to move from one career field to another, and advises in the use of both in-service and outside training and education programs to reach career goals. The counselor needs more than the word of the training specialist that T&D is effective.

Meeting the Trainer's Self-Fulfillment Needs. In the hierarchy of human needs, psychologists say that self-fulfillment is the ultimate aspiration. A trainer cannot go on indefinitely teaching well unless he or she is convinced that the training is meeting a need in the organization and that the participants are profiting from it. Evaluation data can provide the source of pride that the trainer must feel to maintain his enthusiasm for what he is doing. Without any measurement system, the trainer is likely to become lackadaisical in his attitude toward his work.

Limitations of Existing Evaluation Methods

First, a few words about the prevailing methods of measuring the results of T&D: Unfortunately, it is my experience that true measurement of T&D results is seldom realized. This is true for a number of reasons. It may well be that there are never enough dollars to do all that needs to be done because, to some, evaluation seems like frosting on the cake. But suppose that a system of determining whether or not the astronauts ever really reached the moon had not been built into the plans for the space launches. Many taxpayers would still be wondering and debating the question, charging that it was all a lot of government propaganda. Instead, the planners engineered a way for the general public to sit before their own television sets and watch the critical phases of the rocketry, including the launch, moon landing, and splashdown in the ocean. This kind of evidence is needed in T&D, too, but the commitment to make the necessary investment apparently is not compelling.

Typically, T&D programs are evaluated by the people who plan and administer them. Too often the evidence of success consists of meager and superficial testimonials from participants who are moved to respond to simple questionnaires that include such items as strengths, weaknesses, best part, poorest part, and a three- or five-point scale for an overall rating. Such evidence is collected during or immediately after a particular T&D activity has been concluded. There is no effort to look into behavioral change or organization development impact at significant intervals after the T&D experience. There is no control group of persons whose performance is observed despite the fact that they receive no training. There is not even a post-training canvass of the participants to see if they perceive the T&D experience as having been beneficial (or detrimental) to their work. There is no study to see how a series of such T&D inputs may be affecting the career advancement and upward mobility of participants.

Limitations of Measuring

A summary of the major limitations of such evaluation as exists might be better labeled as a list of its deficiencies.

Lack of Objectivity. Attempts at measurement, such as they are, lack objectivity. The principle of check and balance is not used. People who design programs obviously have a self-interest to protect.

Lack of Professionalism. It is doubtful that many T&D specialists even have the skills necessary to design a truly professional approach to T&D evaluation. Test and measurement standardization is a specialized discipline within the field of psychology, and not very many T&D specialists are qualified to administer or judge the results of such evaluation. The cost of a sophisticated measurement system is prohibitive in most situations and its application is beyond the capability of the in-house T&D staff.

Participant Selection System. Many participants who need and could benefit from a particular T&D program are never selected for it. The experience is either poorly timed or supervisors think they lack the qualifications to benefit from it. Frequently, this is due to the fact that most selection systems are based on crude selection standards and the prevailing notion that the T&D staff *has to accept what the nominators nominate.* The nomination system is, unfortunately, fully capable of "making the rich richer and the poor poorer." Every conceivable bias can enter into nominations. Then, when an autocratic supervisor or manager fails to respond to a one-week course in something like "Effective Supervision and Management," observers cannot understand why the training experience has made no behavioral change. Perhaps 20 minutes of time with a professional counselor would have had a better chance to reach the individual.

Performance Appraisal System. Performance appraisal systems are generally as ineffective as T&D evaluation systems. The federal government made a big issue of "Efficiency Ratings" about 30 years ago. Under the sponsorship of the U.S. Civil Service Commission, annual conventions were held in which several thousand delegates from departments and agencies would gather for an all-day dialogue on the philosophy and techniques of rating civil servants. Refinements were constantly being made in an evolving system and these progressed from a numerical result as a final rating (such as 83.5) to a five-adjective scheme, to the present system, which is basically the three-adjective choice of "Outstanding," "Satisfactory," or "Unsatisfactory." The three-adjective plan was virtually the end of a meaningful performance appraisal system in the federal government, since 98 percent or more of federal civilian agency employees are placed in the "Satisfactory" category. The supervisor or manager who makes an extra effort to justify an "Outstanding" or "Unsatisfactory" rating does so at considerable risk. The animosity created when peers do not receive the highest rating can be disruptive; pressing charges against an employee on the basis of an unsatisfactory rating can be explosive, and results in the supervisor's being put on the defensive.

The existence of weak or nonexistent performance appraisal systems is significant from several standpoints. Performance systems should point to specific individual needs for T&D. They could be a benchmark from which the tangible results of T&D could be measured. They could be a constructive guide to future recruitment, selection, and placement. Obviously, they could aid the curriculum development staff by letting it know where training is helpful and where it is not.

Participant Feedback. The principal source of data on many T&D programs is what the participants say about them during and immediately after the programs end. Participants obviously have a vested interest to protect. Often they have asked for the training, have been excused from productive work, and have traveled at the employer's expense to get it. Moreover, they may want further training at a later date. To admit weakness of the program may suggest weakness as a learner. Why, therefore, should they say the training was worthless? The most frequent conclusion expressed by participants is that "It was good stuff but it should have been given to my boss!"

Lack of Follow-through. The ultimate effectiveness of any T&D effort depends heavily on the final phase, which is follow-through. This phase is seldom if ever undertaken. Lacking this final step, existing evaluation systems are probing for results from only a partially delivered T&D service. Granted that follow-through is difficult and expensive, it would probably be better to dispense with a well-designed evaluation plan than to neglect the follow-through. Actually, both could be combined, for the acid test of evaluation is on-the-job performance as perceived by the participant, his supervisor, his peers, and any subordinates.

Inadequate Resources. A fragmentary evaluation effort made for lack of adequate resources is little, if any, better than a fragmentary evaluation effort made for lack of honest intent or know-how. The validity of evaluation results depends upon the execution of a design that has merit under the particular circumstances. Money spent on a token effort might be better spent on additional training of an unknown quality.

Evaluation Undertaken as an Afterthought. When evaluation occurs because of a challenge such as "How do we know the training is any good?" the results are of questionable value. The planning of evaluation needs to be an integral part of the planning of the T&D activity itself. The execution of the evaluation plan needs to be sequenced, some while the program is in progress, some as it ends, and some at later dates when performance results can be measured and related, if possible, to the T&D effort. These steps cannot be taken systematically if they are not conceptually designed at the outset.

Suggested Approach

Soundly conceived T&D routinely begets soundly conceived measurement of results. All the limitations or deficiencies discussed above, and others not mentioned, are dealt with in the course of doing the T&D job—quietly, efficiently, and almost unconsciously. Objectivity, professionalism, better selection standards, and better performance appraisal, all these and other facets of a total evaluation system become an integral part of the ongoing T&D activities. Evaluation is not a separate or optional accessory to the main vehicle. It is an indispensable and integral part of the program, budgeted for, professionally staffed, and executed.

The cornerstones of a sound evaluation program therefore can be identified by the following characteristics.

Career-System Related. Evaluation processes must operate within the context of a career development system. This means that each T&D experience will be used as a *purposeful building block,* not as an incidental happening in the haphazard movement of an individual through an organization. For some, the movement may be a revolving-door type of experience, in and out, with little or nothing learned and without one's marketable skills and abilities having been enhanced one iota. If evaluation is conceived as an integral part of T&D, and made to function accordingly, then it becomes not only a measure of T&D, but also a test of whether or not the career system is accomplishing the objectives for which it was intended.

The Warp and Woof of People Development. Evaluation is a continuing part of the T&D effort, from the beginning of conceptual design of the program itself until the follow-through and a reasonable number of post-training performance appraisals have been examined. It is as interwoven as the warp and woof of a good fabric. It has a feature inherent in the routine of skillfully driving an automobile or airplane. The driver or pilot doesn't read the gauges *casually, after the trip;* he checks them before the trip for proper performance; he monitors them continuously as the trip progresses; he takes corrective action as required, even to the extreme of aborting the trip; and he records and analyzes the data collected after the trip is finally ended. Finally, he takes the recorded experience into consideration as he plans other trips involving comparable objectives, equipment, and conditions.

This means that the evaluation planning must include such steps as careful job analysis to determine what the participant needs to know and what he needs to do on the job to be successful; further, it must consider what conditions are most conducive to effective performance. This may mean special study of a sample of fully trained and proficient employees who are now performing similar kinds of work, in order to identify desirable behavioral characteristics so that the T&D can be designed to reproduce these characteristics in others.

Phasing. The evaluation steps should be introduced in a manner that will make them flow naturally and rhythmically into the stream of all T&D activities. They should not be abrupt, awkward, and strange events that take the participants by surprise and put them on the spot of having to attest to the worthiness of the trainer's effort to teach. "Final examinations" of the conventional type in our educational experience are often thought of as a test of one's ability to recite what the teacher best likes to hear—a replay of his or her lectures. One of the great advantages of experiential methods of teaching, such as role playing, is that the participant begins to interact naturally with the subject matter and with other participants, thus allowing the trainer to observe to what extent the training may be having a behavioral impact on the learner. Small-group buzz sessions help mold and remold attitudes as the social pressure of the group increases on particular individuals. Feedback from such sessions by group-appointed reporters provides a measure of how well the principles and permanently useful generalizations are being absorbed. The trainer's observations through these informal means can be unceremoniously ratified by properly timed evaluation instruments.

Checks and Balances Through a Board of Visitors. The academic world has traditionally subjected its work to the review of an external mechanism called "board of visitors." It is part of the effort of each secondary school and each institution of higher learning to keep in good standing with the community it serves and the accrediting association whose standards it must continue to meet in order to enjoy accreditation. Accreditation is as vital to educational institutions as a pure water supply.

There is no good reason why the T&D arm of both public and

private organizations should not employ the principle of a board of visitors, at least in modified form. On the contrary, there are several excellent reasons why the concept would be a splendid idea. First, the parent organization is much more likely to gain an impartial assessment of T&D activities. Secondly, the importation and exportation of ideas and techniques, methods, and devices through the catalytic effect of the board of visitors is a constructive practice. Thirdly, the involvement of the academic community in the evaluation of an organization's T&D work can further its objectives by having in-service T&D programs recognized by colleges and universities, so that the employees can, if they wish, be awarded credits that further career advancement or qualify them as candidates for academic degrees.

The board of visitors should have balanced representation in order to yield maximum benefit from its reviews and reports. For example, in the review of a federal department or agency, or a major element thereof, the board might consist of representatives from local colleges or universities, the U.S. Civil Service Commission, the federal roster of T&D directors, interested committees of the Congress, state and local government agencies, the private sector, and the citizen lay public. The report of the board, which need not occur annually, should receive wide distribution within the organization. It should be digested in appropriate media, such as the annual report, house organs, and public media releases. It should be seriously considered in preparing both short-term and long-range budget proposals.

The board of visitors evaluation project should be regarded as a necessary supplement to, rather than a substitute for, the organization's continuing internal T&D evaluation efforts. Ideally, the board should be joined by selected observers (nonvoting status) from the organization itself. Subject-matter experts, top management representatives, the T&D staff, operations elements, labor organizations, and employee groups are appropriate sources from which observers might be invited. The availability of resource people as well as adequate staff support can improve the chances of the board's making a fuller and more accurate set of findings.

Doctrine. Every evaluation, regardless of how superficial or comprehensive it may be, should make some effort to determine the doctrine behind the T&D effort, if any, and to what extent the participants are assimilating the doctrine and responding behaviorally. For example, suppose the doctrine being taught in supervision and management courses is one of tough but fair treatment of subordinates. Participants may not be in sympathy with this doctrine and may be doing just the opposite—practicing a gentle and participative style with subordinates. Or, the doctrine may be one of teaching work simplification to supervisors with the admonition that they should get all the participation they can from employees in developing better work methods. Supervisors may scoff at this doctrine and ignore employee participation in their search for work simplification results.

A Negotiative Matter. Labor unions and employee organizations may have missed the boat in limiting their all-out bargaining to pay and fringe benefits. What is more significant in the long-range future of an employee than a career system and T&D opportunities administered equitably within the context of civil rights legislation and merit system concepts? It is all well and good that the messenger continue to enjoy his cost-of-living increases and the standard package of fringe benefits such as retirement, leave, and medical insurance provisions. But if he continues as a messenger year after year, without any upward mobility, without any enrichment of his skills and abilities, he is still "poor" and will remain so in relation to his potential. This assumes, of course, that the messenger is both educable and trainable.

Managements have tended to play this card close to their chest. They say that the decision to train or not to train is a management prerogative. Perhaps so, but it ought to be negotiable and the evaluation system ought to have provision for examining the T&D objectives and plan of action to determine to what extent the current status of T&D activities is the product of honest negotiation with the employees' duly authorized spokespersons.

Communication with Other Management Specialists. Evaluation should look at the T&D effort from the standpoint of its interdependency on other management disciplines in the organization. Does it operate as a "watertight compartment"? Do the other management specialties ignore it, or consult with it and share the burdens of planning and problem solving? Career development of an individual can be realized only through the cooperative efforts of a number of people working cooperatively—the T&D staff, the employee utilization staff, the counselors, the position classification staff, and others. The evaluation effort should therefore probe to try to identify these interdependencies. Collaboration with other management disciplines should be built into its planning by the T&D staff, and should be reflected in the curriculum materials.

Records, Statistics, and Reports. No T&D programmatic or evaluative effort can be very professional unless it generates a reasonable amount of records, statistical data, and reporting practice. A program void of these things would be as helpless as a medical clinic without clinical records. Many organizations have reached the stage of growth and development where they can afford to computerize their T&D records. This means a loss of much hard work unless time is set aside for the careful analysis of the data contained in these basic records. The periodic evaluation by a board of visitors is a good time to schedule a thorough analysis of T&D data.

Some Special Cautions

This chapter ends with the same general caution offered in its beginning—evaluation can be overdone. It is not the intent of this chapter to try to "beef up" evaluation efforts for the sake of beefing them up. Instead, it is my hope that reflective reading of this chapter will help to improve the *quality* of evaluation. Managements need more than a tiny trickle of testimonials from participants to assure them that the T&D activity is healthy and productive. They need to put in place some machinery for making evaluation completely objective and constructive.

Another caution is that the dynamism of change may require new criteria with every new evaluation. The state of the art in T&D is far from static. Social, economic, managerial, and technological changes require frequent adjustments in T&D activities.

Finally, one must constantly be alert to the possibility of the Hawthorning effect of increased attention to the human element in organizations, namely, that employees respond to what they identify as increased attention, more empathy, and compassion. Evaluation should try to sort out which responses are due to the Hawthorne effect and which are truly derived from T&D. This is not an easy task, but it is an important one and an organization is foolish to ignore it.

Conclusion

Organization leaders have every right to expect a dollar's return from training and development for every dollar spent on it. Therefore, they should exercise the oversight necessary to ensure check and balance in the approach to evaluation and require that a steady flow of objective data come from people development activities. It is not enough to see testimonials of a few participants. The leader's support and continuing commitment of resources should depend on the progress that objective evaluators report. However, allowance should be made for the fact that instant results are not obtainable in some training and development programs such as executive development programs.

20

Following Through

ONE must never lose sight of the fundamental purposes of people development in the business world. Primarily, the process aims to aid in accomplishing organization goals—economy, efficiency, productivity, general effectiveness of mission, and profit. Secondarily, it aims to further the individual's realization of his goals, aspirations, and special interests. As in radio communication, the operator can hardly be sure of a message sent without evidence of a message received. In training and development (T&D) work, the test is human performance—behavioral change for the better.

Completing the Loop

Look back quickly at the principal steps leading up to the need for follow-through. They include:

Specific needs determined within the context of organization goals
Conceptual design of the T&D program
Program planning
Curriculum materials development
Assembly of appropriate T&D aids and equipment

Arrangement of appropriate facilities—the environment for learning

Selection of participants according to specific qualification standards

Conduct of the T&D program

Evaluation (initial phases)

Preliminary evaluation evidence may show that a T&D program had some major defects. What is to be the ultimate result of the program if there is no follow-through? It may well be counterproductive if the participants have no opportunity to be set straight in the concepts, methods, or techniques offered in the original training. This can spoil their attitudes toward management's investment and that of their supervisors and managers. How can the program be refined without the necessary feedback from participants who have had the training and tried to apply it? How can other participants be attracted to the program, persons who may need it even more, if "the word" is that the program is marginal and has serious limitations? How can the T&D staff improve its own performance if it never gets the "echo" back from the top? Obviously, some follow-through is called for. There is room for differences on how much is economically feasible and professionally adequate. This chapter offers a suggestion on this point. It also underscores the need for having the follow-through get the employee moving, or moving at a faster clip, on a program of self-education, self-training, and self-improvement.

Again be reminded that the loop is not complete until the T&D director or responsible members of his staff can accurately answer the questions as to whether or not the specific T&D program advanced organization goals and contributed to the participants' career development in a purposeful way.

Reading the Indexes to Organization Development Effectiveness

Since effective performance is the stated purpose of T&D, it is well to take a routine reading of the barometers that are most sensitive to changed behavior in the people affected. If the program were nothing more than a straightforward refresher course for marginal typists, it would be easy to take these readings (look at the before-and-after-training production and error rates). If it were a safety training course, the results might begin to reflect in lower accident rates soon after the training.

But what if it were a basic course for new supervisors? Obviously, no single barometer can tell the follow-through specialist much, regardless of the elapsed time after training. Multiple indexes must be examined. The behavioral changes even months later may be imperceptible, and if any have occurred, they may be subtle. The subordinates' production may have improved, but might it not have improved without the supervisor having had the training? The subordinates may be reacting to a "Hawthorne" effect, thinking that management has at last sensed their need for a new supervisor. The unit may be operating more economically and efficiently, but this may be attributable to change in technology or system.

The unit may have become more responsive to its patrons, and is therefore more effective in its job, but this change in direction may have originated with new leadership at the top. The grievance rate may be down, but this could be the "honeymoon" phase following some successful bargaining by labor and a new agreement, the terms of which leave less latitude for complaints. Safety measures instituted by safety engineers may have had an impact on accident rates, so the new supervisors can hardly claim any credit for this improvement. The point is that, as one looks at the logical indexes of organization performance, one must assess apparent improvements within the context of the total environment in which performance is considered. After making the necessary allowances for non-T&D factors, it is fair to credit the program with a reasonable net gain.

In the case of manager training and executive development, it is even more difficult to sort out the variables from the constants and reach an equitable judgment on what credit can be given to a T&D program. The notes that a follow-through specialist takes in routinely checking specific indexes should be regarded as merely a working hypothesis, subject to further inquiry. Essentially, the process of follow-through is like any other investigation. One must examine a number of sources and compare the results until a pattern emerges which the weight of evidence supports.

Using Diverse Follow-through Methods

Follow-through is in reality not a task for a single individual who suddenly appears, like a bank examiner or postal inspector, and goes through some secretive set of routines to try to trap an embezzler. The follow-through process can be integrated into the routine operations of a diverse alliance of institutionalized groups in the organization. I am a firm adherent to the check-and-balance principle of administration, and therefore believe that the most convincing evidence will be collected by groups other than the T&D staff.

One such group that has a natural interest in improved organization effectiveness, efficiency, and economy is the management improvement staff. It is continually making surveys, instituting change, and making cost/benefit analyses. It has an established network of contacts among both line and staff personnel. Such staffs are showing an increased awareness of the potential in people development programs. The T&D director can systematically apprise the management improvement staff (it may be called industrial engineering staff in industry) of the objectives, scope, and personnel affected by T&D operations. Follow-through can become a collateral part of its normal operations, and in this way the follow-through becomes a smoother, less precipitous event.

Internal audit groups are another good possibility. These groups are interested in verifying the accountability and the degree of mission effectiveness, and the extent to which authorized funds have been used within the limitations imposed by appropriating bodies. They are pleased when they discover, on repeat audits of any operation, that conditions have improved and that the management people have been responsive. It is of no great concern to the auditors how the turnaround was accomplished, so they are far more impartial observers of the impact of T&D programs than would be the T&D staff itself. Both the auditors and the management improvement analysts are in an excellent position to act as catalysts in the formulation of T&D programs and methods.

Budget analysts are more or less in the same category. They are, in effect, the "bankers" for every group of spenders in the organization. The comptroller or budget director puts his or her reputation on the line at least annually when testifying before examining and appropriating bodies. He or she vouches for the soundness of whatever program that seeks continuance of funding or new money for the first time, and attests to the ability of client groups to deliver the products and services enumerated in the narrative justification. When a group misses its delivery target, has catastrophic cost overruns, or generates a lot of flak from its public, the budget people are humiliated in the next round of hearings. It is their responsibility, as budget periods progress, to monitor organization performance as a whole and that of each of its elements; to control for overexpenditure and underexpenditure; and to ensure compliance with laws, regulations, and policies; also to verify compliance with the legislative intent of the appropriating body. Budget people are delighted to see sound T&D programs instituted because this reinforces their program objectives.

The cornerstone of any good follow-through program has to begin and end with supervisors and managers. It is they who are closest to individuals who have participated in a specific T&D experience, and they are the first to share with the participant the delight of being able to perform at a higher skill or conceptual level. Supervisors and managers have to be trained to a new level of awareness, however; specifically, to realize that a training program does not end when the last formal session of the program ends. Further, supervisors and managers must accept the role of being an extension of the formal T&D staff, with responsibilities to coach, guide, encourage, question, suggest, recognize new accomplishments, show compassion when failures occur, and the like.

The work scene is the true field laboratory for testing the theories and methods presented in the classroom. Supervisors and managers are the field lab overseers, and cannot neglect the obligation to observe, listen, and report informally to the training director. Actually, they have a dual responsibility. They have an instant, spontaneous obligation to do what is indicated at the work scene when the post-training participant puts his new knowledge and skill to work. Secondly, they are obliged to communicate through the normal channels about the results obtained from the application of new knowledge and skill.

The T&D staff can, in limited ways, be a part of the follow-through process. While it is usually understaffed for the mission it is charged with, it can employ methods that are economical in the use of staff time. For example, it can use questionnaires on a scientific sample basis to gather data from supervisors, managers, participants, and others. It can call a given group of participants back for a trailer session or meet them at a mutually convenient place. It can use mail-outs to clinch key points and to provide additional information. It can encourage an open-door policy so that former participants may be more inclined to visit, call, or write to express their special needs, concerns, and suggestions about the program they attend.

The staff can also use the house organ to clarify points that follow-through feedback suggests are causing difficulty. The house organ can also run feature articles from time to time on the gains from T&D programs, which means that the reporters are doing some of the follow-through leg work. Letters to the editor, if such a column is carried, may provide a few straws in the wind as to how the training is going.

Coaching Weak Participants

The diverse media approach to follow-through should help in isolating former participants in T&D programs who are having some difficulty adjusting to new concepts and methods taught. The T&D staff has as much obligation to these individuals, if not more, as they do to participants just beginning a training program. A variety of things can be done to reinforce training, some on an individual basis and some on a group basis. It may be possible to communicate with supervisors of such participants and suggest how they can provide the remedial instruction. It may be also possible to arrange for certain institutional groups, such as counselors or systems analysts, to give supplemental help. A subject-matter expert may be willing to meet with selected participants who can profit from a question-and-answer session or a demonstration of methods and equipment.

The T&D office may have a system of providing packaged loan material or self-instructional materials and devices for participants who need refresher training. A good in-house library can be enlisted to offer technical assistance.

The T&D staff may have a network of T&D representatives throughout the organization who are available as resource people to former participants. This would be only an incidental part of their regular duties, but their assistance would be particularly helpful because they are more cognizant of T&D operations than is the typical operator. In this sense, they are, within the context of this book, as much people developers as the T&D staff itself. Therefore, they take a special interest in providing informal advice and assistance to former participants, as well as in identifying individuals with potential for further development.

The T&D staff should always be open to visits, calls, and written communications from former participants who want additional help. The need for individual casework should, of course, diminish as the staff perfects its approach to effective teaching.

Soliciting Help from Former Participants

It is not unusual for a group of participants from scattered geographic and organizational locations, who are brought together for a substantial period of time in a common-need T&D program, to express the desire to keep in touch with each other. They may even ask the program director to arrange a future gathering of the group so that they can swap experiences. As a minimum, they want the names, mailing addresses, and telephone numbers of each participant for future reference. This common desire to avail themselves of a newfound network of professional friendships can be used for follow-through purposes by the T&D staff. For example, if it gets word through any of its channels that a particular member of the group is in trouble in his attempts to apply the material taught in a program, other selected members of the group may be invited to lend a hand.

Another way in which participants can help each other is through contributing case history and critical incident material to a clearinghouse service operated by the T&D staff. This is essentially the system used by the medical profession. That is, theory is learned in medical school but it is practiced only as doctors provide medical services to their patients. Significant conclusions gleaned from the practice are published as articles in medical journals. T&D specialists should use the same strategy in their own professional development, and to a much greater extent than they do. A small minority of T&D practitioners tend to do all of the writing for publication. If they would urge, as standard operating procedure, that all participants in programs contribute to a case history and critical incident "bank," it could serve a dual purpose. The participants could draw on the bank for problem-solving assistance, and the T&D practitioners could use choice material from the bank as a basis for contributions to professional publications.

The director of any T&D program is usually able to identify several participants who genuinely "catch fire" or, as some might say, are "turned on" by the substance of the program. They are naturals for receiving some additional training to qualify them as trainers. These trainers are probably equally good in one-to-one follow-through and in group-training situations. The T&D staff can conserve staff time, cement its relations with the key participants identified as trainers, and reinforce the learning of weaker participants by asking such trainers to do a special assignment. It obviously requires diplomacy and tedious orchestration, but nothing is accomplished without effort and this is an effort well worth making.

The same technique can be useful in the conduct of T&D programs of varying kinds. This especially applies in the case of executive-development and management-training programs. Key individuals who respond favorably and creatively to a particular program can be invited to make guest appearances in subsequent runs of the same program they were exposed to and in other related programs. The old sales technique of using testimonials of satisfied customers works equally well in T&D work. It lends credibility. It improves communication. It gives a change of pace. It essentially is follow-through insofar as the resource people are concerned.

Introducing Advanced Ideas

Follow-through should not be limited to the task of clinching the material presented in the classroom or formal phase of a particular program. It should be conceived as an opportunity to build onto such knowledge and skill with additional material so that new vistas and increasingly responsible performances can be realized by the individual. As in music or any of the arts, one must continually reach new plateaus of learning in order to maintain one's interest and sense of self-fulfillment.

There are many ways in which to introduce new and advanced ideas to former participants. Chapter 10 enumerates and briefly describes an assortment of such methods. I am convinced that far too little use is being made of individualized instruction in the T&D world. Countless dollars are literally wasted by transporting people great distances and excusing them from production on the assumption that *group* instruction is required for results. B. F. Skinner proved a generation ago that this is not true. The oldest form of individualized instruction—correspondence courses—is still alive and well in the marketplace. Programmed instruction and teaching machines were an outgrowth of Skinner's teachings, and they will be with us indefinitely. The computer age brought a special form of individualized instruction called "computer-assisted instruction (CAI)."

Additionally, there are countless informal methods of passing along new ideas and techniques to a target audience with whom communication has already been established. Once the audience can "speak the language" of a given body of subject matter, the follow-through capability need not depend so heavily on multimedia instruction. Even the lecture method may suffice. And one need not be so particular in choosing the size of the group in relation to the instructional source.

Creating a Presence

Family reunions among the members of private families are not much different from "family reunions" of persons interested in a specialized field of human endeavor. The losers are the members who fail to appear at such reunions. T&D staff members have a special obligation to create a presence at places and on occasions where they are likely to encounter former participants. These places include social and recreational occasions sponsored by the organization, field conferences, general staff meetings, professional society activities, fairs, exhibits, and the like. The T&D staff can watch for opportunities to be a part of the agenda, again to create a presence and to demonstrate its availability for consultation and special assistance. A T&D staff with a passion for anonymity is no more likely to realize its full range of objectives than is a sales force in the merchandising world likely to meet its sales objectives by not working its markets.

The T&D staff need not monopolize these extracurricular activities. It can create a presence just as effectively by managing to feature some of their star participants. For example, if an organization has a special program for young professionals, it may be more effective to have one or more of the current or former participants featured on the program. A living presence to exemplify the benefits of the T&D program not only helps the advancement of the program's image, but also gives selected participants another growth experience and presumably accelerates their maturation. It is a useful follow-through technique.

Encouragement to Become Active Professionally

The shortcomings of some of the professional societies that seek earnestly to serve professional groups in the public and private sectors are not incurable conditions that their respective constituencies have to learn to live with. The need for strong professional societies in today's world, at all levels of government and private enterprise, could not be greater. Here are some of the specific reasons:

—A growing need for professionals who are skilled in the art of functioning in a dynamic (even unstable) climate

—The lack of professionals who understand grant management and have the perspective to promote wholesome federal/state relationships without sacrifice to federal standards or state objectives

—A need for professionals with the communication skills and knowledge to articulate sound approaches to economy, efficiency, and general effectiveness in government, and to help in interpreting such programs to the citizenry

—The failure of professional societies with the ability, resources, and courage to reorient administrators who are objective enough to listen, and to wage a fierce campaign against those who prefer to apply their premeditated bias when they move from one sector to the other or from one industry to another

—Minimal effort to take advantage of the innate urge in people, particularly professionally trained people, for self-expression and creativity, which is not fully satisfied at all stages of one's growth and development in bread-and-butter jobs. Professional societies can provide an alternate theater in which this need can be expressed.

The needs to which professional societies can advance solutions will remain unmet as long as some of these organizations remain in the hands of caretakers and are unable to enlarge their active membership. Bootstrap operations are difficult, to say the least. They can be given a tremendous assist by the people developers who are everywhere, if the latter will only make it a regular practice to encourage people in all professions and specialized areas of work to become active in a professional society or the equivalent in the crafts. It takes commitment, strategies, campaigns, courage, resources, and a meaningful program that attracts and holds members through maximum involvement and earned rewards. Therefore, professional societies working closely with people developers not only can contribute to the health and rebuilding of marginal professional societies but also can help individuals find new avenues for growth and expression.

It is an established fact that people who are active in such organizations tend to advance faster and farther in their careers. Since all interested parties tend to gain from participation, it is exceedingly important that the follow-through process in T&D reflect this thought. Incidentally, one of the standard things done for U.S. government-sponsored foreign nationals by International Training Office of AID is to help them identify with an appropriate professional society and to subsidize an initial membership for follow-through purposes when the participant has returned to his or her home country.

Encouraging the Pursuit of Self-Development

In the final analysis, people's careers are largely self-developed. Those who have the basic intelligence will learn when they want to learn, and work at it. Teachers, beginning with parents and siblings, merely assist in the process by answering questions, showing, cautioning, and encouraging. Adult learning is not much different. Without the determination to advance one's knowledge and skill, and the self-discipline to explore new vistas for broadening and deepening one's career opportunities, an individual will fall into a rut and vegetate. He or she may even become a menace to society, for without marketable skills and someone to lean on for sustenance, there is not much left except to take forcibly from others. The root of much of the street crime is lack of marketable skills, and this inadequacy is usually the result of the criminal's failure to be self-starting or to be near enough to people who can and will encourage and guide him or her into channels of self-development, self-training, and self-improvement. Unfortunately, the first prison experience in our society too often turns off the career opportunity clock permanently.

Self-development is a life-long chore for everyone. It does not cease to be a responsibility at age 21 or on landing the first job. Nor is it complete even at retirement from the first career, for one then needs to turn to a second career or to hobbies in order to meet economic or emotional needs that will continue to the moment of death.

The T&D community has a special obligation to follow through by guiding participants into channels of self-development—to let them know where to go for further help. It has the knowledge and experience for doing this. Unfortunately, its resources are always much too limited to do all that it knows needs doing. The key to its making the maximum use of the resources it does have is *involvement of others* in its follow-through activities. Obviously, it must use every possible strategy for getting the multiplier effect. This chapter merely introduces some of the many possibilities. Readers will see others.

Program Refinement

Follow-through by any good T&D staff gleans ideas and material for making programs better and for validating the whole mission. If a training program neglects it, then organizations, both private and public, have misappropriated much of their spendable income on a dead-end venture. Too much capital invested in physical assets, expansion, and maintenance leaves relatively little for developing human resources, without which no organization can function. The point here is that follow-through not only ensures the success of the whole T&D effort, but also ensures the success of the organization.

Conclusion

Organization leaders should require the training and development staff to conduct a follow-through on the job performance of the participants in the program. The "loop," beginning with a recognized need and the conceptual design of a solution, is completed when technical assistance enables the participant to make desired behavioral changes. Each participant should view every training and development experience as a solid cornerstone on which to build more sophisticated work experiences. Without the program refinements that result from follow-through, an organization cannot fully realize the return on investment to which it is entitled, nor can the trainee or trainer be sure that efforts expended in the program have been worthwhile.

21

Establishing a Training Center or Institute

THE federal government has a long history of establishing and operating staff colleges and training centers to meet its specialized needs. The most notable example is its operation of educational institutions for the development of leadership for the Army, Navy, and Air Force.

Some Background on Training Centers

In 1921 a "Graduate School" was established by the Secretary of Agriculture to provide continuing education for Department of Agriculture employees and those of other departments. This facility functions on a large scale, offering both evening and daytime continuing educational opportunities. Other federal facilities include: the Foreign Service Institute, the Army Management Engineering Training Agency, a network of Internal Revenue Service training centers, the FBI Academy, a law enforcement training school for Customs and several other agencies, the Federal Aviation Agency Center, the Postal Service Training and Development Institute, Air

Force and Army centers for training civilian personnel staff members, the Federal Executive Institute and several executive development centers and institutes run by the Civil Service Commission, and others.

All these facilities doubtless serve a useful purpose, some offering unique learning opportunities that are available nowhere else. They are not-for-profit institutions and are not governed by the standards of academic accrediting associations in the establishment of their curricula. They have wide latitude, limited only by available resources, to acquire or build space and housing accommodations; develop or contract for the development of curriculum materials; hire faculties and administrative staffs; and furnish and equip their quarters.

Each department and agency maintains a posture with respect to its education and training facilities which very much resembles that of a sovereign nation. This means that the multitude of federal staff colleges, academies, schools, training centers, institutes, and other facilities—by whatever name they are known—are relatively free to duplicate each other's curricula and exert little or no effort to coordinate the use of common-need faculty, staff, space, curriculum materials, equipment, library, and other resources.

The public interest is not served by having such a vast empire of education and training facilities operating on a laissez faire basis. The Bureau of Training, U.S. Civil Service Commission, is on call for technical assistance, but it is in no position (and probably should not be) to exert a strong hand of coordination and control to get the necessary public accountability. Since there is no threat of "loss of accreditation" from a self-policing association such as secondary schools and colleges and universities have to contend with, the federal community of education and training facilities can perform unbridled maneuvers. It is time for this arrangement to be reviewed, as a matter of public policy, with a view to taking corrective action to the extent desirable.

Following the passage of the Government Employees Training Act (PL 85-407, codified as Chapter 41 of Title 5, United States Code), the U.S. Civil Service Commission established a Bureau of Training, which has proliferated courses to the point where it now has a staff of hundreds of employees engaged on a year-round basis in planning and administering its curricula. The initiative for the conceptual design and start-up of such courses rests with the Commission. The offerings presumably are limited only by the economic principle of "what the traffic will bear." There is minimal collaborative effort between the Commission and its customer agencies in terms of advance review and approval of projected offerings. The Commission is inclined to bombard agencies with course announcements until it has enough nominations in hand to make a given course viable from an economic standpoint. If the course is a failure in cost/benefit terms, the sending agencies have lost their capital and the Commission is free to "go fishing" again.

There are many questions of public policy that could be examined in relation to the Commission's and other federal agency ventures into the training business. For example, the question of government in business, the methods of instruction in relation to the existing state of the art, quality of leadership, the degree of efficiency in utilizing each facility, possible duplication and overlap of effort among the many federal centers, and objective measurement of results obtained are some of the quality questions that need hard answers.

The U.S. government is not alone in its venture into the practice of concentrating continuing programs of education and training in some type of facility in larger agencies and in certain central agency facilities to serve the entire federal establishment, and even state and local government agencies. Incidentally, such facilities travel under different names. The key word is usually "college," "institute," "training center," "academy," "facility," or "agency." The department or agency name is usually included, and the full title of the school may be quite long; for example, as in "Industrial College of the Armed Forces," or "Army Management Engineering Training Agency."

There are staff colleges in western world countries in Europe well over a hundred years old. The British and French civil service systems have long generated civil servants in such facilities for specialized government functions such as postal, telephone, and telegraph. Underdeveloped countries are trending toward some form of post-secondary school system for training civil servants for their specialized careers on a work/study basis. The foreign aid program of the United States has funded the establishment of such facilities in a number of underdeveloped countries, calling many of the new facilities a National Institute of Public Affairs (NIPA).

There has also been a parallel of growth of the private sector in the United States in the number of in-house training centers that focus on continuing education and training. Both public and private agencies continue to expound the principle that most training should be accomplished as on-the-job (OJT) effort, that the first-line supervisor is responsible for the training of his/her subordinates, and that the staff training specialist is paid primarily to advise and assist in this OJT process, allowing himself the option of organizing special courses when the training can be accomplished more efficiently and economically.

Presumably, the rationale for establishing training centers follows the same reasoning, for there comes a time in the history of many large organizations when they become disenchanted with what they are getting for their dollar investments in outside education and training institutions. Then they begin a dialogue on creating their own training centers. Those that do finally make the move argue that "whatever _____ University can do for our people, we can do better."

This trend accelerated in the 1950s and 1960s because some companies almost panicked when they realized that their executives were aging and would soon need replacement. As a result, they began to stampede the middle-management class that had executive potential into outside educational institutions. After they got the bill for this adventure, and as they watched the post-training performance of managers who had been exposed to the executive development "artists" (some were better entertainers than anything else), corporate heads decided there must be a better and cheaper way.

So, they went to work planning and breaking ground for their own centers. Western Electric, one of the companies with the oldest and most secure reputation for people development, highlighted by its great Hawthorne Works experiment in the early 1930s, established a luxury executive development center in New Jersey. One of the most recent (early 1970s) and luxurious examples of this do-your-own club is the Xerox Training Center at Leesburg, Virginia, which reportedly cost in the millions. Its clientele includes sales people, maintenance technicians, and persons with managerial and executive responsibilities.

In the meantime, the American Management Associations has been building a tremendous volume of business by serving mainly the private sector enterprises that have not yet made the plunge on their own. The AMA is to the private sector what the U.S. Civil Service Commission is to the federal government. The Commission has five centers in Washington, one in Charlottesville, Virginia, and a network of executive development centers around the country serving government agencies.

Case History Experience: The Postal Service Institute, U. S. Postal Office Department

The purpose of this chapter is not to explore in depth the reasons why organizations establish training centers. It is intended as a guide to *how* such facilities are brought into being, once the high-level decision has been made to undertake the serious planning necessary to create a viable entity. In order to describe the planning and establishment process with a high degree of accuracy, I have again elected to draw on my personal work experience and relate the essentials of a major case history. In 1966–1967, I had the lead role in the Post Office Department (now U.S. Postal Service) of planning the Postal Service Institute, which was this old-line department's first venture into training centers.

It was my privilege to join the Post Office Department on November 20, 1966. This was shortly after Postmaster General Lawrence F. O'Brien had made the policy decision to establish a "staff college," as it was first called informally. Nominally attached to the Training Division, Bureau of Personnel, as Deputy Director, my sole task for a year was to do the staff work necessary to energize the school, which was officially named "Postal Service Institute" and herein referred to as "Institute." This planning work included curriculum planning, organizing, budgeting, staffing, facilities planning, procurement, coordination with "customer bureaus and offices," reporting, and communications. There was no staff other the faithful secretary Mrs. Jewell Dockery, who did a great deal to assist in this challenging task.

It may be of interest to note at this point that during the first three years of the Institute's history, the Postal Service was to have three postmaster generals (O'Brien, 1966–1967; William Marvin Watson, 1968; and Winton M. Blount, 1969) and also two assistant postmasters, from the Bureau of Personnel (Richard J. Murphy, 1966–1968; and Kenneth Houseman, 1969). Additionally, the Postal Service was to undergo in 1969 a major reorganization and change from Cabinet status to that of a TVA-like public service agency called the "U.S. Postal Service." The new organization had corporate structure and certain independent authority to act without the traditional controls that had been exercised by the Congress, such as postage rate and employee salary fixing.

There was open competition among certain bureaus and offices for the Institute. This contributed to the tensions and delayed decisions. Political forces were at work to establish the Institute on the campus of the University of Oklahoma at Norman, Oklahoma, rather than in Washington, D.C. Other forces sought to pattern the Institute after the United States military academies. In brief, much turmoil surrounded the birth of the Institute. Much of this controversy was reflected in the great debate over what to name it, an issue that reemerges from time to time and has resulted in two official name changes: the Postal Service Management Institute, and Postal Service Training and Development Institute. Such changes have coincided with the naming of a new director.

It is not uncommon for the founding of institutions to be preceded by decades of discussion. For example, staff members of the U.S. Civil Service Commission had worked for many years to establish a federal staff college for the development of civilian administrators, before the Federal Executive Institute (FEI) was founded in Charlottesville, Virginia, in 1968. They claimed that such an institution had been discussed continually since the administration of George Washington. The Graduate School of the U.S. Department of Agriculture, now some 56 years old, was discussed for 23 years before it became a reality in 1921. Measured against these yardsticks, the Institute was the product of almost instant gestation.

Records support the Institute's origination by Postmaster Lawrence O'Brien, whose thinking was strongly influenced in late 1965 by a poll of postmasters in 250 of the largest offices, which emphatically confirmed his belief that training was one of the most pressing needs of the Postal Service. This conclusion was reinforced by his observations during a European trip in the summer of 1966 which made him aware of a century or more of experience of nations such as Britain, France, and Belgium in developing managers for their postal, telephone, and telegraph systems through nationally run staff colleges with up to four-year programs of study.

To ask when and where the Institute really started is like tracing the origin of a river. Summerfield's group, active during the Eisenhower Administration, left behind documentation purporting to show that training in the Postal Service began when it took over in 1953. Before that, however, one discovers that the Donaldson group in the Truman Administration had credited itself with a great deal of emphasis on training. Searching at random still farther back in postal history, training implications are noted in the Annual Report of the Postmaster General for 1863, in which it was stated that the United States (in that year) had participated in an international conference at Paris of some 15 nations and had gleaned much valuable information with which to make future improvements in domestic administration. Finally, a glance at the four-page First Annual Report of the Postmaster General, December 9, 1789, revealed that training was on the mind of Samuel Osgood when he wrote:

> The duties of the Postmaster General at present seem to be as follows: . . . to appoint Deputy Postmasters, and *instruct* them in their duty in conformity to the acts of Congress. [Italics added.]

It should be noted that the dialogue within the postal family through the years was buttressed by vocal outside groups. Large mailers, postal unions, the transportation industry, other federal agencies, states and municipalities, and the public at large were steadily increasing their demands on the Postal Service, and these demands had but one implication—a more efficient service that could to some extent be achieved through training. Such pressures were felt acutely during the two decades immediately preceding the opening of the Institute when waves of articulate management consulting firms seconded the Hoover Commission Report recommendations (1949 and 1955) by prodding the Department to do something substantial about training and career development.

From August through December 1965, memoranda and discussions on the proposed "staff college" were stepped up. These involved the Postmaster General (PMG), the Deputy PMG, the Assistant PMG for Personnel and his training staff, the Office of Special Projects, the Executive Planning Board, and the Office of Planning and Systems Analysis. This discourse climaxed on December 22, 1966, when PMG O'Brien notified President Lyndon B. Johnson by memorandum that the Department was planning an institute. A year of decisions and plans was ahead. The dialogue had ended.

From this date forward the planning machinery was firmly in gear. In the next section of this chapter the 25 steps taken during that year of planning are discussed as the major milestones that had to be passed to accomplish a quick start-up of the Institute. Each step is amplified just enough to give the reader a feel for the administrative and technical tasks and the dynamism of the project.

The staggering volume of work and its compression into such a relatively short period of time made life difficult enough. As one might guess, that was not the whole story. Numerous special circumstances intertwined the situation as honeysuckle invades a hedgerow. A fair sample of the circumstances, as I perceived them, follows here.

The PMG team was of one mind as to the need for an Institute, but they were willing to fight fiercely among themselves, and did, for the right to own and operate the Institute. Competition was the order of the day. Personnel had a vested interest and was determined not to relinquish an attractive piece of the total training and development function. The Office of Planning and Systems Analysis group probably saw it as a logical venture of its own, especially since it needed more substance in its charter.

The Bureau of Research and Engineering would have gladly accepted the Institute had it been offered. R&E sponsored the name "Postal Institute of Technology (PIT)" and advocated a permanent campus idea. The R&E people talked of making PIT a degree-granting institution, and of having it chartered by the Congress and governed by a Board of Regents. They even unilaterally hired a consulting firm in Annapolis, Maryland, manned largely by a consortium of Naval Academy professors, to develop a prospectus of a major institution built around these concepts. The Bureau of Personnel frowned on this effort, so nothing came of it.

The powerful Bureau of Operations had a vast army of employees to be trained, the mail to be moved, and a lion's share of the $7 billion postal budget. Needless to say, its leadership wanted to have (and usually did have) the last word in questions of *what* to teach to *whom, where, and when.*

The Bureau of Finance and Administration had already inaugurated several pilot training programs and was deeply committed to massive computerization, which could fail without proper training. Training could aid greatly in the proliferation and communication of new management information systems, evolving financial management concepts, and new work measurement standards and procedures. For example, that Bureau had adopted the Program Planning Budget System (PPBS), which had been introduced into the federal establishment by Secretary of Defense McNamara.

Finally, there were those who saw the compromise, if not the proper solution, as committing the Institute to the office of the PMG, probably with the Deputy PMG having general direction over it. This competition was settled by a summit-type discussion, with the Assistant PMG for Personnel prevailing.

The internal competition for the Institute was matched by external pressures to have the Institute permanently installed on the campus of the University of Oklahoma. The University had recently acquired a center for adult continuing education through a foundation grant, and it was interested from a financial standpoint in building up a hard core of continuing activities to support the dormitory and instructional quarters. Both the Senate and House appropriation subcommittees on post office and civil service were chaired by Oklahomans, and of course they were not unfriendly to the campaign for the Institute. I was requested on several occasions by postal authorities to do the staff work necessary to support the case for retaining the Institute's base of operations at the seat of national government.

As in so many similar situations, compromise is the basis for resolving an issue and getting on with the business at hand. This matter was resolved, for the time being at least, by establishing on the campus of the University of Oklahoma a maintenance-oriented training and research activity known as "Oklahoma Postal Training Operations (OPTO)."

Another factor that added to the uncertainty and complexity of the year of decisions and planning was the utter lack of duly authorized money with which to launch a million-dollar operation. Was it in fact to be, as the Training and Development Division had first proposed conservatively in August 1966, a mini-institute with a staff of eight and four rooms in the Headquarters Post Office Department building (most likely the basement or attic because of the congestion on other floors)? Was it to have a normal growth in staff annually, as projected, from 43 to 63 to 78 to 103, and beyond, and corresponding increases in funds for other purposes? Was it to have any degree of autonomy over its own destiny or was it to be, as all previous training funds had tended to be in the Department, buried in the appropriations for the Bureau of Operations and the Bureau of Facilities?

Since control so often attaches to the purse strings, money was an urgent issue. Moreover, federal departments and agencies are loathe to start million-dollar projects, especially ones that are expected to grow and continue, without congressional sanction. The General Accounting Office is always in the background to finger errant organizations.

This sticky matter was resolved by the PMG, who called upon the Appropriations Subcommittee just before the spring 1967 hearings on the fiscal year (FY) 1969 budget. He explained the proposal, and asked informally for authority to take the necessary funds from contingency accounts of the Department and apply them as seed money for the Institute, with the understanding that the Institute would be properly budgeted in the FY 1969. Members of the Subcommittee approved immediately. Another hurdle had been negotiated.

One can be so immersed in administrative affairs that little or no time is left to think about, plan for, or manage the substantive program itself. The Institute was presumably being founded to enhance the knowledge, skills, and attitudes of postal managers and supervisors. What was the curriculum to be? Who was to develop what programs of study? And who were the teachers to be?

In May 1967, I convened a task group to come to grips with these questions. Membership was drawn from the Bureau of Operations, the Bureau of Research and Engineering, the Office of Planning and Systems Analysis, and the Bureau of Personnel. A series of informal hearings was held as the six-member group visited the 12 bureaus and offices. Typically, the answer to the fundamental question was, "We know we need training and lots of it, but don't ask us for the specifics."

Actually, the respondents were all under the stresses of administration, too, and they were not training specialists. Some open hostility was voiced toward the Training and Development Division because it had not met training needs in the past and on occasion had blocked their own initiatives. This negative reaction may have been incited by guilt feelings for not having been more aggressive in pressing for training and career development. The division was obviously not sufficiently staffed or funded to do more than implement policy and promotion and make statistical tallies from training field reports. It was evident that because of these limitations, the respondents could not articulate the specific training needs of their respective bureaus and offices and of their field counterparts. This state of affairs is too often the case in dealing with operating people about training matters.

Out of this and other dialogues, I had to draw some conclusions, become the advocate of a modest initial curriculum of 17 offerings, and get it endorsed by all concerned. This was done and the curriculum issue was laid to rest for the time begin. The whole effort for deriving the end product was necessarily limited in scope to about two weeks of discussion at the headquarters level. Had time and staff permitted, a task group would have been in motion for months to isolate training and development needs at headquarters, at regional and sectional center levels, and for post offices of varying sizes. It would also have been an opportune time to begin to relate training to career development patterns.

Another matter that had many ramifications was that of selecting a director for the Institute. Those who wanted the position to reflect prestige preferred a leader who had been a college or university president with a national reputation. When such an individual was found, interviewed, and offered the job, he declined because of salary and retirement considerations.

Needless to say there were in-house candidates, perhaps a score or more. The competition for the Institute itself, resulting in its detachment from the Training and Development Division, spoiled the chances of that division chief and for persons that he might have nominated.

A vacuum seemed to be developing, and I moved to fill it by suggesting, as an interim measure, a two-year reimbursable loan of an individual I had known at the Agency for International Development, Department of State. State was accustomed to such arrangements with federal departments and agencies as a means of keeping its Foreign Service Officer Corps abreast of domestic affairs. A "Dear Bill" letter was prepared for PMG O'Brien to send to A.I.D. Administrator William Gaud. This worked. Edmund F. Overend, the first director, brought to the Institute over 20 years of responsible foreign service experience in international organizations, communication skills, and advanced academic degrees in adult education. He had been sensitized to dynamic situations and was most adept in building institutional image and support by articulating mission and objectives to diverse groups. A great deal of his time was to be consumed by such activity as his staff proceeded with the internal management of the day-to-day operations.

Milestones in Planning and Activating a Training Center or Institute

The 25 milestones discussed below comprise a factual account, with some commentary, of my experience in planning the Postal Service Institute. Any reader who is contemplating a similar assignment should benefit greatly by following the procedural steps in the sequence presented and by devising adaptations of solutions that may apply to his particular situation.

OTHER TRAINING FACILITIES IN THE AREA. One can learn a great deal from an intensive observation tour of neighboring training and development centers. Even a half-day per visit is a worthwhile use of time; up to a week might be justified if the planning cycle is long enough and there are not too many facilities to be visited. In this case, eight visits were made, and letters or calls were made to a number of out-of-town facilities.

What does one look for when making these visits? A good check list will include such data as these:

Philosophy/doctrine of school director and senior staff
Approach to curriculum development
Use of media
Physical facilities (including locale)
Selection and development of staff
Selection of participants
Instructional methods (for example, to what extent are experiential methods and learner-paced methods used?)
Evaluation
Follow-through

During such visitations one can easily gather a portfolio of illustrative materials such as catalogs, annual reports, separate program announcements, space layouts, histories, photographs, forms, registrar literature for new arrivals, organization charts, functional statements, mission, and the like. This material is all worth collecting and preserving for future reference. A key point is to have an appropriate list of quality questions to ask while you are on the scene. Idle conversation is not rewarding for either party.

STAFF PAPERS AS PART OF CONCEPTUAL PLANNING PROCESS. Planning for the establishment of a training and development (T&D) facility can be as fruitless as a conference without a skilled conference leader. Endless talk goes in circles, nothing is decided, and the time of all concerned is lost. Moreover, people become hostile toward the lack of system, and communication with them becomes so difficult that they draw back from the planning process when decisions are really needed.

Nothing surpasses a well-written staff paper for smoking out the issues on a given segment of the larger problem. It identifies and argues the pros and cons of several feasible options, and forces approval or disapproval by a specified reasonable date. A series of such staff papers, systematically walking the interested organizational element people through the planning, establishes the necessary dialogue and discipline, and assures a flow of constructive suggestions and comments, approvals and disapprovals. The planner can see where the support is present and where it is lagging, and by pinpointing areas of concern, can direct the attention of top management to the issues that need reconciliation.

The climax to the staff paper exercise is the draft issuance that the head of the organization will ultimately sign as an order to formalize the establishment of the end product of all the advance planning—a training center or institute.

ACTIVE LIAISON WITH ALL ORGANIZATIONAL ELEMENTS. Coordination in the early stages with all interested parties is a fundamental principle of sound organization and management. Consumer involvement in a facility being planned for the common good is therefore the surest way to ensure the future use of the facility for T&D purposes.

There are many ways to "maintain liaison." One of the least effective ways is by trying to have a continuing series of meetings with a group of people. The turnover of attendees and the tendency to send alternates (sometimes a secretary just to take notes) can be discouraging and counterproductive. A short phone call, a luncheon date, an information copy of some correspondence . . . some informal something is a means of keeping in touch. The method may vary with each key individual, or a periodic report with short, pithy paragraphs on each phase of the planning may suffice for all. The key point is that the planner cannot get too far ahead of his constituency in thinking or in action steps.

ESTABLISH INITIAL CURRICULUM NEEDS. There is a variety of ways to identify the most pressing training needs, regardless of whether the assignment is handled in-house or by an outside consulting firm. Organizational elements can be circularized. A committee can be formed to hold hearings. Performance evaluation reports can be analyzed. The findings of internal and external audit teams can be examined. The question can be made a topic on the agenda of high-level management conferences and retreats. The industrial relations or personnel office can review turnover data and grievance-case histories. Program planners who are responsible for laying out new objectives and operational initiatives can be consulted. Curriculum development specialists can study the curricula of similar organizations. Employee organization and union leaders might be asked for their views. The house organ can carry stimulating articles to alert all employees to the pending development and invite suggestions and comments on curriculum needs. Opinions of customer or client agencies can be sampled.

In this case, the Institute's initial curriculum planning was accomplished by a task group that held an intensive series of hearings with representatives of major organizational elements. While the time frame for the total planning process was much too short, this approach succeeded in reaching a meeting of the minds within a two-week period. One can reason that the way to start an institution about which a great debate has taken place is simply to start and let experience dictate any changes in direction. This is about what happened at the Institute.

DEVELOP CONTRACTUAL RELATIONSHIPS. In many organizations the practice is not to start any new and expensive enterprise without buying the technical assistance of an outside consulting group. This step is made easier by the fact that contractors have a keen sense of "smell" for new developments within their staked out territories, and they will come zooming in from all directions to get a fair share of the new business. This is not to say that the consulting industry cannot contribute at any stage of planning or operating a T&D facility. However, if it is the judgment of top management that external assistance is required, the chief planner should exercise every care in drawing up the language of the request for proposal (RFP). The scope-of-work section is critical in such documents, for a fuzzy delineation of the specific things to be done tends to beget fuzzy and often worthless results from the investment. The sharper the scope of work is drawn, the easier it is to distinguish between well-qualified and marginally qualified bidders, and ultimately to monitor the performance of the contractor.

It may be feasible to engage more than one contractor. For example, one or more can help expand and accelerate the planning effort. Others can be put to work on the development of curriculum materials. Perhaps another can be used in the staff and faculty selection.

Terrible mistakes can be made by selecting either the low bidder or the bidders who enjoy the best public image and reputation in the trade. The ones you want are those who have the knowledge and experience available when you want it (not at the firm's convenience) to do specifically what you want done, by your target date, and who will charge a reasonable price for services rendered.

DETERMINE STAFFING REQUIREMENTS. Two staffs are needed for a T&D facility. One is the staff for planning and administration purposes; the other is the teaching staff, or faculty. Scale of projected operations and scope of curriculum offerings will be the principal factors in staff planning. It is to be hoped that your chief planner can work on the assumption that recognized principles of sound organization and management can be observed in setting up and staffing the facility. For example, will the director of the facility have authority commensurate with responsibilities? Will he/she be expected to delegate as much responsibility as possible? Is communication within the entire staff to be facilitated?

In the Institute case history, some real genius was evidenced by top management in a number of its decisions. The decision to place the Institute in the "field service," rather than make it a part of the headquarters organization, illustrates the point. The constrictions on staff ceilings of federal headquarters elements were never felt by the Institute as it escalated in size from zero to 170 over a four-year period. Furthermore, the frequent changes in administration (three PMGs in three years and one change at the White House) did not greatly affect the Institute because of the insulation of its field status in Bethesda, Maryland.

An example of a bad decision was probably that of not giving the Institute director authority to hire and fire. Numerous other field installations, including the heads of mail bag depositories, had this delegated authority. Moreover, the enabling headquarters circular establishing the Institute granted the director the authority to sign contracts without a dollar limit. Consequences that flowed from this lack of appointing authority had a serious impact on the quantitative and qualitative aspects of the Institute's work that first year.

DETERMINE FUNDING REQUIREMENTS. The essential step of funding cannot be done precisely. It is a matter of making the best possible estimates for the known categories of expense, primarily including salaries, contractual obligations, travel and per diem, supplies and equipment, curriculum materials and devices, space, printing and duplicating, transportation, communications, postage, and miscellaneous services. A contingency fund should be included to cover the items that cannot be anticipated in advance.

Two kinds of budget presentations are advisable. One is for the fiscal year immediately ahead, or for such portion of it as may remain when the work of the T&D facility begins. The other budget should be a long-range set of fiscal needs, ideally those projected for a five-year period. The latter will need to be updated from year to year.

Maximum involvement is desirable in determining the funding requirements. Customer agencies, top management, the central budget office, the staff of the facility, the parent organization's professional planning staff, the central personnel or industrial relations staff, and other appropriate groups should all be consulted. It is through such exercises as budget formulation that rapport is established with a facility's overseers, clients, and its own staff.

DETERMINE EQUIPMENT REQUIREMENTS. The fast-flowing stream of office furniture, fixtures, and A/V aids is as hazardous as the rapids over a river bed. One must be able to negotiate this step with extreme caution. For example, one of the most significant decisions to be made is the design and color of the chairs that participants will occupy in the institution. Hard, uncomfortable, unstable, awkward, or drab chairs detract from the effectiveness of the instruction. There are some well-designed, attractive, and moderately expensive chairs on the market. One needs only to visit the showrooms of a reliable supplier to see the range of possibilities.

Selection of equipment can especially benefit from visits to other T&D facilities. Usually, they will gladly share their inventory listing and tell you how their experience would lead them to change procurement methods in the future.

A wise step to take in connection with the A/V portion of equipment requirements, time permitting, is to watch for A/V shows and exhibits where the various makes and models are displayed and demonstrated. One should remember in equipment planning that the faculty and participants are the principal people to be accommodated. If any group is to have less, it should be the administrative staff. Investments in classroom furniture and fixtures need to be not only highly functional but also attractive enough to appeal to the participants and the general public. They reflect what top management thinks of employee T&D needs. The investment can be amortized over a longer period than office equipment, which can be upgraded as surpluses and excesses occur in other parts of the parent organization.

DETERMINE INTERIM SPACE REQUIREMENTS. It is not easy to make a close approximation of the square footage needed for administration, supporting services, mass assembly, and instruction. The estimate has to be made in the light of such factors as curriculum plans for the immediate future, the expected scale of operations, the mood of the client groups with respect to allocating travel funds and to committing candidates to T&D tours at the facility. Other costs included are the square-foot cost of available space in desirable locations, cost of space maintenance, flexibility requirements (for example, clusters of small group breakout rooms to support conventional-size classrooms), self-sufficiency requirements such as food service, housing, recreation, storage, A/V production capability, laboratories, simulation and computer-assisted instruction facilities, and other physical provisions.

Regardless of the interim space determination, there should be provision for expansion. An organization would probably be foolish to use anything other than interim space for the first several years of T&D center experience. Like one's private residence, it is said that it is not until at least the second house is built that one knows how to tell an architect about one's private home requirements and special preferences.

A critical factor in space estimates and design is the philosophy that will control the teaching methods. If the idea is to run a highly regimented and disciplined school, the design will be one way; if the T&D experiences that employees are to receive at the facility are to be a mix of informal, experiential, individualized and learner-paced, and participative type of experiences, the space requirements will be considerably different for each, as will be the furniture and fixtures.

RECRUIT TOP STAFF. The manpower pipeline at the Institute was extremely sluggish. Nominations often collapsed somewhere in the circuitous path that they had to take at headquarters of the Postal Service. Unfortunately, they had to cross the desk of several individuals who had been emotionally involved in the competition for either the Institute or the directorship, or for both. The situation was compounded by an effective moratorium that prevented the detail of employees from other parts of the Postal Service except through exhaustive justifications that had to survive long delays. This complication had grown out of some congressional relations over a number of postal employees who had complained to their congressmen about excessive details away from their regular jobs without commensurate change in job title and pay.

An extremely important position for which to begin recruiting after the directorship has been settled is that of Executive Officer. While at the Institute I had the dual role of being a member of the director's senior staff and at the same time directing a support-service staff. A flat organization was created by replacing the assistant director in the chain of command. This simplified communication between the director and his senior staff and also supported a higher grade and pay for the executive officer and the four program division heads. Hence, the recruitment effort could be aimed at persons with higher qualifications and more experience in T&D activities.

The ideal choice for a senior position in a T&D center is an individual who has current knowledge of the state of the art, is seasoned in adult education and training, and also has some competence, experience, and professional training in a relevant field, or fields. For example, an engineer with T&D experience was needed to head the Postal Engineering and Technology Division of the Institute. Such applicants are not easily found unless one has plenty of time to comb the sources and even advertise in the public media. One person for a senior staff position at the Institute was identified through a U.S. Civil Service Commission register. He was located in Pakistan as an educational adviser, but interviews coincided with his home leave, and negotiations were concluded satisfactorily. As in the case of contractors whose interest is stimulated, there will be a flow of job applications when the word is spread that a new T&D facility is opening.

When a facility begins operation too quickly, a general shortage of personnel may affect its teaching methods. This was the case at the Institute. In the early stages it was capable of nothing more than the stage management of courses taught by borrowed experts. It combed the postal headquarters for resource people who could be mobilized for classroom duty. A few were available from the field for ad hoc faculty appearances, sometimes in connection with their own course attendance. During the first quarter of calendar year (CY) 1968 alone, 237 individuals appeared at the Bethesda podiums to assist in presenting courses, and another 200 postal supervisors were teaching their peers in the field. Of the 237 who taught in Bethesda, 185 (78 percent) were postal specialists or administrators.

This "talk show" type of operation took its toll in quality teaching. Many administrators are not accustomed to teaching. Some were saturated in their subject. Others had been away from postal operations too long. Some were well equipped from every standpoint except that they were distracted by the pressures of their regular work—pressures from which they were not relieved. For them, it meant a 12- to 14-hour day instead of an 8-hour day, and lesson plans could not be prepared in advance. Obviously, the Institute could not build a solid basis for continuity in its teaching program. It was difficult, sometimes impossible, for the course coordinator to coordinate the presentation of one guest faculty member with the presentations of those who had preceded him or were to follow. Dominating the whole classroom scene was the old-fashioned, traditional lecture method. There was simply not enough interaction of the student with the subject matter, the instructor, or other students.

As time passed, this situation was corrected and the Institute was able to build balance in its faculty between guest instructors and hard-core faculty members who knew both their subject and how to teach it.

PRODUCE FIRST CATALOG. A catalog is a traditional way for education and training institutions to announce their history, broad goals, curriculum offerings, schedules, costs, faculty credentials, leadership, standards for admission, degree or certificate programs, and related matters. This publication should be treated in the same way as any other public or customer relations objective, namely, in good taste, in readable writing with appropriate graphics, and with a convenient shape for mailing. Above all, it should be prepared well in advance of the scheduled distribution, and it should be meticulously checked for accuracy and proofread carefully. The official clearance of the manuscript is tedious and time consuming.

DEVELOP OFFICE LAYOUT AND SERVICE REQUIREMENTS. The planning of the physical layout is not a task for an amateur. The senior T&D planner who is abreast of all the developments and decisions on the facility should have a series of conferences with a qualified space planner to interpret for the latter the institution's requirements. Similar meetings should occur between the T&D planner and communications technicians to discuss telephone service, intercom systems, and any computer linkages and telecommunications networks that may be needed.

Housing, transportation, food, vending machines, parking, equipment repairs, banking, postal service, and pickup and delivery services are some of the obvious service requirements. One of these services neglected at the Institute, which caused some embarrassment, was the lack of a delivery dock. Truckers and vehicular traffic resent an organization that forces trucks to park in the street and unload heavy items from truck to ground level.

Everything connected with layout and service is the concern of the Executive Officer, at least when the services become operational. Ideally, this individual should be hired well in advance and given the responsibility for coordinating the planning.

LOGISTICAL FACTORS THAT START FLOW OF PARTICIPANTS TO FACILITY. There is a mass of detailed paperwork entailed in getting ready for people and in arranging for their transportation from various locations to a T&D facility. A registrar is a good addition to the staff early in its history, someone who is capable of managing the interpersonal relations, review of candidate qualifications, individual housing accommodations, records and reports, social and recreational activities, emergencies (including deaths), and assorted other personal matters.

Concurrently, as these arrangements are being made, the faculty and its support staff will be busily engaged in collating packages of handout materials, requisitioning texts and A/V aids, and having newly developed curriculum materials reproduced. Furniture and fixtures may dribble in from suppliers. Literally, the coordination of all these details may create acute anxieties. The Institute director expressed it well when he said, "We were painting the sets as the curtain went up!"

ASSEMBLE RESOURCE PEOPLE. It is well to inventory the potential resource people who work within the parent organization and a number of those who work outside. They represent insurance against the eventuality that the hard-core faculty will suddenly need to be augmented for one reason or another. After the inventory comes the process of winnowing and making selective use of these resources. Persons about whom the most is known in terms of their subject-matter knowledge and their teaching competencies should be tried first.

The art of extending the invitation, the briefing, the presentation of the individual to his participant group, the way in which the person is released from the teaching role and thanked for the service rendered, all this requires some advance thinking and planning. Some provision will need to be made to provide feedback from participants about the resource person's performance, but such data should be handled most discreetly.

ESTABLISH SUPPORTING SERVICES. When layout and other requirements were considered, decisions were made concerning the supporting services. It is now time to put these in place. A bureaucracy has ground rules that control these procedures. For example, who will guard the building and its contents when the staff and the participants are not there? Hundreds of thousands of dollars of property may be ripe for vandals in the early stages of a facility's operation. They may see trucks moving it in, and it is easy enough to "case" the place during daylight hours because there are so many strange faces around that the staff cannot distinguish between participants and would-be vandals. The Institute was a theft victim shortly after it opened and before guard service was in place.

In addition to guard protection, another critical requirement is a shuttle service to ensure the timely arrival and movement of participants, staff, and faculty. The vending machine business is highly competitive and has to be handled with caution, since it is almost as vital to participants during their rest breaks as toilets. Unreliable suppliers have to be weeded out and others found. Many of these vending machine companies are accustomed to sharing a percentage of the profits or gross income from the machines placed with employee welfare and recreation associations. Such agreements have to be negotiated, preferably with the advice of an attorney. An in-house illustrator is an essential service, one who is responsive and can turn out instructor aids such as overhead visuals almost on a service-while-you-wait basis.

These are but a few examples of the supporting services that have to be in place and capable of functioning efficiently when the T&D facility's doors open daily.

CONTINUE FORWARD PLANNING. Planning is a continuing responsibility. Once the decision is made to have a T&D facility, the entire management hierarchy is stimulated. The decision makers seem to expect a full-blown curriculum, instant results in behavioral change of the participants, and sudden expertise. Internal and external pressures continue on curriculum, procurement, staffing, funding, contractual relationships, organization, leadership, teaching methodology, and other facets of the facility's existence long ofter it opens for business. Moreover, the day-to-day experience in the classrooms, and the response from participants and their sponsors, start an accumulation of data that has to be handled competently.

If staffing complements allow, there should be a forward planner whose full-time job is to review the evidence and weigh the options within the context of the facility's mission, objectives, and cost guidelines. Otherwise, a steering committee composed of key members of the senior staff and faculty has to assume the responsibility. Of course, division or department heads will be doing forward planning for their respective segments of the curriculum, and the executive officer will be translating plans into dollar requirements. Beyond these specialists, a coordinator is needed, someone who can make parallel lines converge toward the overall goals and objectives. This role was assigned to me as the assistant director at the Postal Service Institute.

DEVELOP PROSPECTUS FOR PERMANENT FACILITY. It is never too early to begin translating long-range objectives and modern educational and training technology into specific plans for brick-and-mortar construction of a permanent facility. It may be a long time before the permanent facility becomes a reality, but preliminary sketches and thoughts about how it should look and function may be invaluable in a dynamic setting. The initial success of the facility in interim quarters may be so significant that there is mounting pressure to go forward with the ultimate plans. Political factors, loss of a lease on rented quarters, a new airport opening, relocation of the parent organization's headquarters or its organizational realignment, and a variety of other factors can precipitate a change. Having a prospectus is being a leg up on this aspect of the facility's long-range planning.

COOPERATE WITH PUBLIC RELATIONS OFFICE. The staff of the public relations office works for a living too. It is their assigned task to present the organization and each of its elements, including the T&D facility, in the best light possible. In order to do this, people "in the know" from the facility must cooperate in the drafting and review of press releases, public service announcements for radio and television, photographic services, contracts awarded to produce A/V programs, responses to public inquiries, annual reports, and other public relations matters. It is time well invested when help is given to the public relations staff in order to help them do their job more accurately and with the timeliness and interpretive qualities they aim for.

REPORT ON PROGRESS. Top management will have risked capital and reputation on the T&D venture. It will be eagerly awaiting signs of progress. These signs may take the form of statistical data on attendance, word-of-mouth and written testimonials, the trend of demand for space in new runs of old courses and initial runs of new courses, agency performance indexes (for example, the accident record if safety training is a part of the curriculum), customer reaction to newly trained employees, and the attitude of high-level conferees toward the new facility, as evidenced by their discussions of operational problems to which the T&D facility might contribute a solution.

The preparation of regular and special progress reports should not be viewed by the reporter as a thankless chore but as an opportunity to interpret meaningfully the work of the new facility and to help management see clearly both its progress and its unresolved issues and needs.

APPROACH TO JOB APPLICANTS AND CONTRACT ASPIRANTS. Each new applicant should be dealt with as if he or she may be hired and may one day become the T&D facility director. This is an integral part of the public relations image the facility builds step by step. If the findings from due-process consideration of a candidate support rejection, it is better to level with the candidate by saying something like, "We don't think you are ready yet for the position here," than it is to lie to the applicant by saying something like, "It wouldn't be fair to hire you because you are overqualified for the position."

Some of the job applicants and contenders for contracts may be referred by top management. The T&D staff should not be misled by this because management may be no more interested in the people than the T&D staff is after it has duly considered them. However, the staff may find itself in very hot water if it summarily or arrogantly or dishonestly turns such people away, for some of them at least will have been referred to top management by the political and commercial worlds. The point is that *all* job applicants and contract contenders should receive courteous, objective, and timely consideration. Any fair-minded sponsor can accept the rejection of his client if it is done diplomatically and on valid grounds.

DEVELOP AND STANDARDIZE OPERATING FORMS, RECORDS, AND PROCEDURES. A good management analyst or systems engineer and a member of the T&D facility's senior staff who understands the mission and the thrust of the curriculum should develop forms, records, and procedures. Among the many forms to be developed are the application/nomination form, the format for separate program announcements, the certificate, evaluation forms, statistical report data forms, permanent records, housing reservations, requisitions, a participant locator card, and a classroom reservation register.

It will not be possible to perfect all forms required or to anticipate a comprehensive list without some operating experience. The assembly of basic data on each participant, from the start, is essential to any future research or smooth functioning of career development systems. Further, as the time comes for computerizing the data, a well-conceived application/nomination form will pay good dividends. It is important in forms design to strike a good balance between unduly abbreviated and overly complex forms.

OCCUPY THE INTERIM SPACE. After as much planning has been done as the planning cycle will permit, the T&D staff and faculty will occupy the new quarters and endeavor to make the transition as smoothly as possible. It is impossible to anticipate every need in planning, so there will probably be some awkwardness until things settle down. This is a time for each member of the staff to show patience and understanding toward others. It is not the time or place to indulge brittle personalities or to find fault.

The participants in the first programs run in the interim space may encounter the worst inconveniences. The facility planners could hardly have known how much air conditioning would cool a room containing 25 people when the afternoon sun was beaming through undraped windows on a 94-degree day. Neither could the interference of an exhaust fan in a classroom without carpeting or other acoustical control qualities be observed until such conditions were present. Regardless of such unexpected occurrences, a knowledgeable planner will include tolerance limits in making projections for equipment use under variable conditions. Certainly he or she would know that rugs and drapes help to control excess heat or noise.

The early shakedown use of space for T&D center purposes should be attended by the watchful eye of the original space and T&D specialist planning team, and also by the supporting services, communications specialists, and others who will have played a part in the total planning of the facility. Deficiencies can be caught and remedied before human relations are very much impaired.

DEVELOP FUNCTIONAL STATEMENT. In order to avoid controversy with other organizational elements, a precisely worded functional statement should be prepared, approved, and issued in the organizational manual or other appropriate medium. The statement defines the parameters of the facility's work and tends to keep down "border disputes." For example, to what extent does the facility's curriculum in safety training (if any) displace or supplement the work of the safety engineer who periodically conducts training courses? To what extent, if at all, does the facility's curriculum in automatic data processing displace or supplement the work of the computer management people who periodically conduct training courses? Countless other dilemmas can be anticipated and perhaps settled before they become raging controversies.

SETTLE DISPUTES OVER FACILITY NAME. Even after a year or more of planning for the opening of the T&D facility, it may be identified under several different names, depending on where one is when the subject arises. Since a descriptive functional name cannot be chosen until the function itself is defined, it is not a choice made arbitrarily. It is best accomplished by getting the principals of the representative units in a room, face to face, and discussing the subject. After each delegate has made his or her proposal, the moderator may find a consensus or may conduct a vote to settle the issue.

Unless the decision is loud and clear for a particular name, the moderator must resort to a recommendation, set forth in a staff paper forwarded through channels to the head of the parent organization for ratification or modification. This will settle the matter for a few years perhaps, or until a new administration wants to make its presence felt by changing the names of organizations.

PLANNING AND STAGING FORMAL DEDICATION. Nothing is a more fitting climax to all the thought and hard work that has gone into the initial stages of the T&D facility than a well-planned and properly conducted dedication. It is a time for the political forces, top management, community leaders, the facility's staff and faculty, and some participants to gather in the auditorium and dedicate the mission of the training center. The occasion should be recorded on videotape for future reference, and programs should be distributed.

The public media should be invited and given a briefing, and a tour should be conducted before the ceremonies. Following the speeches and remarks, a reception might help people to get better acquainted.

The date set for the dedication should be carefully selected, and should, if possible, have some significance in the life history of the parent organization. Every effort must be made to mark this as a memorable event.

Conclusion

Managements of large organizations should assess their policies with respect to the use of outside institutions and private agencies for training and developing their scientific, professional, managerial, and executive personnel. They need control over the doctrine, content, scheduling, and cost of such training. If and when the decision is made to develop a single training center or institute, or a network of such facilities, the first step is to survey relevant experience of representative training centers in both the public and private sectors. The 25 milestones reviewed in this chapter should be very useful in identifying and solving conflicts that may arise in the course of planning and instituting such facilities. In effect, the case history recited here is a capsule review of all elements discussed in this text. It is a real-life example of all the knowledge and expertise that is necessary in organizing and conducting a successful career development and training program.

Appendix I

The Federal Establishment and Its People Problems

THE people of our nation depend heavily on the 2.9 million federal civilian employees. Their citizen needs cover today's problems and those anticipated for years ahead—national security and foreign policy, individual liberties, economic affairs, housing, food, health care, employent opportunity, crime and justice, energy, transportation, welfare, the environment, education, taxes, the problems of the elderly, research, recreational facilities, space exploration, and a host of others.

Significance of the Federal Service in the Citizen's Life

Unfortunately, the people's expectations are not being met. Apathy in national elections, with only slightly over half of the eligible voters voting, is one of the barometers. Their concerns are many. Complicated, unrealistic, and bureaucratically conceived guidelines, policies, regulations, and procedures emanating from the federal government without necessary citizen input are often a root problem. Lack of common courtesy in face-to-face contacts and lack of simplicity in government correspondence are others. Intended recipients of federal help too often find the service inadequate, late, and not of top quality. Their irritation stems from such sources as the episodes of poor mail service, their individual dealings with government representatives, and the glaring inequities they see in the administration of federally operated programs.

These routine daily sources of frustration were topped off in recent years by the shocking revelations of Watergate and a series of congressional scandals involving federal officials at the highest levels.

The following table, for which data are taken from the Civil Service Commission monthly release in September 1976, presents the picture of federal employment.

FEDERAL EMPLOYEES AS OF JULY 1976

Washington, D.C.	361,550
Outside D.C.	2,413,331
Total U.S.	2,774,881
Overseas	125,174
Grand total	2,900,055*

DISTRIBUTION

Executive branch	
Permanent	2,440,770
Temporary	181,836
Part time	148,289
Intermittent	78,238
Total	2,849,133
Legislative branch	39,667
Judicial branch	11,255
Grand total	2,900,055*

*Excludes CIA and NSA. Federal civilian payrolls for July 1976 amounted to $3,754,648,000.

The American people have tried to work out a reasonable balance between two distinctions in federal civilian employment. On the one hand, they want the successful political party in presidential campaigns to have responsibility for establishing and defending federal policies and programs, and for selecting a relatively small group of noncareer executives. This is vital if the dominant party is to be really accountable to the people and if it is to carry out effectively the mandates and promises upon which it was elected. The other requirement is for a body of carefully selected, nonpartisan employees in the federal service to carry on the day-to-day operations and to provide for continuity during the transitional period between outgoing and incoming leadership. The alternative is the "spoils system," with massive turnover and accompanying instability.

That balance is hard to achieve, but it is realized to some extent by the federal civil service system in which federal civil servants are given opportunities to keep their knowledge, skills, and abilities updated through intelligently conceived and administered training and development programs.

Occupations and Places of Work

Employees of the federal establishment are working in almost every conceivable occupation and location. A classification system of the 1930s had them neatly subdivided into four occupational classifications and pay scales: Professional and Scientific, Clerical/Administrative/Fiscal, Subprofessional, and Custodial. Today, there are three major pay systems, with employees distributed as follows:

General schedule and others (58%)	1,675,204
Postal (23%)	675,653
Wage board (18%)	529,751
Total (as of June 1976)	2,880,608

Source: Sept. 1976 Monthly Release, United States Civil Service Commission.

There are 21 major occupation groups established by the U.S. Civil Service Commission for the General Schedule:

GS-000	Miscellaneous
GS-100	Social sciences, psychology, and welfare
GS-200	Personnel management and industrial relations
GS-300	General administration, clerical, and office services
GS-400	Biological sciences
GS-500	Accounting and budgeting
GS-600	Medical, hospital, dental and public health
GS-700	Veterinary medicine science
GS-800	Engineering and architecture
GS-900	Legal and kindred
GS-1000	Information and arts
GS-1100	Business and industry
GS-1200	Copyright, patent, and trademark
GS-1300	Physical sciences
GS-1400	Library and archives
GS-1500	Mathematics and statistics
GS-1600	Equipment, facilities, and services
GS-1700	Education
GS-1800	Investigation
GS-1900	Quality assurance, inspection, and grading
GS-2000	Supply
GS-2100	Transportation

The duty stations of this civilian army are spread around the world. Many federal activities are staffed 24 hours a day, 7 days a week. They are assigned to a vast complex of departments and agencies that have a tall, totem-pole type of organizational structure. We, the citizens, take it for granted that the mail will continue to flow; that a customs officer will be on duty when we arrive from abroad at an international airport; that the Coast Guard is ready on a moment's notice to help with emergencies; that veterans' hospitals are always open; that the Bureau of Engraving and Printing will continue to print paper money and that Fort Knox will be guarded constantly to protect the gold bullion that backs up the currency; that the FBI and other investigative agencies are alert; that federal prisons are managed around the clock; that federally operated museums, parks, and libraries are open during hours convenient to the public; and that airway traffic controllers are at their posts in domestic control towers to safeguard us when we fly domestically. There is literally no one in the nation whose life is not touched from birth to the grave by the federal service. Copies of birth and death certificates are faithfully reviewed and tabulated by the National Center for Health Statistics, Health Resources Administration.

Who Are the Public Servants and Where Do They Come From?

The federal service is staffed by Americans who, collectively, represent the diverse ethnic mix from the American scene. The "departmental service," which represents the combined headquarters elements of the federal government, has traditionally been staffed under civil service regulations requiring the use of an apportionment scheme, which, with a few exceptions, gives all states representation in accordance with their population. The "field service" (that part away from headquarters) is staffed by individuals from every hamlet and urban area who meet the published qualification standards without regard to the legal residence factor. The Civil Service Commission researches, with the help of departments and agencies, the qualification requirements of the various occupational groups and specific series of classes and even grade levels of positions. Its large *Qualifications Standards Handbook, X-118,* has long been the bible for federal personnel management specialists.

The federal service probably gets its fair share of people making their initial entry into the job market. First-career seekers tend to enter directly from high school, trade school, community college, or universities. A first-career entry may be a young person just out of high school who takes a clerical position or may be a graduate of a university ready to launch a career in one of the professions such as engineering, forestry, law, or economics. On the other hand, he or she may be someone who is neither interested in nor particularly qualified for a desk job. This person's first assignment may be as a forklift operator in a General Services Administration warehouse or as a mechanic's helper in one of its vehicle repair shops, and he or she may even have been a dropout from an elementary grade school.

The federal service also attracts many people who are shifting from one career to another. An accounting clerk in the private sector may have been taking night courses and can now qualify as a junior-level programmer in a government computer operation. He or she may be someone who had prepared to become a teacher and did teach for a short time until displaced by the shrinking school population, and then decided to start a new career in the U.S. Office of Education. A third person may have decided that the long hours and uncertainties of running one's own business should be exchanged for a 40-hour week in the Small Business Administration. Regardless of the motivation and circumstances, the federal government is constantly absorbing into its ranks many fine people whose careers started elsewhere.

There is also a category of people in the federal service who can be considered transients. They are not career seekers. Many are "between jobs" and only need a temporary assignment pending the culmination of other plans, such as marriage, the birth of a child, military service, an overseas assignment, retirement, or getting other members of the family through school. They may be the second breadwinners in families, working merely to earn some money to raise the family's standard of living. They may be back at work for a time merely to overcome boredom and the confinement of four walls at home. This transient group of people, while challenging the personnel officers to find the effective way of utilizing their talents, are deserving of opportunity and should not be underestimated. They may require special handling, but their potential for productivity and general effectiveness can equal or far surpass that of career people. The federal government has used little or no imagination in how to utilize part-time and transient people.

Finally, there is a distinct category of people for whom the American people have a special feeling of responsibility. Uncle Sam tries to be a good example to other employers, so he takes the lead in finding a place for the physically handicapped and even for the mentally retarded. The government has made a start with the upward mobility concept. In some cases, it has taken persons, some of whom were functional illiterates (unable to read, write, or do simple arithmetic), and substantially upgraded their basic education skills and eligibility for more rewarding work assignments. Equal opportunity measures have been taken to establish a better balance in the work force by introducing more women and members of minority groups. The federal government faithfully adheres to the long-standing Veterans Preference Act requirements by favoring veterans, especially disabled ones, and their widows in certain ways in its personnel regulations. Any federal director of personnel can recite a long list of case histories in which a meaningful job experience has evolved for someone whose chances of competing in the open job market were severely limited. This effort on the part of the federal establishment is the direct result of pressure from groups of American citizens whose views finally become public policy as expressed in laws and regulations.

Specifically, What Do Federal Civilian Employees Do?

The Department of Labor's *Dictionary of Occupations* is well represented by the diverse occupational skills required to keep the federal service going.

It even includes undertakers and the federal service has undertakers. The range is from jobs requiring minimal skills—jobs such as messenger, laborer, driver, guard, and janitor—to ones that require postdoctoral education in science, mathematics, economics, medicine, or other specialized fields.

Actually, the spectrum ranges from many of the relatively simple tasks performed by thousands of employees, such as those at General Services Administration who clean the floors in public buildings, to highly sophisticated work such as that of space scientists at NASA, medical researchers at the National Institutes of Health, entomologists at agricultural research stations, professional foresters who ensure our future wood supply, environmentalists, economists, statisticians, accountants, highway engineers, criminologists, transportation specialists, demographers, foreign service officers, safety engineers, and countless others. Additionally, about 10 percent of the public service is composed of individuals whose work is primarily supervisory, managerial, executive, or administrative in character.

The challenge of public work is in sharp contrast to comparable work in the private sector, where the success or failure can be measured on the profit-and-loss scale. The safeguards built into civil service laws and regulations against arbritrary removal—and to more nearly ensure equal opportunity in selection, promotion, and career development—also increase the stress and tension on supervisors and managers.

Public service has another dimension. Much of it involves a direct face-to-face encounter between the government employee and the concerned citizen. Take the social worker who must visit the home and examine personal circumstances of claimants; the customs officer who must evaluate the credibility of the American tourist's declaration and decide whether or not he or she is a smuggler or cheater; the postal inspector who must check out a neighborhood to determine who is stealing Social Security checks from the mailboxes, or must even spy on window clerks of his own postal service to catch an embezzler. The long list continues with the civilian in the Department of Defense who must be a messenger of death to inform families of the loss of a loved one; the decision maker in the Department of Health, Education and Welfare who must weigh and decide whether or not a given community gets the grant it wants for a community development project; the Food and Drug people who have to confront a pharmaceutical manufacturer with a cease-and-desist order on a very lucrative product; the Veterans Administration official who has to decide for or against an application for a loan from a struggling young veteran who probably wants it to continue his education, buy a house, or start a business.

These and numerous other public servants at the federal level obviously have to face up to their responsibilities. They can procrastinate for a time, and many do, but that tends only to complicate things. They are in deeper trouble if they have a deficiency in knowledge, skill, or basic understanding of their role—all requisites that a continuing program of training and development can reinforce.

How Are They Trained and Developed?

The overwhelming majority of federal employee training experiences take place on the job, from day to day. That is as it should be, provided the supervisor or designated trainer has the time and knowledge to do a thorough and accurate job of training. And provided, further, that the trainer is in position to train in the best known way for performing each task to be learned.

Unfortunately, the odds are against an adequate job of training being done on the job. Competing demands on the trainer's time and other factors too often leave new employees, or reassigned employees, or employees with some new duties to shift for themselves. This means they either have to turn to a buddy or feel their way along by trial and error. The "buddy system" and the trial-and-error approach to learning are hazardous. They perpetuate the methods and attitudes that can be picked up around the work scene, be they the best or the worst. There is no uniformity, no quality control, no basis for objective performance appraisal, counseling, or removal when things go seriously wrong.

There are numerous methods of federal in-service training which can be used reliably to prepare an individual properly for his or her duties and responsibilities. These are covered in depth elsewhere in this book. They range from informal methods such as apprenticeship, understudy, and internships to formal instruction that takes place in schools the federal government has organized in many of its larger departments and agencies. Examples of such schools include the Foreign Service Institute, Army Management Engineering Training Agency, Postal Service Institute, a school for law enforcement agencies, Industrial College of the Armed Forces, Federal Executive Institute, a network of staff colleges run by the Civil Service Commission, and various civilian employee schools run by the Department of Defense in specialized management fields. The IRS has a school for training its special agents in Crystal City, Virginia, and the FBI has long had a school for training its agents in Quantico, Virginia.

Besides the informal on-the-job training and the formal schools that some agencies operate, these and all other agencies have a system of in-service training courses, training conferences, seminars, and workshops as means of providing for the continuing training and development of their staffs. When it is not economically feasible or administratively practicable to meet such needs within in-service resources, they may apply for available space in the facilities of sister agencies or may go to central facilities of certain agencies such as the U.S. Civil Service Commission, the General Services Administration (GSA), and the Interagency Auditor Training Center of the Department of Commerce.

Many agencies buy outside education services from colleges and universities to enhance the performance capability of their employees. This education, under the law, is not supposed to be primarily for the purpose of obtaining degrees. The Government Employees Training Act (GETA) admonishes all federal employees to continue their own self-education, self-training, and self-improvement, for self-help is only to be *supplemented* by federally sponsored training at public expense. One rarely finds a federal employee who has not taken some night courses or is without plans to do so. To their great credit, countless public servants have bootstrapped their way by hard and diligent effort from a high school diploma to a college degree, from an undergraduate degree to an advanced degree, or from a general education to a marketable specialty.

Where Does the Training Lead?

The question of upgrading suggests one of the major difficulties with the present system, or lack of system, in employee training and development. A training experience is too often not a purposeful building block in a carefully planned career field. It may not even be relevant. It may simply be the result of an executive's having been persuaded that all employees in a given group or all employees whose duties are similar, such as those who write letters or use the telephone, absolutely need and must be subjected to a particular "canned" course. Some officials have even sent troublesome subordinates off to school to lessen their own administrative burden. Others have done so to reward faithful employees—a bonus for good behavior.

The performance appraisal system in most federal agencies is a farce, and is nothing more than a superficial effort to meet statutory requirements. Therefore, a specific training experience can hardly be an outgrowth of the counseling that should accompany evaluation. Career counseling is not done systematically, and few federal organizations are adequately staffed for the task. Effective performance appraisal and career counseling should identify both immediate and long-range training and development needs.

Since appraisal is weak in the federal service, the typical employee is left to work out his own path of advancement and to take whatever steps he deems appropriate to get where he wants to go. John Corson, a former federal official, is reported (unpublished paper in the 1950s) by the American Assembly of Columbia University to have described what he saw as three approaches to promotion in the federal service: the "cream" approach, the "shoe-leather" approach, and the "desk-to-desk" approach. He concluded that career development in consequence was haphazard.

Admittedly, there has been a tremendous expansion both in in-service and in outside training and development facilities since the GETA of 1958. However, these facilities have only compounded the confusion for the employee who has serious intentions of bootstrapping himself to a realistic career goal in the federal establishment. Without guidance, he or she may become a perennial course taker and still stay in a dead-end job leading nowhere except to a state of total frustration. Unless each training experience is a "joint venture" of the employer and the employee *in which each makes some investment and some sacrifice because they have mutually agreed that the experience is a logical building block in a feasible career development plan,* the effort will most likely be counterproductive.

Needless to say, there is a growing number of exceptions to the observation that far too much federally financed training and education leads nowhere. There are some delightful oases in the federal establishment's desert of human resources development. These exceptions are described in other chapters of this book and need not be inventoried here, save one notable example. The Management Intern Program started in the federal government in 1944, following a successful prototype demonstration by the National Institute of Public Affairs, and ran for about 30 years. This program is one of the finest examples of what can be done by careful selection and a well-conceived and -administered plan for intensive development. The program demonstrated conclusively that years can be saved in the preparation of a high-potential individual for positions of managerial responsibility. Unfortunately, the Civil Service Commission canceled the program because it apparently lacked the necessary imagination to cope with the criticism of minorities, probably valid, that culturally deprived individuals were handicapped by the tough examinations used in selection.

Public Policy as Expressed in the Government Employees Training Act (GETA)

Public Law 85-507, effective July 7, 1958 (now codified as Chap. 41, Title 5, USC), was cited as the "Government Employees Training Act." Its stated purpose was: "An Act to increase efficiency and economy in the Government by providing for training programs for civilian officers and employees of the Government with respect to the performance of official duties."

The Congress intended, according to the Declaration of Policy preamble to the act, to have the training *supplement* the employees' own efforts to improve themselves, for such government-sponsored programs were to be continuous in nature. Congress also wanted the programs designed to produce tangible results. Specifically, the training programs were to lead to "(a) improved public service, (b) dollar savings, (c) the building and retention of a permanent cadre of skilled and efficient Government employees, well abreast of scientific. professional, technical, and management developments both in and out of Government, (d) lower turnover of personnel, (e) reasonably uniform administration of training, consistent with the missions of the Government departments and agencies, and (f) fair and equitable treatment of Government employees with respect to training." Finally, Congress said it was holding the U.S. Civil Service Commission responsible, subject to supervision and control by the President, for "the effective promotion and coordination of such programs and of training operations thereunder."

This is good rhetoric and good legislation, except that it has not lived up to the legislative architects' concept. In 1975, a panel of ten experienced training directors (most of them retired from federal departments and agencies after many years of experience) issued a 20-page report of study

made under the auspices of the Training Officers Conference and the
Washington, D.C., chapter of the American Society for Training and Development. This report charged that the Act had not kept pace with the changing times. After extensive hearings, the panel recommended 25 reforms in
the GETA legislation. Many of the recommendations pointed to the need
for new initiatives and stronger leadership from the U.S. Civil Service Commission. Further, it suggested that the original intent of the Act—to have its
implementation subject to "supervision and control by the President"—be
realized. It advocated that a position be established in the Executive Office
of the President to see that the President's wishes are carried out with respect to human resources development in the federal service.

Nature of the In-service Training and Development Function

The GETA charged the head of each federal department with responsibility for "preparing, establishing, and effectuating a program or programs,
and a plan or plans thereunder, in conformity with this Act, for the training
of employees in or under such department by, in, and through Government
facilities and non-Government facilities in order to increase economy and efficiency in the operations of the department and to raise the standard of
performance by employees of their official duties to the maximum possible
level of proficiency." Following an Executive Order issued in 1938 by President Franklin D. Roosevelt, each department has had a director of personnel, and the employee training and development function has always been
interpreted to be an integral part of that office. However, some agencies
redirected the function and have made its head responsible to the same administrator to whom the director of personnel reports. The GETA and Civil
Service Regulations on Federal Employee Training do not state where the
function should reside organizationally.

The limited concept of "training" in the GETA was defined as "the process of providing for and making available to an employee, and placing or
enrolling such employee in, a planned, prepared, and coordinated program,
course, curriculum, subject, system, or routine of instruction or education,
in scientific, professional, technical, mechanical, trade, clerical, fiscal, administrative, or other fields which are or will be directly related to the performance by such employee of official duties for the Government, in order
to increase the knowledge, proficiency, ability, skill, and qualifications of
such employee in the performance of official duties."

The objective of the legislation would be, ideally, to prepare employees
at all levels for performing well in their present work and in some specifically identified assignments that would logically evolve as the employee became more experienced and knowledgeable. In the case of individuals seeking a long-term career in the public service, it would seem consistent with
the spirit, if not the letter, of the Act to lay the foundation for a career in a
field consistent with the individual's demonstrated performance, qualifica-

tions, interests, and, above all, with the current and foreseeable needs of the public service.

Regardless of the intent of the legislation, government attorneys have long agreed that the heads of all departments and agencies have a certain amount of inherent authority to train their staffs in order to accomplish the mission for which they are held accountable by the enabling legislation and the President. Obviously, the head of a department or agency cannot personally organize and conduct the training and development activities. Therefore, every major federal organization has established a training and development arm and has placed a supervisory employee development officer in charge.

The Civil Service Commission, in its publication *Occupational Groups and Series of Classes* (Series 235), defines the employee development function as follows:

> This series covers positions that involve planning, administering, supervising, or evaluating a program designed to train and develop employees. This series also covers positions that involve providing guidance, consultation, and staff assistance to management concerning employee training and development matters. Positions covered by this series require as their paramount qualifications an understanding of the relationship of employee development and training to management problems and to personnel management objectives, methods, and procedures; analytical ability; and a knowledge of the principles, practices, and techniques of education or training.

The Commission issues regulations, provides technical assistance, and operates a network of training centers. Policy, standards, and procedures are formulated at the overall department or agency level. At bureau and division levels, the training and development activities are organized and directed to specific target audiences to meet identified organization development needs and the behavioral objectives set for individual participants.

The numbers of people involved in this total effort, at all levels, might be measured by the number of names on the mailing list of the oldest professional society (1938) in the Washington, D.C., area—the Training Officers Conference. This group started when a half-dozen training specialists of several of the old line departments, such as Agriculture, got together for lunch one day to discuss common problems. Today, the Training Officers Conference has about 800 names on its mailing list in the Washington area. Admittedly, all members may not be officially classified as "Employee Development Officers." Some may have moved on to other duties, but retain an active interest in the function. Others may be working in allied fields such as education, or in other specialized fields of personnel management or human resources development (such as the Office of Economic Opportunity, OEO), or in manpower planning and related fields.

The common denominator term applicable to all this work is "people development," derived from a comment made by a large oil company executive, who observed that every organization has its "people developers." These are individuals, he said, who are scattered about the organization, of all ranks, many of whom will never get to the top themselves. They gain their greatest reward and self-fulfillment from discovering, guiding, and encouraging other individuals to the spots where they can make their greatest contribution. I have used the term throughout this text because of its inclusiveness with respect to all training and development programs.

Outside Resources for Training and Development

Clearly, the intent of the GETA was, and still is, to get the training and development job done in the department or agency where the individual is employed. The next recourse is to bid for space in a sister federal organization's training facilities. When federal possibilities are exhausted, the employee's needs can be met by the use of outside facilities. Educational institutions in the United States have recognized this market and have made many adjustments in their traditional formats to accommodate the federal training market. One of these is commonly known as the "campus without walls" concept. For example, some of the universities in the Washington, D.C., area hold classes in as many as 35 to 40 federal buildings—literally, wherever about 12 or more students can be assembled. Its administrative staff is located on campus. The faculty member may be a professor with tenure or a part-time instructor whose primary source of income is a federal position in the specialized field he teaches. Some of these institutions teach in the conventional format, spreading the learning over a trimester or semester, and they may also run intensive seminars and institutes in or away from the central city. They may even conduct their programs on educational television channels, or by correspondence, or by other individualized methods.

Many of Washington's 35 or more institutions of higher learning are competing for the same student body. Moreover, a growing number of universities from all over the United States are hanging out their "shingle" in Washington and in other major urban areas for off-campus business. Examples include Central Michigan University, University of Chicago, University of Oklahoma, and the University of Southern California. Some of the Washington-based institutions have begun to reciprocate by finding markets for their curricula elsewhere in the world. The University of Maryland is a good example; it has followed United States military services around the world, providing off-campus courses that can lead to a degree.

Many of these campus-without-walls institutions almost let the student write his own ticket with respect to the course mix, sequencing, and pacing. One institution permits a student to complete a 3-semester-hour course in two weeks of intensive effort. The key points are flexibility and catering to the needs of *organizations and people* instead of letting the curriculum, faculty, and instructional methods be the master.

The commercial world is another rich source of outside assistance. This source includes publishers, producers of audiovisual aids, and companies that specialize in the production of courses, curriculum materials, systems, and equipment. Manufacturers often include in their contract to supply technical equipment a provision for training operators and mechanics.

Complicating Factors

Perhaps the force that presses the hardest for a continuing program of training, education, and development—a force almost comparable to the tremendous pressures generated by the oceanic tidal system—is the evolution of occupations in this rapidly changing world of the management, social, and natural sciences, and the technologies associated with these sciences. The twentieth century has been a momentous one, to say the least. Automobiles, airplanes, radio, television, radar, computers, nuclear energy, and space vehicles are just samples of the great scientific and industrial discoveries. Social revolutions, wars, political upheavals, and economic disasters have added another dimension to change. During the past two decades alone, the individual employee in the United States has steadily been confronted with new and more complex phenomena in his or her work, which demand a new level of knowledge, skill, and understanding. For example, a worker must (1) install, operate, maintain, or manage far more sophisticated systems and capital equipment; (2) work within a vastly more decentralized organization; (3) interact as a member of constantly changing racial and ethnic mixes of people; (4) face physical hazards constantly growing out of the environment, new technology, and unprecedented crime in urban areas; (5) perform within very sensitive and elaborate labor/management contracts and agreements; and (6) observe new laws and court rulings that have narrowed the discretion of supervisors and managers in decisions where the civil rights and individual liberties of employees are involved.

All these shifting stresses require adjustment on the part of people who have to produce the gross national product. Training and development can do three things to facilitate smooth adjustments to social, economic, and political change: improve knowledge, skill, and attitudes.

Another complicating factor is that of insufficient funding. Traditionally, the Office of Management and Budget has taken the position that money for training and development should be taken out of regular appropriations—essentially, that training should pay its way. Such a policy might be equitable if it could be administered uniformly. The tendency is for training to be the first function trimmed, if not eliminated, when there is a cutback in funding. Training suffers far more than a proportionate reduction. The fiscal shortage may be in only one category, such as travel. Hence, a mere 10 percent shortage of travel funds may force a 100 percent curtailment in training and development programs. When there is a move to economize and reduce the work force, it is inevitable that the training function will be one of the first functions to be abolished or reduced drastically. Moreover, the reduction-in-force regulations are arranged so that the last in are the first to go from the federal payroll.

The total investment in high-potential young career recruits in any department or agency (or in the federal government as a whole), and the intensive training they may have received during the early months or years of their service, can be wiped out by a ripple in the economy or by the political whims of an incoming administrator or regime. It can be as serious as the wanton act of going to our national forests and ripping out all the saplings that have been planted to ensure the supply of wood several decades ahead. *It is a national disgrace that the U.S. Civil Service Commission has never put forth any workable plans for protecting young career recruits who represent future leadership in the federal service.*

Still another complicating factor in the federal service is the fact that there are no special preparatory schools to assure a continuing source of qualified recruits in many specialized fields. If a person expects to enter a professional field such as agriculture, law, medicine, business administration, education, journalism, engineering, or commercial accounting, it is easy enough to identify a choice of colleges and universities where one can get a good educational foundation. There are countless occupations in the federal government where this is not the case. Where can one prepare for intelligence work? For work in the investigative agencies? For the tedious work of developing guidelines and criteria to regulate federal/state relations on grants and matching fund projects? For the work of a horde of analysts? For public accounting and auditing? For handling the inquiries and complaints of private citizens, small business men, veterans, and others? For working interculturally with foreign nationals, and particularly with those of underdeveloped nations? For examining patent applications and applying patent law in the Patent Office?

When federal employees are compelled by circumstances to acquire the knowledge and skill they need for such roles by depending on the buddy system or by trial and error, everyone involved is shortchanged.

The Human Consequences of Shortfall in the Training and Development Effort

IMPACT ON PEOPLE. Individuals who cast their lot with the public sector are most unfortunate when they find themselves with an employer who cares too little or not in the least about the idea of systematic training and development programs, true merit principles, and other aspects of sound personnel management. They may find that this situation is the cause of a whole series of self-initiated transfers from agency to agency. Eventually, the individual reaches some age, such as 40, that categorically disqualifies him or her, in the eyes of many federal managers, for positions holding much promise. This moment of reality leaves an individual with a feeling of utter futility, about the same feeling the occupants of a busy household have when the electricity suddenly goes off on a hot night during a rainstorm. Everything shuts down in the home and the electricity may not be restored for hours. In the life of the individual whose career opportunities are blocked by lack of training and development opportunities, nothing much may happen for *years*—if ever.

Research done at the time of the transformation of the Post Office Department into the quasi-government corporation known as the U.S. Postal Service revealed that 80 percent of the postal employees were retiring from the same job to which they were hired. The postmaster in a small town was never considered for promotion to postmaster of a city. The GSA guard tends to remain a GSA guard. A high-speed typist in the Pentagon may have a few superficial changes in title, but his or her value as a high-speed typist tends, from the viewpoint of supervisors and managers, to disqualify this employee for a more substantive line of work that would offer promotional opportunities and the reward of self-fulfillment. A Census Bureau clerk can get buried in the routines of perennial censuses and statistical surveys. A library aide can become a permanent "acquisition," like the books on the shelves.

These are but a few examples of what actually happens to people in the federal civil service, all because there is such an inadequate career management system. The fact that it does happen to people, who get lost and overlooked in the vast federal establishment, detracts from the luster of the human beings who make up the side of the "fabric" seen by the general public. It causes public servants to become listless, callous, and indifferent toward their work and their public. Moreover, it obviously erodes human dignity and is degrading.

IMPACT ON PRODUCTIVITY. Failure to fully train and develop federal employees has immediate and progressive effects on productivity and the general effectiveness of the public service. Federal employees are constantly being admonished, particularly when new political regimes take charge, to be more creative and innovative. While many are superior and significantly better producers than their political bosses consider them to be, and may even be better qualified than the bosses themselves, a great number are mediocre, indifferent, and lackadaisical. They do not give a full measure of their time and talents because there is no incentive system and no chance for upward mobility or career development. Some have to hide their incompetence by passing the buck, bluffing, or procrastinating. Take, for example, a postal-window clerk approached by a customer who wants to buy some commemorative stamps. The clerk, often having had no training in the philatelic program (one of the few moneymakers for the Postal Service), turns the customer away with the excuse that he or she has only regular stamps. Some window clerks have been known to tear up sheets of 50 commemorative stamps bearing the printer's serial number so that they can say that they have no whole sheets; they may even trade off their partial sheets to other clerks because they lack understanding and appreciation for philately and regard customers of such stamps as eccentrics!

The errors that stem from insufficient training compound waste and public expense. They also lead to organizational pyramiding, for reorganizations are one of the course-of-least-resistance ways of dealing with inefficiency. The Peter principle of promoting individuals to their highest level of incompetence also comes into play as people commit more and more errors, and finally become intolerable in particular positions.

IMPLICATIONS FOR FUTURE RECRUITMENT. The pervasive spread by word of mouth of malfunctioning government agencies cannot but have a long-range effect on the quality of public service. Criticism of public services is rampant and reaches from the lowest level of the public to the highest. Political leaders and candidates for public office at the national level hear it and never try to defend the "establishment." If public service is so generally condemned, if it has no dedicated advocates, how can we expect the federal service to attract its fair share of talent? Government recruiters may eventually have to accept the rejections of responsible employers, and the public will be the great loser. Clearly, the lack of a promise-and-reward component in the present federal training and development system has spawned a massive and uncontrollable morale problem.

New Initiatives Are Needed

The foregoing discussion is only a fragment of the comprehensive subject of human resources development in the federal service. It should be sufficient to stimulate the reader into searching for the reforms needed—now. Some progress has been made since 1958, when the Congress last expressed the general public's concern on this issue by enacting GETA. But in the two decades following the Act, a rapidly changing world has neglected the training, education, and development movement in the federal service. New initiatives are needed, and professional practitioners recognize it. The relevant professional societies recognize it. Federal employees and their unions have long recognized it. There are signs that interested committees of the Congress, the General Accounting Office, and the Office of Management and Budget are beginning to extend the scope of their attention from monetary to people values. Aside from defense materiel, the greater portion of tax dollars goes into salaries of *people,* and it is *people* who make the decisions on how, where, and when 100 percent of the tax dollars are to be spent.

This book is in itself an inventory of the initiatives needed. Each separate chapter is a blueprint for accomplishing a set of reforms to be circumscribed by new initiatives. If there is such a thing as the President's "kitchen cabinet," it had better start cooking up ideas on this vital subject.

The reforms proposed cannot be achieved by isolated training specialists buried in the bureaucracy. Change must begin at the top. Presumably, the people spoke in the 1976 election, and said that they want changes in the operation of their national government. Therefore, the Congress, the Chief Executive, and heads of departments and agencies must make their moves to satisfy this consensus. New policies and objectives, reorganization, revitalization, and zero-based budgeting all require that *people* must take action. Knowledge, skill, and abilities of incumbents will be carefully evaluated, and, where deficiencies exist, training and development will be needed. It is equally true that incoming leaders and people at all levels will need proper orientation and continuing training and development.

A new era may be dawning in the federal service if signs and symbols are reliable indicators, and if those involved in making these changes convert the rhetoric into action that restores the quality of public service.

Conclusion

The people of the United States depend heavily on the 2.9 million federal civilian employees, but unfortunately their expectations are not being fully met. These employees are engaged in a wide range of occupations. They are people who make their initial job entry into the federal service, those who shift from other areas of employment to national government, transients, and special groups.

Federal civilian employees are trained in many ways, both informally and formally. Unfortunately, some training is left to the "buddy" system, which can be counterproductive. Insufficient funding plagues the training and development effort, and even a small reduction of funds can escalate dramatically under certain conditions. Uniformity of pre-entry facilities for educating individuals entering the federal ranks is far from satisfactory.

The human consequences of shortfall in the training and development effort within the federal establishment can severely impair productivity in public services, and handicap future recruitment.

The President needs a human resources counselor who is a people developer at heart, and not committed primarily to a dollar-value development system. If possible, this counselor should be permitted to operate independently, but in any case should not be subordinate to the head of any department or bureau whose function is oriented toward economic rather than humanistic principles. The counselor should explore with educators the possibilities for expanding college and university facilities to meet the pre-entry foundation education needs of certain career groups.

The Government Employees Training Act should be amended to reflect the developments of the past 20 years. The findings and recommendations of a panel of distinguished federal training and development specialists, issued as a report in July 1976 by the Training Officers Conference, Washington, D.C., should be the basis of such amendments.

The basic federal civil service laws and regulations should be amended by the Congress to shelter high-potential career recruits in much the same way as the nation has long sheltered its military veterans.

Appendix II

Some Guideposts for Federal Service Career Seekers

Apparently the popular notion is that one needs only to take a federal civil service examination, make a passing score, and wait for a formal appointment. Most people will have an exhausting wait if they follow this course of action. The U.S. government is nearly always in search of qualified typists, so the test/wait/enter upon duty routine may work in that line of work, but the trouble is that one may work a lifetime as a typist, waiting for reassignment and promotion to a position with greater career opportunities.

Entrance Doors

The door one enters in approaching a career in the federal service is critical. Suppose you are a high school graduate, you are employed as a draftsman in a private company, and you are taking college courses toward an engineering degree, which you expect to receive in about two years. Your mail one day brings a letter of inquiry as to availability for appointment to the position of draftsman in a federal agency at a rate of pay in excess of what you are making. *I advise you to stay where you are.* Answer the inquiry and say that you are not available. Continue your work/study plan until you have your engineering degree in hand. The rationale is this: Once you walk through a federal door to a draftsman's worktable, too many people will tag you "draftsman" and never think of you as an engineer, regardless of how many engineering degrees you may earn later.

Take another case. Suppose you are a secretary to a psychologist in private practice. You are attending night classes at a local university and you are programmed to receive a degree in public administration with a major in personnel management. You are confronted one day with a firm offer to be a receptionist in the personnel office of a federal agency. *Do not take it.* Stay with the psychologist until you have your degree in hand. When you have it in hand, or shortly before, and if you still feel that you would like to move to the federal service, apply for a professional rating in personnel management (Series 235).

The key point is that the "door" is the thing. Federal personnel offices will deny this, and so will supervisors, but my many years of experience in federal personnel offices confirm it. Some individuals have the stamina and initiative to overcome the disadvantage of having made their entry through an inappropriate door. A striking case comes to mind. I recall an individual with a college degree who entered the federal service as a messenger during the Great Depression years. He was so successful in establishing himself during his rounds in carrying official mail from office to office that he was able to convert from messenger to research analyst and to launch a 30-year productive career in the civil service. He was one of those able, affable, extremely conscientious individuals who fit the model of an ideal public servant. Fortunately, his department recognized his potential. This case history is a rare exception to the rule that entering the wrong door is an uphill struggle.

Establishing Yourself

Once you enter the federal service, regardless of the "door" you use, spare no effort to establish yourself as a loyal, industrious, dependable, and cooperative individual. These qualities will set you apart from many of your colleagues, for it is too often the case that persons who enter the ranks of public service do so with the attitude that the federal government owes them something. Consequently, they are inclined not to give a full measure of their energies and abilities. They tend to abuse the hours of duty, the lunch period, the rest breaks, and the leave system. For example, the typical new employee seems to feel that annual (vacation) leave is a right to be exercised on demand whenever the employee chooses. Actually, the law granting such leave stipulates that it is to be used at the convenience of the government, and any employee failing to get advance approval of leave, except in real emergencies, can be placed on leave without pay for the duration of his absence.

One's work habits are just about as important as one's work output. Consistently coming late to a job that involves answering a telephone that the general public or government agencies start using at, say, 8:30 A.M., causes confusion and delays the public business. It is a poor work habit to let incoming calls taken by one's secretary or associates pile up. It causes poor public relations. Failure to meet deadlines, to check outgoing work for obvious errors, and to answer the questions posed in incoming correspondence are other examples of poor work habits.

There is also the matter of how one conducts one's personal affairs. That needs to be considered in establishing a reputation for being a deserving public servant. Personnel offices in the federal service are in constant receipt of complaint letters from creditors of employees. The creditor usually wants the agency to serve as a collection agent or to discipline the employee in some way. The salary of a federal employee cannot be garnisheed, except to meet alimony obligations. This leaves the commercial world to collect bad debts in other ways. Keeping one's credit in good standing is the responsible thing to do, even if it means depriving oneself of some goods and services.

A federal employee needs to keep himself clear and above reproach with respect to involvements that can make him a security risk. The federal government runs a full field security investigation on every employee at the time of appointment, and it updates the investigation as the employee moves from agency to agency or from less sensitive to more sensitive positions. One wrong move that makes the employee a bad security risk can lead to dismissal; and once the record is documented, the employee will find it impossible or extremely difficult ever to be reappointed. In the same category is falsification of one's application for federal employment. Statements made on applications are verified and falsifications are cause for dismissal and prosecution. Therefore, one should be scrupulously careful in accounting for all periods of unemployment and in making sure that all the particulars given in the application are accurate.

Conduct unbecoming to the public service is cause for dismissal. Such behavior need not involve activities affecting one's loyalty to the United States. Excessive use of alcohol, drug addiction, gambling, immorality, and cruelty to members of one's family or others are examples of unbecoming behavior that can come to the attention of the employer and mark the employee as someone to be given limited responsibility or eventually be dismissed.

Getting to Know Your Employer

You can think about your employer as you would about a commuter train providing you with a seat to and from work daily, in which you can sleep, read a newspaper, and wish you were free to do other things. You can take the position that you could not care less about the ownership, management, or financial condition of the commuter line as long as the train you catch keeps running on schedule. But suppose for a moment that there are some startling circumstances surrounding the continued operation of the commuter line. It may be exploiting its personnel. It may be operating with dangerously unsafe equipment and street-crossing signals. It may be indulging in gross tax-avoidance practices. The management may be corrupt. The balance sheet may be hopelessly in the red.

You can assume the same indifferent posture in the federal department or agency where you first go to work. Or, you can set out to explore the many exciting things to learn about a large federal organization and thus gain a background that will make your work more meaningful. Here are some suggestions to guide your exploration:

—Read the organic Act that established your department or agency. It may even have been provided for in the U.S. Constitution. Study the subsequent amendments and the reasons for them.

—Examine the regulations that have been issued by your employer to carry out the legislation. All such regulations have to be published in the *Federal Register,* a daily publication of the National Archives and Records Service, before they are legal.

—If there is a *Policy Manual,* read it from cover to cover.

—Study the issuances on standardized procedures.

—Read the last several annual reports to the President and the Congress.

—Analyze the current budget, including the narrative justification and the congressional hearings in which the budget was defended.

—Examine the *Personnel Manual* that governs personnel actions in the organization and sets forth promotion policy, training and development objectives, the performance appraisal system, and the like.

—If there have been any major investigations of the organization in recent years, try to gain access to them and see what they say. They will probably have been made internally by the Internal Audit group, or by external investigators from the General Accounting Office or congressional committees.

Most of, if not all, these items will be available in your employer's library, or the librarian can arrange to borrow a copy for you. These inquiries will give you insight into what makes your organization tick, how it is viewed by those having oversight over its work, and the direction in which its program is moving. It may point to organizational change, new technology, new priorities, and other impending conditions that could affect your career objectives and opportunities. You will be astonished to find how much more you will know from perusal of the suggested items. All this will cost you nothing except a manageable number of hours of your leisure time. The additional knowledge could pay tremendous dividends.

Charting a Course

Having entered a suitable door, and having begun to establish yourself and acquire some background in the history, current operations, and future direction of your federal employer, you can begin to chart a career course for yourself much more intelligently. This may not be easy. It may take several years of practical work experience before you are in a position to make a definitive choice. Nevertheless, you should work from the premise that career opportunities will not discover you; instead, you will have to take the initiative. Perhaps it should not be that way, but in reality it is.

A good way to start is to do some fact finding. Since you already know why the organization is in business, you can soon figure out what primary occupations are needed to run the organization. For example, if it is a statistical research bureau such as the Bureau of the Census, you can be sure that it relies heaviest on statisticians and people with technical knowledge in the specialized fields in which it does research—population, housing, agriculture, business, industry, foreign trade, and others. The Internal Revenue Service priority will be on investigative skills and selected substantive areas such as law and accounting. Federal functions, such as the Corps of Engineers and the Federal Highway Administration, obviously will value engineering highly in their manning tables.

Your personnel office may be willing to let you see some data on employment by occupational category. With these data you can construct an interesting configuration known as a "career cone." Start with the occupational group that you assume to be the most populous among the primary occupations needed. Assume here that it is civil engineering. On a sheet of graph paper with a vertical line drawn down the middle, you can plot points on either side of the line to represent half of the number of employees at each grade level in the civil engineering group. For example, if there are 20 civil engineers at the lowest pay grade, start near the bottom of the graph and plot a point 10 spaces to the right of the vertical line and another point 10 spaces to the left of the vertical line. Continue plotting other civil engineers in other grades until the senior civil engineer is plotted at the top of the page. Then connect the points and study the resulting configuration. Make a career cone for each additional occupational category in which you have an interest.

Perhaps your analysis of these cones will show that each is significantly different. You will immediately see more career opportunity in some fields than in others. For example, an hour-glass configuration in one occupational field may suggest that the agency gets that type of work done with a relatively large number of "peons" at the bottom pay levels, very few people at the intermediate pay levels, and a large number at the upper levels. It may well mean that it is hiring the upper-level employees from outside sources and leaving the lower-level employees, including you, to stagnate and eventually become turnover statistics. In other words, the published promotion-from-within policy may be just so much rhetoric within the occupational category with an hour-glass career cone. A diamond-shaped career cone is perhaps the optimum configuration from the career seeker's standpoint. Draw one and you will see why this is true.

Another useful piece of research would be that of investigating the extent to which your employer is actually practicing in-service training and development or subsidizing education in outside facilities. Every federal department and agency is required by law to submit an annual report to the

Civil Service Commission, with great statistical detail on its training and development activities. These are consolidated by the Commission into a report to the President. Your personnel office will probably be glad to let you examine its copy of the last annual report and the overall federal report. Your analysis of your own agency's report in relation to the overall report will suggest how active your employer is in the development of human resources. You can compute to find the average man-days of training per employee per year; the distribution by major occupation category, location, and type of training received; and the average duration of training experiences.

In Chapter 15, under the discussion of executive development, the reader will find what I believe is a sound design for accelerated growth and development into positions of leadership. The cross section of a steel "I-beam" is used as a symbol to illustrate the path of advance from entry level to retirement, and the inputs from both employer and employee to facilitate a joint-venture relationship. It is appropriate for anyone charting a career in the federal service to study this model, evaluate it, and either accept or reject it as his philosophy. It is hoped that the reader will find it worthy of adoption and that it will speed his career along.

Forming a Continuing Joint-Venture Relationship with Employer

Many federal departments and agencies enter into training agreements that have the effect of intensifying training experience and assuring a schedule of semiautomatic promotions until a target career grade is reached. Essentially, the agreement is a three-way contract among the employing organization, the Civil Service Commission, and the trainee. Each party is bound to meet certain specified conditions.

Obviously, one should not enter into an agreement to train for a line of work in which one has little ability or interest. That is why the earlier steps recommended in this Appendix II are so important. If one is unsure of one's aptitude, basic educational foundation, or interest in a field in which training agreements are being used to develop people, it may be a good investment to confer with a local university and take advantage of whatever testing and counseling facilities they offer. Some federal organizations have testing and counseling facilities, but there is a certain advantage in protecting the privacy of one's test scores. Should you do poorly, test data could become a liability in the personnel office where you work.

As you look about and learn what the in-service training and development opportunities are where you work, you will want to be very selective, unless you are working under a training agreement that specifies the in-service and outside courses you are to take. Employees who become perennial course takers are not regarded in the best light. Each course should be a logical building block that leads to a realistic career goal. Your supervisor may consider it a sign of lack of motivation if you ask his or her permission to take every course announced. It is well to view the relationship you have with your employer, insofar as training and development is concerned, as a joint-venture relationship. The supervisor must excuse you from productive time when you are participating in a program of instruction. Presumably, the instruction will improve your productivity. As a demonstration of good faith, and as a means of matching your employer's effort to accelerate your growth and development, you should work out a plan of self-education, self-training, and self-improvement.

In the same category as training agreements, you may find internships and apprenticeship programs available in your organization. If you prefer to follow the blue-collar trades in the federal service—and there are some very fine programs there—the apprenticeship route is sound. The Bureau of Apprenticeship, Department of Labor, certifies federal apprenticeship programs just as it does industrial apprenticeship programs, and your credentials should be interchangeable should you move from government to private industry. Internships usually prepare employees for work at higher levels in the professional, scientific, technical, or managerial fields. Once you are selected for an internship, your chances of rising to intermediate and senior levels are far greater than if you take your chances on moving up by the desk-to-desk approach.

Many federal organizations are installing learning centers in which employees may individually acquire new knowledge and skills at learner-paced rates. These facilities are normally supervised by either the in-service training and development staff or by the library, or both. Programmed instruction and teaching machines are demonstrably effective as a means of learning many subjects. They usually provide audiovisual presentation and self-testing capability within a semiprivate module of space called a "carrel."

You should not overlook the library as a tremendous resource to keep yourself abreast of your field of interest, current events, and overall developments in your agency which may not reach your desk in the normal course of business.

Staying Mobile

I constantly counsel employers to use planned mobility as one of their prime methods of developing talent. This means that employees who want to be developed at an accelerated rate, and to have their highest skills utilized, must stay mobile. This does not mean that every move has to be one that takes you halfway around the world. It may be a move across the city or to a neighboring city or state. It may mean a transfer from a headquarters position to a field position. Perhaps it is a change from staff work to line operations work, or vice versa. At another point in your career, it may be a change from nonsupervisory to supervisory duties, from supervisory to managerial, or from managerial to executive.

Some of the chances to practice mobility will not necessarily involve a permanent change. It can be a detail for up to 90 days to another position. You may be asked to take charge of a project on an "acting" basis, due to unexpected circumstances. Many federal employees have the positions they have because they were willing and able to assume the acting role for a time. You may be invited to serve on a task group, the work of which will take you into other parts of the organization temporarily and diversify your duties and responsibilities. This will probably give others a chance to see you in action, thus broadening your contacts and enhancing your chances for moving ahead as openings occur.

Mobility is usually synonymous with growth. You may well be cheating yourself and those who depend upon you for sustenance if you play it conservatively and resist mobility. Admittedly, it is more comfortable to continue your routines day after day—things like the car pool, lunchroom chatter, the bowling league, and your chores at home. You owe it to yourself, particularly during the formative stages of your career, to be more pragmatic and mobile—to stay in step with the dynamism of your federal employer and to try to position yourself where the action is, whenever possible.

Measuring Your Progress

One simple measure of progress is to ask yourself whether or not you are still growing on your job. Are you being paid a fair wage or salary for the work you do? If not, why not? Are things likely to get better or worse?

Theoretically, the performance appraisal system in the federal service should objectively measure your progress and report to you annually with respect to how well you are measuring up to the predetermined performance standards of your job. The system does not work very well, and therefore it is not a reliable yardstick for determining your career progress. Some supervisors do not have the courage to level with subordinates on their deficiencies, and often inflate ratings to make sure there is no reaction.

On the assumption that the official performance-rating system will stay more or less the same, you can still find out where you stand with your supervisor. The best time to talk with your supervisor about your performance is not at the end of a year but project by project. When you finish a piece of work for which there was a definite beginning and end, have an informal chat with your supervisor. Ask a few questions that cannot be answered with a simple yes or no. You may need to prime the discussion with some self-evaluation. For example: "I wish I had suggested we pretest that new form for which I wrote the procedures. How do you feel about it?" Through a continuing dialogue on a series of projects, you should glean a good feel for the way your supervisor perceives your performance.

Periodically, you may wish to initiate a discussion with your supervisor to get the benefit of his counsel on the direction your career is taking. The purpose should be to arrive at a meeting of minds on what your short-term and long-range training and development needs are. Remember that your employer feels no obligation to engage in employee training for the sake of training. Public service is its primary function. You have a viable proposition when you and your supervisor can mutually agree that there is additional knowledge and skill needed in the organizational element where you work, and that you are the logical person to obtain it. If your office is relying on the buddy system for continuity of its operations, you should be able to reason with your supervisor that it is well to go outside from time to time for training in the best known way of doing your kind of work.

How fast you are being promoted in grade may be a crude measure of your progress. Some federal employees look forward annually to more take-home pay from three sources: incremental increases for longevity reasons, a promotion in grade, and a cost-of-living adjustment based on the consumer price index (CPI). None of these factors is fully automatic. The incremental increase is dependent on a "satisfactory" performance rating. A grade increase is dependent on your promotion to a position with more responsible duties and responsibilities. There has to be a vacancy and you have to prevail over your competition as well as have the support of your supervisor, his management, and the personnel office. The CPI may not always increase, and the President's recommendation can suspend or affect the amount of the increase for cost-of-living reasons.

You are as good a judge as anyone as to whether or not your progress in grade is commensurate with your performance and growth in your work. One federal executive worked out a novel formula for judging the progress of federal employees. This placed age over grade, with a minimum score of 3 as satisfactory progress. For example, a 36-year-old person should be at least grade GS-12, and a 45-year-old person should be at least grade GS-15 on his scale. He considered 1's and 2's as exceptional, and 4's and 5's as "over the hill." Obviously, this official would have been hard pressed to defend his formula as a basis for passing over individuals who failed to meet his arbitrary standard. He continued to use it as his informal yardstick for judging potential and promotiveness of applicants and subordinates.

Putting Down Roots

Your staying power in the federal service will pretty much depend upon your ability to put down some roots. If your sole strength lies in the work you do at a certain desk, in a particular building, for the same federal organization where you have always worked, you may not be long for the federal scene. Federal entities are kaleidoscopic. They get reorganized, conglomerated, and shifted about geographically. Technology and leadership change.

There are several things you can do to solidify your position in the federal service. Above all, strive to establish a reputation in your field of specialization. Professional societies, like all organizations, have their limitations, but they are an excellent place for a young person to establish contacts and to find out what the trends are in his line of work. Literature, positions of leadership, opportunities to develop one's communication skills, and other means of growth await those who join and actively participate.

Employee organizations and unions offer another avenue for extending one's scope of influence, contacts, and awareness. It is illegal for federal employers to coerce employees into joining or not joining unions.

The community is an excellent place to put down some roots. This arena for self-development was discussed at some length in Chapter 15 on Executive Development. It is equally applicable to all federal employees, regardless of whether they aspire to executive-level positions or not. Civil service regulations permit federal employees to run for nonpartisan offices and to engage actively in local government. This is a means of reinforcing one's reputation and self-reliance.

Developing Leadership Qualities

Some of the most important years in one's career growth are those in which the individual is working as a first- or second-line supervisor or as a middle manager. It is during these years that one can most easily make or break one's chances of making dramatic progress in the organization. Failure in these capacities can bring almost irreparable damage to one's reputation. This phase is the threshold to the arena with the greatest reward in terms of income and feeling of self-fulfillment, that is, to the executive ranks.

A central thesis of this text is that organizations are studded with "people developers," and that these individuals serve as a strong supplement to on-the-job training and to formalized systems of in-service training and career development. If this is true, one of the finest ways one can develop leadership and influence is by becoming a people developer. Many of those with whom you will be associated will go on beyond your highest level of attainment to positions of greater responsibility. By influencing their thinking and their development on the way up, you will be enhancing your standing and building a more gratifying career.

As you begin to write for publication in your organization and in professional or trade journals, or even in the employee house organ, you will be exercising some leadership. As you take on teaching assignments and special assignments, such as committee and task group roles, you will extend your influence and leadership potential. You may find yourself as manager of a recreational program sponsored by your employer, head of your local union or employee organization, or chairperson of a campaign for bond sales or a charitable cause. These roles may seem to detract from your official duties, but at the same time they let your employer see you in a different light. Your success or failure in these special roles can be an indicator of your leadership potential, and you can be sure they will not go unnoticed by your management.

Keeping Good Balance and Planning Ahead

Maintaining a favorable balance in one's life seems to be as important as a favorable balance of trade is to the economic health of a nation. It is doubtful that federal employees with problems such as the following can give a full measure of their energies and talents to their work:

Serious health difficulties

Overextended financial capability

Serious domestic relations problems at home

No recreational interests

No provision for the future with respect to health maintenance, insurance, savings, investments, self-development, housing, vacations, and the like

Waste of fringe benefits that accrue, such as leave, options to participate in insurance and health maintenance plans, and outside education courses

No proper advanced planning for imminent retirement

It seems very important to me that the individual who elects public service as a career should begin early to build balance into his or her life. There will be disturbed periods to endure. These may stem from such root causes as public hostility to the program of which you are a part, weak supervision and leadership under which you are placed, inadequate resources with which to do the job the way you know it needs to be done, labor/management difficulties with a fallout effect on you, inequities imposed on you and/or your associates, and temporary personal troubles. If you have no other interests to fall back on while these difficulties are being corrected, your depression may affect your work to the point where your work and your problem merge—you become part of the problem—and then you begin a downhill slide from which you may never recover.

Your common sense, coupled with a determination always to be looking ahead and reassessing your total past performance, is a part of the task of keeping good balance in your life. Remember that your career depends on it, and perhaps the careers of countless others.

Conclusion

The door one enters in approaching a career in the federal service is critical. Once on the federal payroll, there are a number of things one can do to establish oneself in the eyes of supervisors and managers. It is also well to get to know one's job by doing some research on its history, policies, practices, and future direction.

Next, a federal service career seeker should attempt to chart a career course for himself with whatever career counsel he may find available in the organization. A number of different career field positions and the organization's training and development policies and practices should be examined in terms of whether or not they provide realistic avenues for advancement within a reasonable time frame.

The committed public servant should form a continuing joint-venture relationship with his employer and make good faith inputs into his own development, stay mobile, objectively assess his progress periodically, and put down roots for security purposes. It is also important to develop and demonstrate leadership qualities by such methods as teaching, writing, and influencing the development of others. Good balance in one's life and thoughtful planning for the years ahead add another very useful dimension to one's career pursuits.

Students and others interested in a career in the federal civil service should personally explore the possibilities by face-to-face contact soon after such interest begins. Such contacts should preferably be with operating officials who are fully grounded in particular federal programs. Career seekers should realize that finding and taking advantage of meaningful career opportunities in the federal service are mostly the results of exerting their own initiative, as things stand now. Once a job opportunity is found, the guidelines detailed in this chapter should help any career seeker maximize his staying power and compensations. Federal departments and agencies should reexamine their personnel management systems and overhaul them, where necessary, to conform to sound personnel management concepts.

Appendix III

The Trainer's Guide

THE trainer's guide has as its overriding purpose the firm establishment of control over the content, emphasis, sequencing, and instructional strategies of the program as a whole and for each session thereof. A good set of specifications for producing a guide would read something like the following:

1. Preface: To be written for the signature of an official of the organization, or the director of employee training and career development.

2. How to Use the Guide: A clear explanation, as brief as possible.

3. Timetables:
>Entire program
>Weekly
>Daily
>Session

4. Introductory Page: The page on which *each session* starts should contain the following information:

Identification of "instructional unit(s)" to be covered. An "instructional unit" (IU) is considered to be the lowest common denominator of material to be taught. For example, equal opportunity in employee selection might be one instructional unit; equal opportunity in staffing, a second IU; and equal opportunity in handling employee grievances, a third IU. Collectively, these three IUs might comprise a session.

The identification would include the following information:
>Specific objectives of session
>Presentation methods
>Participant interaction methods

414

Participant feedback methods

Home assignments

On-the-job (OTJ) assignments

Materials and equipment required for faculty and participant use

5. *First Text Page:* Each instructional unit should include on its opening page the identification of the unit. For example:

Knowledge Block: _____ IU No.: _____

Subject Element: _____ Page __ of __

Beneath the identification block, starting at the left margin, the following information is entered: minutes allowed, IU broad outline points and key points the trainer is to cover. Standardized cue symbols to facilitate the user's coverage are interspersed in the broad outline column as necessary. For example, a hand symbol will cue the trainer to hand out materials to the participants. Sufficient white space is allowed on the page to encourage annotations that will enrich style of presentation without compromising emphasis, sequencing, or content. The material should be arranged on a page 8½ x 11 inches (commercial size), and the format of the introductory text page and those pages following should be uniform throughout. Notes and footnotes should also follow a uniform pattern. The information may be arranged in a table form for each IU or in an outline with numbered steps to indicate sequence.

6. *Subsequent Pages of Each IU:* In the upper corner of each page, show the IU number and the page number.

7. *Last Page of Each IU:* The last page should contain a brief summary of the major points presented. It should also list permanently useful generalizations (PUGs) that the participant should take back to the job, adapt as necessary, and use when the timing and other factors in the job setting are right for their application.

8. *Other Technical Specifications:* The pages of the copy for final reproduction should be on white paper for ease of reproduction. The pages should be numbered sequentially, as described in item 6 above.

An easily read, open-faced type should be used, and it should be large enough so that the trainer can readily follow it from a sitting or standing position while teaching from the guide.

All pages of the finally produced guide should be prepunched for use in three-hole binders so that later revisions or additions can be easily inserted.

INDEX

Civil Service Commission, U.S. (*cont.*)
  training weaknesses of, 398
  see also government; merit system
classrooms, 130
clerical employees
  in department stores, 6
  training for, 283–284
  in training support staff, 323–324
closed-circuit television, *see* television;
  videotapes
coaching
  in follow-through, 352
  in method selection, 177
  of supervisors, 274–275
colleges, *see* universities and colleges
Columbia University, 38, 392
Commerce, U.S. Department of, 57
committees
  assignments to, 176
  to identify training needs, 45
  in structuring development pro-
    grams, 63–64
  see also task groups; teams
Common Cause, 25, 243
communications
  in cultivating pride, 257–258
  in production-oriented teams,
    27–28
  supervisory skills in, 247
community
  building bridges to, 68–69
  executive participation in, 276
community colleges, 84–85
comprehensiveness, in development
  programs, 67
computer-assisted instruction, 176,
  188, 298, 305–306, 354
  for blue-collar employees, 283
computers
  Census Bureau's first use of, 25
  manual operations altered by, 26
  training of operators for, 7
conference rooms, 94
conferences
  in identifying training needs, 45
  in method selection, 181

conflict, Follet's theory of, 248
Congressional Record, 25
Consolidated Federal Law Enforcement Training Center, 86
Constitution (U.S.), 22–23
construction of audiovisual aids,
  208–210
consultants
  in civil service, 315
  in helping establish training center,
    372
  as help to training unit, 88
  in identifying training needs,
    43–44
  in recruiting personnel, 126
  work simplification versus, 28–29
consultations, in method selection,
  176
consumer movement, 25, 47–48
content of training programs, 224
continuing education, 273
contracting
  for audiovisual aids, 210
  in establishing training center, 372
  for production of curriculum ma-
    terials, 196
contractors
  as help to training unit, 88–91
  for human resources development,
    51
contracts, union
  in assessment of development
    needs, 30–31
  day-to-day business and, 80
  seniority in, 10–11
  see also unions
cooling, 133
coordinating, Gulick on, 262
coordination, in development programs, 67–68
copyrights, 193, 309
corporations, by-laws of, 23
correspondence courses, 149, 187,
  305, 354
  for blue-collar employees, 283
Corson, John, 392

heating, 133
Herzberg, Frederic, 67, 247
hierarchies, organizational 259–261
high schools, 85
hook-and-loop boards, 201
Hoover Commission (U.S.)
    on continuing training, 34–35, 71
    on job rotation, 269
    on management training, 275, 277
    recommendation to Post Office
        Department by, 365
hotels, 96–97
Houseman, Kenneth, 363
house organs, 177–178
    in follow-throughs, 351–352
housing
    at learning environments, 135,
        145–146
    management of, 7, 10
human resources
    assessing needs of, 69
    development of, 2–4, 5–21
    marshaling of, 107–109
    see also personnel; recruiting;
        staffing; training and develop-
        ment
Hutchinson, John G., 261

identification, of equipment, 214
illustrators, 378–379
in-basket analysis, 46, 183–184
incentives
    administrative decisions on, 226
    in participative management, 268
incidents
    analysis of, as method, 184, 197
    in identifying training needs, 46
indexes of effectiveness, 348–349
individualized instruction
    computer-assisted, 176, 188, 283,
        298, 305–306, 354
    by correspondence courses, 149,
        187, 283, 305, 354
    programmed, 16, 188–189, 193,
        283, 305, 354

by teaching machines, 136, 161–
    162, 188, 299, 304–306, 354
Industrial College of the Armed
    Forces (Defense Department), 81
industrial engineering staffs, 350
industrial engineers, 98
information, delivery systems for,
    53–54, 148–171
in-service courses, 181
    teaching assignments for, 189–190
institutes
    designing environment for, 141–
        146
    establishing, 334, 359–383
    in off-job training, 182
    personnel for, 316, 324–326
instruction
    computer-assisted, 176, 188, 298,
        305–306, 354
    development of teams for, 228–230
    different techniques for, 15
    for large and scattered audiences,
        221, 298–315
    programmed, 16, 188–189, 193,
        283, 305, 354
    units for, 168, 414–415
    see also individualized instruction;
        teaching
instructional aids, see audiovisual
    aids; training aids
instructors, 114
instructor's guides, 309
interchangeability, of audiovisual
    aids, 212–213
Intergovernmental Personnel Act
    (U.S.), 18
    sharing of training facilities under,
        38
IRS Training Center, 141
International Personnel Manage-
    ment Association, 124
International Training Office
    (Agency for International De-
    velopment), 295, 356
internships, 187, 287, 408
    see also apprenticeships